MOVING FRONTIERS: ECONOMIC RESTRUCTURING, REGIONAL DEVELOPMENT AND EMERGING NETWORKS

Moving Frontiers: Economic Restructuring, Regional Development and Emerging Networks

Edited by
JUAN R. CUADRADO-ROURA
PETER NIJKAMP
PERE SALVA

Avebury

Aldershot · Brookfield USA · Hong Kong · Singapore · Sydney

Published by
Avebury
Ashgate Publishing Limited
Gower House
Croft Road
Aldershot
Hants GU11 3HR
England

Ashgate Publishing Company
Old Post Road
Brookfield
Vermont 05036
USA

British Library Cataloguing in Publication Data

Moving Frontiers: Economic Restructuring,
    Regional Development and Emerging
    Networks
    I. Cuadrado-Roura, Juan R.
    338.9

ISBN 1 85628 905 2

Library of Congress Cataloging-in-Publication Data

Moving frontiers: economic restructuring, regional development and
    emerging networks / edited by Juan R. Cuadrado-Roura, Peter Nijkamp,
    and Pere Salva
        p. cm.
    ISBN1-85628-905-2 : $67.95 (est.: U.S.)
    1. Regional economics. 2. Regional economic disparities.
    3. Space in economics. I. Cuadrado-Roura, Juan R. II. Nijkamp,
    Peter. III. Salva, Pere, 1959–
    HT388.M68 1994   94-10772
    338.9--dc20   CIP

Printed and Bound in Great Britain by
Athenaeum Press Ltd, Newcastle upon Tyne.

Contents

Figures and tables

Contributors

C. Albessart
Service of Survey & Statistics
Place Leopold 12 D
Namur
Belgium

C. Anderstig
Institute for Regional Analysis
P.O. Box 12519
S-10229 Stockholm
Sweden

M. Borman
University of Strathclyde
Management Science Department
Richmond Street
Glasgow G91 1XH
Scotland

R. Camagni
Dept. of Economics
University of Padua
Via del Santo 28
Padua
Italy

D. Campisi
CNR
Via Manzoni, 30
00185 Roma
Italy

R. Capello
Universita Commerciale Luigi Boccani
Via R. Sarfatti 25
20133 Milan
Italy

S.S. Cohen
University of California, Berkeley
Institute of International Studies
2234 Piedmont Avenue
Berkeley, California 94720
USA

J.R. Cuadrado-Roura
Alcalá University
Rafael Calvo, 17
28010 Madrid
Spain

T. Dignan
Institute of Public Policy
George Mason University
Fairfax, Virginia 22030-444
USA

C.E. Garcia
University of California, Berkeley
Institute of International Studies
2234 Piedmont Avenue
Berkeley, California 94720
USA

M. van Geenhuizen
Economic Geography Institute
Erasmus University
P.O. Box 1738
3000 DR Rotterdam
The Netherlands

A. Gillespie
CURDS
The University of Newcastle
Newcastle upon Tyne NE1 7RU
England

P. Hall
The Bartlett
University College of London
School of Planning
22 Gordon Street
London WC1 H 0QB
England

K.E. Haynes
Institute of Public Policy
George Mason University
Fairfax, Virginia 22030-444
USA

J.C. Houard
Service of Survey & Statistics
Place Leopold 12 D
Namur
Belgium

B. Johansson
Department of Regional Planning
Royal Institute of Technology
S-100 44 Stockholm
Sweden

P. Leo
Université de Bordeaux
32, rue d'Alsace-Lorraine
31000 Toulouse
France

N.G. Lundgren
Luleå University of Technology
Department of Industrial Economy and Social Sciences
S-95187 Luleå
Sweden

R.R. MacKay
School of Accounting, Banking and Economics
University College of North Wales
Bangor, Gwynedd LL57 2DG
Wales

M.C. Monnoyer
Université de Bordeaux
32, rue d'Alsace-Lorraine
31000 Toulouse
France

P. Nijkamp
Free University
Faculty of Economics
De Boelelaan 1105
1081 HV Amsterdam
The Netherlands

G. van Oirschot
Free Univesity
Faculty of Economics
De Boelelaan 1105
1081 HV Amsterdam
The Netherlands

A. Oosterman
Free University
Faculty of Economics
De Boelelaan 1105
1081 HV Amsterdam
The Netherlands

C.R. Pathak
Dept. of Architecture & Regional Planning
Indian Institute of Technology
Kharagpur, West Bengal
India

J. Philippe
Université de Bordeaux
32, rue d'Alsace-Lorraine
31000 Toulouse
France

L. Qiangsheng
Institute of Public Policy
George Mason University
Fairfax, Virginia 22030-444
USA

P. Salva
Department of Physical Planning
University of the Baleares
Palma de Mallorca, Mallorca
Spain

J. Taylor
University of Strathclyde
Management Science Department
Richmond Street
Glasgow G91 1XH
Scotland

C. Tesauro
Instituto di Pianificaziane e Gestione de Territorio
CNR
via P. Catellino 111
80131 Naples
Italy

R.W. Vickerman
University of Kent at Canterbury
Centre for European, Regional and Transport
Economics
Cornwallis Building, The University
Canterburg, Kent CT2 7NF
England

A. Vulterini
Instituto di Pianificaziane e Gestione de Territorio
CNR
via P. Catellino 111
80131 Naples
Italy

L. Westin
CERUM
University of Umea
S-901 87 Umea
Sweden

H. Williams
University of Strathclyde
Management Science Department
Richmond Street
Glasgow G91 1XH
Scotland

Acknowledgements

The following organizations have to be thanked for their support to the Fourth World Conference of the Regional Science Assocation International in Mallorca, which offered an inspiring source for composing this volume:

- Govern Balear (Regional Government of the Baleares Region), Department of Economy and Finance
- CICYT (Spanish National Commission for Science and Technology), Madrid
- AECR (Asociación Español de Ciencia Regional)
- Universitat de les Illes Balears
- Caixa 'Sa Nostra'
- Banca March
- Consell Insular de Mallorca

Preface

The title of this book, *Moving Frontiers: Economic Restructuring, Regional Development and Emerging Networks*, does not only call attention to the geographical-political changes in our world, but emphasizes also the need for new analytical departures in regional science research.

In many countries, urban and regional systems exhibit indeed complex and turbulent developments fluctuating between growth and prosperity on the one hand and decline and recession on the other hand. These spatiotemporal developments are often due to *structural changes* and *differential dynamics* at various levels of a complex spatial system comprising a multiplicity of diverse actors and decision makers.

In recent years, a great deal of attention has been paid to spatial dynamics in order to explain drastic changes in regional and urban agglomerations (for instance, with regard to growth rates of income *per capita*, average urban unemployment, in- and outmigration ratios, the economic base structures, and capital and trade flows).

Regional economies are currently going through a new, often revolutionary phase in their economic transformation process. The Industrial Revolution in the last century implied already completely new ways of organizing production and transport, accompanied by continuous innovations in technology, which led to large-scale mass production and transport. The current economic - technological revolution generates new roles for services and even more radical ways of producing, performing and organizing industrial enterprises. This radical transformation is induced by increased speed, capacity and reliability in information handling and knowledge creation. New technologies have created many opportunities for increasing the efficiency of large firms and also for enlarging the potential of small scale production.

The changes we are observing nowadays have several important dimensions, each relating to and interacting with a number of others. *Spatially*, it implies reshaping the location of goods handling activities (and also the location of information-handling activities) between and within regions and nations. *Sectorally*, it incorporates both the growth of tertiary activities, and the changing relationship and blurring differentiation between manufacturing and service industries. And finally, from an *organizational* perspective, it reflects important changes in the nature and forms of the relationship between enterprises, and the ownership and control of these enterprises.

It is noteworthy that a uniformly valid theory describing and explaining structural changes in a multifaceted spatial system does not exist. A study of the literature reveals a great diversity in economic theories and explanatory frameworks. Nevertheless, the role of a region (or urban area) as a nodal activity area is still unquestioned, as:
- a region provides a breeding ground for the exchange of ideas, desires and products
- a region contains a great potential for selling products and for receiving or distributing information
- a region has usually a large labour and capital pool
- a region often exhibits a large industrial diversity that favours technological changes
- a region has normally a relatively high concentration of (economic, physical and social) infrastructure (or social overhead) capital
- a region is a 'natural' territorial unit for public policy and creative entrepreneurial strategies in a network society.

The recent revival of *Schumpeterian* views on current spatial economic restructuring phenomena has increasingly induced scientific interest in innovation and economic transformation. Both the behavioral stimuli and the selection environment for the creation and adoption of technological and organizational change in firms have become a subject of intensive research. In this context, a rich field of economic research has recently been developed, for instance, long waves analysis, network configurations, technogenesis conditions, impact studies on small and medium sized enterprises, neo-Fordist structural approaches, labour market dynamics, and the growth potential of high technology industries. Various studies have been devoted to the seedbed conditions of new technologies, especially in the context of small and medium sized firms. In this context, different frameworks of analysis have attracted much attention, such as the spatial incubator hypothesis and the spatial product life-cycle model.

In the same vein, also *industrial dynamics* has received much attention. Normally, an 'upswing' of a certain regional economic sector will be based on (1) a rise in demand for its products, (2) an associated technological innovation favouring this change in demand, (3) a sufficient implementation of required productive investments, and (4) a satisfactory supply of public capital supporting this growth process. A reverse development takes place during a 'downswing'.

It should be noted, however, that in the Schumpeterian view entrepreneurial innovation is not an exogenous determinant of economic growth, but an endogenous force in a profit maximizing economy. Thus, the profit motive, which is crucial to survival in a competitive system, is the main driving force of adopting and generating innovations and hence of cyclical economic patterns. Clearly, the discontinuities associated with the adoption and diffusion of innovations may lead to perturbations in a spatial-economic system.

A necessary condition for a structural change taking place in a spatial economic system is the presence of *seedbed conditions* for technological innovation, the so-called incubator potential. This potential which was originally referring to new firm formations in general is also equally relevant for innovation creation. In this context, all over the world there appears to be a strong tendency for agglomeration and geographical concentration of the location of information and R&D centres. There are sound reasons for such agglomeration forces. The information intensive nature of technological activities and the resultant need for face to face communication favour those places that offer (1) high levels of competence, (2) many fields of academic and cultural activity, (3) excellent possibilities for internal/external communications, (4) widely shared perception of unsatisfied and growing needs, and (5) a general situation of structural instability facilitating a synergistic development. These conditions for 'regional creativity' can be translated into more conventional policy stimuli, but in general, they focus on three main elements: (1) the presence of professional and technical labour competence, (2) urban agglomeration, or a threshold size of a place where cultural activity and communication will be heightened, and (3) conditions that promote synergy or instability.

An important phenomenon that has recently emerged in the economies in many countries and regions is the emergence of a *network society*. A network is a particular organization of an economy based on synergy via actor dependency and operating mainly via nodal economic regions connected by various modes. Especially the rise of the *information economy* has caused this new structure in the evolution of spatial economic systems. Such networks are also the vehicles par excellence for rapid transition, diffusion of technological innovation, international mobility and knowledge transfer.

All the above issues have formed a major ingredient at the Fourth World Conference of the Regional Science Association International, held in 1992 in Mallorca. This conference, organized in close cooperation with the AECR (Asociación Español de Ciencia Regional), provoked much attention in the above mentioned issues. A selection of the great many papers focusing on the theme of *economic structuring, networking and spatial dynamics* has been brought together in this volume complemented with a few additional papers to ensure sufficient cohesion.

The book is organized according to three major themes. The first part of this volume is concerned with recent economic and technological changes and their consequences for the space-economy. The changing positions - and resulting socioeconomic disparities - of regions and cities are discussed, in both the developed and developing world. The next part of this book comprises contributions to the spatial dimensions of physical and non-physical networks, including their economic, technological and organizational barriers. The final part of this volume deals with the design, and application of models for analyzing spatial networks and regional development. All chapters in this book aim to provide refreshing contributions at the interface of spatial dynamics and policy analysis.

Juan R. Cuadrado-Roura, Madrid
Peter Nijkamp, Amsterdam
Pere Salva, Palma de Mallorca

Part A

ECONOMIC RESTRUCTURING AND SPATIAL TRANSFORMATION

1 Regional disparities and territorial competition in the EC

J.R. Cuadrado-Roura

1.1 Introduction. Disparities and winner regions

The arguments in favour of applying regional policies have traditionally been of two types: ethical or moral, and economic. Based on the principle of equity, ethical arguments have placed their emphasis on the tenet that it is unacceptable to allow broad economic differences and lags in welfare between the different regions of a country or a set of countries in the process of integration. Solidarity with the poorer regions or those that have trouble with reconversion has thus been considered necessary due to the social and political implications of inequalities.

Arguments of a more economic nature have been based on efficiency. Faulty mechanisms of adaptation and development in some regions lead to insufficient or poor use of certain resources. The end result is that the standard of living of the entire population is held below what might reasonably be reached. Though economic efficiency may improve if market forces are allowed to act freely, there is no lack of reasons for holding that the possible losses in real production stemming from regional aid policies may perhaps not be too high a price if they succeed in achieving better use of initial resources.

European countries' experience and the approaches of the European Community (EC) itself in regional policy exhibit a mixture of both types of arguments, although those of an ethical nature have clearly tended to domineer. The chain of argument has generally been quite simple: 1) There are differences in well-being between different regions; 2) Such differences are neither politically nor socially acceptable, nor is it acceptable to allow a specific sector problem seriously to affect a given area; and 3) The way the system works fails when these problems must be solved. Therefore the basic goal of regional policy should be: to reduce interregional disparities by boosting the development of more backward areas and/or recovering areas that are backsliding or have trouble reconverting.

Understood as part of income redistribution policies, under the redistribution focus, or simply as the system's aid or compensation for trouble areas, under the compensation focus, in the end regional policy is justified by its possible effects in furthering greater interregional equality. Regional income disparities have thus become policy's main reference point, and the situation of each

3

region 'with respect to' an average has very frequently served to determine the right to obtain certain benefits and aids.

To a very broad extent, theoretical debates have also hinged upon regional disparities and their possible evolution. Positions have been held based on the neoclassic model, which favour the free circulation of factors, goods, and services, reasoning that this will inexorably lead to regional convergence. Criticisms have arisen in opposition to this view which rather heterogeneous (accumulative causation, polarization, unequal development, etc.) but coincide in the end in asserting that market mechanisms and the free behaviour of economic agents tend to lead much more toward interregional divergence than to convergence.

In the last twenty years, elements have appeared and tendencies have been observed which pull toward a new approach to regional problems. Some regions which used to be considered backward and peripheral have experienced very substantial growth and important changes in their future outlooks. Quite a number of central regions have had to face problems of structural change and deindustrialization, and not all of them have managed to recover their former standing. The internationalization process and the world-wide extension of economic relations have also altered the expectations of some countries and regions, and the same has happened in the European sphere with the advance toward closer economic integration.

Of course, regional differences persist, both within countries that already exhibited very marked disparities and within the EC. For various reasons their downward trend has even stopped in recent years. But concealed under this lies behaviour that differs widely from one region to another. The determinism entailed in both the theses on the inexorable advance toward interregional economic convergence and those theses that support the permanence of the periphery with respect to the centre may be questioned. In short, it seems that there are regions that are able to use their competitive advantages to develop their potential, attract investments and conquer markets for their products. These regions are the winners of the game, and they are not necessarily the traditionally most dynamic or richest regions.

Our purpose is precisely to stress the importance of these changes, which suggest a revision of some traditional regional policy viewpoints and allow the validity of certain conventional theories to be questioned as well. To that end, in our next section we will analyse the recent evolution of regional disparities in the EC, and we will reflect on their meaning. In section three, we will zoom in on the differing behaviour of a number of regions both inside the group of the more backward regions and among those that the EC does not consider problem regions. Their different responses and some coincidences between them will allow us to point toward a possible process of regional inversion which may be compared with that experienced in the United States (Suarez–Villa, 1992; Cuadrado-Roura and Suarez-Villa, 1992). We will then present certain selected cases as examples (section four) and reflect on the factors behind their dynamics.

The future continuity or interruption of the changes discussed here is not clear. There are a number of unknowns and changes under way in the European sphere whose consequences are difficult to evaluate. In a context as competitive and innovative as the current field, emphasis on the dynamic

4

processes of growth must needs lead to an evolutionary approach to spatial dynamics (Camagni, 1991; Nijkamp, 1993). But what at any event does seem clear in the light of recent experience is that simplistic centre-periphery views are not that applicable, nor may they be discarded for the neoclassical focus.

The subject is complex and tinged with shades of meaning which we cannot explore here, as our emphasis is on the more general traits. The contents set out here are based on a continuing comparative study of European regional cases and the results of completed group work which will be mentioned.

1.2 Regional disparities in the 70s and 80s. What do they tell us?

Any discussion of regional differences or disparities entails two problems from the very start. First, what disparities shall be discussed, and therefore what indicator shall be used? Second, to which regions shall the discussion refer, since scale, in terms of size, inevitably affects results?

As far as indicators are concerned, the possibilities are many,[1] and the choice of one or another leads to varying results. Here we will use the GDP per inhabitant, since, on the one hand, it is a good sign of the evolution of the level of development, whether for a country or a region, and on the other hand, as what is of interest here is the economic behaviour of regions, the significance of the GDP seems more pertinent than other indicators such as available net income.

On the question of regions, we will, when referring to either the EC or individual countries, take the EC's NUTS II as our reference. Nevertheless it must be pointed out that these regions' sizes are very heterogeneous, and this will to some extent influence comparative results. In addition, there are regions – though few - whose basic magnitudes are especially affected by the way production figures are attributed or by the region's small size.[2]

In the EC as a whole, the differences existing between regions today in the early nineties are extremely important. The Community's ten leading regions have a GDP per head equivalent to something more than three times that of the ten regions sitting at the bottom of the hierarchy, and between the leader and the last-ranked region there is a difference of 400-500 per cent.

Inside EC countries, the situation is quite different and comparatively less dramatic than that of the EC as a whole. Taking figures for GDP per inhabitant in ECUs and purchase power standard, Germany (not including the new East German *länders*) displays one of the lowest difference levels (weighted standard deviation 14.7% of the average), while France (29.3%), Italy (26%) and Portugal (25%) are the leaders, followed by Spain and Great Britain.

The evolution followed by disparities over time is without a doubt more significant than any still portrait. Of particular interest is the trajectory traced by these disparities from the late sixties until now, since this will afford an opening into the aspect on which special emphasis is to be laid here.

In the sixties, the regions of the EC as a whole registered a considerable convergence to one another in terms of GDP per inhabitant as well as GDP per job. The component stemming from different national behaviour explains something more than 50 per cent of this tendency, as shown by Molle et al.

(1980). Migratory movements from lower-income countries (regions) toward richer, more industrialized zones practically explain the rest. Inside these different countries, evolution during this same period was similar, and especially marked in the cases of Spain, Portugal and Italy.

In the early seventies, the regional convergence process continued, but the impact of what came to be called the oil crisis (an impact which was not identical for all regions, but was widespread nonetheless) triggered an interruption and then an inversion of the tendency. The practically general drop in the growth rates of European regions, whether rich or poor, and the interruption of migratory movements both inside the less-developed countries (Ireland, Portugal, Spain, Greece) and from these countries toward northern central Europe lie at the bottom of this change. And the events observed later, in the eighties, were not exactly a return to the past tendency toward convergence, despite the important economic recovery they produced, but made for stability in the world-wide position of the EC (Table 1.1). Between 1980 and 1990, regional disparities inside the EC were practically at a standstill, on the whole, though they did worsen in several countries (the United Kingdom, France, and Italy), albeit not seriously.

Table 1.1
Evolution of interregional disparities
in GDP per head 1970-1990
(Weighted standard deviation)

	EC12	UK	W.Germ	France	Italy	Spain	Port.
1970	.435	.133	.124	.285	.271	.285	.369
1973	.414	.126	.130	.266	.250	.280	.352
1975	.399	.120	.144	.260	.230	.270	.333
1978	.433	.119	.148	.256	.236	.273	.343
1980	.371	.130	.145	.252	.232	.231	.287
1983	.360	.127	.158	.283	.215	.230	.274
1985	.361	.130	.162	.289	.240	.231	.248
1988	.360	.150	.149	.296	.255	.224	.252
1990*	.363	.154	.147	.293	.261	.226	.250

* Estimate: Advance figures.
Data-base: NEI and Regio. Values in ECU, NUTS II level. Own calculation.

The significance of this evolution and its future may be subject to several interpretations, of which we may simply take a few samples.

As Barro and Sala (1992) have shown, the neoclassic model predicts that GDP per capita will converge. However, their own estimates for the U.S.A. suggest that while the gap between the rich states and the poor states of the Union has tended to shorten in the long run, it has done so at a rate much slower than theory predicts, taking into account the additional fact that the United States have an integrated economy featuring ample internal factor mobility. For Europe, these authors suggest similar evidence as well, again in the long view (Barro and Sala, 1991). Nevertheless, what we have seen above with regard to the events of the last two decades would allow only a very slow convergence process to be considered, if indeed it can still be considered at all.

Then there are Emerson et al. (1990), who interpret the change in Europe's interregional convergence process more in terms of the conditions of the moment. Convergence shows a tendency to intensify, they say, during periods of heavy growth, and to weaken in phases of stagnation. This is due to the existence of sensitive sectors and marginal small business in weaker regions, and to the fact that these regions usually receive a relatively large share of public investments as well as fresh private investments, which are more sensitive to the changes buffeting the economic climate.

Lastly, the movement back toward more pessimistic positions on the difficulty/impossibility of regional convergence (from Myrdal to Holland) is also gaining supporters, especially in view of not only recent evolution but also the possible consequences of the Single Act and the EMU. Begg and Mayes (1992) stress the all-too-simplistic nature of the centre-periphery focus in understanding regional changes; but they do also indicate, like others, that the persistence of inequalities is linked to the disadvantages accumulated by more unfavoured regions, and that the liberation and integration of markets tends or will tend to exacerbate problems. Some symptoms already appeared in the eighties and may be confirmed in the nineties, as the march toward greater European economic integration presses on.

In its more general aspects, the subject of regional convergence/divergence is then food for controversy, and for speculation as well. But, in our opinion, if we hold to the overall level (be it Community-wide or even nationwide), the data do not reveal too much. What is more, we lose sight of an important event of recent years: different regions have actually shown rather different behaviour. While some have grown little or gone stagnant, others have achieved performances earning them a place in the winners' category. Furthermore, there are examples of both tendencies among the most developed regions and the most backward, or those which have had to face serious reconversion problems.

1.3   Behaviour differentiated by regions. A new map of Europe?

Differences in regional economic dynamism have stood patent in the last twenty years. In a number of cases, the phenomenon has been perceivable since the early seventies or even somewhat earlier. By that time, East Anglia, South West and East Midlands in Great Britain, the *länder* of southern Germany, and the area called 'Terza Italia' had already registered performances relatively better than those of other areas in their respective countries. Most of all, they showed evidence of renewed dynamism and a talent for drawing in industries and services.[3] The regions forming the Mediterranean hub of Spanish growth are also reaching growth rates above the European average. On the other hand, quite a number of long-standing industrialized regions (i.e. Nord-Pas-de - Calais, Nordrhein-Westfalen, South Yorkshire, Strathclyde, Wallonie, etc.) have growth rates far below the European average (EC-12); and while the problems of regions of this type are relatively similar (Quevit et al. 1991), their renovation and reaction capacities have differed.

In the eighties, the unequal behaviour of regions persisted, almost along the same lines as it held in the seventies. Several regions belonging to the poorer Community countries worsened, as in Greece, Portugal and even Italy. At the same time, some of the regions located in the European heartland (in Great Britain, the Netherlands and Germany) and the southern European reaches that were already considered economically emergent (Italy, France and Spain) improved. In fact, a more painstaking analysis of the behaviour of the EC's 'objective 1' regions (that is, the more backward regions given higher priority in receiving Community aid) in the 1980-1990 period shows that this group as a whole has achieved overall growth at rates close to the Community-wide average in terms of GDP per head, and some regions actually grew at quite clearly higher rates. Ireland (considered as a single region); the regions of Abruzzi and Molise, Italy; Eastern Macedonia and the Ionian Islands, Greece; the Centro region of Portugal; and the vast majority of the Spanish regions included in this group (Andalusia, the Canary Islands, Castile-La Mancha, Comunidad Valenciana, Extremadura and Murcia) reached higher-than-average growth rates, even while undergoing considerable demographic increases at the same time. Almost all of them have improved their relative position inside the Community. This has not occurred in other backward regions such as Corsica, France, and Basilicata, Campania and Calabria, Italy (GREMI, 1991).

In the block of senior industrialized regions having trouble reconverting (the EC's objective 2 regions), wh8ich have an average level of income per inhabitant higher than the preceding group albeit with ample differences, growth in the eighties was below the European average. Yet here also there are variations in behaviour; while regions of this type in the UK, the Saarland and Bremen regions of Germany, and Limburg, Belgium, have improved their positions, others, such as Nord-Pas-de-Calais and Lorraine, France, Liège and Hainaut, Belgium and Cantabria, Spain, are experiencing backslides.

The rest of the EC regions with generally average or above-average incomes have also experienced higher-than-average increases in terms of GDP per inhabitant. The regions whose performance truly stands out, however, are southern Germany, "Third Italy," southern Great Britain, and the Spanish regions lying in the Mediterranean hub (Catalonia) and the Ebro River Valley (Aragon), as well as the Balearic Islands and Madrid.

If we run this comparative analysis using product values per employed person, the results are quite similar. Even so, some points of interest do crop up in the last decade. Firstly, in the more backward regions there has been a considerable increase in the productivity per worker with regard to the average. This generally reflects the current adjustment process, with its costs in terms of higher unemployment. Secondly, the varied panorama of the industrialized problem regions is not changing, but neither is productivity being boosted above average, which reflects the industrial adjustment process (the exceptions are Lorraine, France; Limburg and Overijssel, the Netherlands; Munster and Weser-Ems, Germany). Thirdly, the rest of the regions offer a highly varied panorama, from the fine progress of Hamburg, Brussels, and the Balearic Islands, practically all the way to the performance of the Dutch regions and Schleswig-Holstein, in Germany, below the European average.

8

Table 1.2
European regions with higher performance
1970-80 AND 1980-89 (*)
(GDP (PPS) relative performance, EUR12=100)

EUR-12		1970-80 100	1980-89 100
OBJECTIVE 1 REGIONS			
Abruzzi	(It.)	124	117
Molise	(It.)	139	110
Puglia	(It.)	119	102
Sicilia	(It.)	104	103
Sardegna	(It.)	108	102
Eastern Maced.	(Gr.)	122	140
Galicia	(Sp.)	126	109
Castilla-La Mancha	(Sp.)	102	104
Comun. Valenciana	(Sp.)	119	112
Andalucía	(Sp.)	116	112
Murcia	(Sp.)	125	114
Canarias Ils.	(Sp.)	112	134
Centro	(Po.)	109	135
Lisboa-Tejo	(Po.)	127	104
OTHER REGIONS			
Baden-Württ	(D.)	101	103
Bayern	(D.)	101	106
Lombardía	(It.)	104	105
Emilia-Romagna	(It.)	117	100
Nord-Este	(It.)	115	113
(Trentino, Véneto, F.Venezia. Giulia)			
Centro	(It.)	118	105
(Toscana,Umbria,Marche)			
Lazio	(It.)	105	129
East Anglia	(UK.)	102	128
South West	(UK.)	102	126
Madrid	(Sp.)	105	110
Catalonia	(Sp.)	103	114
Baleares Ils.	(Sp.)	105	129
Aragón	(Sp.)	101	114

Source: Regio and NEI data base. Own calculation.

(*)Note: Regions with performance below 100 in one of both periods have
been excluded.

This mismatched regional dynamism over the last two decades, particularly in the eighties, draws a map of Europe on which development seems to be lining up gradually along what has come to be called the big megalopolis,[4] which runs from the traditional European economic heartland (the triangle between London, Paris and the Ruhr area) through southern Germany to Italy's Lombardy, with offshoots toward central Italy (Tuscany, Emilia-Romagna), southern France, and the Spanish Mediterranean axis (Camagni, 1991; Gaudemar and Prud'homme, 1991; Cuadrado-Roura, 1988 and 1991b). The groundwork studies of the Europa 2000 program (C. of EC, 1991) reinforced this thesis, providing numerous elements of support from both the outlook of changes noticed in the location of industries and services, and the demographic viewpoint on urban and communications networks.

1.4 Some cases and the explaining elements

Not all the different cases of winner regions mentioned above can be analysed. Of course, it must be acknowledged immediately that the differences between them in terms of performance, production structures, and more decisive factors are important. It would thus be risky to hazard generalizations. There are, however, certain elements and points in common that seem to have been determinant in winner regions' greater success in a world of increasingly competitive territories - at least, this is the conclusion that may be deduced from a series of 16 regions that we have been able to study in greater detail.

From this set of regions, we have chosen three cases that are illustrative and will allow us to draw conclusions. They are the southern Mediterranean 'region' of France (including the NUTS-II regions of Midi-Pyrénées, Languedoc-Rousillon and Provence-Alpes-Côte d'Azur), the state of Baden–Württemberg (Stuttgart, Karlsruhe, Freiburg and Tübingen) in southern Germany, and the two most significant regions of the new Spanish Mediterranean axis, Catalonia and Comunidad Valenciana. The latter is the poorest of all them in Community-wide terms, and is included among the objective 1 regions, while Baden-Württemberg numbers among the ten leaders. The rest lie below the European average in GDP per inhabitant, though above the threshold of the regions included in objective 1.

These are - in a very synthetic form - some of the most significant traits of these three examples.

1.4.1 Baden-Württemberg

The south German state of Baden-Württemberg (35,000 sq. km., 9.5 million inhabitants in 1990) has, as is well-known, a long industrial tradition evolved from the very first textile initiatives, a tradition featuring an especially outstanding entrepreneurial spirit and a high level of education and labour specialization that got its start as far back as the ducal era. Its industrial base has always been comprised of a broad variety of small, highly innovative businesses (Bade and Kunzman, 1991), but the Stuttgart cluster is also the main headquarters of various important firms such as Mercedes Benz, Bosch, SEL, and IBM. The state has a rather thick-lain network of cities that, while not exceedingly large, do offer a high level of services. These conditions and characteristics, plus more attractive physical surroundings than in other areas of Germany (it is not hampered by activities in an obvious recession, and it has a good standard of living) have over the last twenty years converted this *länder* into the most prosperous in the country. Industry is responsible for 39 per cent of its GDP (33 per cent is the Federal average).

Although a true analogy may not be drawn, some traits of Baden–Württemberg may be held to resemble those of Italian industrial districts. Small business is the base here as well. There are local schemes of innovation giving rise to two types of cooperation: horizontal cooperation (in R&D, marketing, personnel training, and other areas) among firms operating in activities that are not directly concurrent; and vertical cooperation between customers and suppliers, such as the cooperation between a big company like Bosch and its suppliers and subcontractors (Gaffard, in Savy and Weltz, 1993). The amount of effort poured into R&D and human resources is undoubtedly one of the state's key points, and one on which business and regional authorities cooperate. Regional authorities have also established a network of alliances with other European regions (Rhône-Alpes, Lombardy, Catalonia), one of whose goals is technical cooperation between companies and the attainment of funds for R&D from specific EC programs (Morgan, 1991).

There are several factors to be emphasized when explaining this *länder*'s recent dynamism and allure. In a comparison of this case with the state of Nordrhein-Westfalen (N-W), which has traditionally been the industrial heartland of Europe but has been going through serious restructuring since the early seventies, Bade and Kunzman (1991) stress some of these factors. In the first place, there is the nonexistence of and lack of proficiency in traditional heavy industry, forming a heavy burden for N-W and other regions in a number of ways, making for a certain labour environment, unattractive surroundings, less initiative, and dependence on political decisions, as opposed to the greater agility and flexibility of mid-sized, more innovative industries. The second factor favouring this *länder* is, as in other regions such as Bayern, the availability of a qualified labour force. This has favoured not only industrial development in the form of fresh initiatives, but also the development of services. Furthermore, the existence of well-established, respected technical universities in the southern states has also been a supportive factor, especially as formal and informal linkages have formed between institutions of higher learning and local industries, ensuring a practical exchange of knowledge and technologies.

The fourth factor to stress due to its contribution to winning regional results is the existence/development of producer services. Services such as strategic planning, R&D, data and information processing, and marketing are essential preconditions for innovative and competitive capability in business. Moreover empirical results prove that there is an obvious correlation between the high level of producer services in southern German regions (essentially B-W and Bayern) and these regions' economic performance.

Two additional important factors seem to have been, on the one hand, the availability of space, as opposed to in more congested northern areas, and, on the other hand, the sociopolitical climate. Southern Germany is traditionally conservative from the sociopolitical point of view, and labour unions have never played a heavy or conflictive role, unlike in older, now problem-saddled industrial zones. Potential foreign investors have clearly valued these factors, and this has also favoured and driven local decisions. To this we may also add regional government's clear support policies: financial aid for businesses, welcomes for potential investors, support for vocational training and specialization, measures favouring small business' use of consultancies, as well as the opening of new markets, technological innovation, and measures to reduce environmental pollution.

Lastly, the superior image of south German regions plays no mean part. This is especially so for southern cities, both culturally and environmentally in general, and in terms of international prestige. The subregions of B-W share this positive factor with their neighbours. Stuttgart thus takes a place alongside Munich, Frankfurt, Karlsruhe and other smaller cities of the southern states that hold cultural and environmental prestige, making them attractive.

1.4.2 Midi-Pyrénées and the Mediterranean Regions of France

Southern France, especially the area made up of the Midi-Pyrénées, Languedoc–Rousillon and Provence-Alpes-Côte d'Azur regions (8.6 m. total population), is a very different example from that given above, but it too offers some interesting conclusions and explanations for its dynamism.[5]

In the late sixties, the area had but a modest industrial base - all regions had a value-added percentage below the national average - and concentrated mainly on traditional sectors common throughout the Mediterranean area (textiles, footwear, wood, food, paper and graphic arts, and so forth), dominated by small business. Tertiary activities were, on the contrary, more highly developed in relative terms, though there were shortcomings among the more advanced branches. The area had a series of important, relatively well-equipped cities (Toulouse, Montpellier, Marseille, Aix-en-Provence, and Nice), in addition to other, smaller cities, though it was handicapped with a decaying hinterland.

Of course, things did not change radically from then to the end of the eighties, but some noteworthy events did occur. The first is that the growth rates of several departments in the area rose regularly above the average for France. The second is that the installation of prominent foreign businesses operating in what were considered advanced sectors contributed to creating new industrial environments, while at the same time an innovation milieux of considerable interest developed (Hansen, 1990). The third is the development in the area of a technopolis complex (Sophia-Antipolis) and technological parks (Toulouse, Montpellier, Marseille, etc.) which have tried to contribute toward altering the zone's expectations, making it attractive to new industries and local initiatives. And the fourth is that, despite the already high degree of tertiary development existing in the area, services have continued to advance faster than the French average during the last decade (employment went up by 24 per cent from 1976 to 1988).

Gaudemar and Prud'homme (1991) and the IFRN report (1993) have highlighted some causes of the area's greater dynamism. The balance between industry and services is one, as is the fact that small business dominated the manufacturing sector. The educational level also appears among the weightier

12

factors. In the early eighties, the share of people age 15 and up holding a graduate degree (post high school qualification) was about 7.5 per cent, compared with 6.5 per cent for France (not counting Paris) and 5.9 per cent for the northeast regions. The fine university offer in the area and the development of research centres forms another decisive factor, supported by the local network of cities.

Of course the area's more traditional industries have had to deal with problems and adjustments. Some basic industries and their respective surroundings have also suffered, particularly in the Marseille-Fos area. Employment in consumer product industries fell over 23 per cent from 1976 to 1988. However, intermediate and production goods have almost held steady in terms of employment, and they show good results. The aeronautics industry (Toulouse, Midi-Pyrénées), the electronics industry, computers and other technology-intensive products are responsible for this.

In the search for an overall explanation of relative success, four key findings (Figure 1.1) seem to be instituted policies, the educational level, the business climate, and the development of services. (Gaudemar and Prud'homme, 1991).

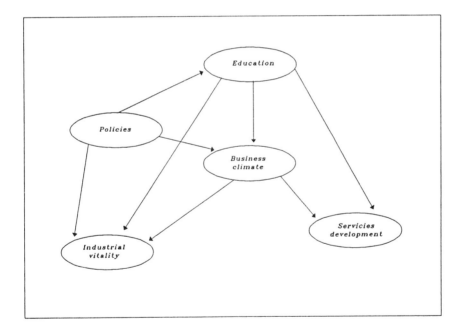

Figure 1.1 Factors in the development of the south

Source: Gaudemar and Prud'homme, 1991

13

From the economic policy point of view, the Mediterranean south has benefitted from aid from both the French government (subsidies, company moves, and research support) and the Community. The south's high educational level has in turn allowed businesses to obtain a qualified or at least more easily specialized labour force. The effort put into research here has also been more intense than in other areas of France, the ratio of researchers to the total labour force being 2.6 per cent here and 1.5 per cent for the rest of France (except for Île-de-France).

The good educational level, the predominance of small business, the zone's trading tradition and probably the climate and environment of the area as well have worked in favour of the existence of a good business climate, giving rise to not only a reaction among local businesses but also the attraction of other, larger outside companies (IBM, Ford, Alcatel, Matra, Motorola, and Thomson).

Lastly, services, most particularly business services, have also contributed to and clearly helped feed the economic vitality of the south. Between 1976 and 1988, the increase in the tertiary employment most closely linked to the manufacturing industry was striking: +47 per cent for financial services, +31 per cent for personnel in producer services, +16 per cent for telecommunications - always far above the French average.

Furthermore, the south Mediterranean region is equipped with a good roads system reaching eastward to Italy, northward to the Rhône-Alpes region (which is richer and also very dynamic), and southward to the Spanish northeast, which has also shown itself to be highly dynamic economically in recent years.

In the last two decades, the economic and regional map of Spain has performed a flip-flop. The north, with its important foundation of mining and industry, entered a hard phase of recession and reconversion. The result: deindustrialization, particularly in the Basque Country, but in Cantabria and Asturias as well, and low growth rates. On the other hand, the Ebro River Valley (the regions of Aragon, La Rioja and Navarre) and the Mediterranean axis (from Catalonia to Murcia, including a certain outgrowth into Andalusia) have displayed greater economic dynamism, better adaptation to their new circumstances, and timely use of opportunities stemming from Spain's opening up to the outside.[6] Apart from these two areas of growth, some poorlydeveloped regions have also managed to show excellent performance in the 80s, as indicated in the section above.

We will take as our examples two of the regions considered part of the Mediterranean axis, Catalonia and Comunidad Valenciana.[7] Catalonia (6.1 million inhabitants and 20.3 per cent of the Spanish GDP) is one of Spain's rich regions, though its GDP per head is barely 90 per cent of the EC average. Comunidad Valenciana (3.85 million inhabitants and 10.5 per cent of the Spanish GDP) is one of the EC's 'objective 1' regions, since its GDP per head is under 75 per cent of the Community average.

Catalonia has a long-standing industrial tradition and quite a diversified production base. Its trailblazing role in Spanish industrialization lasted long into recent times, under the import substitution model that Spain was able to develop due to its political circumstances. Although part of Catalonia's industry suffered the impact of the oil crisis and Spain's aperture, Catalonia has seen heavy growth in the last twenty years. In the 80s, the average rate of growth was 3.8 per cent, and between 1985 and 1992 it reached an annual accumulative rate of 5.1 per cent (7.1 per cent between 1985 and 1989), clearly above the Spanish average, and of course, the EC average. Moreover, the region is a leading receiver of innovations at the international scale. This role is due largely to foreign investments (from 1985 to 1990, Catalonia received 24 to 40 per cent of the annual Spanish total), but its own businesses have also gone international. Catalonia's fat share of Spanish exports (19.8 per cent in chemicals; 19.8 per cent in machinery; 17.1 per cent in transport equipment) is one consequence. Services are highly developed, and the capital city, Barcelona, features quite a varied range of producer services which are also available in other cities of the region.

Comunidad Valenciana, which laboured under a certain historical tardiness in its industrialization process and featured considerable agricultural production, has leaned more heavily on small and mid-sized industry in traditional sectors. Nonetheless, some multinationals (Ford, IBM) have located there, and in some manufacturing sectors important renovation/innovation processes have also taken place (e.g. in construction materials, wood, decoration, food, footwear and metallurgy), though not all businesses have participated. The development of tourism and tourism-linked construction have worked and still work with specialized agriculture to play a respectable role in the achievements of the last two decades. In the 70s, the region's average growth rate was slightly above the Spanish average, and in the 80s, always above (4.7 per cent, annual accumulative average for 1985-92).

An analysis of the recent behaviour of these two regions and the causes behind their dynamism in comparison with both Spain and the EC brings at least eight relevant factors to the fore.

The first two are of a geographic/infrastructural nature. The fact that the natural corridor formed by the Mediterranean coast is outfitted with a relatively good communications network including roads, motorways and international airports has facilitated the zone's access and functional and productive interrelations. Added to this is a microclimate that allows excellent, highly profitable export crops to be cultivated, in addition to providing location-related advantages for industry and services and the development of tourism.

Closely linked to this physical framework is the system of cities dotted throughout the two regions. In addition to important, influential cities such as Barcelona and Valencia, a full network of medium-sized cities as well as smaller but relatively well-equipped towns form a good basis for decentralized, specialized industrial development and the services offer (Pedreño, 1988).

The fourth trait they hold in common is their having commanded a diversified production base. Agriculture here is intensive, intended for exporting, and increasingly capitalized. In their small-business-run industry, virtually free of big businesses operating in the base sectors, two scenarios have taken shape. One, an intraindustrial scheme, features larger shares of participation in the industries that used to be redoubts of the EC's more industrialized countries, industries where a diversification process is now being developed. The other scenario is interindustrial, where the more traditional industries play a part in

15

company with their problems due to cost competition from third countries now undergoing industrialization.

Aperture to foreign trade is another major trait. As a group, Catalonia and Comunidad Valenciana are not only big exporters (43 per cent of all Spanish industrial and agricultural exports), but they have also been especially attractive to foreign investment and the gradual development of intraindustrial commerce. Support from regional authorities (new technologies, design, commercialization, fashion, marketing, vocational training, etc.) has allowed them to maintain and sometimes recover their competitiveness. On this point, their respective regional governments and agencies have counted on businessmen and sought their participation in policymaking.

The entrepreneurial base, which features a proven capacity for renovation and noteworthy innovative tendencies, has been and is a relevant factor in the regional development and dynamism observed in Catalonia and Comunidad Valenciana. Aperture to other countries has facilitated contacts and networks, given access to new markets and made the introduction of new technologies easier. The dynamism of local investment has been proven through empirical analyses (Aurioles and Cuadrado-Roura, 1989).

The availability of a relatively specialized labour force and a high educational level are two more favourable elements. Joining them is the fact that the costs of the labour factor in these regions used to lie considerably under the European average (approximately 60% of the 1985 average), although they are losing this advantage as they gain ground on the advanced countries.

Lastly, the sociopolitical aspects must not be underestimated. Labour conflict has been modest in comparison with other Spanish and European regions. Furthermore, regional governments have enjoyed growing autonomy, which has allowed them to develop initiatives supporting industrial activity (spreading of technology, development of parks, technological institutes, spreading of information, support for international cooperation, etc.) in both Valencia and Catalonia, though under somewhat different formulae.

1.5 Regional changes and territorial competition. Some final remarks

The revived dynamism - or sometimes the awakening - of certain European regions is a much more interesting phenomenon than the mere evolution of interregional disparities. The coincidences between certain changes both in the EC and at country-wide levels are enough to perceive the existence of a regional inversion process whose sustaining factors have already been pinpointed elsewhere (Cuadrado-Roura andSuarez-Villa, 1992).

The different behaviour of and relations between Community regions might perhaps be better understood through the idea of territorial competition. In the new international economic surroundings, there are competitive companies and noncompetitive companies, but there are also territories that are more competitive and those that are less so. A company is competitive if it can survive and win or obtain an advantage in the increasingly crowded market. Success depends, at the most primary level, on the firm's own internal conditions of production, organization, and so forth, which allow it to compete in a given sector or product range, but the company's surroundings also help shape its competitiveness.

Territories in general, and regions and cities in particular, are clearly all fighters in the ring of competitiveness. There are factors or elements that are necessary in order for production activities to be truly 'localized'. Some are simply not moveable, such as environmental quality, infrastructure, and urban networks. Others are, in practice, hardly subject to relocation, as are the availability of qualified labour, potential subcontractors, research centres, authorities' own autonomy, and so forth. The existence of these features and advantages in a given territory makes it more attractive to foreign investment and makes conditions more favourable toward its mobilizing its own potential. In short, it makes it more competitive.

Our analysis of various cases gives an idea, first of all, of the variety of situations. Furthermore, it highlights certain definite coincidences and conditions in order for one territory to outstrip another in competitiveness. Obviously, not all these coincidences and conditions must be present in the same proportions, but those European regions that have shown better performance and attracted/developed new activities in the last twenty years all meet said conditions, albeit not always to the utmost.[8]

Since some of these conditions have already been reviewed, we shall merely list them briefly.

1 Evidently some regions hold certain initial advantages location-wise, such as climate, nearness to high-growth areas, and natural advantages; but in order to take advantage of them and be competitive, these regions decidedly must have an adequate, if not an advanced, communications infrastructure including roads, international air connections, an advanced telecommunications system, and so forth. Said infrastructures and networks do not provide growth, but the reverse is also true: there is no possibility of growth nor use of advantages without these infrastructure systems. In the three cases analysed above as well as in all other cases studied, this condition is clearly met.

2 The urban system also plays an important role. A big, well-equipped city with a good image and a system of the right kind of complementary urban nuclei form an especially favourable foundation for development. Competition between regions easily becomes competition between cities. Europe has fine examples of this,[9] and the cases cited here also amply cover this requirement.

3 The availability of human resources with a stable offer of qualified labour and a high educational base is a factor in which all winner regions coincide. If in addition relative salary and non-salary labour costs are moderate, the region may hold an extra advantage. In some regions of France, Portugal, and Spain, this latter factor has played a positive role in attracting investments in recent years. Nonetheless, in an ever-more - integrated European market, this advantage is tending to shrink. The presence of prestigious centres of higher education and their relations with industry are, however, much less volatile.

4   The presence of big business in regressive sectors has operated in almost every case to expel trade, while a predominance of small businesses in a variety of activities coincides as a positive factor, even when the more traditional factors hold sway. Furthermore, the dominant presence of small business is often a sign of a local business base that is right for new initiatives, possibilities of subcontracting, etcetera.

5   Another key is the region's accessibility: market accessibility, access to the country's or the EC's political and economic decision-makers, access to technical developments and innovations, and so on. Certain instruments, such as information centres, technological institutes, and scientific and technological parks, act as channels and networks to facilitate said access.[10] At the same time, there must be a response in terms of receptivity to the signals sent in from outside the region. In a recent analysis on the accessibility and receptivity of Community regions to ideas and innovations (Cadmos, 1992), practically all the regions we have highlighted for their fine performance appear among those with an average or high level of access and receptivity to innovative ideas and investments.

6   Availability of advanced producer services, such as strategic planning, technological consultancies, design, commercialization/exporting, financial services, and R+D, also appears as a positive condition for territorial competitiveness. Though these services may be offered and/or acquired outside the region, it is a fact that nearness, frequent contact and adaptation to one's requirements are very positive factors for both ordinary use and real effectiveness.

7   As some European experiences prove, institutional aspects are not only important but decisive. The existence of a regional authority with autonomy from state authorities and a system of cooperation between the different authorities on the one hand, and on the other, between authorities and civil institutions (chambers of commerce, business and social associations) proves especially clinching. A competitive territory, whether a region or a city, requires a good organizational foundation and practical use of support strategies (Cheshire and Gordon, 1992). The more autonomous regional governments have been able to apply measures and develop initiatives that clearly go beyond the possibilities of central authorities. In a number of cases, one consequence of action coordinated by the local environment itself is the creation of a good image abroad.

8   Lastly, though the relationship may not be considered categorical, the relative attractiveness of a region in drawing in foreign investment or activating local investment also bears a relationship with a peaceful, cooperative social climate. Normalization, stable dialogue with labour unions, and freedom from conflict are requisites in order for one territory to gain a competitive jump on others.

We said at the beginning that regional disparities tend to persist in the EC and its member countries, but that some regions among the backward, the intermediate and the rich are managing to reap better results and would seem to be changing or strengthening their position within the whole. Taking certain cases and the events of the last twenty years as our basis, we have suggested one explanation of these facts in terms of territorial competitiveness.

If this explanation is right, neither centre-periphery determinism nor inactivism, no matter how neoclassical, are right. Authorities may work along with each region's social forces to advance in making their territories more competitive, concentrating their efforts on the conditions competitiveness requires. Of course, some regions start out at higher levels or with more advantages than others, but, as we also stated at the beginning, in a competitive and innovative context, emphasis on the dynamic processes of growth leads to a concept of spatial changes that can by no means remain static, and this is what recent European reality seems clearly to uphold.[11]

References

Aurioles, J. y Cuadrado-Roura J.R. (1989), *La localización industrial en España. Factores y tendencias*. FIES, Madrid.

Aydalot, Ph. and Keeble, D. (1988), *High Technology Industry and Innovative Environments: The European Experience*. Routledge, London, New York.

Bade, F.S. and Kunzmann, K. (1991), Deindustrialization and regional development in the Federal R. Germany, in Rodwin, L. *Industrial Change and Regional Econ. Transformation*, Harper, Collins, London. Chapter 3.

Bagnasco, A. (1977), *Le tre Italie,* Il Mulino, Bolonia.

Boeckhout, I.J. and Romkema, S.A. (1989), 'Shift of Economic centres of gravity in North-West Europe: fiction or reality?'; Paper to AEGEE-Congress, Groningen.

Barro, R. and Sala i Martin, X. (1991), 'Convergence across states and regions', *Brookings Pap. Econ. Activ.*, pp. 107-72.

Barro, R. and Sala i Martin, X. (1992), 'Convergence', *J. Pol. Econ.*, n.100, pp. 223-251.

Begg, I. and Mayes, D. (1992), 'Cohesion, Convergence and Economic an Monetary Union in Europe'. *Regional Studies*, vol. 27.2, pp. 149-165.

Brunet, R. (1989), *La France dans l'espace européen*, Gip-Reclus, Montpelier.

CADMOS, (1992), *European Scenarios on the Technological Evolution and the Social and Economic Cohesion in the E.C.*, Fast Program; mimeo, Brusells.

Camagni, R. (1991a) (ed.), *Innovation Networks: Spatial Perspectives*, Bellhaven, London.

Camagni, R. (1991b), 'Regional deindustrialization and revitalisation processes in Italy', in: Rodwin, L. and Sazanami H. (ed), *Industrial Change and Regional Economic Transformation*, Harper Collins, London, Chapter 5.

Cheshire, C. and Gordon, R. (1992), 'European integration: Territorial Competition in theory and practice', Paper for the North American Conference of the RSA, Chicago, mimeo.

Comm. of the European Communities (1991), *Europe 2000. Outlook for the Development of the Community's Territory*, Brussels.

Cuadrado-Roura, J.R. (1988), 'La crisis económica y la redefinición del mapa económico-regional español', in García, D, *España. Economía*, Espasa, Madrid, Chapt. 19.

Cuadrado-Roura, J.R. (1991a), 'Structural Changes in the Spanish economy: their regional effects', in Rodwin, L. and Sazanami, H. (ed), o.c., chapter 6.

Cuadrado-Roura, J.R. (1991b), *El crecimiento regional español ante la integración europea*, Int. Est. Prospectiva, Madrid.

Cuadrado-Roura and J.R.Suarez-Villa (1992), Regional Economic Integration and the Evolution of Disparities, *4th. World Congress RSAI, Palma*, mimeo, (forthcoming in *Papers in Regional Science*).

Datar-Gip/Reclus (1989), *Les Villes européennes*, Paris (R. Brunet, director).

Emerson, M. et al. (1990), Marche Unique, Monnaie Unique, *Economie Européenne*, n° 44, octobre (monographic issue).

Gaudemar, J.P. and Prud'Homme, R. (1991), 'Spatial impacts of the deindustrialisation in France'; in, Rodwin, L. and Sazanami, H. o.c., chapter 4.

Gremi (1991), *Development Prospects of the Community's Lagging Regions and the Socio-economic Consequences of the Completion of the Internal Market*, Rapport to the ECC.

Hall, P., (1991):,'Structural Transformation in the regions of the U.K.', in Rodwin, L. and Sazanami, H (1991), o.c., chapter 2.

Hansen, N. (1990), 'Innovative Regional milieux, Small Firms and Regional Development: Evidence from Mediterranean France', *Annals of Regional Science*, 24, pp. 107-123.

IFO (1990), 'An empirical assessment of factors shaping regional competitiveness in problem regions'. Cited in EC (1991) *Europe 2000*, Brussels.

IFRN (1993), Evolution Prospective des Régions de la Méditérranée Ouest. Rapport to the C. of E.C., mimeo, 215 pp.

Illeris, S. (1991), 'Urban and Regional Development in Western Europe in the 1990s: Will everything happen in the London-Brussels-Frankfurt-Milan 'Banana' ?' Paper to the meeting *IGU Commission on Urban Systems and Urban development*, June, mimeo.

Kunzmann, K. and Wegener, M. (1991), *The Pattern of Urbanization in Western Europe 1960-1990*, Institut für Raumplanung, Dortmund, WP, n. 28.

Molle, W. et al. (1980), *Regional Disparity and Economic development in the European Community*, Saxon House, Westmead, Farnborough UK.

Morgan, K. (1991), 'Innovating by Networking. New Models of Corporate and Regional development', W.P., Dpt. of City and Regional Planning, University of Wales. Cardiff.

N.E.I. (1991), Production and Location Patterns, in: EC, *Europe 2000*, Brussels.

Nijkamp, P. et. al. (1993), 'Regional Networks, Science Parks and Regional Development: An International Comparative of Critical Success Factors', included in this book.

Pedreño, A. (1988), Un eje de expansión económica, Cataluña-Mediterráneo.in, García Delgado (ed.), *España. Economía*, Espasa-Calpe, Madrid.

Quevit, M. et al. (1991), *Impact Regional 1992. Les Regions de tradition industrielle*, De-Boeck, Bruxelles.

Savy, M. and Veltz, P. (1993), *Les nouveaux espaces de l'entreprise,* Ed. de l'Aube, Paris.

Suarez-Villa, L. (1992), Twentieth Century U.S. Regional and Sectorial Change in Perspective, *The Survey of Regional Literature*, pp. 32-39.

Suarez-Villa, L. and Cuadrado-Roura, J.R. (1993), Thirty years of Spanish Regional Change: Interregional Dynamics and Sectoral Transformation, *International Regional Science Review*, 15, no. 2, pp. 121-156.

Notes

1. The indicator used may range from the GDP per inhabitant and per employed person to the net income available per individual, the unemployment level by regions, certain social well-being indicators, such as those having to do with housing, family belongings, health, etc., or a synthetic indicator like that used by the Commission of the European Communities.

2. The cases of the Hamburg region, where a considerable number of residents from neighbouring regions work, or Groningen, which includes the natural gas extracted in its territory, as well known.

3. See Hall (1991), Boeckhout and Romkema (1989), Bagnasco (1977), Camagni (1991b), Cuadrado (1991a), the Commission of European Communities (1991) and the *Third* and *Fourth Periodic Report on the Social and Economic Situation and Development of the Regions of the Community* (Brussels, 1987 and 1991).

4. The literature on this subject has increased in the last four years. See, Brunet (1989), Datar-Gip Reclus (1989), Aydalot and Keeble (1988), Kunzman and Wegener (1991), Illeris (1992).

5. We have found in our participation in the EC project **Prospective Evolution of Western Mediterranean Regions** (IFRN, 1993, coordinated by J.P. Guademar) highly useful, since it allowed us to enter into and discuss certain facts and traits of French Mediterranean regions. In addition to this we have incorporated direct complementary information.

6. See Cuadrado (1988) and (1991b); Suarex-Villa and Cuadrado (1993). In 1992 the journal *Papeles de Economia* published a volume dedicated to the Mediterranean Arc, with excellent detailed contributions. See also IFRN (1993).

7. The regions of Murcia (1.04 million inhabitants) is usually included in the 'Mediterranean arc' of growth as well. It is also an 'objective 1' region for the EC. Although its characteristics do have some points in common with Comunidad Valenciana and Catalonia, they are somewhat different. That is why it is not included here as an example. However, it does have quite a dynamic economy, and some of the traits stressed as explanations for Catalonia and Comunidad Valenciana are perfectly applicable to Murcia.

8. Some recent analyses of tendencies in industrial location (IFO, 1990; NEI, 1991) clearly show greater freedom of location then in the past, less constrained by raw materials and natural resources.

9. See Cheshire, P. and Gordon, R. (1992), Datar/Gip-Reclus (1989); Kunzman, K. and Wegener, M. (1991).

10. See Nijkamp, P. et al. (1993), in this volume.

11. The current economic recession is causing a pause in prior (that is, pre 1990/91) regional behaviour. The uncertainties clouding the advance toward the EMU suggest no few unknowns as well. Big macroeconomic decisions have asymmetric effects at the regional scale which may of course be very important, for the areas that will derive some benefit for those that will suffer damage.

2 The disappearing city

P. Hall

2.1 Introduction

Are cities destined to disappear? Some may say that this is an old, tired question: there were articles with titles like that coming out of America even in the 1950s, reaching a peak in the work of writers like Berry and Vining (Berry 1976; Vining and Kontuly 1977; Vining and Strauss 1977; Vining 1982); yet, even there, cities are alive even if they are not well. But it is I think a question worth asking, because the fact is that the predictions of the deurbanization school seem to have proved right. Everywhere, during the twentieth century, there has been a persistent and growing tendency for cities to decentralize and suburbanize. The tendency, once restricted to the Anglo-American group of countries - the United States and Canada, Great Britain and Australia - is now affecting all of western Europe.

Recently, also, another and quite separate trend has manifested itself: many cities also appear to be losing their economic base. They no longer seem to exert the attraction they did for many traditional economic activities. Not only manufacturing and port activities and warehousing, but also the newer office and laboratory-based service activities, seem to be deserting them, leaving large tracts of cities as economic wastelands. If cities lose people and also their economic base, in what sense can they be said to survive? This question has long been evident in some older industrial American cities, where the central city has now become a kind of relic area, a zone of repulsion that no one visits. There is a threat that it could be happening to European cities also.

In order to comprehend what is happening, we need to make a rather careful distinction. There are at least four separate processes happening all at once, and they interact in confusing ways. There is *deconcentration* of people and jobs from central cities to suburbs. There is *deindustrialization*, or more accurately the shift of advanced nations from a goods-handling, resource-based economy to an information-handling, knowledge-based one. There is *reconcentration*, a shift from large metropolitan cities to smaller adjacent ones. And there is, more questionably, a *regional shift* from both the oldest, densest central urban regions and the most remote peripheries to new growth bands and growth corridors, located in certain favoured rural regions of each country. In this talk, I want to review briefly the operation of these four trends, both worldwide and particularly with reference to Europe. Then I want to ask what, in combination, they spell for the future of European urban life.

2.2 Deconcentration

In the United States, just over a decade ago, Daniel Vining wrote a celebrated series of papers arguing that there, demographic trends indicated what he called a complete break with the past: the two-hundred-year old pattern of movement from farm to city had been reversed, so that for the first time in record so-called nonmetropolitan areas - basically, areas outside the sphere of influence of major cities - were growing faster than metropolitan areas (Vining and Kontuly 1977, Vining and Strauss 1977, Vining 1982). And, almost simultaneously, research from the Rand Corporation showed that though about one half of this growth represented a fringe phenomenon, whereby people moved to areas just outside the statistically-defined metro area, about one half consisted of the growth of genuinely small and remote places, well away from the major urban areas (McCarthy and Morrison,1977).

Since then, the American experts have been arguing. Some have pointed out that data for the 1980s point to a sharp slowing of the growth of the nonmetropolitan areas, partly because many of the fastest-growing counties have been absorbed into the metros in the latest redefinitions. William Frey has shown that during 1980-85 the larger metropolitan areas have started to grow again, though not nearly as rapidly as in the 1960s. Further, there now seems to be very little difference in growth rates between the largest metro areas [with 1 million and more people] and smaller ones, or between metro and nonmetro areas. What does emerge is a very strong regional effect, whereby in the 1980s metro areas of all sizes [and also nonmetro areas) in the south and west grow much faster than those in the north (Frey 1988, 264-66). Even Vining has accepted that what he calls core regions - which are very large aggregates, consisting of entire United States Census regions- have again resumed growth in the 1980s (Cochrane and Vining 1988, 223-4).

However, none of this alters the fact that core cities in the United States have continued to lose massively by out-migration to their suburbs. And very powerful evidence now suggests that this process has spread across Europe. Paul Cheshire and Dennis Hay have continued the work that Hay and I started during the 1970s, and have analyzed urban trends for the EEC countries on a comparable basis, at least as far as the data allow: this is the Functional Urban Region [FUR], a concept very similar to that of the familiar Metropolitan Statistical Area [MSA] used by American analysts. They conclude that "Decentralization has tended not only to 'spread' from larger to smaller FURs, it has also spread from the countries of Northern Europe to France and northern Italy and later to the countries of Southern Europe" (Cheshire and Hay 1989, 145; cf. Hall 1988, 116-120). This pattern has proved remarkably stable over time: Cheshire and Hay predict that losses of core city populations, which occurred in northern Europe by the early 1970s [and in the UK as early as the 1950s] and in France and Northern Italy by the late 1970s, will occur also in southern Europe by the 1990s. By 1980, both the UK and Germany were dominated by population decline of their entire major urban regions, accompanied by continued out-movement from core to ring (ibid.)

2.3   Deindustralization

Everywhere, we are seeing the realization of the hypothesis that Colin Clark advanced in his book *The Conditions of Economic Progress*, almost half a century ago: the movement of employment from manufacturing to services, and the shift from an economy based on the processing of goods to one based on the processing of information (Clark 1940). So-called advanced industrial countries - the very term is now a misnomer - now count at least 60 per cent, and often more than 70 per cent, of all workers in the tertiary sector. As a result, we need a new taxonomy of industries and occupations. Robert Reich has recently suggested a useful threefold distinction: old-fashioned production; what he calls the manipulation of symbols; and consumer services (Reich 1989). This is close but not identical to the more conventional distinction between manufacturing, producer or business services, and consumer services. If we do not even know how to classify the newly-growing activities, still less do we understand the rules for their location. Our location theories, whether neo-classical or Marxist-based, are still obsessed with manufacturing and other forms of goods-handling. The most notable, that of Alfred Weber, was published here in Germany as long ago as 1909 (Weber 1929 (1909)). Many of you will remember his famous locational triangle, in which the location of an industry was determined by locational weights that depended on the bulk and the transportation costs of the raw materials and finished product.

There is a similar kind of Weberian triangle for the information industries, depending on the costs of information transfer, whether in the form of packages, or electronic impulses, or the physical movement of brains and the rather weightier bodies that unfortunately have to travel with them. There is also an equivalent for his famous agglomeration principle, but it is now rather more subtle. Agglomeration for Weber depended on economies external to the decision unit, generally in the form of a range of specialized services, markets and pools of labour, access to which cheapened the costs of production. But agglomeration for the information industries has a quite other dimension: it actually contributes to the growth of these industries, through a process of constant innovation in what the late Philipe Aydalot called an innovative milieu (Aydalot 1986; Aydalot and Keeble 1988; cf. Andersson 1985, 1986). The basic insight here goes quite beyond the static framework of neoclassical economics: it hinges on the processes first identified by Joseph Schumpeter, in a work ironically published exactly two years after Weber's, and then deepened by him in his best-known works of the 1930s and 1940s (Schumpeter 1939, 1942).

A homely example, for academic readers, may illustrate the point. You wish to research a new subject. You have various choices. You may take the traditional course and visit the best library available to you. Now the density of information available in this way has a remarkable spatial gradient, which descends very rapidly from information-rich places like London and Greater Boston down to smaller and more isolated university cities. If you work in one of these latter, you may need to take my brain for a day or a week or a month to a bigger centre of learning, which costs time and money. Alternatively, you can phone or fax your academic colleagues and ask them to send you photocopies. Or you may conduct a very expensive, and often very frustrating, computer search of a distant data base, inevitably located, for some reason, in Palo Alto, California. Or you may go to a gathering like this one, and obtain "unprogrammed" information from colleagues you meet in the corridors and wine bars. If you are lucky and belong to a big university in a big city, you may get this kind of information on a daily basis, but most academics have to spend time and money to obtain it. And this is important, because it is this kind of information that is most likely to lead to fundamental innovations. Conferences are temporary innovative milieus, but great intellectual cities are permanent ones.

Now all this suggests that cities have not yet had their day. Electronic information moves cheaply, though often access to value-added data bases is expensive. The post represents good value too, though express international mail is relatively expensive. But, despite continuing technical advances like the high-speed train, moving people is time consuming and expensive.
So there are economies of scope and well as economies of scale in the big places.

Why, then, the paradox? For the evidence is that not merely the goods–handling activities, but some of the information-handling ones, tend to be leaving the cities. More precisely, a rather fine re-sorting is taking place. Those activities that can be spun off to distant locations will be so spun off, because it is cheaper to do so. This is why we see huge suburban office centres springing up around all the great metropolitan regions of the world: in places like Reading 70 kilometres west of London, Stanford in Connecticut a similar distance from midtown Manhattan, the so-called I-680 corridor in the San Francisco Bay Area, places like Tyson's Corner in the Washington DC area. They handle two major kinds of process: research and development, and large–scale routine electronic data input, processing and retrieval. Activities requiring a great deal of skilled judgement or creative activity, in contrast, continue to command expensive space in the cores of the metropolitan cities. So there is a constant tension, in these places, between the centripetal and the centrifugal principles. But, because the more routine part employs many more people, the tendency in general is for activity to migrate out.

Cheshire and Hay confirm that this process has been occurring in Europe, though they cannot measure this as comprehensively as they can measure population movements, because of data problems. They do conclude that "there does appear to have been a significant relationship between specialization in industry at the start of the period and a poor measured performance for the urban region" (Cheshire and Hay 1989, 151). Everywhere, they find, service employment is growing at the expense of manufacturing, though the process still had a long way to go in the mid-1980s. The implication, clearly, is that the cities that are going to do best - or perhaps we should say the least badly - are those that earliest made the transition to the advanced service economy.

One way of looking at this is to concentrate not on the problem cities that everyone talks about, but on those that seem to have few problems. Cheshire and Hay analyze them comprehensively. They quote four cities as examples of "healthy growth": Bristol, Nancy, Norwich and Strasbourg. And they quote five as examples of "healthy decline": Amsterdam, Bologna, Copenhagen, Frankfurt and Hamburg (ibid., 121). All these are service-based cities, two of them smaller national capitals, the others regional capitals. They correspond quite closely to a longer list of such cities I produced earlier (Hall 1987, 10). There I described them as the European equivalents of what Stanback and Noyelle, in the United States, term regional nodal cities (Noyelle and Stanback 1984, Stanback 1985): "city regions with populations ranging from a few hundred thousand up to about two million in population, that act as service centres for prosperous, traditionally rural hinterlands". "All have this common quality", I wrote, "traditionally service cities, they have enhanced that role, and thus have more than compensated for any decline in their traditional manufacturing functions" (ibid.) So there are some rules, but they are not binding; individual circumstances alter cases, and successful urban policies may promote one place while another languishes.

2.4   Reconcentration

Below these medium-sized cities in the urban hierarchy, Western Europe has well over one hundred smaller FURs with less than a quarter of a million people, many of them administrative centres for rural areas, or resort and retirement towns. Nearly three-quarters of them showed population gains in the 1970s; more than two in five had gains of 5 per cent or more. [They are not however the smallest places, many of which are losing both people and employment]. Again, many of these small-medium places showed losses in their urban cores; but, even then, many of these places are growing as employment magnets. These fastest-growing areas, whether larger or smaller, are for the most part semi-rural: the hinterlands of the cities are quite rural in appearance, but they are not remote. On the contrary, they are often next door to the places that are both deindustrializing and deurbanizing. It is a reciprocal process: the big industrial cities' loss is their gain. We can speak of it as a process of recentralization of jobs in these smaller places, with local concentrations of residential populations around them; the resulting commuting distances are generally quite short, certainly much smaller than in the giant metropolitan centres whence these people came.

This is very clearly shown in South East England. There, London has been losing both population and employment for the last quarter-century. But a ring of about twenty FURs, all around it, have gained massively. And the wave of growth is spreading ever farther outward, to engulf places 150 kilometres and more from the capital. In fact, the conventional South East Standard Region is no longer an adequate unit for analysis; we have to talk of a Greater South East, extending into the adjacent South West and East Anglia standard regions. Within it, maximum growth is now concentrated right at the perimeter, largely in those other regions. The fastest-growing belt in Britain - you may call it the Golden Belt, or Sunbelt - extends from Cornwall up through Somerset and Wiltshire to Northamptonshire, Cambridgeshire, Suffolk and Lincolnshire: every one a rural county.

The evidence is compelling that the whole process is started by movements of people in search of more housing space at prices they can afford. But then, the jobs follow the people. More accurately, the jobs themselves for the most part do not move; rather, the local economies expand to absorb the newcomers. A study published in 1986 estimated that by the end of ten years, well over one half and perhaps three-quarters were absorbed in this way (Buck et al 1986, 45, 97). This seems to be a very important conclusion. But we do not understand the reasons why: in these places, local economies grow in ways that need much more research.

We do know that these centres of job growth can actually be created by deliberate agency. We did that in Britain with our original new towns, just after World War II. Those around London were extraordinarily successful, returning many times the original public investment in them. The French paid their neighbours a compliment twenty years later, by adopting the same formula around Paris, with the same results. Much more recently, there has appeared a distinctly American variant, developed by private capital. Places like Arlington between Dallas and Fort Worth in Texas, or Mesa outside Phoenix in Arizona, have recently been cited as examples of "supersuburbs" or "edge cities" (Dillon, Weiss and Hait 1989; Garreau 1991). Like the example of Tyson's Corner, which I mentioned earlier, they are huge new commercial centres having many but not all of the attributes of a traditional downtown. They have come into existence almost overnight: Tyson's Corner, a supermarket and grocery store only twenty years ago, is now the largest downtown in Virginia. They signify the fact that informational activities, deconcentrating from traditional metropolitan centres, almost immediately find the need to recapture the traditional advantages of agglomeration - even when, as in several of these cases, they thereby recreate the same traffic congestion that they thought they were leaving behind. These supersuburbs - they have also been called urban villages - are in many ways the most startling recent American contribution to the evolution of urban form. The problem is that all too many of them are one-sided: they are pure agglomerations of office blocks, whose sole advantage is that they are cheap to rent. For the people who come to work in them, they may represent a parking lot and a corridor to the office, nothing more.

It is true that there is also another remarkable urban innovation, also developed in North America but copied in Europe: the super-shopping mall, represented by North Edmonton Mall in Canada and by Metro Centre, Meadowhall, Merry Hill and Lakeside in England. This is nothing less than the attempt to create a new kind of urban place, which combines shopping and entertainment: a kind of shopping centre in a theme park, again created instantly on an open site. [Three of the four English examples, incidentally, are not true greenfield sites but pieces of restored derelict land]. Since they seem to have been successful, we can expect to see more examples - though both in France and in Britain, governments have given notice that they intend to be very restrictive about such developments in future. The fact is that, so far, no one seems to have thought to combine these two urban innovations into one. The new suburbs therefore tend to be determinedly polycentric: wealth is produced in one place, consumed in another.

2.5 Regional shifts

What seems to be happening, as a result, is the development of belts of fairly widespread growth in basically rural areas of many European countries. The English "Sunbelt" is one example: the south German corridor from Heidelberg via Stuttgart and Ulm to Munich is another; the Mediterranean coast of France and Spain, from Monaco to Nice and on to Barcelona and Valencia, is another; so, on a smaller scale, is the so-called Interstate 680 corridor in the San Francisco Bay Area. I find it difficult to form any meaningful generalization about such belts of growth. Some, like the south German example, follow major and very old-established corridors of movement by road and rail; others, like the British example, actually cut across the grain of the major corridors. Some can be regarded as "central" in terms of the major established urban centres; others appear to be "peripheral".

But what is central, and what is peripheral, depends on the geographical scale that is being used: the Nord-Pas de Calais region is peripheral in French terms, but central in terms of the European Economic Community; the Copenhagen region is central to Denmark, peripheral in relation to Europe. Therefore, I think that it is difficult to argue - as Cheshire and Hay at one point do - that in Europe the periphery is becoming relatively more remote. Some parts of it, like Northern Scandinavia or the Scottish Highlands or the Italian Mezzogiorno, do suffer from a combination of long distances and sparse population, which makes it difficult for them to achieve the necessary economies of scale to compete in the new informational economy. But other regions, peripheral in a European sense - the Spanish Mediterranean coast, central Italy - have been relatively quite dynamic areas. The geography of urban change simply cannot be reduced to a core-periphery basis.

Another point needs stressing about these new growth areas. In one sense, they do represent the formation of vast, sprawling Megalopolises, as Lewis Mumford forecast fifty years ago (Mumford 1938, 223-299). The urban centres increasingly form a set of interconnected functional urban regions. A husband may leave the home in one direction to work in one such centre, a wife may leave in the opposite direction to work in another. They may find it almost indifferent as to where they do their weekly shopping. They may eat in a restaurant in one place one weekend, in another the next. They may imbibe their news and their culture from national newspapers and television broadcasts. Their patterns of movement represent a kind of doodle on the map. There is no coherence, of the sort that geographers have always sought when they mapped daily urban systems. It is the Nonplace Urban Realm, forecast by Melvin Webber in a celebrated paper from California over a quarter century ago (Webber 1962, 1963).

But there is a profound sense in which the Mumfordian nightmare has not been realized, and probably never will be realized. The cities remain physically quite separate and quite small. They are surrounded by wide areas of open countryside. Indeed, that is part of their attraction: they remain country towns. There is a clear physical identity, even if functionally there is none. The Nonplace Urban Realm, in this sense, proves to be a myth. So does the idea of a continuous linear megalopolis, hundreds of kilometres long, as described by Jean Gottmann in 1960 (Gottmann 1961; Hall 1988). Emotionally, too, people are very attached to the places where they live - as witness the growing importance of local environmental issues, in political life all over Europe, as in the United States.

2.6 Conclusion: the end of the metropolis?

Put together, these trends seem to spell a new and deep threat to the traditional great city, especially to those great cities that owed their rise to the manufacturing and port activities of what Patrick Geddes and Lewis Mumford called the palaeotechnic era (Geddes 1915, 60-83; Mumford 1938, 143-222). Economic activities, it appears, no longer need such cities. People want to get out of them, or perhaps have to get out of them. The people and the jobs come together in smaller places arrayed in belts of growth, typically in places little touched by earlier industrial revolutions. To an extraordinary degree, in Europe today we are seeing a partial return to pre-industrial patterns of urban settlement: a return to the medieval urban hierarchy, based on historic trade routes.

Yet this does not mean a mass retreat from the city. On the contrary: it represents a shift from one kind of city to another. Cities that depended on the winning of coal or metals from the earth, or on simple production of the industrial goods that other places could soon imitate - first cotton textiles, then ships, then cars - found themselves left behind by history. Cities that can readapt into the informational economy do not. As Cheshire and Hay stress, urban prosperity is by no means synonymous with urban growth: cities can decline successfully. And, not far away, other places may be growing successfully too.

Clearly, in making a successful adaptation, some of the larger and more problematic cities have a harder road than others. The key is that hardly any city any longer depends, as many cities once depended, on a unique resource inheritance. Cities do not arise and thrive because they are located on coal seams or on deep navigable water. The locational factors that help or hinder them are more subtle, and to a considerable degree they are capable of being created by human decision. A new airport or a new high-speed railway junction, a teleport or even a new fibre-optic link may create the conditions for large-scale private investment in the informational industries. Restored historic industrial or port buildings, coupled with the amenity values of a waterfront location, may similarly provide the basis for development of tourism, including that important variety, business tourism. A revived public transportation system, coupled with vigorous policies to civilize the private automobile, may create the right environment for a range of related activities, including retailing, tourism and entertainment.

All over the advanced industrial world, we can see successful models of these kinds of inner-city revival. Everywhere, waterfront areas - London and Manchester docklands, the Boston waterfront, the old harbour in Rotterdam - are being redeveloped for a mixture of housing, services, tourism and what has come to be known as leisure shopping or festival marketplaces. The model is provided by what James Rouse so successfully did, first in Boston, then in Baltimore, in the late 1970s and early 1980s. It has been followed by other models, so numerous now as to be almost beyond count; almost every older American city has its revived waterfront or warehouse area.

The most interesting point about this model is that it represents a deliberate attempt to restore urbanity to the heart of a great city that had lost it. The downtowns of many American cities, by the 1970s, represented nothing so much as urban disaster areas: the last remaining commercial buildings, relics of an earlier building wave of the turn of the century, stood isolated amidst a sea of derelict sites and parking lots. Baltimore, the most successful case of readaptation, was actually one of the earliest and the worst affected by this downtown blight. It successfully redeveloped both its downtown and the adjacent waterfront, which - as in Boston - had the happy fortune of being next door to each other. There is no doubt about the success of the formula: Baltimore's Inner Harbor is one of the major tourist attractions in the United States, rivalling the California Disneyland. Visitors and their children flock to it, enjoying a kind of synthetic urban quality that is, as they say in the hotel bathrooms, sanitized for their convenience. They are reacting against the dull sameness of the new suburban America, where so many of them now live and work.

It is very interesting to compare this model with that presented by the traditional European city. For it is being actively followed in those European cities that have been most drastically affected by the collapse of the old goods–handling, resource-based economy: places like Glasgow and Liverpool, Manchester and Rotterdam. But, as already seen, there is another kind of European city that was always service- and information-based, and has not suffered the same trauma of adaptation. Some of them suffered in a different way, from the destruction of war; and some few of those happened to have the good sense to rebuild their shattered patrimony. It is significant perhaps that some of those that did not, such as Frankfurt am Main, have actually begun to rectify that mistake in recent years: they want their history back. Everywhere, however, these cities have sought to breathe new life into their city streets, by pedestrianizing them and by improving public transport. Munich took something of a world lead in this respect, at the time of the 1972 Olympic Games; and many other German cities have paid it the sincerest form of flattery.

The result is something rather extraordinary: a city that retains all its historic qualities, including the rare prize of accessibility without access to a private automobile. But you should notice that it is a quality shared, to a considerable degree, with those transatlantic urban innovations: festival marketplaces and supermalls and theme parks, too, are places designed to be enjoyed on foot; all of them depend on the creation of a unique environment, in their case engineered, in which the street becomes a kind of theatrical show. In fact, one of the keys to urban success is now to achieve just this kind of physical and cultural quality.

The fact is that, in their role as consumers, people come to these places to enjoy a particular kind of urban experience, which they are not going to find anywhere else. It is fairly easy to preserve and enhance that experience in Europe; in most of North America, it is almost necessary to create it ab initio. In Europe, and in certain places in America, they will be able to find a certain urbanity in the smaller country towns that are being progressively embodied

31

into the new polycentric megalopolitan structure; and here they will resort for most of their regular weekly shopping and other personal services. But these places will not convey the undefinable sense of being in the heart of the big city; for that, they will have to return to the great cities. They fact that they are doing so - as occasional visitors, as tourists and as business tourists - is ample evidence that these places give them something unique to enjoy.

These places are uniquely serving the third of those functions that I earlier cited from the work of Lester Thurow: that of providing consumer services. And, with increasing affluence and discretionary spending, this becomes a central function for urban places. The key may be to combine it successfully with the other distinctive role of the post-industrial city: the production of informational services, the manipulation of symbols in Thurow's terminology. I am not sure that many places have got this combination quite right - though a few, like San Francisco, Toronto and of course Munich, come close. The problem is that the two functions have different locational and above all space requirements. Offices demand integration and bulk, either vertically [the skyscraper] or horizontally [the so-called groundscaper]. Neither structure sits well in a traditional urban fabric, such as is needed for consumer activities: both will prove completely overbearing.

This problem is easier in North American cities, where there never was much of a traditional urban structure and where - as Chicago showed - the gridiron street pattern early proved favourable to skyscraper construction. Here, it may be possible either to fit shopping streets into the spaces between office towers, as in San Francisco, or to build completely new enclosed malls - the suburbanization of downtown, as seen variously in Vancouver, Calgary and Atlanta. Elsewhere, above all in European cities with their delicate urban fabrics, it may be necessary to exclude large-scale office developments from the centre, in order to guarantee its survival.

2.7   Conclusion: the new urban form

We can thus see the emergence of a new urban structure, which is growing out of the old one like a butterfly from a chrysalis. Many of its elements are physically old elements, which are restructured to serve new purposes. Others are new, but in intimate relationship to the old.

The cores still constitute the old downtowns. First in Europe, somewhat later in North America, their position as centres of information exchange and processing will be suddenly and dramatically enhanced by the new high-speed trains - surely the true transportation technology of the twenty-first century. The places that become hubs on the new system, in particular, will play a unique role in the new system. A similar role will be played by nodes of advanced telecommunications, which are likely to occur in the same places. Private capital will inject large investments around these new hubs in the form of office concentrations, with attendant hotels. The major rivals to these revived downtowns will be new or existing airport hubs, wherever these can in turn be interconnected to the high-speed trains - as is certain to happen at Paris Charles de Gaulle and Amsterdam Schiphol, and perhaps some other places. But, with the general switch to train for journeys of up to 500 kilometres and even more, there will not be room for many of these giant interchanges.

In rather different places will be found the centres of conspicuous consumption in the new economy. Some will be revived medieval cores of major cities, including those special enclaves that have traditionally served as the places for night-life: Schwabing here in Munich, Sachsenhausen in Frankfurt, the Burg in Nuremberg. Some undoubtedly will be new centres. For the great bulk of the population will continue to disperse into smaller cities and towns and into their surrounding areas. A minority of these, in turn, will commute back to the cities for work; but a majority will find both homes and jobs there. A substantial number of the bigger or more attractive of the towns in these rural belts will almost certainly acquire an enhanced role as service centres, some perhaps even rivalling their larger cousins. In particular, towns with special roles - such as administrative or university centres - may be able to offer a range of services much richer than their size alone would signify. Places like Oxford, Cambridge, Marburg or Tübingen will successfully compete with London, Frankfurt or Stuttgart over a wide range of consumer services. And some new university centres - Louvain-la-Neuve in Belgium, Santa Cruz in California - may be able instantly to create the unique quality that evolved over centuries in their older counterparts.

Meanwhile, of course, the third of Thurow's sectors - production - will continue to provide the economic base for certain places and certain regions. But even it will be increasingly information-based, so that it will progressively gravitate to the places where knowledge is being generated. That is why, all over Europe, production is increasingly allied with research and development in precisely these rural belts of growth that I have earlier been describing: the western crescent of southern England, from Southampton and Portsmouth to Reading, Oxford and Cambridge; the very similar research belt south of Paris; the Cote d'Azur; and the Munich-Stuttgart-Heidelberg corridor. In other words, production is now being driven by information, and the factors of location for the one sector increasingly become the same as that for the other.

It poses an obvious challenge for the resource-based goods-producing cities of the earlier generation. But they too can find their niche, so long as they ally imagination with the will to invest. Public and quasi-public investment will surely be one of the main drivers of urban and regional change in the coming generation, as they lay down a new infrastructure of telecommunications and high-speed ground travel. It is vital that, both at the national level and above all the level of the European Community, we appreciate just how momentous these decisions are going to be.

Note

This paper was originally published in German as: Gibt es sie noch - die Stadt? in: Schabert, T. (ed.) *Die Welt der Stadt*, 17-42 (Munich: Piper, 1990), and was earlier delivered as an invited lecture at the Carl Siemens Foundation, Munich. Minor revisions have been made to this version.

References

Andersson, Å.E. (1985), Creativity and Regional Development. *Papers of the Regional Science Association*, 56, pp. 5-20.

Andersson, Å.E. (1985), *Kreativitet: StorStadens Framtid*, Prisma, Stockholm.

Aydalot, P. (ed.) (1986) *Milieux Innovateurs en Europe,* Paris: GREMI (Privately Printed).

Aydalot, P. Keeble, D. (ed.) (1988a), *High Technology Industry and Innovative Environments: The European Experience*, Routledge and Kegan Paul, London.

Berry, B.J.L. (1976), The Counter-Urbanization Process: Urban America Since 1970. In: Berry, B.J.L. (ed.), *Urbanization and Counter-Urbanization*, Sage Urban Affairs Annual Reviews, 11, Sage, Beverly Hills and London.

Buck, N., I. Gordon, and K. Young (1986), *The London Employment Problem*, Oxford U.P., Oxford.

Cheshire, P.C., and D.G. Hay, (1989), *Urban Problems in Western Europe: An Economic Analysis,*Unwin Hyman, London.

Clark, C. (1940), *The Conditions of Economic Progress,* Macmillan, London.

Cochrane, S.G., and D.R. Vining (1988), Recent Trends in Migration between Core and Peripheral Regions in Developed and Advanced Developing Countries. *International Regional Science Review*, 11, pp. 215-244.

Dillon, D., S. Weiss and P. Hait (1989) Supersuburbs, *Planning,* 55, pp. 7–21.

Frey, W.H. (1988) The Re-emergence of Core Region Growth: A Return to the Metropolis? *International Regional Science Journal*, 11, pp. 261-268.

Garreau, J. (1991), *Edge City: Life on the New Frontier*, Doubleday, New York.

Geddes, P. (1915), *Cities in Evolution.*, Williams and Norgate, London.

Gottmann, J. (1961), *Megalopolis: The Urbanized Northeastern Seaboard of the United States*, Twentieth Century Fund, New York.

Hall, P. (1987), The Flight to the Green, *New Society*, 7 January.

Hall, P. (1988), Urban Growth and Decline in Western Europe, in Dogan, M., Kasarda, J. (ed.) *The Metropolis Era*, Vol. I, *A World of Giant Cities*, Sage Newbury Park and London.

Hall, P. (1989), *London 2001*, Unwin Hyman, London.

McCarthy, K.F., Morrison, P.A. (1977) The GottmannChanging Demographic and Economic Structure of Non-Metropolitan Areas in the United States. *International Regional Science Review*, 2, pp. 123-42.

Mumford, L. (1938), *The Culture of Cities*, Secker and Warburg, London.

Noyelle, T.J. and T.M. Stanback, Jr. (1984), *The Economic Transformation of American Cities*, Rowman and Allanheld, Totowa.

Reich, R. (1989), As the World Turns, *New Republic*, May 23, pp. 23-28.

Schumpeter, J. A. (1939) *Business Cycles*, New York: McGraw Hill. (Reprinted 1982, Philadelphia: Porcupine Press).

Schumpeter, J.A. (1942), *Capitalism, Socialism and Democracy*, Harper, New York.

Stanback, T. (1985), The Changing Fortunes of Metropolitan Economies, in Castells, M. (ed.) *High Technology, Space and Society.* (Urban Affairs

Annual Reviews, 28). Sage, Beverly Hills.

Vining, D.R. and T. Kontuly, (1977), Increasing Returns to City Size in the Face of an Impending Decline in the Size of large Cities: Which is the Bogus Fact? *Environment and Planning, A*, 9, pp. 59-62.

Vining, D.R. and A. Strauss (1977), A Demonstration that the Current Deconcentration of Population in the United States is a Clean Break with the Past. *Environment and Planning, A*, 9, pp. 751-8.

Vining, D.R. (1982), Recent Dispersal from the World's Industrial Core Regions. In: Kawashima, T. (ed.) *Urbanization Processes: Experiences of Eastern and Western Countries*, Pergamon, Oxford, pp. 171-192.

Webber, M.M. (1963), Order and Diversity: Community without Propinquity. In: Wingo, L. et al, *Cities and Space: The Future Use of Urban Land*, Johns Hopkins, Baltimore.

Webber, M.M. (1964), The Urban Place and the Nonplace Urban Realm. In: Webber, M.M. et al, *Explorations into Urban Structure*, University of Pennsylvania Press, Philadelphia.

Weber, A. (1929 (1909)) *Alfred Weber's Theory of the Location of Industries*, (Translated by C.J. Friedrich), Chicago U.P, Chicago.

3 Learning from California: The macroeconomic consequences of structural changes

S.S. Cohen and C.E. Garcia

3.1 Introduction

Suddenly, something has gone very wrong with the California economy. To a far greater extent than reported in official and conventional analyses, the problem is structural - not just cyclical. Consequently, a moderate national recovery will not translate into a comparable California recovery. Geographic trickle down will prove no more effective than the 'supply side' trickle down America tried for the past dozen years. California's economy is performing far worse than the national economy and, as the U.S. recovers, albeit tepidly, from recession, California doesn't. Unemployment is almost one-third-again higher than the national average, and is likely to exceed 150% imminently.[1] Instead of adding some 250,000 new jobs per year as it did regularly throughout the eighties, California is losing jobs - and not just low-end jobs - in big batches, some 550,000 to 800,000 jobs[2] in two and a half years. Indeed, over 35% of total job losses in the United States between June 1990 and December 1992 were in California, and over 25% of the national job loss was located in the four contiguous Southern California metropolitan areas centred around Los Angeles.[3]

At one level, diagnosis of the California problem - job loss - is simple. Everything went wrong in the same place at the same time. Cyclical forces ranging from a seven year drought with severe economic consequences, through the US national recession, which hit California late but hard, through corporate downsizing and the end of the real estate boom, played a major role. So did structural or California-specific causes ranging from the out migration of jobs through severe cutbacks in defense procurement. This paper argues that official and conventional efforts to understand the problems of the California economy significantly underestimate the importance of structural changes, especially those related to cutbacks in defense spending. A major reason for this is the built-in tendency of macroeconomics to underestimate the macroeconomic impacts of structural changes. Structural change that has made California's recession both more severe and prolonged than the national recession.

California is the most important regional economy in North America. Its GDP makes it a G-7 nation.[4] Big enough and, critically, diverse enough to withstand the sectoral and cyclical shocks that beset most fast-growing regions, for decades California has been the very model of a successful and dynamic regional economy - relentlessly growing faster than the national economy in which it is embedded. Of course the Golden State was rich from the very beginning, and it has stayed rich because it has always been more modern.

The importance of California is not only quantitative. In both myth and reality, California is the place that invents the future, and, of course, markets it to the rest of the world. As legend has it, if it is happening in California today, it will hit New York in six months, and London, Munich and Tokyo next year. The rest of the world dutifully follows the autonomous and incessant inventiveness of California in phenomena that extend from new products - from plastic surf boards, to lap top computers - through new organizations; from entrepreneurial high-tech firms to religious movements; new weapons; new fashions; and, most important, new attitudes and styles, including even entire *"life styles"* (itself a California concept). For Americans, California has been the ultimate and seemingly permanent expression of the American dream. And that *"take,"* as they say in language-inventive California, has been shared by most of the world, often as dream, sometimes as nightmare, always as market.

During the late 1980s - just yesterday by the rhythms of American academic publishing - a substantial literature in regional science appeared to extrapolate, analyze and explain California's special success.[5] The element most often singled out was its high-tech industrial base; California was not weighed down by the industries of the past like steel and autos with their flat or declining futures and their outmoded industrial and social practices. California's industrial base was built instead on advanced electronics, aerospace, biotech, and advanced services such as film making, music making, auto design, and software development. Even California agriculture had a strong base in advance technologies with its tight ties to the University. Californians had created a uniquely flexible economic and social system. It spawned high-tech entrepreneurship to route electrons and digital codes into new products and new applications. It could provide the entrepreneurial flair to take advantage of the cheap immigrant labor that poured across the Mexican border to produce apparel and furniture, and at the same time organize battalions of scientists for giant technology projects such as space shuttles, missiles and stealth aircraft. It has been, we are told, the special California culture, flexible, innovative, based on risk and fun, that provided the atmosphere out of which new demands would first be perceived and new organizations created to take economic advantage of those new demands that could not happen in more hide bound cultures that encapsulated other great economic regions like the Ruhr or Detroit or Washington. Californians were always starting out fresh. They had left the past behind.[6] They have now caught up with their future. And for the first time in memory, the California future looks worse than the California past.

3.1.1 Californias

Economically, as well as culturally and politically, California divides rather neatly into three distinct zones: the Central Valley, Northern California (the San

Francisco Bay Area), and Southern California, centering around the Los Angeles basin and sprawling down to the Mexican border.

The Central Valley, Steinbeck country, has its economic base in agriculture, with over half the state's agricultural jobs (167,000) and 80% of food processing jobs (40,500).[7] It is the smallest of the regions, and is growing rapidly in part through 'spillover' growth of jobs and housing from the Bay Area. Although the Central Valley currently suffers from high unemployment rates, it has absorbed only about 1% of the state's substantial job losses since 1990.[8]

Northern California circles the San Francisco Bay with San Francisco as its traditional centre through San Jose, some forty minutes down the freeway (at night) has now grown larger than San Francisco. Between them stretches Silicon Valley, with some quarter of a million high-tech based jobs. The Bay Area economy has been growing faster than the rest of the nation for several decades. Its success has been based on those high-tech industries as well as financial, and international services. Its high-tech base is dominated by its two great Universities, Berkeley and Stanford, and their offsprings of young companies, mostly in electronics, which typically began as venture firms. Silicon Valley counts well over two thousand such firms at any given moment. Some of them, such as Hewlett Packard, Intel and Apple, have grown quite large but the Silicon Valley culture and industrial structure is still that of a community of smaller, entrepreneurial firms. It is the symbolic antithesis of an economy dominated by a few large employers, with a monocultural industrial base. The pace of innovation and the creation of new firms remains lively. Northern California is now the world's leading centre for biotech start ups. But it is neither immune to fierce competition from Japan and the Pacific nor recession proof. Its high cost structure puts it at a great disadvantage, not for start ups, but for job creating expansions of firms. Its share of total California job losses is about 14%, while its share of California's employment base is about one fifth.[9]

Finally there is Southern California, four Standard Metropolitan Areas (MSAs) centred around Los Angeles and extending down the coast to the Mexican border. It contains about half of California's 30 million people, a bit less than half of California's officially counted 13 million jobs, and about eighty percent of California's job losses.[10] One very big town, metro Los Angeles accounted for over half the state's job losses between 1990 and 1992 but over one fifth of the national job loss.

3.2 Los Angeles on the nature of the economic decline in california

Los Angeles makes myths, music, movies and missiles; together they dominate the world. But the missiles dominate the LA economy. Of course, as in all modern metropolitan areas, service jobs in health, education, FIRE (finance, insurance and real estate), and retail trade, etc., provide the vast bulk of employment. But it is Los Angeles, not Detroit, that is the biggest manufacturing centre in the U.S.[11].

The economic base[12] of Los Angeles is dominated by four major sectors: (1)

Real Estate and Construction, (2) Light Manufacturing, (3) Advanced Services and (4) High-Tech and Aerospace (including military industrial firms).

1 Real Estate and Construction. Real estate was LA's first industry, its first export product. In 1870 the population of Los Angeles was five thousand; today it is well over ten million.[13] The first folks out drew lines on the ground, printed brochures about the new paradise, and sold lots to the next arrivals, who conveniently came with money. They, in turn, sold lots to the next, and so on, and all prospered, albeit unevenly. Today over 55,000 people are employed in the real estate business; promoting and processing transactions. Construction is the next step. It employs about 110,000 people.[14] This sector, as we will soon see, is severely depressed, and will stay depressed for several years at least.

2 Advanced Services. LA, like the other great world metropolises, is a centre for advanced and high-end services, especially, finance, law, international business, and corporate control. It is America's second financial centre, though well behind New York. Los Angeles also has some economic specialties all its own in high-end services. First, of course there is the entertainment industry. LA is the unrivalled world capital of The Entertainment Industry. The motion picture segment alone employs about 100,000 people. It is also the world's capital for the music business and for television. And each of those segments generates a broad range of high value-added services that stretch from costume design and sound engineering through deal making, subsidiary rights negotiations, talent agents and particular kinds of intellectual property definition and protection. LA is also a major world design centre, for a host of goods ranging from swim suits and clothing through automobiles for producers from Japan as well as the US. This complex sector of advanced producer services is in perfectly fine shape and continues to play a major role in supporting the LA economy.

3 Light Manufacturing. Light manufacturing - furniture, apparel, textiles and printing - occupies a substantial place in the Los Angeles economy. Apparel dominates this sector, 100,000 Los Angelenos earn their living, often meagre, in the garment trade, making Los Angeles a major American garment centre. Furniture production is another large sub-sector, employing some 25,000 people, while printing and publishing, as would be expected in a world commercial metropolis, is a major employer of some 55,000 people, about half of whom are in commercial printing, tightly connected to advertising and multifarious hype. Statistics on light manufacturing in Los Angeles are probably the least reliable of the various categories of employment, reflecting the industry's tight connection to the City's large immigrant population, both legal and illegal, and the new social structure of LA.

4 High-technologies and Aerospace Industrial Complex. Los Angeles is also the "aerospace capital of the world".[15] Beginning well before World War II, Los Angeles began to work at making itself attractive to the Big Casting Director at the Pentagon. The creation of Caltech, which differed from other universities in its focus on science that had definite military potential, and its innovative tight relations with the Military (and then NASA), was a major building bloc. It paid off for LA, in a big way. In the phrase of Mike Davis', stimulating book about L.A., "Caltech, together with the Department of Defense, substantially invented Southern California's post-war science based economy."[16] Los Angeles has continued to develop its primacy in Aerospace and Industrial Military firms. It is the site of the prime contractors for stealth aircraft, space shuttles, Trident, Midgetman, and various cruise missiles, as well as the advanced electronics, location guidance, detection and communications systems that add value to those flying platforms.

LA is America's most important manufacturing centre, and aerospace is mostly what they make. Writing in 1990, regional planners Peter Hall and Ann Markusen remarked "there is as yet no sign that the region (Los Angeles) has lost the creativity, the innovative capacity, that was the basis of its meteoric industrial rise to become the aerospace capital of the world".[17]

In corporate organization, industrial behaviour and, crucially, the structures and dynamics of their markets, high tech in Los Angeles is quite different from high tech in Northern California. In terms of industrial structure, LA high tech is overwhelmingly dominated by giant, DOD prime contractors: Rockwell, McDonnell Douglas, Hughes Aerospace, TRW or CalTech itself (with a regular inflow of over $1 billion in prime contracts). These firms have a particular organization and conduct. They do project, or mission, research and development. Speed to market, low cost R&D and low cost production are not top priorities, and are not particularly present. But fastidious bureaucracy is. The prime contractor firms have created their own internal bureaucracies and procedures that match - as they absolutely must - those of the monopsonist buyer, the Pentagon.

In Northern California, the market structure for high technology is quite different. With a few notable exceptions (Lockheed, FMS and Ford Aerospace) high-technology industries are commercial; markets are competitive; entrants are many and swift; foreign competition (from Japan and the Pacific basin) is brutal, prompt and sometimes devastating. There are no monopsony buyers, no dominant buyers. The "Founding Myths" in Northern Californian differ from those in Southern Californian high tech: down South it is the Manhattan Project and Man on the Moon - heroic and gigantic missions marked by truly vast mobilizations and organizations of scientific resources; up North, it is Steve Jobs creating the personal computer in his garage - small scale, entrepreneurial, market driven. Firms are self-consciously non-bureaucratic in their organization, and strive, sometimes in almost comical ways, to avoid the reality and appearance of bureaucratic organizations in their behaviour. Turnover of product, technology, personnel and firms is substantial and rapid.

High Tech in Southern California is in trouble, and so, therefore, is California. The preliminary diagnosis is simple. Defense spending in California has fallen, from a high of about $60 billion at the height of Star Wars in 1988 to about $51 billion in 1992 (inflation adjusted).[18] That decline was concentrated in Southern California, and it is continuing, with no end in sight.

41

3.3   The 1980s "A Golden Age": a review

The l980s were years of rapid growth in jobs, population and asset values for California in general, and for Southern California in particular. About one fourth of the total national population increase during the decade of the 1980s, some 4.8 million people, took place in California, mostly in Southern California; that proportion rose to about one third for the period l983 and 1990. During the eighties, the California economy added, about one quarter of a million new jobs per year, year after year. Real Estate values soared: the median price of houses sold in Los Angeles house rose from $119 thousand in 1982 to $215 in 1989.[19] Adjacent Orange country experienced a very similar increase. In the judgment of regional economists Allen Scott and Alan Paul, the 1980s were "a golden age for the Southern California economy." They neglected to note that so were the 1940s, l950s and l960s. Golden ages are nothing new to California; what is interesting is the comparison among them.

As California golden ages go, the 1980s had a distinctly bronze bottom. Because as population, employment and asset values increased, real average wages did not. Across the entire decade, from 1980 to 1990, average wages did not rise more than consumer prices, so that adjusted for inflation, average wages, both in California as a whole, and in Los Angeles, actually fell slightly, about one half a per cent.[20]

The population influx was not the motor of growth. nor even of the dramatic rise in real estate values during this period. Growth was motored by an influx of money, not people, and the impetus influx came from the Pentagon and Real Estate investments.

Defense spending rose rapidly during the 1980s from about $30 billion in 1982, to about $60 billion in 1988,[21] and almost three quarters into the four Southern California MSAs.[22] Employment in industries dominated by defense contractors soared, from to 600,000 in 1980 to 720,000 in 1989,[23] and we should note, that employment in Defense dominated sectors pays far more than average wages in manufacturing, let alone services. Average weekly wages in Aircraft and parts in LA region came to $729.10, while average wages in manufacturing were $463.50.[24] An increase in Aerospace employment in LA has, therefore, a much more important multiplier effect on the economy, than a comparable rise in general manufacturing or services. So as we will see, does a decline.

Real Estate, prompted by changes in tax laws, quickly responded accelerating the boom. Demand began to spin off from the defense build-up quickening the pace of new construction and transferring substantial portions of the new money into rising prices for houses. Then Construction spending took off on its own, beyond the pull of demand. It was pushed by floods of new money that began to pour into Los Angeles, as it so often has. Real Estate became a second, quite independent river of funds into LA. It itself had several tributaries. The Savings and Loans system shovelled money out the door into ambitious new construction projects, and LA got more than its share of this new form of creative spending. Beginning in the mid-eighties, Japanese investors burdened with vast quantities of strong Yen bellied up to the table and paid for yet another round of construction of prime office and commercial space. By the end of the eighties Los Angeles had become the prime locale for fresh Japanese investment in US real estate. Official statistics show Japanese ownership of California real estate rising from $5 billion in 1987, to $6 1/2 billion in 1988, to $10 billion in 1989 to $13 billion in 1990 and to $18 billion 1991.[25] Note this is ownership, distinct from bank mortgage loans. California also became the prime locale for Japanese banks with their coffers full and interest rates low back home, to compete, with their weaker American rivals, by aggressively pricing and financing real estate loans to buy market share. They got it, faster than Toyota. Unofficial sources have it that Japanese banks originated more than half the commercial real estate loans in California during the years 1989-91. Fresh money also flowed in through overseas Chinese networks in significant amounts. But as it tended to come through family networks, and typically in smaller chunks than the Japanese corporate placements, it seems to have completely escaped tabulation by U.S. government statisticians.

The impact of these diverse flows of new money for construction was impressive. Employment in construction rose from about 350 thousand at the trough of the 1982 recession to 650 thousand by the end of the decade in the State. And in California, construction, especially in the office segment, pays well: construction in general pays 160% of the average LA manufacturing wage.[26] Employment in real estate in California, that is in the promoting and processing transactions, soared: from about 125 thousand at the beginning of the decade to about 205 thousand at the end of the decade.[27] Perhaps the best and most impressive measure of the boom in new construction of commercial properties is the inventory of office space in LA County and adjacent Orange county, which rose from 67 million square feet in 1980 to 252 million sq. feet in 1991, and price in office rose from $234 in 1985 to $303 in 1990.[28]

The selling price of the median existing single-family home in Los Angeles rose from $119,260 in 1982 to 215,000 in 1991 (an increase that was itself not much smaller than the total price of the median house in the Mid West or Texas at the end of that decade). The production of new housing units exceeded 200,000 every year from 1984 to 1989, topping 315,000 housing units in 1986. The rapid rise in housing prices-in its turn, generated a dramatic increase in household wealth, at least perceived wealth. The LA habit of rapidly trading up, from house to house, or refinancing, to draw spendable money out of real estate appreciation, plus of course, the spurt in new construction, spilled over throughout the economy.

During the late eighties much was made of the growth of financial services in Los Angeles and the shift of finance jobs out of San Francisco, California's traditional centre for finance, for consolidation in the larger LA market. These moves generated more headlines (mostly in San Francisco) than jobs in LA.[29] But jobs were added and with them a new definition of LA, as the Capital of the Pacific Rim. For during the eighties LA emerged not only as the leading California centre for financial services, but as the rapidly rising number two in the US, and as a major world centre for extremely innovative and mega-scale finance for national corporations. LA's share of origination of major corporate financing showed an incredible rise, but behind the statistics lay not so much the rise of a new financial centre, but the meteoric rise of one firm, Drexel Burnam, and its leader, Mike Milken, who created and ruled the junk bond markct. During the eighties, Drexel more than boomed; it went, as they say in

LA, "off the charts", and the money sloshed through the LA system, beginning with Mr. Milken's own annual income of over $500 million. A good chunk spilled out of Drexel's fancy headquarters in Beverly Hills onto local construction and services.

Light manufacturing was an obvious beneficiary; new construction and housing turnover generated a sharp increase in demand for household and office durables such as furniture. And the LA furniture industry boomed. The rapid growth in light manufacturing was taken by many as an indication of the extraordinary flexibility of the LA economy and system of social organization.[30] The furniture industry combined local demand, local entrepreneurship and immigrant labor to create thousands of low end jobs. The LA furniture industry boomed. Employment rose from about 33 thousand in the trough of the 1982 recession to about 43 thousand by 1988.[31] Employment in apparel also spurted, rising from about 75 thousand officially counted in the early eighties, to about 100 thousand by the end of that decade. And so did printing, it grew from 60 thousand to over 70 thousand during the 80s. Light manufacturing provided a strong case of the possibilities of creating new jobs, in new industries, for new classes of people, especially all those poor and low skilled immigrants from Mexico. They kept pouring in, in unstoppable streams. The garment industry expanded on a similar base, compounding the employment effects, and compounding also, the dual wage, dual society structure that so rapidly developed in Southern California during the 1980s. Wages in apparel are about one third of aerospace wages, and furniture about one half.[32]

3.4   The 1990s

LA ended the 80s rich, proud and confident of its unique, innovative prosperity, its ability to absorb newcomers from all over the world, and of its technological and creative prowess. In March 1990, The UCLA Business Forecast for California began with the heading "near term outlook remains good.

The 1990's - thus far - have not been kind to LA; and the near future does not look much better. California, but essentially Southern California, is seriously under performing the US economy. This is out of character. Typically California outperforms the US economy. Income rises faster. When recession hits, California recovers faster. This time it is recovering - if it is recovering at all - far slower (See Table 3.1 and Chart 3.1).

And the key indicator of underperformance is job loss. It is not just an economic fact; it is a political fact.[33]

Cyclical factors and forces experienced by the whole nation: - the U.S. recession, corporate downsizing, the end of the great real estate boom - combined with structural, or California specific factors - such massive defense cut backs and shifts - hit California at the same time. But this all encompassing observation obscures as much as it explains. Because the crisis of California, which is essentially a crisis of southern California, is most fruitfully understood in structural terms. Let us first review, quickly, the different forces at play, and then focus on the structural elements.

44

Table 3.1
Present change of U.S. GNP and
California employment (annual)

Year	U.S GNP [1]	Employment in California [2]
1961	2.6	4.1
1962	5.3	4.7
1963	4.1	3.6
1964	5.3	4.1
1965	5.8	4.7
1966	5.8	5.1
1967	2.9	4
1968	4.1	4.1
1969	2.4	3.6
1970	**-0.3**	**-2.3**
1971	-2.8	2.1
1972	5	4.7
1973	5.2	4.9
1974	**-0.5**	**1.6**
1975	**-1.3**	**2.3**
1976	4.9	3.9
1977	4.7	7.2
1978	5.3	5.7
1979	2.5	4.6
1980	**-0.2**	**0.9**
1981	1.9	1.4
1982	**-2.5**	**1.8**
1983	3.5	1.6
1984	6.5	6.1
1985	3.2	3.8
1986	2.9	2.5
1987	3.1	3.7
1988	3.9	3.6
1989	7.5	3.9
1990	0.8	2.1
1991	**-1.2**	**-3.1**
1992	2.1	-1.9

Source: 1 Bureau of Labor Statistics
            2 California Department of Finance

45

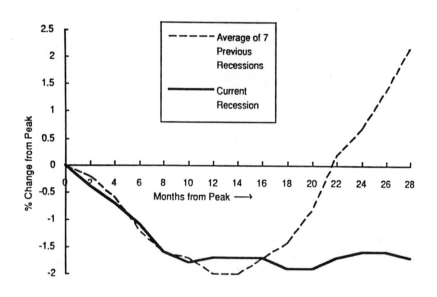

Source: Bureau of Labor Statistics and Joint Economic Committee

Chart 3.1 The job recession. Change in payroll employment from Cycle
Peak

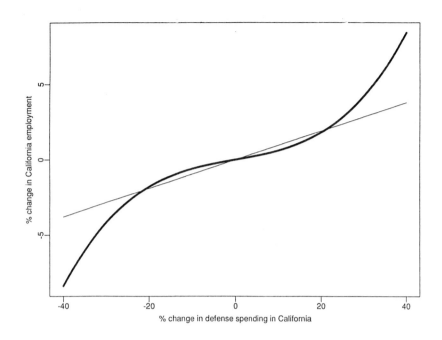

Chart 3.2   The presence of nonlinearities and threshold effect

3.4.1. Cyclical or national factors

a   The recession
The national recession hit California late. It did not just descend uniformly on the country, but made its way around, like a flu epidemic, from region to region. It is responsible for the largest part of California job loss. The State Commission on Finance attributes about 50% of job loss to the recession;[34] as will become apparent below, we find this figure to be too high.

b   Corporate downsizing
Intellectually quite distinct from a traditional recession, but certainly part this recession is the national (or perhaps world scale) morphological phenomenon conventionally called "corporate downsizing". Companies are reducing employment, but not in traditional, temporary "lay offs", with expectations of rehirings once business conditions pick up again. This time expectations for rehiring are feeble to nil. Companies are reorganizing to shed staff permanently. The Fortune 500 companies employed about 19 million in 1982; by 1992 they employed about 12 million and the downward trend is continuing. Behind this strong trend is a confluence of diverse forces: companies that lost market share and margins to foreign competitors, a la GM; companies that suddenly found their industries "deregulated" such as airlines and utilities; companies involved in major consolidations, such as Bank of America and First Interstate Bank in California, that resulted in the elimination of thousands of positions in California's financial sector; companies that suddenly lost profitability in key segments of their market a la IBM. But the tendency is also manifest in companies whose sales are not contracting, and are doing quite well. Some companies are replacing regular employees with temporaries, or sub-contractors that pay lower wages and often no fringes. But more fundamental changes seem also to be at play. It appears, that we are now beginning to experience the long awaited productivity payoff for information technologies which, only when coupled to concrete reorganization of the production process and the corporate organization, seem to permit of a good deal of "jobless recovery" and perhaps "jobless growth".

c   Real estate and construction
The real estate bust is another localized impact of a national (or world cities) phenomenon. After the great late 'eighties boom' in commercial real estate values and construction activity, the bubble burst and both indices crashed. In LA's central business district, average prices paid for commercial property fell from about $300 per sq. foot to under 200 per sq. foot between 1990 and 1992; and they are still falling. Rents followed a similar path.[35] Even the value of houses, after nearly doubling between 1982 and 1991, turned and have begun to decline; the decline seems to be gathering momentum. The median price of houses sold in LA in the first quarter of 1993 was more than 5% lower than in 1992.[36] Employment in construction (a high multiplier sector) plummeted: from 154,000 in 1990 to 100,000 in the first quarter of 1993, and is continuing to fall.[37] And as the pipeline empties there is little reason to expect a sudden improvement. By 1992, the value of new building permits was down to about 20% of the 1989 level.[38] Vacancy rates are above 20% in LA,

48

and San Diego.[39] The bursting of the real estate bubble is not particular to California. Comparable implosions have hit London, New York, Dallas, Connecticut, Paris, Madrid, etc. We can consider it part of (inter) national level, cyclical, forces.

3.4.2 Structural or California Specific Factors

a The out-migration of jobs and the in-migration of poor people

Much is being made in California about an exodus of jobs to other American locations and to Mexico as a result of California's oft-criticized high cost, high regulation business environment.

The out-migration of jobs takes two distinct forms. The first, simplest, most dramatic, but smallest, is when companies move out of state. The second, is when California companies expand and add new facilities, typically large factories, outside of California. It is more important. The latter migration accounts for the big numbers of jobs. But these are difficult to count in fundamental, not just tracking ways. Out-migration of that sort is, of course, nothing new to the California economy. One could guess that perhaps most of the many high-tech jobs created in Singapore between say 1975 and 1985 were directly transferred (or induced by transfers) from Silicon Valley and a few other US high-tech locales. High cost, innovative locales typically and classically incubate new products and processes. Then scale ups transfer to lower cost locations, in their nearby hinterland, then further afield. The classic formulation of this "product cycle theory, " which is a pillar of regional analysis was made by Vernon and Hoover, in the 1950s for the New York Regional Plan.[40] Out-migrations, of labor intensive, or pollution intensive activities, as well as major manufacturing expansions are part and parcel of the dynamic of a rich and innovative economy; they will not, and should not, cease.

Nonetheless, there are indications, - however suspect the data - that something new is going on, and that it might have negative and significant impacts on the California economy, especially in the Los Angeles region.. Studies based on analysis of 1035 documented cases of business migration from California over the past decade estimate job loss between 168,000 to 224,000.[41] Mexico received over one fourth of those cases. Analyses point to the obvious factors: environmental regulations in the LA basin that simply shut down certain kinds of industrial processes; high overhead costs such as workers compensation which costs 3 times as much as in neighbouring Oregon, or litigation costs that have risen by 300% on a per case basis over the past decade; high rents; high insurance, etc. And the overwhelming fact that cheap Mexican labor is cheaper in Mexico.

Out migration of jobs per se cannot be counted, although we have a goodly supply of estimates.[42] Jobs, especially expansions, are always migrating out. Some kind of net difference comparison with previous periods is required to give the notion any meaning whatever, let alone dimensions.

In-migration of people, however, continues, the overwhelming mass consisting of poor and unskilled immigrants (legal and illegal) from Mexico.[43] Migration flows are often sensitive to economic conditions; a downturn in cmployment often slows the flow. But migration is a decisive factor in

49

reshaping the structure of the California economy. At the simplest level, and the one with the greatest potential for political backlash, the demographics of migration and the large dependency ratio of people to jobs in the immigrant population, creates substantial "fiscal drag" for the troubled finances of the State of California, which pays the costs of education and most other services to this population. These questions are rising rapidly on the California and American political agendas, and not only in pleasant ways. Migration at this scale also reshapes the structure of the California economy, as well as the society, towards low wage, low skill activities. California risks becoming a dual society, living uneasily together, competing with Japan in high level activities and Mexico in lower skill, lower wage activities, perhaps unsuccessfully on both counts.

b Defense: Structural Change as Distinct from Marginal Changes

Defense cut backs are the key to understanding the relative severity of California's recession. Defense spending (measured in constant 1992 dollars) declined from $60 billion in 1988 to $51 billion in 1992.[44].. We estimate that cutbacks in defense procurement and R&D, which are still accelerating, have already been responsible for better than one third of California's job loss. This calculation ignores other reductions in defense spending such as direct payroll reductions or base closings, but it does include ripple effects. The official estimate, (as well as most conventional estimates) is about 22%.[45] This disparity demands some explanation because if our avowedly preliminary estimate is even approximately correct, it calls into question our understanding of the structures of the California economy, especially as regards its dependency upon Federal government procurement, and the likelihood of a modest national upturn translating into an end of recession in California.

First, estimates are based on input-output relationships labor under two onerous difficulties. The first of these is that estimates for California input–output relations are derived from national input-output tables and for the most part, those national input output tables are based on modified 1982 relations.[46] Rapid changes in technology, plus reorganization of production into new, regional based "flexible production systems, that have become keen objects for study by microeconomists, argue strongly for substantial changes in these inter–industry relationships.

Second, the official state estimate (and several non-official efforts at estimation) equates the defense budget with defense spending for a given year. That is, it ignores the crucial time-lag represented by the defense "pipeline" between contract awards and changes in actual spending. This time-lag is especially consequential for estimating employment effects when awards - and later spending - hit an inflexion point, from an upward to a downward trajectory.[47]

We can correct for these problems in the following ways to produce a simple, alternative estimate of total job loss in California due to cutbacks in defense procurement and their ripple effects. Such a preliminary alternative estimate is built on two assumptions: (1) A lag time of two years between contract awards and employment effects and (2) Treat changes in defense procurement in California as an exogenous variable.[48]

50

Under those conditions we simulated total California annual employment changes on the assumption of no changes in DOD procurement between 1988, the inflexion point, and 1992, in constant (1987) dollars. We excluded all other variables and treated that change in procurement and R&D as exogenous. We then compared it with a simulation based on actual (but lagged) cuts in procurement and R&D spending, again excluding all other variables and treating procurement change as exogenous.

The difference in total employment between 1990-1992 in both sketch simulations represents a preliminary estimate of job loss due to defense cutbacks - procurement and R&D - in California. In that first and simple analysis the total job loss in California associated to changes and cuts in defense spending arising to 230,000. In contrast the last official estimate provided by the Commission on State Finance concluded that about 180,000 jobs have been lost in the past two years due to the military industrial cutbacks.[49]

The numbers of our estimate represent a higher regional employment multiplier of the aerospace industrial complex. But the implicit assumptions - especially changed inter-industry relations and spending time lag - are quite consistent with empirical reality, the difference in results should be taken not as the final, correct number, but as a prompt to reconsider our understanding of the macroeconomic implications of structural change in a major regional economy. However they are not efforts to re-do multipliers for California aerospace, although they do call those conventionally received multipliers into question. Rather they aim, not at better "marginal multipliers," representations of total employment effects of adding, or subtracting, say one thousand jobs in the aerospace sector. They are back of the envelope sketches of something we can call "structural multipliers," indictions of what happens to an economy if a major industry is excised. To repeat a bit, it does not address the question, What are the employment consequences of shedding a few hundred or even a few thousand jobs in a big sector? Rather it addresses the question, What happens if that sector undergoes a structural transformation: it shrinks beyond the marginal; it is off-shored. Here, it is perfectly reasonable to believe that the structural effect is something inherently different than a simple summing of marginal effects. A thousand person decline in aerospace employment will not close down the specialized equipment industries that provide capital goods to aerospace; a structural change in aerospace will induce a structural change in aerospace equipment, and the rest of the supplier chain.

Reconciling these findings with other studies. Our estimate of employment repercussions of the substantial, structural, cuts in defense spending in California are substantially higher than those conventionally available. They are, indeed, far higher than most regional multiplier effects. Why? As noted above, we do not aim at estimating marginal employment multipliers, the purpose of traditional exercises. We aim at responding to questions of structural change. Here, there is some external work that is quite apposite. Recently a major effort to recalculate national multipliers for various manufacturing industries has been made (Baker and Lee, 1993).[50] They used some methodological and traditional assumptions in regional multipliers, but most important, they counted capital requirements (on a depreciated basis) for each job, something that seems reasonable, but is not part of the conventional approach. They also counted Government effects, at all three levels of government, something again, not part of traditional practice. Then, on the basis of readily available BLS statistics, they calculated direct plus indirect employment effects. They got multipliers for aircraft, etc. far in excess of traditional multipliers for those industries: numbers around 4 rather than 2.5. The implicit intellectual basis for the Baker and Lee analysis, is not to be found in the techniques or the data sets employed in the recalculations. It is in the basic assumption. What they look at is the total impact of a sector, starting at the very top of the chain. It contemplates the up-rooting (or complete installation) of an industry and its supplier chain. In this sense, we find it a good deal closer to our central problem of estimating the impact of a massive cut-back in a particularly well developed industrial chain: defense industries in California, than an exercise involving extending marginal multipliers beyond their dimensional and structural limits.

3.5   Prognosis and conclusion

If our preliminary estimate of the role that cutbacks in defense procurement played in California's job loss is correct - or more accurately, if it is even in "the ball park,"- it bodes ill for expectations of a modest national economic recovery bringing with it comparable recovery to California. Structural factors, indeed, exogenous non-cyclical factors, have played a much larger role in California employment and wealth expansion, and in their subsequent contraction, than conventionally thought. Medium size cyclical uptakes will not compensate for that structural drag. Defense procurement is on a long term downward trajectory. Furthermore, the important time lag factor that we emphasized compounds that pessimism: the negative effects of recent DOD cutbacks will just now begin to make themselves felt. And over the middle term, these will be compounded by cutbacks in defense spending in California that are quite separate from procurement, such as the closing of major military bases with substantial civilian payrolls and substantial local spending. To this dispiriting reconsideration of structural problems, one must add the continuing effects of the collapse in commercial real estate. The extent of the overhang of unrented commercial properties, and the free fall in building permits, indicate a bleak middle term for construction in California. Simply put, there will be absolutely no recovery in commercial construction in California for at least five years, probably longer when traditional rules of thumb about space needs are adopted to changes in corporate organization and resources. And commercial construction and defense procurement, were the great motors of Californian, but especially Southern Californian growth in the eighties. When they kicked into reverse, they were the key variables in determining the relative severity and persistence of California's recession.

A modest recovery in the United States economy will not translate smoothly into a comparable recovery (or perhaps any recovery) in California where major structural, problems compound the cyclical. And much of the structural problem lies at the doorstep of the Federal Government. Absent, large scale, regionally targeted stimulus packages, the middle term prognosis for California in general, and for Southern California in particular, is dreary. Construction will pick up substantially only in response to a targeted public works program. And here the problem is scale. A few hundred million dollars will not go very far.

Despite much hope, and some rhetoric to the contrary, the defense industrial complex that dominates the Southern California economy, will not succeed in converting itself into a large and competitive commercial high-tech sector. Conversion at a scale that will matter will have to be conversion to civilian - as distinct from commercial - markets, and that points right back at Washington, in its traditional role of creating a market through purchasing policy. And here Washington confronts the same, recalcitrant problem of scale: offsetting a $10 billion annual cut in one region is politically unlikely. Simply put it won't happen.

Notes

1. Unemployment figures for summer 1993 show 6.8% for the U.S. (down two tenths of one percent from the previous month), and 9.8% for California. Source: Department of Finance, 1993.

2. There are fundamental problems with the basic numbers for the key period 1990 to 1992 that underlie all analysis - and all the politics - of job loss in California. The estimate has been revised repeatedly. In June 1992 the Bureau of Labor Statistics made its official revision to national job losses. It substantially increased the estimate. This provided the basis for the estimate of California job losses at 800,000 (That figure is basic to all subsequent analyses by the State of California, Commission on State Finance. See for example, their *Impact of Defense Cuts on California*, Fall 1992; and its 1993 up-date) .Subsequent preliminary revisions followed, for both national and California totals. These encompassed a range of almost 300,000 for California. At the time of this writing (July 93) a provisional rectification of 575,000 has been made by the Department of Finance.

   The governmental statistical agencies messed up, real bad. (colloquialism appropriate.) The somewhat ludicrous, but nonetheless important saga of the repeatedly revised, but incurably inaccurate, official estimate of job loss, became the object of a special *New York Times* article (7 May 1993):.which reported:

   "The department [of Labor] says it overstated by 540,000 the number of jobs that were created in the late 1980's.[nationally] And then it overstated how many jobs had disappeared in the recession."

   "Not until early this year did the Labor Department realize that any of these figures were incorrect, and that data processing companies that deliver payroll information to the Government had miscounted:..."

   [In June 1992 the Bureau of Labor statistics officially revised its count of job losses in the 1990-1991 recession and" stated that the job loss had been 1.7 million, not 1.2 million. The bureau had issued what it now says was an incorrect correction... Somehow a number of the data processors made similar mistakes: among other things they were counting paychecks rather than people so that a person getting a paycheck and then an overtime check came out in the data as two workers." [Software was changed at data processors in 1992 and] "the new software had corrected, in one swoop, most of the 540,000 overcount."

3. California Employment Development Department.

4. California GDP for 1991 was $724 billion; For G-7 GNPs for 1991 see *World Competitiveness Report*, 1992, World Economic Forum, Lausanne, pp. 282. Recent currency fluctuations will have likely moved California up in the league standings.

5. See for example: Storper, Michael, and Scott, A.J. eds., *Pathways to Industrialization and Regional Development*, London, NY, Routledge, 1992; Scott,A.J. and Paul, A.S.,"Industrial Development and Regional Growth in Southern California, 1970-1987," in Mitchell, D.J.B.,& Wildhorn, J., eds. *Can California be Competitive and Caring?*,Institute of Industrial Relations, Monograph Series, no. 49 UCLA 1989; Scott, A.J., "The Role of Large Producers in Industrial Districts. A Case Study of High Tech Systems Houses in Southern California," *Regional Studies,* 1992, Vol.26, no. 3, pp. 265-275; Goodnough, R., "The Nature and Implications of Recent Population Growth in California," *Geography*, April 1992, vol. 77, no. 335, pp. 123-133; Shallbit, Bob, *California:Triumph of Entrepreneurial Spirit*, Northridge, Ca., Windsor Publications, 1989; SRI International, *Understanding Changes in the Southern California Economy*, June 1991, Menlo Park, Ca.

6. In this theme see Carey McWilliams, *California, the Great Exception*, New York, 1949; for the latest reprise of this theme see, Joan Didion, "Trouble in Lakewood," *The New Yorker*, July 26,1993.

7. UCLA Business Forecast.

8. Commission on State Finance, *Quarterly General Fund Forecast*, January 1993, p.9.

9. *Ibid.*

10. Munroe,Tapan, *PG&E Economic Outlook*, Spring 1993, p. 9, Pacific Gas and Electric Company, San Francisco.

11. *Metro, City and County Data Book*, 1993 County and City Extra: Bernan Press, Lanham, Maryland pp. 875 and 952: shows LA with about three times Detroit's manufacturing employment. See also Bank of America, *Economic and Business Outlook*, Nov. 1990, p.4

12. The concept of economic base is a mainstay of regional economics.For a review of its development, see, Richard Andrews, "the Mechanics of the

Urban Economic Base: the historical development of the base concept, *Land Economics*, XXIX, August 1953, pp. 161-167; Homer Hoyt, "Homer Hoyt on the concept of Economic Base," *Land Economics*, XXX, August 1954, pp. 182-186.

13. US Census, *Compendium of the Ninth Census*, 1870 shows Los Angeles' population as 5728.

14. California, Employment Development Department, *Monthly Labor Market Bulletin*, April 1993, Table 5. All Los Angeles Employment numbers are from this source.

15. Hall,P. and Markusen,A. (1992) "The Pentagon and the Gunbelt" in A. Kirby ed. *The Pentagon and the Cities*, Newbury Park (CA): Sage Publications, 53-76, page.66.

16. Davis, Mike, *City of Quartz:Excavating the Future in Los Angeles, New York, Verso, 1990.*

17. *Op.cit.*, p. 68.

18. Commission on State Finance,*.op. cit.*,Fall 1992.

19. Data provided by California Association of Realtors, 1993; more anecdotal sources hint at far sharper declines during 1993, especially in the luxury housing segment: see, for example, Didion, *op. cit.*, p. 60.

20. Wages from BLS C-13; California consumer price index from UCLA Business Forecast

21. Commission on State Finance, *Defense Spending in the 1990s: Impact on California*, Summer 1990, p.14. Let us recall that this is a conservative figure. It does, not for example, count "black" or secret projects, such as stealth aircraft and SDI (Strategic Defineses Initiative or Star Wars) which were big ticket items, and done in the region. For example the California Commission on State Finance remarks: "Nearly all of the SDI contract awards for the next several years are for R&D. The exact share of SDI funding entering California is unknown, since the location of work for many SDI contracts is classified. However, we do know that California has traditionally garnered about one-third of *all* research and development funding, and data on unclassified awards shows that California firms such as Rockwell International, McDonnell Douglas, Lockheed, Aeroject, and Science Applications are major participants in the program" Commission on State Finance, *Impact of Federal Expenditures on California*, Fall 1989, p.4.

22. Commission on State Finance , Fall 1992, *Op. cit.* The proportion rises to 80% for prime contracts.

23. An increase that represents about the 80% of total jobs added in manufacturing industries between 1980 and 1989.

24. California Employment Development Department, *Monthly Labor Market Bulletin*, April 93, table 23.

25. U.S. Department of Commerce,Economics and Statistics Administration, *Foreign Direct Investment in the United States, Benchmark Survey, Final Results*, 1993, table d 21,California.

26. California Employment Development Department, *Monthly Labor Market Bulletin, op. cit.*April 1993.

27. The UCLA Business Forecast, annual averages.

28. Centre for Real Estate and Urban Economics, University of California at Berkeley, *California Real Estate Opportunities in the 1990s*, September 1991.

29. See for example, "Gold Rush, Los Angeles-style; urban giant overtakes San Francisco as financial centre," *Christian Science Monitor*, 30 Jan 1987,p.3;or *Business Week* of 11 Nov. 1991, p 173ff.

30. Scott,Allen and Paul,Alan (1989) "Industrial Development and Regional Growth in Southern California, 1970-1987", in Mitchell and Wildhorn eds. (1989) *Can California Be Competitive and Caring?*, Institute of Industrial Relations, Monograph and Research Series no.49, UCLA.

31. BLS, ES 202

32. California Employment Development Department, *Monthly Labor Market Bulletin*, April 1993.

33. For non American readers California has 54 electoral votes. Presidents are elected by electoral, not popular votes. In a two candidate race, if a candidate gets 49% of the votes in California, he gets zero electoral votes.

34. Commission on State Finance, *Quarterly General Fund Forecast*, January 1993, p. 6.

35. National Real Estate Index, *Market History Report*.

36. California Association of Realtors,1993.

37. California Employment Development Department, *California Labor Market Bulletin*, April 1993.

38. *PG&E Economic Outlook*, Spring 1993, p.7.

39. *PG&E Economic Outlook*, Spring 1993, figure 23.

40. Hoover,Edgar and Vernon,Raymon, *Anatomy of a Metropolis*, Harvard University Press, 1959.

41. *California Industry Migration Study*, October 1992, prepared for Los Angeles Department of Water and Power, PG&E, Sand Diego Gas and Electric Company, Southern California Edison Company and Southern California Gas Company.

42. *The Economist*, relying on the California Industry Migration Study cited above, reports that 5 to 10% of total California job loss is due to out–migration of jobs, but that out–migration is responsible for 40% of industrial job loss . Vol. 328, no. 7820, July 17, 1993, p. 24

43. Data on illegal immigrants are notoriously unreliable. Official estimates are subject to mood swings, and revisions. The latest is the US Bureau of the Census revision of its estimate of illegal immigrants residing in California. In July 1993, it was doubled, from one to two million, although California's proportion, about one half the national total, was kept constant. Official publication is anticipated by the end of 1993. See, *San Francisco Chronicle*, 7 August 1993, p. 1.

44. Commission on State Finance, Fall 1992, *Opus cit.*exhibit 10, p. 21

45. Commission on State Finance, *Quarterly General Fund Forecast,* January 1993, page 6.

46. US Department of Commerce, *Regional Multipliers*, Appendix II, "Detailed Industries for which Multipliers are Available" states that "the detailed industries are based on the 1982 benchmark input-output accounts"; these data are what generate the multiplier for aerospace industries.

47. An alternative way around this problem is to use national level data for actual expenditures by SIC category and adjust accordingly as in the WIA model used in the UCLA Business Forecast model.

48. See Olivier Blanchard, "Consumption and the Recession of 1990-1991, *American Economic Review*, May 1993, vol. 83, no.2, p. 271 on treating government spending as exogenous.

49. Commission on State Finance, Fall 1992, *Opus cit.*

50. Dean Baker and Thea Lee, "Employment Multipliers in U.S. Economy," Economic Policy Institute, Washington DC, 1993.

4 Regional inequality, economic integration and automatic stabilizers

R.R. Mackay

4.1 Introduction

"Tradition seems to require that economists argue forever about the question whether, in any disequilibrium situation, **market forces acting alone** are likely to restore equilibrium. Now this is certainly an interesting question. But as social scientists we surely must address ourselves to the broader question: is the disequilibrium situation likely to be corrected at all, by market or nonmarket forces, or by both acting jointly? **It is our contention that nonmarket forces are not necessarily less 'automatic' than market forces.**" (Hirschman, 1959, p.63) Emphasis in the original.

Hirschman and Myrdal insist that we fail to understand regional inequality if we confine our attention to market forces. Any tendency to regional equality may owe more to nonmarket forces than to price signals and the search for maximum profit. The balance between pressures which promote and reduce regional inequality alters over time and is heavily dependent on state action.

Particular to Hirschman is the idea that nonmarket forces emerge naturally, inevitably and even without conscious volition. When the market fails to achieve reasonable balance, society will recognize and will sense the gap and state policies and social institutions will evolve in an attempt to bridge it.

The process of closer integration within Europe gives freer play to market forces. These concentrate growth and resources on the more advanced sectors and regions of Europe at the expense of poorer and more backward parts. In addition, closer economic and monetary union implies that nations become more like regions. Regions cannot devalue or reduce interest rates, impose quotas, or act independently to raise the level of demand and so ensure that regional resources find reasonable opportunity. With removal of tariff barriers and reduction of non-tariff barriers, protection is removed from national markets. Entry to the Exchange Rate Mechanism limits the opportunity to devalue; a common currency, even more a single currency, involves significant loss of independence for the nation state.

Resource transfer (fiscal transfer) is important in containing regional inequality within nations. Resource transfer is also important to economic and monetary union. Fiscal transfer (support for weaker regions) produces a reasonably fair distribution of the gains from economic union and thereby helps to maintain political unity. Fiscal transfer provides a degree of insurance against the risks inherent in restructuring: one likely effect of closer economic and monetary union is to accelerate restructuring.

The MacDougall Report (sponsored by the European Commission and published in 1977) predicted that fiscal transfer would grow in importance with economic and monetary integration. Transfer would be essential (Vol.1, p.59) in holding the Community together. The Report anticipated a need for change in the scale and direction of the Community budget. Sixteen years later and as we pass the key date for the Single European Market (1 January 1993), the budget remains below 1% of Community GDP, is still dominated by agriculture and has no clear redistributive role between richer and poorer parts of Europe. How do we explain an apparently inevitable evolution (resource transfer between nations and regions without the Community) that fails to evolve?

Section 4.2 of this paper uses United Kingdom (UK) experience to give empirical content to the Myrdal-Hirschman theme that success and failure provide secondary reactions which drive the regional system away from balance.

Section 4.3 outlines the importance of the main response to regional inequality within nations; that response involves public expenditure above taxes in poorer regions and in regions with trade problems. Section 4.3 builds on the evidence provided by the MacDougall Report.

The MacDougall Report is dated and it relates to a notably different economic climate. Section 4.4 considers one important component of fiscal transfer (welfare benefits) and looks at the impact on regional inequality in the 1970s and 1980s. In doing so it illustrates an essential difference between automatic (built in) stabilizers and regional aids at the discretion of central government.

Section 4.5 provides possible explanations of the puzzle set in the introduction. Hirschman suggests that closer union necessarily implies a deliberate and major effort to protect weaker regions. The MacDougall Report underlines the potential role of fiscal transfer. From birth the European Community recognized the importance of "reducing differences between regions" (Treaty of Rome, 1958). The Commission remains consistent in recognizing the attractions of regional convergence. The Padoa-Schioppa report (1987, p.25) describes "economic benefits" as the "cement of an economic community". If those benefits fail to reach all parts, the Community lacks stability. The declared objectives of the Single European Act include "reducing disparities between the various regions". There remains a gap between intention and reality. The most important aid to regional balance at national level (fiscal transfer to poor regions and communities) remains of limited importance at Community level. The concluding section provides a number of explanations. Political themes are central to understanding.

4.2   Uneven development

"The counter-forces which are continually defeating the forces which make for economic equilibrium are more pervasive and more deeply rooted in the constitution of the economic system than we commonly realise ... Every important advance in the organisation of production ... alters the conditions of industrial activity and initiates responses elsewhere in the industrial structure which in turn have a further unsettling effect. **Thus change becomes progressive and propagates itself in a cumulative way**". Allyn Young (1928, p.533) Emphasis Added.

"The cumulative process goes in both directions ... [and] if not regulated, will cause increasing inequality." Myrdal (1957, p.12).

The two quotations lead into a central theme of uneven development. There are sympathetic interactions between firms and between firms and communities. These often ensure that secondary change is in the direction of initial movement. There is an established tradition in economics which suggests that supply and demand analysis is not particularly helpful in understanding these broader aspects of increasing returns. Indeed, equilibrium, stability and regional balance prove misleading metaphors which flow from limiting attention to reactions which develop in the opposite direction to inequality.

Hirschman and Myrdal are part of that admittedly, unorthodox tradition. Hirschman refers to development as a chain of disequilbria, to backward and forward linkages and to one investment inducing others. Myrdal explains uneven growth in terms of the "principle of circular and cumulative causation". Growth and decline develop direction and momentum from initial change - positive or negative. Inequality may be self-reinforcing. The market giveth and the market taketh away, but success breeds success and failure promotes decline. The secondary movements which support and amplify initial change involve increasing returns (external economies), demonstration effects and multiplier impacts (linkages).

The decline of major industries will have secondary impacts, notably on firms that supply industries in decline. As value added declines in base and supporting firms, the initial and secondary impacts spread to the service sector. Taking UK evidence, in the 1980s (see Figure 4.1) employment gains in service industries provide compensation for employment loss in manufacturing. Compensation proved notably more generous in regions where loss of production jobs was limited.

Figure 4.1 points to regional development that is highly uneven. All regions lose jobs in the production industries (including manufacturing and mining), but the decline ranges from less than 15% in East Anglia to over 30% in the North, North West, Scotland, Yorkshire and Humberside and the West Midlands. In Figure 4.1 the regions are ordered according to growth in service employment and this differs from over 30% in East Anglia to less than 10% in Scotland, the North West and the North.

The subtitle for Figure 4.1 could be manufacturing matters. At national level, trade in services fails to compensate for manufacturing decline. The consequence is a balance of trade deficit of embarrassing proportions. At regional level, the regions with the heaviest loss in manufacturing (production) employment show limited growth in service jobs. The regression equation[1] suggests that each additional 1% decline in regional production employment reduces service employment growth by 1%. The relationship is imperfect but far from random. Many service activities develop close to consumers. Employment is distributed according to population and disposable income with expansion depending on success in other sectors.

The five regions with the lowest growth in service employment (North, North West, Scotland, Yorkshire and Humberside and Wales) are the Outer Regions of Great Britain. They account for two fifths of total employment in 1979, but only one fifth of employment growth in service industries. If the enterprize society relies on the service sector for salvation, results are more encouraging in Inner Britain.

"Within broad limits" Myrdal suggests (1957, ps 26-29) "the power of attraction of a centre has its origin mainly in the historical accident that something was once started there, and not in a number of other places where it could equally well have been started, and that start met with success". The demonstration effect is perfectly illustrated in Map 1. Wales has the biggest concentration of Japanese jobs and Japanese investment in Western Europe. The Japanese plants develop and interact in two tight groups within Wales (along the M4 corridor in South East Wales and in North East Wales). Industrial movement, like human migration, involves imitation and contact with those who have moved. Movement and growth develop from earlier, successful decisions.

We can only understand cumulative causation and increasing returns, Myrdal insists, if we give these terms the broadest possible interpretation. With Japanese plants the standards they set for suppliers, for industrial relations, for training and for reducing the barriers between blue and white collar workers may be important. The impact is not necessarily local. More generally, increasing returns include skills and know-how; ease of contact and communication; the spirit of new enterprise; the emergence of specialist firms; and the differentiation in product and process that evolves from capturing market share.

A last example concentrates on labour quality. When considering development we cannot simply take the quality of resources as given. Attitudes to schools, further education, qualifications, training, employment counselling, government schemes are not uniform across labour markets. As the Ashton and Maguire (1986) study of young adults effectively demonstrates, ambition, involvement, commitment and aspiration expand with opportunity. The key argument for regional policy is (and always has been) that human resources remain latent, untapped and unexplored potential in the absence of positive signals. A similar point is made by Myrdal (1957, p.88) when he optimistically claims that inherent in circular and cumulative causation is the idea "that the final results as measured in the rise of production and national income should be many times greater than the initial costs implied in getting the system under way and keeping it moving".

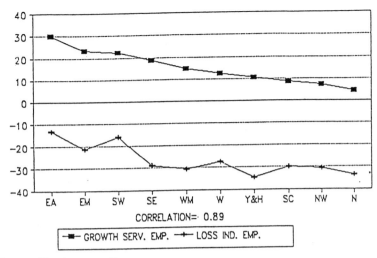

Source: Employment Gazette

Figure 4.1 Industrial decline - service growth, % change in employment - 1979 - 1989

Map 4.1 Japanese plants in Wales. The demonstration effect

4.3 Fiscal transfer - automatic stabilizers

"Fortunately there exists one important policy instrument that is available to an underdeveloped region: the allocation of public funds through the national budget." (Hirschman 1968, p.20).

"A main explanation of why these few countries can now be characterised as highly integrated is to be found in the complex networks of systems of state interferences, preventing any region, industry or social group from lagging behind in its development." (Myrdal, 1957, p.47).

"In 1964 net transfers of benefit offset differences in per capita regional product to the extent of about 47 per cent ... In this important financial respect we have indeed a United Kingdom." (Brown, 1972, p.66).

Fiscal transfer is an expression of national identity: it derives support from the sentiment of national unity. It also compensates weaker regions for being notably vulnerable to competition. Regions lack some of the principal policy instruments available for development at national level. The level of demand in a nation state will always be a compromize, leaving margins of unused capacity which differ across regions.

The region is part of a political community with national standards for public services and welfare and a common base of taxation. Those national standards ensure taxes below public expenditure in low income regions. They also guarantee that regions receive assistance whenever trading relations with the rest of the country deteriorate. There is automatic support when the region's share of national income and national product decline.

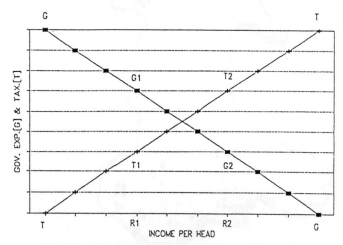

Figure 4.2 Public finance as a regional stabilizer

An outline of fiscal transfer is illustrated in Figure 4.2. Two functions of regional fiscal transfer are implicit - redistribution and automatic stabilization (immediate response to limit the impact of structural decline). Low income regions gain more from government expenditure (GG in Figure 4.2) than they pay in tax (TT in Figure 4.2) - the net transfer for region R1 is G1 T1 in Figure 4.2. Given a shock to the regional economy, given loss of markets and income, government expenditure in the region is increased and taxation is reduced. The budget balance adapts - without the need for conscious decision. Automatic stabilization provides a cushion which absorbs shocks and acts to contain the cumulative impact of structural decline. If there is balance between regions, Myrdal suggests (1957, p.48), it is contrived or "created harmony".

The MacDougall Report demonstrates that fiscal transfer is significant in developed nations. It emerges naturally as a product of national standards for public services and a common tax and welfare base. Figures 4.3 and 4.4 are drawn from data provided in the Report.

Figure 4.3 shows the relationship between fiscal transfer and relative income[2] in the United Kingdom, West Germany and Italy. In all three countries relative income is the key to fiscal transfer. Low income regions enjoy fiscal gains (they pay less in taxes than they receive in services and benefits); high income regions provide support. In each country the degree of regional transfer is sensitive to regional income: the relationship between relative income and transfer is remarkably strong. Moreover, the levels of support at similar levels of relative income are surprisingly similar in all three countries. Notably different systems of redistribution provide results that are compatible across countries. Italy provides the highest levels of support to weak regions, but this is a product of greater diversity in regional income.

Figure 4.4 (for Italy and West Germany only) shows that low income tends to go with trade deficits. It also shows fiscal transfers to regions with trade problems. The region that fails to develop or loses its export base, automatically receives a degree of protection from the tax and welfare system. Standards in declining areas are protected by redistributing income and by maintaining the level of public services.

Figures 4.3 and 4.4 indicate that regional stabilizers are sensitive to regional differentials: they are built-in and they respond naturally to relative decline. The reality of automatic stabilization is remarkably close to the model of Figure 4.2.

The effect of transfer is described as "quite powerful in the direction of equalisation" in the UK: in West Germany it contributes "considerably in equalising regional per capita income and in preventing regions becoming 'bankrupt'"; in Italy transfers are of "high level when compared with ... other European countries" (MacDougall Report, Vol.2, ps 21, 97, III). In all three countries they act to check the cumulative process of disequilibrium at regional level.

Italy and the UK are perhaps unusual in providing clear examples of North/South (Inner/Outer) differentials which remain persistent over time. But the message of the MacDougall Report is that fiscal transfers are sensitive to regional income in all the countries studies. The Report provides considerable detail for five federal states (Australia, Canada, West Germany, USA, Switzerland) and three unitary states (France, Italy and United Kingdom). The general picture that emerges is as follows:

1   Regional economies are notably open and highly vulnerable. Instability of

65

employment and disposable income is more probable for the region than the nation.

2   The region cannot counter balance of trade problems with trade barriers, exchange-rate adjustment or interest rate reduction. In compensation for loss of independence, trade and income decline leads to fiscal compensation. To the extent that central government maintains effective regional demand, it does so by transfers.

3   Wage adjustment as between regions is insufficiently sensitive and inadequately persuasive to produce balance.

4   There is continuous redistribution of income from richer to poorer regions. Net flows of public finance in the range of 3-10% of regional product (income) are common for low income and high income regions. Net flows of up to 30% of regional product occur in exceptional circumstances.

5   The flows reduce regional income inequalities by an average of 40% in the countries studied: they provide a powerful check to the regional multiplier and a major role in limiting cyclical fluctuations. "One half to two-thirds ... of loss in primary income ... may be automatically offset" through lower taxes and higher benefits. (MacDougall Report, Vol.1, p.12).

6   Regional policy (narrowly defined) is relatively unimportant, at least in expenditure terms.

7   The nature of redistribution varies from country to country. There is no clear role model. There is more variation (as between countries) in the instruments of redistribution than in the changes it brings in inter-regional income differences.

8   Redistribution at European Community level is negligible.

Fiscal transfer between regions appears important in all advanced, market economies. The pattern outlined by the MacDougall Report gives substance to Hirschman's claim (1959, p.63) that "nonmarket forces are not necessarily less 'automatic' than market forces". The shocking suspicion, introduced by Hirschman and Myrdal, is that any tendency to regional equality may owe more to policy than to markets. The MacDougall Report provides partial confirmation.

In unitary states (Italy, France, UK) the regional stabilizers are all the more impressive for emerging without conscious planning or clear regional intent. In Italy (MacDougall Report, Vol.2, p.106) "the redistributive effect is achieved almost automatically ... there is no explicit redistributive intent". In France, (MacDougall Report Vol.2, p.31) redistribution "is not deliberate and takes place ... with little or nothing known about the relevant mechanisms". In the UK it emerges (Wilson, 1975, p.119) from the normal activities of government, taxing and spending, "without any explicit expression of intent, and probably without any statistical calculation". In federal states redistribution is more likely to be open, clear and acknowledged. An appropriate example is West Germany, where budget equalisation between Länder is designed to raise the tax capacity of the poorest Länder to 97.5% of the West German average.

The transfers, both hidden and open, are of particular interest to economists in the Keynesian tradition. They imply that balance between spread effects (forces that reduce regional inequality) and backwash effects (forces that add to inequality) depends, in large measure, on the nature of the fiscal adjustments

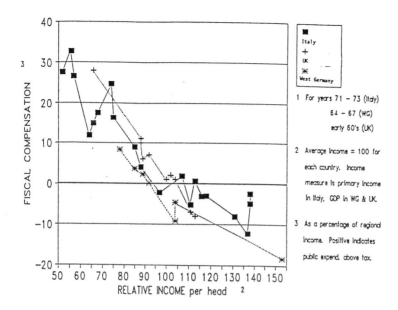

Figure 4.3 Regional transfer, Italy UK, W. Germany[1]

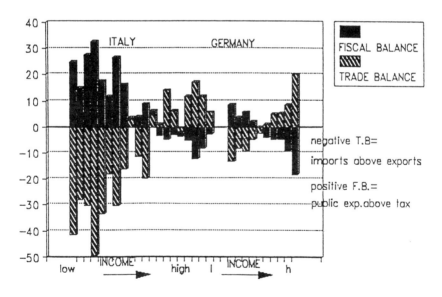

Figures 4.3 and 4.4 from data in MacDougall Report (1979)

Figure 4.4 Trade and fiscal balance, % of regional income - Italy and Germany

that emerge to counter decline and redistribute income and opportunity. They also imply that fiscal transfer has a role to play in all open economies. That role becomes potentially important within the Community as the barriers between national economies are reduced.

The process of integration brings about two effects. One is the reallocation of market area and the redistribution of production in favour of the most efficient and best situated firms. This implies increasing geographic specialization. The second is the opportunity provided to realise increasing returns which follows from extending and enlarging market area. Static gains lead to dynamic benefits and the process differentiates between superior and inferior location and trade routes.

"The need for redistribution" (MacDougall Report, Vol.1, p.60) emerges because economic integration is expected to add to Community wealth and to regional diversity. Uneven distribution of regional benefit includes the possibility of "net losers". A system of redistribution is required to divide benefits in a manner acceptable to different parts of the community.

Without transfer the process of integration falters. The Report recommends a menu which includes (1) budget equalization (fiscal transfer) for weaker member states to bring fiscal capacity up to 65% of the Community average, (2) cyclical grants to local or regional government, (3) counter cyclical aids for weak member states and (4) a community unemployed fund. In order to counter extremes of income distribution within the Community, the Community budget would have to rise to between 2 and 2.5% of Community GDP (MacDougall Report, Vol.1, ps 16-17). Transfer would have to be strongly redistributive and capable of a "sensitive and large-scale response to short-term changes in the economic fortunes of regions and states". (MacDougall Report, Vol. 1, p.20).

Integration adopts a notably different form. The entry of Spain, Portugal and Greece adds to regional inequality (and implies larger transfers between different parts of the Community, if inequality is to be contained). The Community Budget remains below 1% of Community GDP. It is not strongly redistributive between regions. It does not act as a sensitive, or automatic stabilizer. The remarkable fact is that next to no progress has been made. If explicit transfers are required in a more open Community, the Community is notably more vulnerable in 1993 than in 1977. A reasoned plea for public debate and political consensus on the mechanisms for transfer has produced nothing of substance.

4.4   Regional inequality and welfare - the UK

"The most general service of the compassionate state is to supply some income to those otherwise devoid. As an intensely practical matter, nothing more effectively limits freedom, including freedom of expression, as the total lack of money." Galbraith J.K.

Can a state become less sympathetic without its citizens losing charity? In recent years we witness compassion fatigue; a perception that stresses individual responsibility rather than collective action or common risks.

The MacDougall Report is dated. Some might argue that it was dated when published. The data used relate to an economic climate that had disappeared by the late 1970s. The 1970s and even more the 1980s, provide a shift in the balance of private and public emphasis. In these years "people returned to worry primarily about their private interests, the more so as the easy forward movement that had marked the earlier period gave place almost everywhere to uncertainty and crises." (Hirschman, 1982, p.3).

Rational generosity is perhaps made possible by growth. Redistribution is more accepted and less readily questioned, when economies are successful in delivering growth and greater security. The shift in public-private sentiment links to the lower growth rates from 1973.

The balance between backwash and spread effects depends not only on the level of development, but on success in achieving growth. Myrdal (1957, p.38) is explicit: "A boom [growth, low unemployment] will always increase the relative strength of the spread effect. A depression [low growth, high unemployment] will decrease it."

Experience in the European Community is consistent with Myrdal's claim. Within the Community, the period of high growth and low unemployment is the period of convergence. Regional differences in income and opportunity diminish. From 1973, unemployment rises throughout the Community, but settles and concentrates on particular regions. The nature of unemployment alters, with long-term unemployment emerging as an issue of real importance. The years of slow growth and high unemployment (from 1973) add to regional divergence. The growing contrast between regions involves both unemployment and income: it is evident within and between countries.

Extra unemployment concentrates on regions where unemployment is already high. Between 1976 and 1985 unemployment rose by 4 percentage points in the 25 Community regions with the lowest unemployment rates. The increase in the 25 regions with highest unemployment was 13 percentage points. The unemployment gap at the extremes of the community triples in only 10 years (for greater detail, see Third Periodic Report on the Regions of the Community).

Similar effects are identifiable within the United Kingdom. Convergence gives way to divergence and unemployment increase tends to concentrate on the regions where unemployment is already high. The male unemployment gap between the Inner and Outer Regions climbs from 1.2 percentage points in the years 1959-76 to 5.5 percentage points in 1977-88. That gap grows every year between 1979 and 1988. By 1988 an extra eight out of every 100 men are unemployed when we compare Outer Regions with Inner Regions.

Regional divergence grows in the 1980s. The question remains: does fiscal transfer play any role in checking the trend to regional inequality? A partial answer can be provided by considering the role of social security is in redistributing income within the United Kingdom. It is partial because social security is only one part of regional stabilization.

Employment reduction is severe in the Outer Regions of the UK (including Northern Ireland) and also in the West Midlands (see Section 4.2). Figure 4.5 indicates the growing Opportunity Gap between the Outer Regions and the Inner Region Core (South East, East Anglia, South West, East Midlands) and between West Midlands and the Inner Region Core (IRC). The Opportunity

Gap combines differences in unemployment with differences in participation rates[3] (the percentage of population of working age in employment, self employment or classified as unemployed). It thus provides the broadest, available measure of regional differences in employment opportunity.

The Opportunity Gap between Outer Regions and IRC averages 5.5 percentage points in the 1970s and 10.2 percentage points 1980-1991: it climbs to close to 14 percentage points by 1984-1985. The Opportunity Gap for the West Midlands is only 0.6 percentage points in the 1970s and 7.8 percentage points 1980-1991. Figure 4.5 illustrates that the key distinction is between the 1970s and the 1980s. In all parts of the UK measured, disguised unemployment rises but increases are concentrated in the Outer Regions and the West Midlands.

As we move to the 1980s there are two relevant impacts on the role of social security as a regional stabilizer. First, higher unemployment acts to increase social security expenditure, with additions particularly marked in the regions of major employment loss. Second, there is a desire to contain public expenditure, with social security a target for cuts and for changes in regulations which limit access. The automatic stabilizer operates against the background of a policy and ideology which emphasizes individual improvement and private welfare goals.

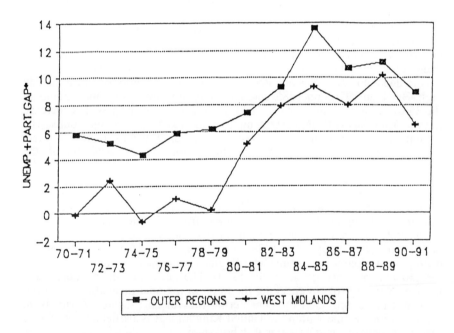

*   Positive indicates unemployment rates above and participation rates below Inner Region Core (IRC)

Source: *Family Expenditure Survey and Employment Gazette*

Figure 4.5 Opportunity gap OR and WM compared to IRC

Figure 4.6 compares Outer Regions with IRC in terms of (1) earnings for those in work (top line), (2) household income with social security (middle line) and (3) household income without social security (bottom line). In the Outer Regions, in the 1970s, household income is 87% of the IRC level and household income without social security is 85%. In the Outer Regions, 1980 - 91, household income is 79% of the IRC level and household income with social security is 74%. Social security adds only 1% to relative household income in the Outer Regions in 1974-75 and 6% in 1984-85.

The gap between relative earnings in work and relative family income without social security (top and bottom line of Figure 4.6) indicates the importance of differential access to employment. For most of us, our most important property is our own labour. The fall in the relative value of that property is indicated in Figure 4.6: Outer Region income without social security falls from 87% of the IRC level in 1976-77 to only 70% in 1990-91.

In the 1970s Outer Region earnings are close to IRC levels: differential access to the necessaries and conveniences of life is largely explained by differences in employment opportunity. In the 1980s the earnings gap between the Outer Regions and the IRC grows. Both price (wage) and quantity (employment, unemployment, participation) adjustment occurs. The quantity adjustments are even more of a problem than the wage adjustments. The main burden of the more difficult macroeconomic environment falls on those who fail to sell labour.

Unemployment increase in the European Community and in the UK, tends to concentrate on the regions where unemployment is already high. The exception in the UK is the West Midlands. Figure 4.7 indicates a growing earnings gap between the West Midlands and the IRC. It also shows that social security begins to play a role in maintaining relative income in the West Midlands in the 1980s.

Social security expenditure covers more than payments to the unemployed, but the increase in social security expenditure as a share of UK household income - from 6% in 1974-75 to over 14% in 1982-83 - is largely the result of unemployment increase. That increase is important in explaining why public expenditure has proved difficult to contain. It is particularly marked in the Outer Regions and in the West Midlands.

One attraction of automatic stabilizers is that, once introduced, they work without conscious political decision. Between 1975 and 1985 the real value of regional aid to industries in the United Kingdom is reduced by two thirds. By contrast, after allowing for inflation, the social security expenditure gap between Outer and Inner Regions climbs by a multiple of over three (See MacKay, 1991). The growing importance of social security in containing differences between the regions does not follow from government policy. This has sought to reduce dependence on the state and to cut back public spending. Figures 4.6 and 4.7 indicate the power of automatic stabilizers against a background which has not been over-sympathetic to those who rely on the welfare state.

This section is in the nature of a self denying ordinance. One may long for an economy where higher employment is a real target - not something to be addressed only when inflation is finally conquered. One might hope that labour economists would recognise that a labour market policy which addresses

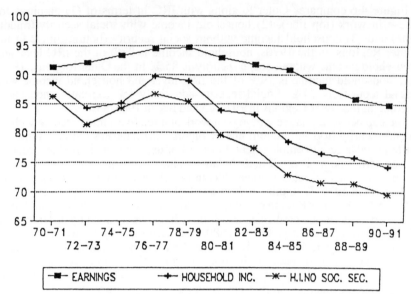

Figure 4.6 Earnings & household income gap. Outer regions as % IRC

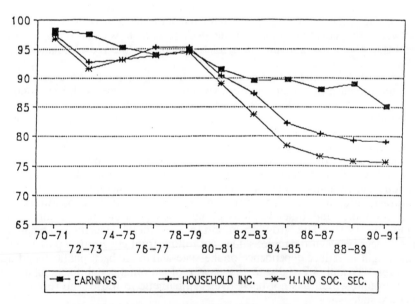

Figure 4.7 Earnings & household income gap. West Midlands as % IRC

Source: Figures 4.6 and 4.7, *Family Survey* and *New Earnings Survey*

mainly long-term unemployment is a response which is too late and notably ineffective (See MacKay, 1992 and MacKay and Jones, 1989). One might even seek greater emphasis on the right to work and less stress on the right to benefit, but that shift also depends on opportunity. Human resources are the key to economic development, including regional development. The underlying problem, at least in the UK, is an uneasy co-existence of a labour surplus and a labour shortage. Labour scarcity relates to quality, to the absence of education and skills which permit effective competition. Traditionally regional development policies concentrate on physical capital: on public infrastructure and on financial incentives to create jobs. A more ambitious approach embraces 'software' development tools, that is job skills to sustain a momentum that will also require capital investment.

These are dreams. This section has a more limited objective. It accepts the reality[4] of lower growth, greater emphasis on the individual and a confined public purse. These contribute to tax and welfare changes which reduce the strength of regional transfer. In spite of compassion fatigue, one built-in stabilizer (social security) grows in importance as a means of limiting income differentials between regions.

There is a critical difference between automatic stabilizers and regional policy. UK regional industrial policy relied on directing and guiding manufacturing expansion away from regions with full employment to regions with unused capacity. For effect, regional policy required low unemployment, growth and manufacturing firms with a commitment to expansion. Automatic stabilizers become more important when these favourable conditions are absent. The drift from regional policy is not confined to UK. Läpple (1985, p.52) refers to a silent but comprehensive retreat throughout Europe. Commitment to regional balance proves a victim of lower growth: loss of belief is part of Hirschman's wider withering of public meanings (Hirschman, 1982).

Involuntary unemployment is the product of a cumulative process which is triggered by initial decline in key sectors of the local economy. Modern unemployment takes its characteristic form from the employment relationship within large industrial and mining units. Such employment required a clear separation between formal and informal economy: a clear divide between organized and casual work. When this form of secure employment disappears, a gap emerges within the community and for the individual. That gap is the essence of unemployment (see Piore, 1987).

Modern economies are not accurately described as a series of small scale gambles or naturally compatible with contestable markets which guarantee ease of entry and exit. They are marked by heavy, sunken costs, by long term commitments and by pronounced specialization of physical and human capital. Failure to recognize this allows economists and others consistently to overstate the speed with which resources transfer between employments, especially in generally slack economies.

Transfer, including regional transfer, is not just about compassion. Automatic stabilizers are deeply embedded in advanced, mixed economies. They provide greater stability, greater security than would otherwise exist. They are a response to a weakness of capitalism. Given the loss of major industries, it takes time to prepare for useful investment. Given loss of markets and reduced valuation of human and physical capital, built-in stabilizers provide time and opportunity to find a new sense of direction. Without transfer and guaranteed support at the earliest possible stage, cumulative forces of decline may be set in motion which prove extremely difficult to check until they have run their course. To be effective, regional transfers must be available before the full impact of decline becomes visible.

Regional transfers are important to open economies. Why do they fail to emerge within the Community as national economies become increasingly open to trade and exchange?

4.5 Conclusion

"The changing pattern of production and exchange that characterises an integrated Community typically brings gains to some but losses to others. To make integration acceptable to all participants may thus require an explicit distributive mechanism to divide the gains from integration in a politically acceptable way. Failure to attend to this matter may at the least result in a stagnation of the integration process, and at the worst result in secession and dissolution."

There are gains from economic and monetary union. The benefits are unevenly distributed. Some regions, possibly those on the periphery, may lose as trade creation redistributes markets and opportunities. The clear intention of economic union is to add to restructuring and thus to trade imbalance within Europe.

Fiscal transfer has a key role in spreading the potential benefits of market unification. It provides a 'shock absorber' by reducing the intensity of economic decline in vulnerable regions. Transfer is central to the spread effect provided by nonmarket forces. It gives potential substance to Hirschman's claim that economic policies will naturally emerge wherever the forces that promote inequality and imbalance are powerful.

Hirschman even claims (Hirschman, 1981) that countervailing policies are already strong within the Community. These community responses are, he suggests, additional to national policies. The reality is notably different. The resources provided by the European Community are slight. They are not always additional to national efforts (see MacKay, 1991). These are in decline. That decline emerges against a background of growing regional inequality.

Substantial development of fiscal transfer was anticipated and thought necessary to hold the community together in the process of integration. The puzzle is that it remains neglected, unexplored and still-born.

There are a number of possible explanations. They include (1) the threat to the periphery has been exaggerated, (2) there is no clear model for fiscal transfer, (3) enlargement of the community ensures that it takes a contrary direction and (4) transfer depends on a degree of political unity that is beyond the reach of the Community. Transfer depends on shared values and objectives that emerge within a nation, but not necessarily within a community of nations.

The distinction between Outer and Inner Regions in this paper implies, even when it does not underline, a core-periphery contrast. The major benefits emerge at the centre of the Community, in regions that are already relatively

74

prosperous. It is producers on the periphery who are particularly at risk. The counter argument is that infrastructure and human capital are more important than location in determining growth. As Kaldor reminds us (1970), resource endowment and natural advantages grow less important over time and created advantages grown in significance. Extreme locational disadvantage has been no bar to Korea and Japan in accumulating human and physical capital. What is peripheral is not given. It depends on decisions, including those made for the public sector. In a paper that is clearly informed by the MacDougall Report, Jacques Delors (1989, p.83) develops a similar argument. The United States has seen pronounced growth "at its geographical edges". The core regions may be more prosperous in Europe, but there is no universal pattern. Even in Europe there are significant exceptions. Many anticipate that Spain will be one of the most successful countries in adding to market share.

The qualification is important, but not entirely convincing. Greater freedom of location of choice does not imply stability. Production has become more mobile in space and less stable in location. Specialization implies risk and closer economic union adds to specialization. Exchange value and productive power are at the mercy of a division of labour which adjusts to competitive forces beyond the control of the individual and the local community. An extended market produces uncertainty as well as wealth.

In Europe, additions to unemployment concentrate on regions where unemployment is already high. But even in UK, a country noted for its consistent pattern of regional imbalance, there are exceptions. The West Midlands, once the heartland of industrial prosperity, loses its relative position. Fiscal support emerges automatically. The appeal of fiscal transfer is that, unlike regional policy, there is no need to predict which regions will lose. Fiscal compensation produces automatic support given decline. Fluctuations in personal income are smoothed, without the need for conscious policy response. Moreover, compensation is, as Delors claims (1989, p.84) "Both a product of, and source of the sense of national solidarity which all relevant economic and monetary unions share."

Delors (see 1989, p.82) points to our second explanation of fiscal transfer failing to emerge. There is no clear national model for budget transfer. Reform can follow a number of different evolutions and there is no good reason for selecting one. In federal nations, regional transfers can be explicit. In unitary states they may remain hidden, rarely measured and a source of surprise. Within these two broad groups there are substantial contrasts in the way regional transfers emerge. As an explanation this is true, but limited. There are many plausible models (see MacDougall Report) and there is one common result. Advanced economies rely on fiscal transfers. In the countries studied these reduce regional income inequality by an average of 40%. It remains difficult to envisage a deeper union without fiscal compensation. The real mystery relates not to the absence of a complete system (such systems evolve only slowly within nations) but to zero progress.

With the Community, as with a bicycle, motion is required. The direction of movement, from seven member states in 1977 to twelve member states in 1992, adds to the degree of regional diversity and renders effective transfer more difficult. Within a land area more limited than the United States, regional differences are more pronounced. The search for economic and social cohesion

75

includes regions and localities with different life styles, living standards, structures and expectations. The Commission calculates that merely raising the budget capacity of the four weakest nations to 75% of the Community average would involve tripling the Community Budget. Transfer on this scale for such a limited objective, is perhaps not going to happen. The political will is absent. There is, in other words, a real contradiction between deepening and enlarging the Community. It is difficult to combine both.

The most recent addition to the Community alters the nature of the argument. East Germany receives transfers from West Germany which are over 3% of West Germany's product. The scale of transfer is above the level anticipated for the Community in the early stages of integration. Common burdens are accepted within the nation state. The harmony of interests, and of shared risk, is confined within national boundaries - albeit extended national boundaries in the German example.

The great attraction of built-in stabilizers is that, once introduced, they work without conscious political direction. Their great problem is that such commitment depends on consensus and on shared values. "The welfare state is nationalistic" is Myrdal's phrase (1957, p.49). As the Germany example underlines, regional transfer and created harmony derive support from the sentiment and strength of national solidarity.

There are obvious differences between individual countries and the European Community. The latter lacks independent sources of finance and the political integration that provides the background for taxation and distribution. Financial and democratic deficits flow from a common source. The sense of belonging that binds different parts of a nation together is not as strong between nations. We reach the paradox that perhaps explains the logical evolution that fails to emerge. Closer union may require fiscal support for weaker regions: fiscal transfer depends on closer union.

The patterns, the general explanations and the social facts provided by Myrdal and Hirschman add to understanding, even when they do not provide predictions that are precise and accurate. This paper develops questions of political economy. The absence of effective regional transfer has many partial explanations but political themes are more important than economic. Closer union between countries provides a difficult test for Hirschman's claims. Fiscal transfers compensate for loss of independence, but their counterpart is a mature political structure. Voice and institutions are important in converting a vague desire for balance into policies that have impact.

References

Ashton D.N. and Maquire M.J. (1986), 'Young Adults in the Labour Market', *Department of Employment Research Paper No. 55*.

Brown A.J. (1972), *The Framework of Regional Economies in the United Kingdom*, Cambridge University Press.

Commission of the European Communities (1977), *MacDougall Report*, Report of the Study Group on the Role of Public Finance in European Integration, Vol. 1, General Report, Vol. II, Individual Contributions and Working Papers.

Commission of the European Communities (1987a), Third Periodic Report from the Commission on the Social and Economic Situation and Development of the Community (The Regional Report), Com 187k, 230 Final, Brussels.

Commission of the European Communities (1987b), 'Reform of the Structural Funds', Communication 87, 376.

Delors J. (1989), 'Regional implications of economic and monetary integration', pp. 81-89, in Committee for the Study of Economic and Monetary Union, Report on Economic and Monetary Union in the European Community. Office for Official Publications of the European Community, Luxembourg.

Hirschman A.O. (1958), *The Strategy of Economic Development*, Yale University Press, New Haven.

Hirschman A.O. (1968), 'Industrial Development in the Brazilian North-East and the Tax Credit Scheme of Article 34/18', *The Journal of Development Studies*, 1968.

Hirschman A.O. (1981), 'Three Uses of Political Economy in Analysing European Integration', in Hirschman A.O., *Essays in Trespassing. Economics to Politics and Beyond*, Cambridge University Press.

Hirschman A.O. (1982), *Shifting Involvement*, Princeton University Press.

Kaldor N. (1970), 'The Case for Regional Policy', *Scottish Journal of Political Economy*, Vol. 17, pp. 337-48.

Läpple D. (1985), 'Internationalisation of Capital and the Regional Problem', in Walton (ed), *Capital and Labour in the Urbanised World*, Sage, London.

MacKay R.R. and Jones D.R. (1989), *Labour Markets in Distress: the Denial of Choice*, Gower Press.

MacKay, R.R. (1991), 'European Integration and Public Finance - The Political Economy of Regional Support', *SABE Working Paper Series No. 91.6 University of Wales, Bangor* and to be published in proceedings of Regional Studies Association Conference, Haldiki, Greece.

MacKay, R.R. (1992), 'Labour Market Adjustment in Wales', in Verhaar, C.H.A. and Jansma, L.G. (eds.), *On the Mysteries of Unemployment*, Kluwer, The Netherlands.

Myrdal, G. (1957), *Economic Theory and Under-Developed Regions*, Duckworth, London.

Padoa-Schioppa, T. (1987), *Efficiency, Stability and Equity. A Strategy for the Evaluation of the Economic System of the European Community*, Oxford University Press,

Piore, M.J. (1987), 'Historical Perspectives and the Interpretation of Unemployment', *Journal of Economic Literature*, Vol. XXV, pp. 1834 - 1850.

Wilson, T. (1975), 'Economic Sovereignty', in Vaizey, J. (ed.), *Economic Sovereignty and Regional Policy*, Gill and Macmillan.

Young, A. (1928), 'Increasing Returns and Economic Progress', *Economic Journal*, December 1928, pp. 527-42.

Notes

1. $$S = 41.9 + 0.999 P$$
    $$(3.9) \quad (0.18)$$
    where S = % change in service employment and P = % change in production employment. The relationship indicated in Figure 3.1 has links to the base-service multiplier. A base-service multiplier would attempt to separate service activities that cater for wider markets (national, international) from those that are tied to local/regional demand. For detail see Brown (1972).

2. The measures used identify income generated from regional resources.

3. Hidden unemployment - particularly of males - increases in all regions in the 1980s. It is notably severe in the regions of major employment decline. Changes in the classification of unemployment add to the importance of disguised unemployment in the 1980s. For greater details see MacKay (1992).

4. A reality which involves greater emphasis on individual improvement and private welfare goals against a background which denies opportunity to many.

5 The partnership between small firms and metropolitan areas. The response to the challenge of internationalization

M.C. Monnoyer, Py Leo and J. Philippe

5.1 Introduction

The opening of internal European borders represents a widening of horizons but also a reduction in protected economic areas. In the regions which, up to now, have been the economic actors at all borders: large and small businesses, towns and territorial administrations, have felt concerned about this, because the close proximity of a foreign rival, whoever it may be, underlined what was at stake. For businesses, and more particularly for small firms, the possible development of export markets disappears when faced with the fear of seeing the local market becoming highly prized. As for the towns, they are afraid of losing their capacity to attract interest when faced with a dynamic foreign neighbour.

Faced with these facts as well as the challenge of internationalization, it seems to us that towns and small firms should become aware of their solidarity. Today, small firms still represent the heart of a region's economic structure and are the economic base of regional metropolitan areas. The report on European towns[1] underlines the weakness of French metropolitan areas. Lyon, which is the top regional metropolitan area, is relegated to the fourth group[2], a long way behind Milan, and Marseille, Strasbourg and Toulouse fall to group 5, behind Turin, Barcelona, Frankfurt, Stuttgart and Geneva. Other French metropolitan areas do not appear until group 6.

The opening up of French metropolitan areas cannot rely on international functions such as embassies, commercial delegations and offices of large companies, which are automatically situated in capital cities. Neither can they count on multinationals which do not select regional metropoles when setting their head offices. In most cases, these are found in capital cities. When setting up their business premises they often prefer less important towns or suburbs because the costs of location and running the business are not so high.

Small and medium sized businesses do not have this possibility of choosing sites. There is a strong chance that their initial location will be definitive, so they therefore constitute an element of stability and a dynamic factor for a regional metropolitan area.

The internationalization of the market modifies the relationship of a small firm with the economic environment. Unlike large multinational businesses which are capable of organizing their economic environment, or even of starting it from scratch by setting up their own services in order to function, small firms are obliged to call upon external business services. This opening up towards the tertiary sector is now widening to include data processing services and is enriching the traditional relationship between towns as places for exchange and contact, and their companies. It can bring a new dynamism to the partnership between metropolitan areas and small firms if both partners are aware of the role that services, and especially information technology services can play in an international strategy.

In order to illustrate this, in this chapter, we will first outline the structuring nature of information in the town/small firm relationship and we will then compare the demand for information from the small firm with the existing supply in the metropolitan area. This will be based on studies carried out among about a hundred businesses in two French regions and their metropolitan areas: Aquitaine and Provence.

5.2   Information as a structuring element in the town/small firm relationship

The dynamism of towns is mainly the result of the growth in activities commonly known as the tertiary sector which employ qualified professionals backed up by office staff. The importance of these activities became apparent through empirical studies carried out on the economic relationships in both inter - and intrametropolitan areas. The largest number of studies has been done in the USA where the impact of services on the very morphology of towns is the most visible in geographical terms.

All these studies have demonstrated a dichotomy between the towns. Some have higher level services and functions as places where economic decisions are taken. In other towns, their economic basis depends on these decisions and any control over development is lost. The problem of the development of regional metropolitan areas, which from many points of view are towns which are economically dependent, must in our opinion, be situated within an approach which brings urban analyses of the transactional economy and modern information systems together.

5.2.1   The contribution of transactional urban economy to the analysis of metropolitan areas

Jean Gottman[3] was the first to use the term transactional urban economy to describe the new situation in metropolitan areas. For a long time, towns were mainly a market place and their urban function is not found systematically either down the ages or all over the world. In the West, the Industrial Revolution saw industry concentrated in towns and throughout the twentieth century, industrialization has borne urbanization in its wake. However, this is no longer the case: industrial decentralization has considerably reduced the towns' manufacturing basis. They continue to grow nevertheless, because they still fulfil the need for centralizing activities that Jean Gottman calls transactional. These activities include judicial and legislative functions as well as decision making, commercial agency, consultancy and university and research activities.

Jean Gottman insists on the necessity of distinguishing between tertiary and quaternary activities. The former consists of higher services and calls upon highly qualified staff. The latter includes transport, communications, distribution, as well as personnel services.

The transactional urban economy is therefore divided into segments which differ according to their impact on urban growth. The services of head offices and services which help in decision making (financial, judicial, management) play a key role because they are at the heart of mechanisms that concentrate and disperse activities. When a certain level of concentration is reached at head offices, international companies, business consultancies and international banks, any decentralization of a head office then becomes impossible. This has been proved in the recent economic history of the USA where very few large firms have changed the location of their head office. Quaternary activities, therefore, develop in a complementary fashion by creating networks of relationships within the metropoles. Tertiary activities linked to the production of goods do not obey this law of mutual reinforcement and instead undergo a process of peri-urban decentralization.

This research has brought a new dimension to the development theory which, until now, attributed the responsibility for the structuring and development of the urban economy to industry and the exchange of goods. Higher services (quaternary) which mainly consume, handle an produce the flow of information of different sorts, can play a similar role. B. Thorngren[4] and G. Tornqvist[5], Swedish geographers from the University of Lund, had this problem in mind when they analyzed the system of contacts between individuals when they were researching groups of individuals, firms and social actors who interact during information exchange. In a society which is undergoing transformation, personal contact between experts and people in posts of responsibility becomes indispensable for the exchange of information. In fact, international cities are places which integrate systems for the production of goods and services networks. The economic base of these metropoles is organized around head offices, government services, international organizations and higher services.

Economic dynamism no longer comes from the capacity to produce goods and to exchange them, but rather from the capacity to decide. Deciding is a consumer activity and produces information. For a town possessing business services which implement this information as a resource, this is a crucial trump card.

5.2.2 The Evolution of Information Needs in Small Firms

Until very recently, very few small firms deemed it worthwhile to devote human and financial resources to finding information. The current rise in demand for information in all its forms[6], the development and the success of regional funds for consultancy aid[7] has led to the possibility of envisaging a real change in behaviour in three main directions[8]: scientific and technical information, knowledge of foreign markets and financial information.

- Small firms are particularly aware of the interest of an information strategy. This would lead to greater efficiency concerning the firms' commercial position when launching new products or else productivity gains realized thanks to the introduction of new technologies or by using new materials. This would then allow
  - either for progress to be made by others and available on the market to be directly integrated into their own product or into their own production process,
  - or for these firms themselves to undertake, in a permanent fashion, improvements in their materials or in the techniques used. All the production units are concerned in the desire to intensify human activity[9] which can be seen in the permanent effort to combine knowhow from different origins.
- The opening of internal European frontiers and the apparent simplification of export procedures which goes with it is leading small firms to take an interest in foreign markets, to undertake market studies for some of them and to discover the information procedures which requires regular exporting.
- The connection made by some small firms between their increasing financial costs in a less inflationary environment and the efficacy of certain cash flow management tools has led many firms to take an interest in the numerous financial products that the banking system proposes, and to widen their range of financial information.

This fresh attention to the problem of information has led small firms to a more active approach towards those suppliers of information which are the tertiary and quaternary sectors. In order to obtain a more precise perception of small firms' demand for information and to widen our knowledge about the relationships which firms establish with their economic environment, we have chosen to concentrate on one of the above three points, which is the information strategy linked to internationalization.

5.3   The need for international awareness and expression

5.3.1   The export chain and its implementation

The economic world is not an empty reference, but a structured stage where certain actors, such as customers and suppliers maintain stable relations with the firm. For those managing small firms, international action raises difficulties concerning the way this world is perceived and the way the firm enters onto this stage. This is due to the non-identification of potential partners and to the presumed instability of business relations. A way to reduce this uncertainty consists in identifying all the operations that businesses carry out when exporting and pinpointing the priority operations. The nature of these operations and the degree of priority determines the export chain.

Logistic analysis is extremely useful for identifying this chain because it supplies "A classing of base operations and support activities by following a logic in the polarization of aims towards the goal of customer service".[10] Logistics valorizes the dominant role of information flows leading to the control of activities that coordinate the flow of goods and the means of payment. But the type of information which is emphasized is that which concerns the running of the business and is fed by data.[11] There are generally written traces because it is linked to the circulation of products: anticipating orders, orders themselves, stock management, production management, delivery notes, invoices, etc.[12]

The export chain must also integrate those operations which create development information.[13] This information is not directly linked to the circulation of products but concerns global information about the target countries as well as information on general sales conditions abroad (product norms and fiscal details) or information about commercial networks. This information is neglected by some small firms which do not see it as being of immediate use. It is, however, indispensable in order to control the future development of exports and to integrate the specifics of foreign markets into the firm's production.

Applying the concept of an export chain means that the line between what is done inside and outside the firm can be drawn. Any subcontracting operation should be supplied by the economic environment, which therefore needs to be in a suitable position to reply to the firm's demand just as the firm itself should be capable of functioning with external partners. The integration of the economic environment into a firm takes place thanks to information and product exchange and is based on the complementarity of different sorts of competence and knowledge. These chains seem to be 'soft' structures or contact systems since product exchange is not predominant and exists alongside information exchange. These structures are nonetheless tricky to set up and the elaboration of such systems is a real difficulty for small firms starting out in exporting. Building and activating a system of external contacts therefore constitutes the first problematic field in the internationalization of small firms. Communication with the economic environment is the second difficulty that they must overcome.

With the aid of those responsible for export in a few firms, a certain number of basic export operations have been listed and those firms were then questioned about their practices.[14] These are shown in the following diagram, from pre- to post-operation. Three types of operations stand out:
- Operations which are inevitable in exporting: transport-transit (most small firms carry this out except for exporters of services and certain subcontracting firms), search for information regarding a client's solvability, prospects.
- Frequent operations: transport insurance, search for information about norms, regulations and fiscality in the target countries, debt recovery, search for information about commercial practices and sales networks, drawing up of contracts, taking out guarantees on payments, collecting general information about the markets, bringing funds back home, insurance and financing of prospects, financing the export operation.
- Operations seldom carried out: feasibility studies for selling the product, mobilizing potential aid, information about French regulations, exporter's guarantees.

Setting up an export chain varies according to the firm, its organization and its capacity to control all the elements in exporting. A first important distinction

concerns the carrying out of operations by the firm itself or their being
subcontracted to outside partners. Out of 17 operations, 15 are subcontracted in
three quarters of the cases. Drawing up contracts and the seller's guarantee are
the only operations that firms prefer to do themselves. These figures show the
extent of the small firms' call upon their surrounding economic environment.

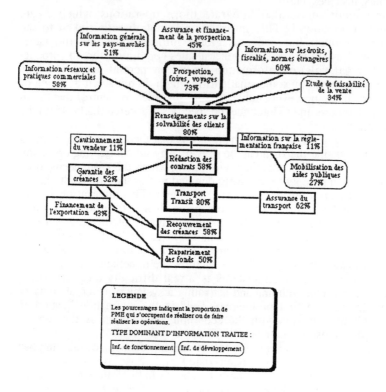

Figure 5.1 The export chain: the operations and firms' practices

Several criteria allow us to identify the predominant behaviour of firms as
regards the export chain. Generally speaking, we can make the following
remarks:
- Small exporting firms with fewer than 20 employees carry out the least
  number of basic operations. The number of operations carried out increases
  with the size of the workforce.
- Small firms that are independent carry out more operations than small firms
  connected to groups. These are characterized by their search for information
  of a strategic nature (which is general and concerns market practices) and their
  desire to limit the risks linked to exporting (information concerning a client's
  solvability, diverse insurances and credit guarantees). Independent small
  firms carry out more operations but they are centred on those actions which
  are essential to exporting (information linked directly to products, prospects,

are essential to exporting (information linked directly to products, prospects, financing).

- Firms which have an export department carry out more operations in the chain than those which do not have a special exporting set up. It seems that job specialization contributes to a better identification of the ins and outs of exporting.
- Experience in exporting does not show up as a determining criterion. We will simply note that the search for development information is an operation that is rarely carried out by firms starting up in export. However, these firms stand out because of their collecting information about foreign norms, about French regulations and about the mobilization of potential aid. The criteria for belonging to a sector and the rate of commitment to exporting do not introduce any significant differentiation.

5.3.2 *Geographical scales in export operations*

The location of these operations determines a firm's geographical scales for functioning. The operations are not all necessarily in the firm's region. A small firm exporting functions on several geographical scales which our study allowed us to examine.

There are five operations which are done for the most part with foreign partners: scale of goods feasibility study, commercial prospects, the search for information about commercial practices and sales networks, obtaining general information about the country and information on norms and obtaining information about the regulations and fiscality of foreign countries. The last two operations are carried out abroad but also in France. Generally speaking there are deficiencies in their implementation.

A second group brings together operations carried out on home ground. These are insurance and the financing of the prospects, information about clients' solvability, collecting information about French regulations, transport insurance, organizing guarantees to cover credit, debt recovery and the transmission of funds back home.

The last group consists of operations carried out exclusively in the firm's region: transport-transit, the financing of exports and organizing potential aid, the drawing up of contracts and establishing the exporter's collateral. Firms function therefore within a geographical area that has a certain coherence:

- Abroad, the search for information about markets with backup in France concerning the search for information about regulations.
- In France, operations which are ancillary to the movement of goods or are linked to logistic information. There is competition between the regions in order for this to be carried out.
- In the firm's area, the transport and finance operations which call upon traditional business services.

Small firms situate their operations geographically according to their possibilities, their interests and from the point of view of efficacy. However, two characteristics exert a particular influence on their choice: their own method of organization on the ground and their status as a business that is either independent or affiliated to a group. A firm's own geographical organization is defined by the number of premises and branches as well as the location of these in France and abroad. If the size and the compact nature of the organization of small firms are to be considered as advantages in the current economic situation because of the flexibility that they thereby gain, as far as international commerce is considered these same characteristics can create specific difficulties. In order to export, distance and more precisely geographical and economic distance must be carefully managed. Firms which have subsidiaries abroad are in a better position to know markets and to penetrate them. Generally speaking, multi-location is an advantage because it means that first hand information can be gathered and different markets and partners can be placed in direct competition.

This advantage is clear when accomplishing operations that have a high information content. All those small firms which have branches abroad carry out in those countries all the operations which collect development information. The same is true for prospects. Those small firms whose premises are in France carry out these same operations much more often in France because the cost of amassing this information limits their choice. Also, it is interesting to note that those small firms which have several branches in different regions of France use the services of those regions certainly to the best of their comparative advantages. They have a power of geographical discrimination especially for operations to do with the movement of goods that compact firms located on one single site do not have.

Small firms linked to groups also have this facility of finding the best information abroad and of being able to select the services of different regions according to their different comparative advantages. We have noticed that this latter sort of firm have the same behaviour patterns as small firms which have branches abroad, even when they consist of one single establishment. Obviously their group serves as a base.

Finally, it must be noted that small firms generally prefer the region where they are established for all those operations which are not carried out abroad. This preference becomes exclusive whatever their status or their methods of geographical organization for operations which are the hard core of the international activity, which are transport-transit and the financing of exporting. The composition and the quality of the local economic environment are therefore factors which contribute to the success of small firms that export.

5.3.3 Using the economic environment

It is stating that the obvious to say that small firms do not export alone but with the help of some of their suppliers, of service suppliers, of banks and also of public or para-public bodies which are likely to help them. However, all the potential helpers are not solicited with the same intensity by the firms, and some are not even known to them. The problem of firms' economic environment can be resumed thus: it must be rich which is to say that it must contain numerous services; also, the services must be efficient. Efficacy can be judged according to two criteria: firms must know them and must use them.

The analysis of the economic environment is often restricted to the public and para-public bodies whose role is to bring help to firms, but if we wish to evaluate the quality of the environment we must also take private bodies into account. Public bodies are not small firm's usual partners because their actions do not enter into the framework of the firms' day to day management. By questioning firms on their knowledge of public and private services located in their region and on the ways of using these services we can obtain a classification of these bodies according to their renown and utilization. The characteristics of firms will allow us to reflect upon this classification and to put forward explanations about the use or non-use of the services these bodies provide. In order to carry out this evaluation a list was drawn up that included 40 names of bodies or professions totally or partially responsible for promoting export and it was submitted to firms. This test has its limits in that certain highly specialized bodies might not be known because they operate outside the field of activity of the firms questioned. This accumulation of intervening bodies gives an impression of abundance and disorder which in fact corresponds to the French system of promoting exports. We find the same situation in the system for aid to innovation. The causes for this state of affairs have been analyzed[15] as has the fact that the bodies in question are underused. The results are pictured in Figure 5.1.

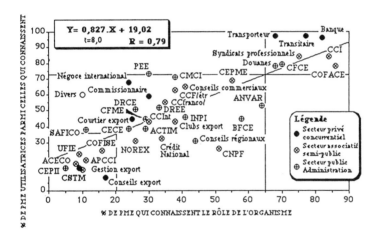

Figure 5.2 Familiarity and use of export linked services

Most small firms know between 10 and 25 bodies but only regularly call upon between 5 and 9. Two interpretations can be made of these low figures: small firms do not have enough time or manpower in order to learn about and to use such devices or else these service propositions are not adapted to their needs.

We have noticed however that certain services are very well known and used on a regional basis. As regards private services this concerns banks, freight forwarders and transporters. For public and para-public services this concerns the COFACE, Chambers of commerce, professional unions, the CFCE and

87

Customs services. On the other thand, we also find bodies whose role most small firms claim not to know: the CEPII, the ACECO, the CSTM, the COFISE[16] (for public services and for private services it is a question of exporting consultancy and management companies).

Familiarity and use are generally linked except for a few bodies like the ANVAR, the CNPF, and the BFCE whose general activities are well known but whose international activity remains confidential. There are other bodies which on the whole are not very well known but are used a lot by firms that know them. This is the case of the ARDEPI in Bayonne and the CMCI in Marseille, (which are shown as a single dot on the graph) as well as Economic Expansion Posts set up abroad. There is also a relationship between intensive use and use in the firm's region, except for bodies which do not exist locally or which, although they have outposts in the provinces are judged as offering a better service in Paris (COFACE, business consultants, professional unions, the CFCE). These same bodies as well as those connected with the movement of goods (customs, freight forwarder, transporter, bank) are also those which are used regularly outside of a firm's home region.

5.4   The metropolitan supply of services

The nature of needs in information and the profile of the demand have now been identified:
- Regional small firms with more than 20 employees need data about all foreign countries and more especially about nearby border regions. The emergence of their demand varies according to their internal organization and the existence of an export department.
- As for border region firms and the French subsidiaries of foreign companies, they require information about the French market and its organization. In order to answer this demand metropolitan areas should organize themselves and get together a human environment of skilled people and decision makers which could gradually grow. Within this process of reinforcing activities and symbolically and physically setting up an international environment, it is a necessary condition that the critical mass of businesses and international activities be reached. Studies carried out on the determining role concerning the attractiveness of the city:
- The function of centralizing information and communication and the expansion of tertiary activities and in particular the resulting business services.
- The functions connected with welcoming and accommodation linked to the business world. These studies also insist on the knock on effects of the development of the regional and urban economic area.

In order to evaluate the adequation of the metropolitan response to the needs expressed by internationalized small firms we have identified 24 services which a metropolitan environment can supply to an internationalized firm, and we have analyzed the way firms behave when acquiring these services. There are three main types of services:
- Logistics services in the widest sense of the term, which transport goods,

passengers, messages and means of payment, as well as their ancillary services (freight forwarding, warehousing, travel agencies, hotels, catering ...).

- Information services where the firm can find development services (trade fairs, international shows, fact finding missions abroad or foreign buyers, information services about countries and their markets, study services and export information, legal or regulatory information, international trading companies, dealers, commission agents and other export middlemen...).
- Economic services have, in theory, a more indirect role but they can influence the quality of the information or logistics services already listed (possibilities of the local employment market supplying multilingual employees, possibilities of local training for export executives, the presence of the head offices of large French firms, the presence of foreign firms' branches, environments that are technical, scientific, sociological, human, historical and cultural, the city's brand image, accessibility and traffic flow, ...). These services belong to the idea of 'externals', frequently used in geographical economics, for by nature they are indivisible and cannot be commandeered by individuals. A city's brand image is a good example: it seems surprising that this should be assimilated to a service for nobody produced it and nobody can lay claim to it. Yet, a city's image is either useful or else it does a disservice as much to an exporter as to those who promote the metropolitan area.

This list of services was submitted to those responsible for export in small firms and it was suggested that they could freely add any activities which seemed to them to have been omitted. Nobody added any different significant heading. They were also asked to give a qualitative appreciation of these services and to name other towns where they had recourse to any of the services.

The answers obtained[17] globally show a high level of coherence with those replies concerning the export chain, bodies and means of information. Generally speaking, those small firms which mobilize the largest number of services to exporting are also those which carry out the greatest number of operations in the export chain. They are the same firms which know and use support bodies the most often just as they are the same ones which are the best organized and which use specialized employees to handle their exports.

However, further to the validation which these replies bring, they also reveal the small firms' opinion of their city. They bring us a structured vision of these urban environments which allows us to characterize them globally and to pinpoint their faults. These responses also reveal the competition which metropolitan regions face not only from other international cities but also from the capital city. Some of the mechanisms of this competition could be analyzed to point up the leading role of the urban system of supply as far as international services are concerned.

5.4.1 The urban environments in practice

The metropolitan environment's degree of efficacy can be measured, among other things, by its capacity to attract and retain a more or less large number of export chain operations. By choosing not to use one or other service locally, small firms are making a judgement in relation to their export procedure. This practice, which might be linked to a call on other service location reveals a hierarchical image of the urban environment where the small firms are located. The comparison between the two regional metropolitan areas of our study shows that the quality and variety of services offered on the spot have a direct effect on the small firms' demand.

5.4.1.1 The use of urban services

In the towns under study the small firms make a precise selection of the services they use. In general, and this is quite clear, logistics services are local ones for most small firms. 'Environmental' services concern much more variable behaviour, while information services are used infrequently within the two metropolitan areas studied.

Table 5.1
Classification of urban services according to the number of small firms which claim to use them for export purposes.

(Bordeaux and Marseilles together)

%	Logistic services	Environmental services	Information services
95	Telecom		
82		Traffic flow,accessibility	
81		General brand image	
80	Transport/goods		
"	Hotel, catering		
79	Freight/Warehousing		
76	Travel Agencies/booking.		
69	Internat.financial services		
68	Internat.missions		
		Environments :	
61		Human socioloiqcal	
56		Technical-scientific	
52		Cultural-historical	
51	Internat.insurance	Hiring bilingual staff	
49			General info about countries
46			Internat.fairs
40			Export.studies/info
37		Training export exec.	Div.export middlemen
36			Trade missions abroad
"			Internat.trading
35			legal and reg.info
20		Foreign subsidiaries	
18		French head offices	

90

Logistics services in the export process are, characteristically, the sort of services that regional metropolitan areas are well able to satisfy. Except for insurance, they are all used locally by more than two thirds of the exporting small firms. They help to move goods that have been sold as well as move business people, buyers and sellers, and finally means of payment which is the final stage in any commercial operation. These services can be considered as the vital minimum to the internationalization of local firms, without which no town or city can claim to have an international dimension.

The common characteristic of environmental services is that they are global, collective and different from one geographical area to another. Most company heads perceive two main components: the ease of traffic flow and the city's general image.

The quality of traffic flow and means of transport in a metropolitan area determines accessibility to its different parts and therefore determines accessibility to the services which are located there. This service has an obvious logistic dimension and businesses which are in contact with abroad are particularly sensitive to this. Any blockage in the traffic system can have direct and pronounced effects on the international strategies of firms depending on their location.

We can question the unanimity of company heads concerning the role of the city's 'brand' image as a support to their international activity. They would thereby be condoning the often criticized city policies of image and promotion. Economic rationalization does not usually place quite so highly such indirect effects of image.

Very few small firms showed any interest in the branches of foreign firms or in the head offices of French companies which might help them to export. In part, this comes from the fact that these two cities have very few establishments of this type. Only 4% of small firms go elsewhere to find such contacts. This clearly shows that 'piggy back' strategies are not yet commonplace. Small firms are also wary, and perhaps justifiable so, of large companies, French or foreign, on whom they wish to depend as little as possible.

Information services are not very much sought after locally: between a third and a half of the small firms questioned used their city for that. The geographical scales on which exporting firms function contribute to this. While it is normal that firms seek their strategic information wherever they might find it, it would be preferable if regional metropolitan areas proposed information services at a level and of sufficient variety to be attractive not only to those regional companies but also to foreign firms come to investigate the French market.. We find between 10% and 15% of firms buying certain services[18], but which seek them elsewhere. For most small firms it is the very idea of buying services which is lacking. Nevertheless, the comparison of the two regional metropolitan areas under study clearly shows that a large proportion of the services demanded by exporting small firms depends on the local presence of a compatible supply, in order for the demand to make itself known.

5.4.1.2 A demand conditioned by the supply

In our study of the two cities it was not possible to carry out a complete survey of the localized service activities forming the supply system connected with internationalized business. A detailed comparison of available services in Bordeaux and Marseille is not necessary either in so far as all the elements gathered by us[19] or by others[20], point up the important difference between the two urban systems, which is the reflection of the difference in demographic size. We have also been able to show[21] how the geographical proximity of services offered to businesses can have an important effect on the small firms expressing a demand for them. A comparison of the behaviour of small firms in the two cities confirms this result.

On average, for exporting, small firms in Bordeaux use 13 out of the 24 services named, 11 of which are local. In Marseille, the equivalent figures are 17 and 15. Companies in Marseille also use more help and support bodies (on average 12 as compared to 10). The local environment, which is more developed, shows itself to be more capable of retaining small firms' demands: 80% of the bodies examined are done so locally against 75% in Bordeaux; 43% of the export chain operations are done with a local partner in Marseille (compared to 35% in Bordeaux). finally, small firms only turn to other cities on average for 1 to 2 services in Marseille and for 1 to 3 services in Bordeaux.

This result, which was observed among the few independent small firms is confirmed by the analysis of small firms which are subsidiaries of larger groups. These were outside the main field of study in this research because they function according to a different logic to that of the independent small firms, but they bring a complementary point of view which is useful when forming an opinion about the quality of a geographical environment offering its services equally to all those located within it.

The behaviour of subsidiaries in the export process makes them stand out from other companies. Because they are better informed via the internal channels of their group they manage their exporting in a more complete fashion than independent small firms, accomplishing more operations in the export chain and also knowing how to mobilize a greater number of bodies and partners for their sales abroad. Their high degree of extraversion serves to set them apart. As a rule the local environment supplies them with a lesser number of partners than for independent businesses. It would seem that their belonging to a group obliges them to judge the efficacy of the services that they call upon in comparison with those of the group and those accessible in other regions. Their choices are therefore all the more revealing. In Marseille more businesses are satisfied with the possibilities of local supply. Their international operations are more frequently carried out there and they use a lesser number of services in other metropolitan areas than subsidiaries in Bordeaux.[22]

The advantage of the Marseille 'supply system' is to be found in practically each of the 24 services listed. They were classified according to the proportion of independent small firms that used them and 9 proved to be very frequently used (more than 75% of the small firms) in Marseille against 4 in Bordeaux. 7 were used frequently (between 55% and 75% of small firms) compared to 4 in Bordeaux 13 services were little used (fewer than 45% of the small firms) in Bordeaux against 6 in Marseille.

In order to satisfy their need for services some firms turn to other cities of international standing. Such an attitude is a handicap for the local development of international services, but it is also, probably, the consequence of insufficiency in the local system of supply of these services.

Table 5.2
Comparison of the use of urban services by independent small firms in Bordeaux and Marseille

B/M	Logistic services	Environmental services	Information services
1,12 1,08 0,99 0,95	Internat.fin serv.(65) Transport/goods (77) Telecommunications (98)	 General brand image (81) Traffic flow /accessibility	 (84)
0,83 0,81 0,79 0,78 0,76	Freight/warehousings Hotels, catering (88)	(86) *Environments :* Cultural-historical(58) Technical-scientific (63)	 Divers middlemen(42)
0,72 0,69 0,67 0,64 0,61 0,59 0,57	Travel ag./booking. (88) Internat.missions (84) Internat.insurance(65)	 Training exp.exec.(47)	 Soc.comm. internat.(42) General info. /countries(58) Law info. (42) Internat missions .(44) Fairs/ internat.meetings(58)
0,52 0,51 0,46		Human socio.(79) Hiring bilingual staff	 Exp.studies/info(53) (70)
0,25 0,05		Foreign subsidiaries (37) French headquarters	 (28)

(Classification according to the Bordeaux/Marseille ratio: B/M; the figures in brackets indicate the percentage of user small firms in Marseille)

5.4.2 Services in competition and protected services

Small firms which buy their services elsewhere must certainly be convinced of the importance of these services for their own development. To trigger this decision for mobility the added cost in obtaining the service which the distance entails should be seen as low with regard, on the one hand, to the comparative advantage offered for this service by the other metropolitan areas and, on the other hand, to the gamble which the good satisfaction of this need represents for the firm. Few services are seen by company heads as both essential to the firm and much better handled elsewhere. Small firms' buying mobility therefore means we can define a hierarchy of urban services, as illustrated by table 3. For metropolitan areas this hierarchy shows the opening up to competition from other cities which is faced by its supply system of international services. These figures show that information services are more open to competition between cities whereas those which describe the general environment seem to be well protected. Logistics services seem to show diverse results but most face weak competition from those in other towns.

Table 5.3
Classification of services according to their risk of competition from other cities

%	Logistic services	Environmental services	Information services
32			Fairs/ internat.shows
28			Legal and reg.info
21		French head quarters	
20			Gen.inform. about countries
19			Internat.trading comp.
"			Trade missions abroad
17	Transport/goods		
16	Internat.insurance		
15		Foreign subsidiaries	
14			Div.export middlemen.
13	Freight/warehousing		Export studies/info.
9	Internat.fin.services		
7	Internat.missions		
6	travel ag. /booking		
3		Training export executives	
		Environments :	
2	Telecommunications	Technical-scientific	
"		Cultural-historical	
"		Human sociological	
1	Hotels,catering	General brand image	
"		Traffic flows/accessibility	
0		Hiring bilingual staff	

(Classification according to the percentage of independent small firms which turn to other towns; total field of the two cities together.)

In theory, the situation of information services seems to be consistent with the under-equipment of regional metropolitan areas in this domain. Firms which need certain precise services and do not find them locally will naturally seek them elsewhere. Nearly a third of small firms turn to other towns whenever there is any sort of international event or fair or specialized show.

Very often, this is the main attempt to obtain information that is undertaken by exporting small firms. These are occasions to make oneself known, to keep ut with technology and to keep up with competitors, to evaluate their competition, consolidate relationships, make contacts, and so on. Similarly, it is not very likely that international fairs or shows which are held in a regional metropolitan area will satisfy all the heads of local businesses. It is however essential that the organizers of these events be aware that they are managing an important tool, not only for local internationalized businesses but also for the international image of the city. Choices which are made will favour some 'actors' to the detriment of others. This is also true for the organization of trade missions, whether it be a question of inviting foreign managers over or accompanying local managers abroad.

All the environmental services (except two)[23] seem to suffer very little competition from other cities. These kinds of services cannot really be

94

dissociated from firms' locations. They are a little like the air we breathe and company heads would never dream of looking elsewhere. A small number of managers claim to do so however. If these services become really bad, then the firm itself will move in order to find better conditions in which to operate.

This behaviour also concerns logistics services, hotels and telecommunications, whose role in the internationalization of cities we noted earlier. These services must not be neglected because it is they which intervene, often in a discriminatory manner, in decisions over firms' locations. Typically, these services combine to form a global economic image of the urban environment.

Logistics services which normally are properly provided locally seem not to be very sensitive to inter-city competition except where repeated industrial action gives rise to uncertainty about the availability and the quality of the service.

The main competition for information services comes from the capital which is way ahead of other cities concerning the use of services by small firms outside their own metropolitan area.

Nearly 80% of small firms which go afield to find services use at least one Parisian service. Besides this, unlike the other towns quoted by the small firms outside their own metropolitan area, Paris is rarely used for just one single service. Between a third and a half of firms which turn to Paris do so for three or more services (between 5 and 6 on average). This is never the case for foreign metropolitan areas nor for other French towns used. Among the independent small firms which use service providers in the capital, nearly two thirds go there for an international event, one third go there for legal or regulatory information, and a third go there for general information about countries or markets prospected. We might reasonably consider that these three fields[24] are the 'loss leaders' of the Parisian supply system. Firms which decide to go to the capital for a specialized show[25] (for example) might take advantage of the capital's different information services on this occasion. This is an ace[26] that regional metropolitan areas will find difficult to match, for their aim, as far as fairs and shows go, might at best be to show that they are the best in a restricted number of specialities.

It is not the same for the two other information services. Except for certain cases, metropolitan areas - and especially those in border regions - should adopt these kinds of services, so that foreign firms do not reproduce the centralization formats acquired by those active in the French economy.

5.5 Conclusion

Geographical proximity is not in itself sufficient for economic 'actors' to obtain a better relative knowledge of the opportunities which a neighbouring border region proposes. This is shown by the mediocre performances in neighbouring markets of our two regions under study. They still incite small firms to take their first steps in exporting in the border region markets.

The complete opening of frontiers intensifies and widens the competition for service activities, which is the new vector for the thrust of urban activities. French metropolitan areas, which for the most part are situated in border regions, do not have at their disposal a sizable core of internationalized activities in order to respond to the information needs of exporting firms located on both sides of the border, whether it be a question of basic information services or more specialized services. This weakness explains in part the withering of small firms' demand for services.

It seems difficult for metropolitan areas to have a complete range of specialized services available because the variety of needs is so great, setting up networks of cities which have complementary services seems to be the right way to reveal and to get going those information linked practices which are likely to confirm the exporting potential of small firms located in border regions, while ensuring the international attractiveness of their metropolitan areas.

Notes

1. GIP Reclus, 1989, Les Villes Européennes, rapport pour la Datar, Documentation Française, Paris

2. Lyon is listed 19th among European cities.

3. Gottman, J., 1970, Urban centrality and the interweaving of quaternary activities, *Ekistics*, Vol. 29, pp. 322-330. Gottman, J., 1983, The coming of the transactional city, Institute for Urban Studies, University of Maryland.

4. Thorngren, B., 1967, Regional economic interaction and flows of information, Proceedings of the Second Poland-Norden Regional Science Seminar, Committee for Space Economy and Regional Planning of the Polish Academy of Sciences, PWN, Varsovie. Thorngren, B., 1970, How do contact systems affect regional development?, *Environment and Planning*, no. 2, pp. 409-27.

5. Tornqvist, G., 1968, Flows of information and the location of economic activities, Lund Studies in Geography (Série B), Human Geography, CWK, Gleerup Pub., Lund.

6. We can note for example the increase in the consultation of data banks accessible through minitel in the upper levels of the professional kiosk. This is largely due to the fact that small firms have no access to computer equipment linked to large service centres.

7. Centre de Gestion Scientifique de l'ENSMP, 1987, Evaluation des fonds régionaux d'aide au conseil.

8. Cohen, R., 1979, The changing transaction economy and its spatial implications, *Ekistics*, no. 274, pp. 7-14. Bonnet, J., 1990, Ancrages territoriaux des services. Communication aux journées "Métropoles en

déséquilibre" organisées par le Plan Urbain les 22 et 23 novembre 1990 à Lyon.

9. Bucaille, A. et Costa de Beauregard, B., 1987, PMI enjeux régionaux et internationaux, Economica, Paris.

10. Tixier, D., Mathé, H. and Colin, J., 1983, La logistique au service de l'enterprise, Dunod Enterprise, Paris, p. 28.

11. Here we find Gregory Bateson's distinction between a datum (a given information) "trace, description or memory of certain events", and a unit of information, "the difference which produces a difference". Cf. Bateson, G., 1977, Vers une écologie de 'l'esprit, Le Seuil, Paris, pp. 14 and 231.

12. Heskett, J.L., 1978, La logistique: élément clé de la stratégie, *Harvard - l'Expansion*, no. 8, Printemps, Paris, P. 54.

13. A fuller analysis of the two types of information used by the firms is presented in Leo, P.Y., Monnoyer, M.C. and Philippe, J., 1990, Métropoles régionales et PME, l'enjeu international, Serdeco, Aix en Provence.

14. 130 firms were questioned in the two regions, Provence-Côte d'Azur and Aquitaine. All the results of this study can be found in Leo P.Y., Monnoyer, M.C. and Philippe, J., 1990, PME - Stratégies internationales, Economica, Paris.

15. Bucaille, A., and Costa de Beauregard, B., 1987, PMI enjeux régionaux et internationaux, Economica, Paris.

16. The action of these bodies is presented in a synthetic manner, by fiche in Leo PY, Monnoyer MC & Philippe, J., 1990, PME - Stratégies internationales, Paris.

17. 110 answers were obtained, divided thus:
- in Bordeaux: 41 independent small firms and 15 linked to large groups
- in Marseille: 44 independent small firms and 10 linked to large groups.

18. This percentage is as high as 21% for fairs and shows. This degree of openness can be quite normal since it concerns one of the methods of obtaining information preferred by small firms.

19. A certain number of points have been brought together. A map analysis is given in Leo P.Y., Monnoyer MC & Philippe, J., 1990, Métropoles régionales et PME, l'enjeu international, Serdeco, Aix en Provence.

20. G.I.P. RECLUS, 1989, Les Villes Européennes, rapport pour la DATAR, La Documentation Française, Aix en Provence.

21. Leo P.Y., Monnoyer MC & Philippe, J., 1990, Métropoles régionales et PME, l'enjeu international, Serdeco, Aix en Provence.

22. On average, in Marseille, small firms which are subsidiaries use 75% of the services listed, of which 94% locally and 6% in other towns. In Bordeaux small firms only use 64% of the types of services mentioned and 17% of the services are sought elsewhere.

23. Which only concern a very small number of small firms, which are those that cannot find large French or foreign firms on the spot on whom they can rely for exporting.

24. Subsidiary small firms also turn a lot to the capital. They concentrate on using practically the same services, except for international shows, which they hardly ever frequent and the head offices of French firms which of course they use a lot.

25. Remember that Paris is regularly listed as the top European capital for international fairs and shows. 80% of the specialized professional shows held in France are in the capital. Paris Chamber of Commerce and Industry, 1988. Les métropoles de services dans la compétition Européenne. Paper presented at the congress of the International Association of French Language Economists, Lille, 30 May-1 June 1988.

26. The financial power of the Paris Chamber of Commerce and Industry, which benefits from the concentration of French head offices, is far from being a minor advantage in this affair.

6 The role of technology and services in restructuring the productive base of the traditional industrial regions of Europe

J.C. Houard and C. Albessart

6.1 General approach of the productive structure of the traditional industrial regions

The aim of the present paper is to underline the structure and performance of the Traditional Industrial Regions that differentiate them from the EEC as a whole.

A word of warning is however necessary: beyond a number of convergences, the Traditional Industrial Regions (TIR) distinguish themselves by a great heterogeneity of their productive networks. That is why we will have to weight their convergences against the regional specificity.

6.1.1 The structure of the TIR's productive networks

The main characteristics of the TIR is the overdevelopment within their productive networks, of metallurgy. It concentrates nearly twice the industrial employment share of the EEC-9 (11.5% and 5.2% respectively). That share in some regions is three times (the Walloon region with 15.6%) to four times as much (South Yorkshire with 19.8%) as in the EEC-9. Table 6.1 presents the distribution of industrial employment among the nine productive 'filieres'.[1] The productive 'filiere' downstream metallurgy and equipment goods are also more important (28.5% of industrial employment) than in the EEC (23%).

In the TIR, the productive 'filiere' metallurgy-electricity makes up 40 per cent of industrial employment (with a peak reached by South Yorkshire, 50 per cent). Strathclyde is the exception with only 25% of its industrial employment in that productive 'filiere' (of which more than 20% is in equipment goods).

Three productive 'filieres' are underdeveloped:

. the chemical 'filiere' with an employment share varying from 4% in South Yorkshire to 9% in the Basque country, in comparison with 11% with the EEC. The Nordrhine-Westphalia is the exception with 15% of total regional employment producing 40% of chemical turnover.

. the electronic 'filiere' concentrates only 12% of industrial employment of the six regions compared with 15% for the EEC. A greater underdevelopment is to be noticed in the Walloon region (8.5%), in Nord-Pas-de-Calais (7.7%) and in South Yorkshire (5%).

the agro industry represents 5.5% of industrial employment of the TIR compared with 12% in the EEC. The Walloon region and South Yorkshire nearly reach the same share as the EEC. Strathclyde is concentrating 15% of its industrial employment in that productive 'filiere' (mostly in the alcohol 'filiere').

Table 6.1
Distribution of the industrial employment
among the 9 productive 'filieres'

Filieres	Metal	Build Public works	Chem	Equip goods	Electr.	Trans.	Agro-indust.	Text.	Wood, Paper	Total
Europe	5.2	5.1	11.4	23.1	16.4	5.8	11.6	11.0	10.3	99.9
126 Regions	11.5	4.4	12.1	28.5	11.6	8.1	5.5	8.3	8.7	98.7
W	15.6	11.4	8.9	21.8	8.5	5.1	11.7	6.8	9.1	98.9
BC	16.0	4.1	9.3	24.8	10.5	9.5	6.7	2.0	10.6	93.5
NPC	10.9	9.0	7.3	19.2	7.7	13.0	1.0	23.0	6.8	97.9
ST	5.1	9.0	6.4	20.6	13.2	13.9	15.3	12.3	9.5	99.3
SY	19.8	9.0	4.1	29.4	5.0	5.5	10.4	7.4	7.5	98.1
NRW	10.1	3.1	14.7	31.4	13.0	6.8	4.2	6.5	10.0	99.8

Source: Michel Quévit and Jean Houard, (1991), "Impact Regional 1992, Les Régions de tradition industrielles", De Boeck; W=Wallonia; BC=Basque Country; NPC=Nord-Pas-de-Calais; ST=Strathclyde; SY=South Yorkshire; NRW=Nordrhine-Westphalia

As a whole, the other productive 'filieres' are the same in the EEC as in the six TIR. The most important features are:
. textile 'filiere': 25% of employment for Nord-Pas-de-Calais, compared with 11% for the EEC,
. building and public works: 11% in the Walloon region compared with 5% in the EEC,
. transport 'filiere': in Nord-Pas-de-Calais and in Strathclyde, 13 % and 14% respectively, while 6% in the EEC.

Table 6.2
The 9 productive 'filieres':
Distribution of the employment among the production stages

	Upstream	-Upstream	-Downstream	Downstream
EUROPE	5.1	17.9	29.1	48.3
6 REGIONS	10.1	20.0	27.2	42.7
W	17.2	17.2	26.8	38.4
BC	15.1	16.8	20.9	47.3
NPC	9.6	22.0	29.3	39.3
ST	5.8	10.8	31.7	51.7
SY	17.2	10.3	30.6	41.8
NRW	9.0	22.6	27.6	41.2

Source: Michel Quévit and Jean Houard (1991), "Impact Régional 1992, Les Régions de tradition industrielles", De Boeck

The second characteristic of the TIR is the specialization in the upstream stages of the 'filieres'. They concentrate from two to three times more employment in these stages than in the EEC (see Table 6.2). Strathclyde presents nearly the same situation as in the EEC.

Finally, specific activities within the productive 'filieres' call for the following comments:
. the diversification of the productive networks in the 6 TIR is less than in the EEC. In decreasing order of employment share, 17 activities are necessary to make up 50% of total industrial employment in the EEC. Only 14 activities are necessary in the Walloon region, 13 in the Nordrhine-Westphalia, 11 in the Nord-Pas-de-Calais, 9 in the Basque country and 7 in South Yorkshire;
. these activities obviously vary from one region to the other. On the basis of the preceding data, 35 different activities were recorded among the 6 regions.

6.1.2 Dynamics of the productive networks

The aim of this section is to identify the industrial portfolio of activities of the different regions. The industrial portfolio of activities means the characterization of the regional productive networks by their medium term economic growth and by their technological dynamism.

The methodology uses two criteria:
. the medium term growth of the economic activities of the TIR (measured by the recorded and sectorial prospects, value-added, with some qualifications by sectorial experts);
. technological evolution associated with their activities. The assumption is made that technical development potential constitutes one of the medium term growth factors. Being unable to directly identify that potential, we assumed that technical evolution may be evaluated by the following double criteria:
-   the rate of investment as an indicator of the capital intensity of the sector;
-   the comparison of the rate of growth of turnover and the rate of growth of investment.

As compared with the average of the EEC, the dynamics in the TIR are essentially concentrated on activities with a growth potential in the medium term, weak to medium but in which the modernizing and rationalizing process was quite important during the last few years.

This characteristic is the direct consequence of the specialization of the TIR in terms of employment in mature economic activities upstream stages. These activities constituted their growth bases until the 70s but their present technical and economic growth potential is thereafter medium to weak:

.   metallurgy-electricity (all regions)

.   the upstream of the building-public works sector (Walloon region)

.   the upstream and the downstream of the textile 'filiere' (Nord-Pas de Calais)

.   the Agro industry (Strathclyde)

.   the transport 'filiere' without the car construction and the aerospace sectors.

During the last few years, much was invested in these activities to rationalize their production structures because these are sectors in maturity with weak growth in the past, a weak demand potential and with great competition inside and outside Europe. This is confirmed by the sectorial experts interviewed. Investment, research and development efforts in the last five years, essentially concentrated on the process rather than on the products, without any real innovation.

If the adaptation effort of the TIR cannot be certain of accelerating their rate of growth, it will, in the future, allow for a better build up of the value-added and increased productivity.

It should be noted that in these activities the decision making centre is mostly local as opposed to other activities which are better located in the portfolio but of which the most important decision makers are national or international groups.

6.1.3   Position of the regional productive networks compared with the present structure of the European supply

6.1.3.1 Average dimension of the firms

As compared with the average European dimension, the TIR concentrates a great share of their employment activities on medium to large firms. The overdevelopment of the transformation industries' upstream stages is the most important explanatory factor of that situation.

 This is confirmed by the fact that the TIR, except in Nord-Pas-de-Calais, have a lower share in activities where the firms of 10 to 20 persons and 20 to 100 persons contribute significantly to the regional value added as a whole.

6.1.3.2 Relative export specialization

A lower share of the industrial employment than in the EEC is located in activities with an already important export rate and export specialization. The exceptions for the export rate are Strathclyde and Nordrhine-Westphalia and for export specialization is Nord-Pas-de-Calais.

6.1.4 Business services

The services activities reviewed are business services as opposed to collective or individual services.

In our general approach to the productive networks by the productive 'filieres', we have to analyze these networks in terms of agents contributing to meeting intermediate or final demand and the dynamic interactions between these agents.

The main assumption is that business services have a structuring effect on productive networks and that there are reciprocal attraction dynamics between these activities and industrial ones.

With this in mind, the question is: what is the availability, quality and exploitation modality of business services in the regional space studied?

6.1.4.1 Situation and perception of the business services in TIR

Business services are faced with no prospect of growing interaction with the industry of which they are one of the conditions for development and dynamism.

Because interaction is much greater between the supplier and the user of the services, the service activities are subject to localized constraints, much more than industrial activities.

Table 6.3 illustrates recent employment development business services in the regions studied.

The first finding is that the employment evolution in services is, in all regions, far more favourable than in the whole of industry and services. This is especially true in the Walloon region, but mostly due to the impact of item 3 - interim Agencies: the growth of which is particularly pronounced in Nord–Pas–de-Calais - and item 12 - general services that is growing in importance in nearly all regions. That evolution corresponds to the trend in industries to externalize their general ordinary services, i.e. cleaning, maintenance, security and collective catering.

It is necessary to distinguish between:
. Operational services; services that are contributing to the normal operation of the regional economy: financial services, insurance, trade services, communications, transport, etc.
. Regulation services; structuring services; which are contributing to the development and the renewal of the economic structure.

In Table 6.3 we observe, among regulation services, a favourable evolution of the:
. accounting and financial services in the four regions for which the data are available
. technical services in Nord-Pas-de-Calais
. advertising and marketing services in the Walloon region and in all regions except the Basque country.

The evolution of the operational services is generally less satisfactory. This

103

means that those services have reached their maturity in comparison with the other ones that are in emergence. In terms of relative weights in total service employment, they are dominant, representing from 72% to 78% for the four regions for which the calculation was made.

Table 6.3
Recent evolution of the employment in the rendered services in the firms

Services	W 1980-84	PC 1979-85	NPC 1980-87	ST 1980-84	SY 1980-84
1. Insurances, credit	+ 4	-12	-12	+ 2	+ 4
2. Accounting	+ 10	n.a.	+ 18	+ 14	+ 35
3. Workforce management	+ 24	n.a.	+ 63	n.a.	n.a.
4. Office services	n.a.	n.a.	n.a.	+ 6	+ 10
5. Technical	+ 1	n.a.	+ 31	+ 33	- 29
6. Marketing	+ 17	- 7	+ 39	+ 31	+ 38
7. Distribution	- 15	n.a.	+ 5	- 6	- 4
8. Data processing	+ 25	n.a.	+109	n.a.	n.a.
9. Transport	- 11	- 3	- 2	+ 7	- 8
10. Communication	- 5	n.a.	- 55	- 6	+ 33
11. Hiring-building	+ 6	n.a.	- 20	+ 27	+ 25
12. General services	+ 28	- 1	+ 18	+ 17	+ 10
Total SRE	+ 20	- 5	+ 6	+ 9	+ 2
Total industries services	- 7	- 8	- 13	- 6	- 6

Source: Michel Quévit and Jean Houard, 1991, "Impact Régional 1992, Les Régions de tradition industrielles", De Boeck.

In other words, services are beginning to take an important place in total employment (industry and services) in the TIR although their share remains lower than in the EEC (from 14% to 18% in comparison with 25% for the EEC).

Another finding is that restructuring services are developing very fast but still constitute a small fraction of total service employment.

6.1.4.2 Accessibility and availability of business services

. **Financial services and insurance**: are practically nonexistent at the firm level, poorly represented at the enterprise level and mostly represented at the group level. External use of these services is locally or nationally oriented.
There is an acute problem with availability of venture capital for small and medium firms, specially in the Walloon region, but that type of service is satisfactory in Nordrhine-Westphalia, South Yorkshire and in Nord–Pas–de-Calais.
In all the regions, the need for technical assistance in preparing credit applications is noted, especially for small and medium firms.
. **Recruitment, training and workforce management**: except for

training in small and medium firms, these services are not well represented in all the regions. The external supply is locally represented, but with a low level of quality, especially in the Basque country and in the Walloon region.

An important finding is the lack of appreciation of local firms of these services; they do not weigh their potential benefit against their high costs (mostly for workforce management).

Concerning training, we noticed a significant supply and demand for short and operational training courses (data processing, communication and trade). The high cost and the standardization of the services are stressed.

. **Office services**: this type of service is mostly internally generated. The external availability is really low in the Walloon region and the Basque country and medium in other regions. This situation is quickly moving with the emergence of small and medium secretarial office services firms.

. **Technical services**: are weakly to mildly represented in firms, except in Nord-Pas-de-Calais or are concentrated in groups as in the Nordrhine–Westphalia. In the other regions, the availability of these services is poor. Here again, external supply lies within national or extra–regional groups. The second finding is that small and medium firms are not sufficiently aware that universities are centres of technical knowledge and may offer technical assistance.

. **Marketing and adverting**: These services are centralized in firms or groups. External supply of this kind of service seems to be the most adequate one at local level by local experts.

. **Data processing services**: are internally generated only to a limited extent except in Nordrhein-Westphalie. The external supply is quite weak at the local level (except in the Nord-Pas-de-Calais). In all cases, it is extra regional firms that are supplying the services.

6.1.4.3 Structure of the regional supply and demand

. Supply is from small local firms or from subsidiary companies of national groups. They essentially supply standardized products (financial services, insurance, formation, technical services), or very specialized services (data processing). Local firms are forced to look for structuring services (marketing, technical assistance) outside their region.

. Demand, especially in the case of small firms, which are insufficiently aware of the very existence of these different services and of their potentially dynamic role in their own activities. Firms, however, increasingly recognize the strategic importance of services for regional development, as testified by the fact that business services are, together with training, the only areas which call for public funding.

. Services appearing to be most important for technological innovation are in decreasing order:
  - Training and recruiting services
  - Technical services
  - Transport and logistic services
  - Communication services
  - Data processing services

- Advertising and marketing services
- Accounting services
- Hiring services and building management
- General services

The main three elements suggested by this rating are:
- the importance of a qualified labour force
- the importance of the financial dimension
- the connection between technological investment and the competitive market.

6.1.5 Conclusion: TIR's development potential

6.1.5.1 TIR's structural characteristics

The qualitative as well as the quantitative analyses of the productive structure brings to light, beyond a measure of convergence, a heterogeneity of the TIR in terms of their activities 'portfolio' and in terms of their development prospects.
   The general diagnosis of the development potential of the TIR might read as follows:
.   the preponderance within their productive networks of the filieres and industrial activities borne during the first and the second industrial revolution:
    - metallurgy-electricity
    - textile
    - building materials - buildings and public works
    - equipment goods
    - transport
.   the firm's environment is concentrated on those filieres.
The main consequences are:
.   activities are focused on the production network upstream,
.   weak diversification regional productive networks,
.   weak regional value-added
.   weak past and potential rate of growth,
.   a great restructuring effort during the last few years inducing:
    - important employment losses
    - significant modernization of the production equipment
    - improvement in profitability and in productivity;
.   a greater dichotomy between
    - larger firms are in a position to build up self financing as well as external funds, necessary for their restructuring.
    - small and medium firms, without those opportunities, are surviving because of their greater flexibility although still dependent on a limited number of clients;
.   classical financing networks in favour of the larger industrial and more traditional firms;
.   public interventions in favour of those same traditional sectors;
.   few opportunities to find venture capital;
.   limited availability and/or inadequate business services except operational;

106

the present formation level in the great sectors is quite high, but totally inadequate in new activities.

6.2 R&D potentials of the TIR

The objective of this section is to evaluate the TIR's R&D potential and to identify possible new ways of adapting their productive networks to technological development.

6.2.1 Technological gap

6.2.1.1 TIR's R&D potential relative to their national and the European space

TIR lag behind their respective country as a whole in terms of R&D efforts. All the regions are below the average level reached by their country (except Nordrhine-Westphalia and the Basque country).
   In terms of European R&D potential, the TIR can be classified in three groups:
.   regions with a high potential for R&D (Nordrhine-Westphalia)
.   marginalized regions (Basque country)
.   intermediate regions where the R&D potential is still weak compared with the European situation, although sufficient to avoid marginalization (Walloon region, Nord-Pas-de-Calais, South Yorkshire and Strathclyde).
   If, furthermore, we use the R&D potential criterion together with the creation of regional wealth, we can distinguish three groups of regions:
.   regions with a high technological potential and a high level of development;
.   regions where both regional growth and the technological level are weak (Basque country);
.   regions with a relatively high level of growth but with a weak technological potential (the other regions).
That classification bring to the fore one major characteristic of the TIR: a relatively important regional growth which was not based on a high R&D intensity. The value added is still too dependent on a productive network with a low technological level.

6.2.1.2 Structural characteristics of the technological gap

(a) A reduced participation of the TIR's firms in the national or European R&D effort
The TIR's R&D effort in the private sector is limited, relative to European R&D, on the basis of the share of R&D investment in the total value added.
   At the national level, the situation is the same, but with a large trend towards concentration of R&D in the metropolitan areas.

(b) Industrial specialization in the R&D effort
The TIR's R&D potential seems to be bound to the sectorial orientation of R&D expenditures and to their industrial specialization.

107

- In the Walloon region 85% of the total R&D expenditure is concentrated in the chemical industry (29%), electrotechnics (29%), mechanical engineering (21%) and stone, clay and glass (6%)
- In the Basque country, 52% of total R&D expenditure is concentrated on machinery (25%), mechanical engineering 18% and the chemical industry (9%)
- In Nordrhine-Westphalia, the chemical industry and mechanical engineering account for a total 57% of the R&D effort
- In South Yorkshire, metallurgy is the most important sector in the R&D investment structure.

Table 6.4
Industrial specialization of the R&D investments of TIR firms (as a % of the regional total)

Walloon region	Basque country
Chemical industry	Non electric machinery
Electrotechnic	Electric machinery
Mechanical engineering	Mechanical engineering
Stone, clay and glass	Chemical industry
Nordrhein-Westphalie	**Yorkshire**
Chemical industry	Iron and Steel
Petroleum processing	Missing machinery
Mechanical engineering	Instruments
	Electronic capital goods
	Shipbuilding
	Tractors
	Textile

Source: Michel Quévit and Jean Houard, (1991), "Impact Régional 1992, Les Régions de tradition industrielles", De Boeck.

6.2.2   Technological orientations

6.2.2.1 Technological orientation and R&D problematic

Technological innovation (products and processes) covers, in the TIR, three distinct processes that are offering prospects for new growth.
- the inclusion of new technologies in the production of the traditional industries
- the creation of new technologies and new applications from R&D in the traditional industries
- the creation of new technologies born from science.

Those different processes show that the TIR are engaged in very diversified technological movements which stem from the technological developments of the major sectors in the regional economy and form the strategies of existing firms.

Technological fields

In this study, will focus more on technological fields than on sectorial specialization. A technological field means the grouping of different technologies around their scientific creation process.
We have chosen six fields for further analysis:
. telecommunication;
. automation;
. data processing;
. new materials;
. energy;
. biotechnology.
These fields will now be investigated in Section 6.2.3.

6.2.3 Predominating technological field

6.2.3.1 General trends

From the six selected technological fields, only four appear to be relatively present in the TIR:
. energy
. automation
. data processing
. new materials
The biotechnological field is present in each TIR but more significantly in the Walloon region, Nordrhine-Westphalia and Nord-Pas-de-Calais. The telecommunication field is not a significant development field in the TIR.

6.2.3.2 Special trends
a   Energy field
The energy field is particularly important in the TIR's R&D potential. This originates in the rationalizing strategies of the process aimed at reducing the costs borne by heavy industry, hence interaction between larger industries and research laboratories. Major R&D efforts are made in Nordrhine-Westphalia and Nord-Pas-de-Calais, less so in the Basque country, the Walloon region and South Yorkshire.

b   Automation and data processing
Automation and data processing are well developed in the TIR, also as a result of restructuring efforts in large industries such as metallurgy, mechanical construction and textile.
In Nordrhine-Westphalia and in Nord-Pas-de-Calais, both are predominating fields, as in the Walloon region, where they are the second most important areas for R&D. In the United Kingdom, and therefore in the two TIR of that country, government policy is making a big investment effort in those special fields. In the Basque country, they are the first R&D field in their magnitude.

c   New materials
New materials are in the TIR, one field with great potential. The larger

industrial sectors find in them a number of diversification and restructuring opportunities of their activities.

In the Walloon region, it is the predominating field. In Nord-Pas-de-Calais, it is not a very developed technological field while in Nordrhine-Westphalia, it is considered with great attention by the authorities.

d   Biotechnology

Biotechnology has a large potential for transferability in a series of industrial activities as a whole. In the TIR, biotechnology is specially developed in the Walloon region, Nordrhine-Westphalia, Nord-Pas-de-Calais and to a lesser extent in Strathclyde. In South Yorkshire and the Basque country it is not significantly developed.

Table 6.5
Predominating technological fields in the TIR as a whole

	NRW	NPC	BC	W	SY	ST
Energy	+	+	-	-	-	n.a.
Data processing	+	+	+	+	+	+
New materials	+	-	n.a	+	n.a.	n.a.
Biotechnology	+	+	n.a	-	-	+

Source: Michel Quévit and Jean Houard, (1991), "Impact Régional 1992, Les Régions de tradition industrielles", De Boeck.

6.2.4   Organization characteristics and technological orientations

Technological specialization is not the only predominating characteristic of the TIR's technological orientation. It also depends on structural and organizational factors.

We may distinguish two important possibilities of the technological transfer of the TIR's traditional technical system. One is centred on new technology creation based on the direct interaction between science and technology. The other is centred on the use of generic technologies as a base for productive networks adaptation to the technological transfer and to the structuring of a new productive system.

Among factors underlying these dynamics, we may mention:
.   the research project's orientation is towards major projects of laboratories, firms, research centres, etc.
.   the R&D potential capacity to participate in a regional or international partners networks
.   the TIR's capacity to absorb their human resources in their productive networks

6.2.4.1 Technological orientation

We identify three main types of research:
.   basic research
.   applied research

110

. pre-competitive research which is a prerequisite for the development of a technological innovation.

Table 6.5 gives, by degree of importance, the distribution of the three types of research in the TIR by technological field

Table 6.6
Technical orientations by research type for the TIR as a whole

Research type			
Technological field	Fundamental research	Applied research	Pre competitive research
Automation	-	=	+
Data processing	-	=	+
New materials]	-	=	+
Energy	=	+	+
Biotechnology	=	=	+
High +; Medium =; Weak -			

Pre-competitive research is predominating in the TIR's five main fields of R&D projects. There is a clear trend to favour the productive networks' technological adaptation. Some regional specificities may be noted:
. Nordrhine-Westphalia has a more clear trend to favour basic and applied research in the energy field. There is also a greater articulation between applied and pre-competitive research.
. Nord-Pas-de-Calais and the Walloon region tend to concentrate their R&D on basic research, specially in the biotechnology field.
For these three regions the opportunities to participate in a technology creation scenario are greater, but only if conditions are created to allow their scientific potential to reach a critical mass sufficient to participate in international research programmes.
. In the Basque country there is no R&D tradition. Nevertheless, the recent take off of these kind of activities is mostly oriented towards the modernization of the industrial structures by the adoption of generic research (applied research).
. In Strathclyde, the decline of productive networks does not favour the development of R&D activities.

6.2.4.2 Partnership networks and international orientations

The renewal of the regional productive networks based on a new technical system requires a measure of interdependence between the agents involved. The constitution of local or regional networks takes the form of partnership networks.
Such practices need support at two levels:
. regional level: associating public authorities, firms and research centres
. international level: favouring the firm's participation in major R&D programmes.

111

a   Partnership networks structure in the TIR
There are three important characteristics in the TIR's partnership networks:
. the aim is centred on the acquisition of knowledge for adapting the technology and not for creating technology;
. the most current organization practice is subcontracting
. the partnership networks often bind local or regional firms
There are some important differences between regions. Nordrhine-Westphalia has developed a large partnership network at the international level while in the English TIR the national dimension is much more represented than in the other regions.

b   Human resources and R&D
Human capital is an important variable of the TIR's technological transfer. In TIR the connection between the human resources supply in R&D and the technological adaptation of the productive networks is quite paradoxical: the TIR absorb a high number of graduates into Science and Technology as compared with their national average. However, in terms of employment creation in advanced technologies, the TIR's position is clearly less favourable.

Table 6.7
Human resources and employment of
higher qualifications of the TIR

	Science & Technology graduates by 10,000 inhabitants	Employment in high technology (EURO10=100)
Belgium	2.3	90
Walloon region	2.3	75
France	6.04	95
Nord-Pas-de-Calais	7.38	49
Spain	2.3	n.a.
Basque country	2.5	n.a.
Great Britain	2.7	101
Strathclyde	6.5	75
South Yorkshire	5.2	52
Germany	n.a.	118
Nordrhein-Westphalie	n.a.	51

Source: Michel Quévit and Jean Houard (1991), "Impact Régional 1992, Les Régions de tradition industrielles", De Boeck.

With the exception of Nordrhine-Westphalia, all regions experience a substantial outflow of their human potential.

6.3   Conclusions

In the last few years the TIR's investments have been concentrated in the old (coal) or traditional (electricity) energy sectors. Nevertheless, in certain regions

some special efforts have been made in new industrial projects:
. the Walloon region
. Nord-Pas-de-Calais
. South Yorkshire
In terms of R&D however, the situation is different:
a TIR's participation in European technological programs is restricted as compared with their economic and demographic weight in the EEC. The reason is the technological gap which confronts those regions. Their technological base is not consistent enough to be competitive at scientific and technical levels.
b In most TIR, universities are the main promoters of R&D projects. Compared with the EEC average the TIR's R&D potential and investments are weak in spite of the obvious presence of universities in all the TIR.
c TIR participate, to a large extent, in sectorial actions oriented towards technical and economic R&D. The main orientation of the projects is thus the direct satisfaction of the market needs (rationalization and modernization) in traditional industrial sectors.
d Some factors limit the participation of the TIR to R&D projects:
- Small and medium firms seem to offer most opportunities for employment creation but they face some important difficulties in acquiring the important means they need in order to be able to develop technological projects (financial, human, etc.).
- The international scientific level is rarely reached by the firms: their first priority is competitiveness.

Notes

1. 'Filiere' is a French word which can be interpreted as a broad sector. The aim is to classify industries into broad functional groups of related industries as opposed to using simple product grouping.

113

7 Regional disparities and development strategies in the developing countries

C.R. Pathak

7.1 Introduction

In the latter half of the 20th century, the developing countries embarked upon nation building development programmes as a step towards self-reliant sustainable economic development. The path of such development planning processes has been far from smooth. The constraints to their development are much more formidable than the advantages. Their low levels of economic development have turned out to be the main stumbling blocks. Even some of the comparative advantages such as untapped natural resources and teeming millions of human resources, can not be exploited effectively because of lack of technical knowhow, capital resources, entrepreneurship and other factors of production. These lagging nations have gradually been emerging to be politically independent but economically, remain very much dependent on developed economies for factor supplies. The factor endowments (if any) can not be dynamized so as to bring about sustainable development. Many economies have become poorer in the process and can not keep pace with the demands of the people.

This very state of affairs in developing countries has led many scholars in the developed world to propound many growth theories which have indicated that the 'development of underdevelopment' in third world countries is a cumulative process and may require a 'big push' to break away from stagnancy.

However, they have also produced some rays of hope by saying that this situation has to change and in the longrun, they would benefit if such economies were opened up for capital investment and transfer of technology from the developed nations and are linked up through international trade. Initially, they may face an unfavourable balance of trade because of high payoffs for the imported technology and borrowed capital resource transfers through multinational corporations. Once the economic foundations of developing countries are strengthened and the domestic market is expanded, the development with multiplier effect could be sustainable.

In some countries, development has been quite rapid with good progress and has been glorified by developing nations by dispensing with the derogatory phrase 'backward countries'. The pace of development however, has varied from country to country depending upon the capacity of such countries'

115

economies to absorb the development programmes.

The scholars from developing countries would probably have different views with regard to the growth path needed for these nations. It has been widely expressed that the opening up of developing economies for international transfers of growth factors from developed economies is a means to perpetuate the domination of the developed economies for a long period. Various protective measures have been put forward to safeguard against exploitation of free market economies and restrictive trade practices have been introduced by choosing technology free from the vices of its impact, experienced in the developed world. In most cases, it has been seen that the disparities in levels of development between developed and developing economies have increased rather than decreased. It is expected that only in the longrun can the development gaps be minimized. This pattern of development at the international level has contributed greatly to the concept of a 'North-South Schism' - developing countries forming the 'South', while the developed countries represent the 'North'. While the 'North' advocates North-South Cooperation to minimize development gaps, the 'South' seeks 'South–South Cooperation' because of similarities in their problems to achieve mutually supportive growth. In fact, the 'North' - the developed economies - have experienced similar paths of progress, i.e., through labour-saving technological and industrial-agricultural economic development. The 'South' consists of disparate economies of various types and are unhappy in their own way. They are economically backward but vary greatly in levels of development with multifarious social problems. There cannot be a single path of progress that could be presented to them.

The concept of a 'North-South Schism' did not, however, develop out of the international pattern of economic growth alone. The regional economic inequality exists irrespective of the developed or developing economies. J.G. Williamson (1965) has put forward the concept from his study of north-south differences in development, by studying 24 countries, including developing countries. This has been further tested in the case of the Italian and Brazilian economies. The concept is a modification of the 'growth pole' concept developed from the study by Perroux and later extended by Kuklinski (1972), etc. in the case of developing countries and by W. Isard (agglomeration economies), and John Friedmann, in Latin American countries. The 24 countries studied include 13 European, four empty overseas European, four Latin American and three Asian countries, including India. Interregional inequality in development has been measured by the Kuznets (1965) indices of inequality based on industrial sectors (see Table 1, J.G. Williamson).

7.2   Regional inequality and economic development

From the international cross-section studies of economic growth, a significant correlation is observed between levels of development and degree of regional inequality. The severity in regional inequality in development increases sharply with the low level of economic development. Williamson (1965) has used various measures of weighted coefficients of variations to measure the degree of regional inequality. He writes: "Divergence of regional income per capita levels should generally hold true for those countries below the middle income group, while convergence should be the case for those above the middle income range. "That is, India at low levels of per capita income and regional disparity should exhibit increasing regional dualism and a rising Vw as she proceeds through her early stages of development." (pp. 118-119.) There will be lower degrees of inequality and imbalance in the United States and in other developed, matured economies. The LDCs would reveal tendencies towards divergence in regional income levels.

The rising trend in regional inequality resulting in divergence between the developed and underdeveloped regional economies in developing countries, depicts not only the early stages of economic development but also reflects the sectoral development gaps. The traditional agrarian sectoral economic development has provided the foundation for regional inequality because regional resource endowment plays a significant role. Recent technological development in agriculture, being localized in geographically favoured areas has probably accentuated the disparity because of productivity differences regionally and product specialization. Williamson summarizes his study with the following sentences: "There is a consistent relationship between the two: rising regional income disparities and increasing North-South dualism is typical of early development stages, while regional convergence and a disappearance of severe North-South problems is typical of the more natured stages of national growth and development". (p.155) And that "regional dualism or inequality is much more extensive within the agricultural than within the industrial sector, and that labour participation rates in part, contribute to regional income per capita differentials". (p.156).

It is not a question of national economic growth at the cost of regional income inequality or vice versa. The more formidable question is whether the pattern of industrial economic development which has started in the developing countries on the weaker and more unstable sociopolitical setup, could be sustained with a further widening of income inequality.

Before we turn to this question, let us examine the case of the Indian economy and the resulting pattern of regional inequality in the post–independence period.

7.3   Regional inequality in India

Williamson has analyzed the pattern of regional inequality, taking the national income per capita for 18 states (Andhra, Assam, Bihar, Gujarat, Kerala, Madhya Pradesh, Madras, Maharashtra, Mysore, Orissa, Punjab, Rajasthan, Uttar Pradesh, West Bengal, Delhi, Himachal Pradesh, Manipur and Tripura) for the years 1950-51, 1955-56 and calculated the weighted coefficient of variation (Vw) i.e., 0.275 which is quite low compared to other developing countries, namely the Philippines (0.556), Yugoslavia (0.340), Brazil (0.700), Italy (0.360), Spain (0.415) and several others. (See Table 1 of J.G. Williamson.) The situation in India has since changed.

In the following paragraph, we analyze the pattern of regional inequality in the 1980s.

Table 7.1
Per Capita Net State Domestic Product
At constant (1980-81 prices, 1980-81 to 1988-89 Rupees)

States	1980-81	Rank	1988-89	Rank
1. Andra Pradesh	1380	14	1692	13
2. Arunachal Pradesh	1557	10	2429	7
3. Assam	1200	17	1558	15
4. Bihar	896	19	1071	19
5. Goa	3145	2	3523	2
6. Gujarat	1970	6	2506	6
7. Haryana	2370	5	3086	3
8. Himachal Pradesh	1664	7	1948	10
9. Karnataka	1612	9	2041	8
10. Kerala	1463	12	1447	18
11. Madhya Pradesh	517	20	680	20
12. Maharashtra	2427	4	2960	5
13. Manipur	1449	13	1775	12
14. Orissa	1231	16	1455	17
15. Punjab	2724	3	3552	1
16. Rajasthan	1199	18	1620	14
17. Tamilnadu	1498	11	2030	9
18. Uttar Pradesh	1284	15	1547	16
19. West Bengal	1612	9	1930	11
20. Pondicherry	3159	1	3067	4
21. All India	1627	-	2082	-

Source: Statement 4, Per Capita Net Doestic Product. Estimates of States Domestic Product and Capital Formation, CS, Dept. of Statistics, Ministry of Planning, Govt. of India, 1990, pp. 10-11.

Table 7.2
Regional Development in Particular Countries
International Cross-Section

Country and Kuznets Group Classification	Years Covered	Vw	Vuw	Mw	Size Sq. miles
Australia	1949/50-1959-60	0.058	0.078	4.77	2,974,581
New Zealand	1955	0.063	0.082	4.93	103,736
Canada	1950-61	0.192	0.259	17.30	3,845,774
United Kingdom	1959-60	0.141	0.156	11.39	94,279
United States	1950-61	0.182	0.189	16.56	3,022,387
Sweden	1950,1955,1961	0.200	0.168	15.52	173,378
Group 1 average		0.139	0.155	11.72	
Finland	1950,1954,1958	0.331	0.276	26.64	130,165
France	1954,1955/6,1958	0.283	0.215	20.80	212,659
West Germany	1950-55,1960	0.205	0.205	16.98	94,723
Netherlands	1950,1955,1958	0.131	0.128	12.45	12,850
Norway	1952,1957-60	0.309	0.253	23.84	125,064
Group II average		0.252	0.215	20.14	
Ireland	1960	0.268	0.271	24.20	26,601
Chile	1958	0.327	0.440	30.65	286,397
Austria	1957	0.225	0.201	18.69	32,369
Puerto Rico	1960	0.520	0.378	42.31	3,435
Group III average		0.335	0.323	28.96	
Brazil	1950-59	0.700	0.654	53.78	3,288,050
Italy	1951,1955,1960	0.360	0.367	30.94	117,471
Spain	1955,1957	0.415	0.356	32.32	195,504
Colombia	1953	0.541	0.561	46.70	439,617
Greece	1954	0.302	0.295	25.56	51,246
Group IV average		0.464	0.447	38.06	
Yugoslavia	1956,1959,1960	0.340	0.444	24.54	95,558
Japan	1951-9	0.244	0.222	19.98	142,644
Group V average		0.292	0.333	22.26	
Philippines	1957	0.556	0.627	29.59	115,600
Group VI average		0.556	0.627	29.59	
India	1950/51,1955/6	0.275	0.580	19.39	1,221,880
Group VII average		0.275	0.580	19.39	
Total Average		0.299	0.309	23.78	

Source: Williamson, J.G. (1965)

Table 7.3
Regional Development in Particular Countries
States/UTs in India by per capita NSDP for 1980-81 to 1988-89

Year	Above Rs.2500	Rs.2000-2500	Rs.1500-2000	Less than Rs.1500
1980-81	Pondicherry(1), Goa(2) Punjab(3)	Maharashtra(4) Haryana(5)	Gujarat(6) H.P.(7) Karnataka(8) West Bengal(9) Arunachal Pradesh(10)	Tamilnadu(11), Kerala(12), Manipur(13, A.P.(14), U.P.(15),Orissa(16), Assam(17), Rajasthan(18) Bihar(19), M.P.(20),
1988-89	Punjab(1), Goa(2) Haryana(3) Pondicherry(4) Maharashtra(5) Gujarat(6)	Arunachal Pradesh(7) Kranartaka(8) Tamilnadu(9) H.P.(10)	West Bengal(11) Manupur(12) A.P.(13) Rajasthan(14) Assam(15) U.P.(16)	Orissa(17) Kerala(18) Kerala(18) M.P.(20)

Figures in parentheses relate to their rank.

120

7.3.1 The data base

The estimates of Net State Domestic Product (NSDP) at factor cost (state income) are available for the years 1980-81 to 1988-89, both at current prices and at constant (1980-81) prices for 25 States/Union Territories. The States of M.P., J & K and Delhi have been continuing with the earlier (1970-71) series and the new series is yet to be published. For Nagaland and Mizoram, estimates are available at current prices. For Meghalaya, the estimates are available up to 1987-88 and for Sikkim, Mizoram, Tripura and Delhi, up to 1986-87. Hence, we have excluded those states whose per capita net state incomes are not available for the year 1988-89 (the terminal year).

Table 7.1 accounts for the NSDP per capita in rupees for the 20 states.

The states have been listed alphabetically, but ranked according to 1980-81 and 1988-89. While the average per capita income for the country is Rs. 1627 in 1980-81, it varies from as low as 517 for M.P. to Rs. 3159 for Pondicherry. There were only seven states having more than the national average, i.e., Pondicherry, Goa, Punjab, Maharashtra, Haryana, Gujarat, H.P. in order, on the other hand, the lowest being M.P., preceded by Bihar, Rajasthan, Assam, etc.

7.3.2 Per capita income

There has been a sizeable increase in per capita income during 1980-81 to 1988–89. The statewise growth was far from stable and fluctuated tremendously. However, the relative position has not changed much. The average per capita income in 1988-89 was Rs. 2082 (at 1980-81 prices). There were again only seven states with higher than national average, i.e., Punjab, Goa, Haryana, Pondicherry, Maharashtra, Gujarat and Arunachal Pradesh with H.P. sliding down and Arunachal Pradesh rising above the national average in 1988-89. There had been steep competition among the higher income states while there is no significant change in the ranking of low income states. Madhya Pradesh remained the lowest ranking state preceded by Bihar, Kerala, Orissa, etc. (see Table 7.1). This has been revealed by a very high rank correlation (0.918) among the states between 1980-81 and 1988-89. In other words, the richer states became richer and poorer states became poorer during 1980-81 and 1988–89.

7.3.3 Net state domestic product

The per capita Net State Domestic Products (NSDP) have been further analyzed by calculating weighted coefficients of variation (Vw) weighted by the share of national population by the state for both the periods. It should be noted that there has been no change in the share of state population in 1981 and 1991. The per capita state income of 1988-89 has been weighted by the 1991 population. The mean per capita NSDP was calculated for 20 states for 1980–81 and 1988-89 which were Rs. 1718 and Rs. 2096 respectively, for statistical analysis, rather than taking the national average per capita NSDP. The weighted coefficient of variation (Vw) for 1980-81 and 1988-89 are 25.38% and 28.46% respectively. In other words, inequality has increased

121

during the 1980s. The results are not surprising as this can be seen in the income growth differential. The regional inequality would have been much greater provided some of the most developed states did not experience setbacks during the latter part of the 1980s, such as, the per capita NSDP for Pondicherry declined by (–)5.67 per cent in 1988-89, Gujarat declined by (–)7.84 per cent in 1987-88 and Haryana by (-)2.52 per cent in 1987-88. Of course, the backward states also suffered at the same time, namely, Orissa, Rajasthan and Bihar and Madhya Pradesh which have experienced fluctuating growth from (+)6.64 per cent in 1983-84 to (-)4.11 per cent in 1984-85. The variations in growth rate per capita NSDP are more revealing in agricultural sectors as government policy supported only the industrial sector by equilibrating the regional disparity which itself is a weak sector in the backward states. In fact, the industrially prosperous states have also experienced positive growth in agriculture. Intraregional (state/U.T.'s) disparities could be measured by district level data but NSDP at district level is not available after 1956. Some scholars used multivariate analysis with district level sectoral data in the 1960s, excluding income data. We have also found that in India, while interregional disparity had been declining in the 1970s, intraregional inequality has been on the increase. For the sake of brevity, we shall not analyze the sectoral contribution to NSDP by states or by districts.

However, the Indian experience in per capita income growth is not unique but an indicator for regional inequality for the developing countries at large. We do not have relevant data for other developing countries to be able to test our hypothesis. While our findings corroborate Williamson's North-West Schism and Kuznets' warning of rising inequality for the LDCs, the conditions or factors contributing to such inequality have remained unexplained.

7.4   Development strategies for balanced regional development

During the post World War II period, the developing countries launched centralized planning for economic development. The efforts were directed primarily towards selfreliant, sustainable development. The constraints to their development were many and the rates of growth were far from satisfactory. Despite the fact that the efforts were quite encouraging, the development was not spread equitably over the economy or regions and the resulting pattern is imbalanced regional development because the chief concern in these countries was overall problems of economic underdevelopment. These countries were quite conscious of the uneven regional development and knowingly had to concentrate on growth oriented economic activities in the favoured pockets with a view to quickly generating basic goods first and thought of distribution of development later. As a matter of fact, the backward regions had, in the process, manifested the problems of underdevelopment expressed in increasing unemployment, shrinking economic activity, low levels of educational development and low labour participation, low income and low productivity, outmigration of young educated people and decaying social capital facilities, etc. (Francis and Pillai, 1973, p. 33). Regional policies directed towards the development of backward areas, adopted by these countries through decentralization of development activities, backed up by concessions and subsidies for backward regions, did not open up the regional economies, nor did the regions benefit from such concessions. Recent trends in the 1990s are directed towards regional development to lift the subsidized, backward economies, to incorporate efficient criteria to bring them into the free market arena. Protective measures have eroded their productive base and perpetuated their dependence on the national economy. Social upheaval and disintegrating forces in the backward regions are the manifestations of cumulative social and economic deprivation. Such regions must rise to the occasion and participate in the national development process in a participatory role rather than resorting to political agitation. What alternative paths of development are left to the national economies?

Accepted theories of regional development are inadequate to influence the growth paths of the backward regions. To break away from backwardness, the 'big push' received tremendous support, but has failed to integrate the regional economy to the industries located in these regions. There might have been some backward link to the regional natural resource base. The forward link was directed towards the national market. The up-quoted multiplier effect on the non-basic sector of the regional economy has not resulted in interregional transmission of economic growth as neither the comparative advantages of factor mobility, nor favourable interregional trade, has had equilibrating effects. "Under such conditions, a region which is less efficient than others in all sectors of economic activity, due either to inferior resources or to inability to realize economies of scale, or both, will be at a general disadvantage and this process could result in the cumulative decline of the region. The final outcome of this process would depend on the relative strength of what Myrdal calls the 'backwash effects' (of the growth process itself) and the 'spread effects' arising from either deliberate public action to stimulate regional economic activity, or from the pressure on resources in the prosperous regions" (Francis and Pillai, p. 39). They further write that "in sum, the tool-kit now available to Regional Development provides nothing more than a set of hypotheses to explain the spatial dispersion of economic activities". (p. 42).

The modern industrialized societies have been experimenting with regional policy making to tackle the problems of regional inequality by injecting growth activities and taking reconciliatory measures between social and economic policies in the relatively backward areas. These experiments of the developed world might provide clues to the formulation of regional development policies in developing countries with checks and balances. There is no easy solutions nor is there a doctrinaire package of regional development that could be recommended for the developing world as such. There is a need for constant searching towards regional development policies and programmes aimed at development or vice versa. Equity measures must be supported by the efficiency criteria as no regional development could be perpetually subsidized. No nation could boast the pride of eliminating regional disparity but some could try to reduce the development gaps with workable strategies for equitable regional development.

7.5 Conclusions

Until recently, the problems of regional inequality in developing countries were not given priority as the national economies themselves were at a low level. Regional equity under such conditions would have led to the sharing of poverty. The question of equity is being raised now because the economic growth process has a tendency to create regional imbalance and economic growth will become polarized. The most relevant strategy should be 'growth with equity' or 'equity with growth'. This concept needs further elaboration and will be dealt with in future research.

References

C.S.O. (1990), Ministry of Planning, Government of India, Estimates of State Domestic Product and Capital Formation, New Delhi.

Francis, J.P. and Pillai, N.G. (1973), Regional Development: Some Issues and Conceptual Problems, in *Regional Poverty and Change, Canadian Council of Rural Development*, Compiled by Gunter Schramm, pp. 31-50 (with comprehensive references).

Hansen, N.M. (1972), (ed.), *Growth Centres in Regional Economic Development*, Free Press, New York.

Kuklinski, A.K. (1972), (ed.), 'Growth Poles and Growth Centres in Regional Planning', *UNRISED: Regional Planning Series*, Mouton, The Hague.

Kuznets, S. (1955), 'Economic Growth and Income Inequality', *American Economic Review*, 45, pp. 1-28.

Myrdal, G. (1957), *Economic Theory and Underdeveloped Regions*, Duckworth, London.

Williamson, J.G. (1965), 'Regional Inequality and the Process of National Development: A Description of the Patterns', *Economic Development and Cultural Change*, Vol. 13, pp. 3-45 (reprinted in Regional Analysis - Selected Readings, 1968, L. Needleman, ed.).

Part B
NETWORKS AND SPATIAL DYNAMICS

8 City networks: An analysis of the Lombardy Region in terms of communication flows

R. Camagni

8.1 Introduction[1]

In a recent paper, one of the present authors supported the hypothesis that the wellknown paradigm of city-hierarchy, based on the works of Christaller and on the subsequent central-place literature, should be complemented by a new paradigm, the 'city-network' one, taking care of other kinds of linkages and relationships that cities entertain among themselves, beyond the gravity-type relationship with the surrounding market area (Camagni, 1993).

The traditional central-place model remains the more elegant, abstract but consistent representation of the hierarchy of urban centres, and the model that better interprets the spatial behaviour of many economic sectors, from retail trade to consumer services and public administration.

Nevertheless, real city-systems in advanced countries have departed in many respects from the abstract Christallerian pattern of a nested hierarchy of centres and markets. The reduction in transport costs and the demand for 'variety' of the consumer have broken the theoretical hypothesis of separated, gravity-type, non-overlapping market areas; 'location economies' à la Hoover and synergy elements operating through horizontal and vertical linkages among firms have generated the emergence of specialized centres, in contrast with the typical despecialization pattern deriving from the theoretical model; high-order functions locate sometimes in small (but specialized) centres where the model's expectations refer only to lower-order functions.

This evidence is not at all new, and the deficiencies of the model are often highlighted; but to change the underlying assumptions would mean to change the model itself, and no other set of clearly defined hypotheses have ever replaced the former ones.

City networks are defined here as systems of horizontal, non-hierarchic relationships among specialized centred, providing externalities from complementarity/vertical integration or from synergy/cooperation among centres. Two types of network relationships among centres emerge from this definition: 'complementarity networks', made up of centres specialized in complementary products within the same sector or 'filière', usually belonging to the same 'industrial district' or 'local production system', and 'synergy networks', made up by centres specialized in similar products or functions, reaching through the network linkage a superior efficiency. Examples of the former type may be found in many polycentric urban systems like the Venetian region in Italy or the Randstad Holland; a good example of the latter type is represented by the network of financial cities, which form an internationally unified stock market operating virtually worldwide in real time (Camagni, 1993).

While the organizational logic underlying the central place model is a 'territorial' one, emphasizing a gravity-type control over market areas, in the network model other logic prevails, referring to long distance competition and cooperation regardless of the distance barrier. While transport costs and economies of scale were the principal forces shaping the spatial organization of functions and centres, in the new logic other kinds of economies come to the forefront: economies of vertical or horizontal integration, and network economies similar to those emerging from 'club goods' (Capello, 1993; Capello and Nijkamp, 1994).

As in the central-place model, also here the spatial relationships among centres emerge from the logic of the economic and spatial behaviour of firms. This logic departs more and more from a transport oriented, market-area philosophy and is more and more shaped by cooperation and synergy goals in the production and innovation spheres, realized both through long-distance, selected network relationships and through local, 'milieu' or 'industrial district' relationships (Camagni 1989, Hansen 1992).

But the concept of network relationships, often utilised in the literature and in spatial policy, especially in Italy and France, was seldom empirically tested with direct methodologies. In fact, what is needed is a different kind of basic information with respect to the usual and available one, namely flow data - on inter-city relationships - as opposed to stock data - on economic or demographic variables.

In this paper, an attempt to identify city-networks within the Lombardy region and the wider Po Valley (Piedmont, Liguria, Lombardy, Emilia-Romagna, Venetian regions) is made, through the use of a matrix of telephone communication data. A network relationship between two centres is hypothesized when actual communication flows exceed significantly the interaction that is expected on the basis of a doubly constrained entropy model: by this in fact we capture all the relevant interaction that happens within the urban structure as a consequence of selected economic relationships, going beyond the simple gravity-type interaction happening as a consequence of size and proximity.

The results of the empirical exercise are encouraging: city-networks as defined here, do in fact exist, and they bear the following interesting characteristics:
- they are not ubiquitous, and they do not substitute for traditional, hierarchical forms of spatial organizations; rather, the two organizational forms may be thought of as complementary. In fact, a super-gravitational relationship appears in the case of Milan with respect to all the big centres of the Po Valley, showing a dependence of these latter for high-order services and functions;
- in the regional context that is examined, city-networks appear in a relevant way in two spatial contexts, characterized by a high synergetic potential:

within a metropolitan area (Milan), among its sub-centres, and within some sub-regional industrial districts, deeply characterized in terms of sectoral specialization and economic 'vocation".

Some of these results were relatively unexpected: network relationships were in fact hypothesized also (or mainly) on a longer distance basis, while the empirical results show that they mainly add to proximity and short-distance interaction. But further empirical research is needed in this respect, based on inter-regional and inter-national flow data.

8.2 Spatial networks in Lombardy towards empirical evidence

8.2.1 Aims of the analysis

Theoretical studies (Dematteis, 1990; Camagni, 1992) and empirical ones (Camagni and De Blasio, 1993) have shown that, over the past two decades, the territorial organization of the production and distribution of goods, services and information in the economic region of Milan has undergone profound and extensive changes, giving rise to a new network organization principle in addition to and often substituting the traditional hierarchical structures.

The use of stock, rather than flow data, a feature common to all these works, allowed to deduct the existence of network-like relations, but could not give evidence of this.

Through a direct analysis of flow data, this study aims to identify and somehow to measure the real importance of the network organization principle with respect to the areal-based hierarchical structure. Results will be drawn within the framework of a comprehensive review of the urban system of the Po Valley region, approaching the analysis at different scales (in fact, it is far from clear to what extent the dominating principle at the micro system level remains such as scales are gradually reduced).

Though recent studies in the field of neural networks suggest interesting perspective in this direction (Fischer, 1992; Fischer and Gopal, 1992), no ready-to-use analytical instruments are available in order to study non–hierarchical networks, therefore this work will use an indirect approach moving from the following thesis: assuming that the object of interest is synergy flows, a spatial-interaction model will be used to esteem gravitational flows, relational networks will then appear by means of comparison between real and expected interaction data.

As for the nature of the empirical data-base (Lombardy telephone flows) used here, this also could be for many reasons considered to be innovative.

In fact the functional relationship can be determined through an analysis of flows of goods, labour, information, money, etc. that are exchanged between urban centres. However, the data that are usually used for this type of analysis involve commuter trips to which gravitational models are applied, which are notoriously dominated by spatial friction and settlement mass effects. The use of these models assumes that the territory is based on a hierarchical organization and relationships between urban centres reflect plain dependency.

Instead, since this study intends to investigate the possible presence of new

129

types of relationship in the territory, such as the formation of spatial functional networks between families and companies and therefore between urban centres, it is appropriate to select non traditional data and analysis methods. In particular, in order to overcome an areal-based logic, the distance factor should be negligible, as occurs for immaterial information flows. In this study phone traffic data are used, which also have the advantage of continuous detection (making it possible to quickly update study results).

8.2.2   The telephone flow data

In the present study, data obtained from SIP (the national telephone carrier of Italy) are used, describing telephone traffic as an origin/destination matrix, relative to year 1990 and to the Milan compartment (covering the whole territory of Lombardy administrative region).

Firstly, a little terminology concerning this kind of data is needed: *sector, district* and *compartment* are telephone service areas of increasing dimensions, among which communication traffic is measures. The standard international unit for measuring phone traffic is *Erlang*, whose exact definition will be given later.

As it was said, the structure of the data is twofold, allowing for both a macro (district level) and a micro (sector level) approach: in this work both levels of the analysis are faced, and a comparison of results will appear quite useful.

At the sectors' level, an origin/destination matrix of intersector telephone traffic intensity is given, covering the territory of the compartment of Milan (approximately equal to Lombardy).

At the districts' level data are available, which describe, besides the interdistrict origin/destination matrix of the compartment, also flow intensity going out from each district of the compartment of Milan to every other district of Northern Italy; unfortunately neither flow data coming into the districts belonging to the compartment of Milan are available, nor those exchanged among districts to this compartment.

The matrix values are measured in Erlang during the average morning peak–hour. Erlang is defined as the telephone traffic value that is processed by a circuit that is continually engaged for the duration of one hour. We preferred to use morning-time data, implicitly selecting business traffic (as distinguished from family traffic).

The territorial organization of the telephone service in Italy is divided into four levels of increasing aggregation: urban networks, sectors, districts and compartments. Urban networks are becoming obsolete, and will not be considered hereafter.

The following table indicates the number of these different subdivisions in Italy and in the Milanese area.

The boundaries of these different levels do not exactly correspond to the territorial administrative levels (regions, provinces and municipalities). The Milanese compartment includes a part of the Piedmont region (province of Novara), whilst districts in Lombardy are more than double the provinces. The sectors are much less than municipalities: on average the ratio is 10 municipalities and 50 thousands inhabitants for each sector, the latter appearing to be a much more significant scale of analysis compared to the administrative.

This discrepancy between telephone and administrative regions must not be forgotten when interpreting results.

Table 8.1
Definition and number of telephone service areas

	Italy	Compartment of Milan
Compartments	21	1
Districts	232	34
Sectors	1399	178
Urban networks	1898	222

The two matrices used (the one of inter-district flows, and that of inter-sector traffic) show a concentration of flows in the row and column of Milan, and a very sparse character elsewhere, corresponding to a strong gravitational effect of the regional metropolis, which will be outlined in the following section.

8.2.3 Empirical reality vs. gravity model

Telephone communications may be considered as a peculiar instance of spatial interaction: other well-known and well-studied examples include commuters flows and flows of expense for goods and services. There is a long tradition of studies on such sort of flows, and a wide literature is available, as well as a number of interpretative models. Telephone flows, however, are in many ways different: studies making use of this kind of data are very scarce and only recently an analysis by means of forecasting models has been attempted (Fischer and Gopal, 1992). There seem to be good reasons for this inattention by modellers: spatial interaction phenomena are usually studied by means of gravity models, based on two mass terms and a distance decay factor:

$$T_{ij} = k \cdot W_i \cdot W_j \cdot f(c_{ij});$$

where:
T_{ij} measure of the interaction between zone i and zone j
K constant of proportionality
W_i flows generation potential in i
W_j flows absorption potential in j
c_{ij} cost of the interaction between i and j (often assumed to be equal to time or distance)
$f(c_{ij})$ decay function (decreasing with c_{ij})

This functional form tends to give reason to a hierarchical territorial structure and is especially apt to study this kind of organization. Telephone communication flows, because of their own nature, seem to be rather distance independent and one could expect them to be poorly simulated by models based on a gravitational logic. From the point of view of the available techniques they could not be regarded as a promising research direction. But changing one's own point of view, and moving from the consideration that the characters to be outlined by this study are not the hierarchical ones, but those proper of a network-like structure, flows data free from the old areal paradigm rise in the researcher's interest. Unfortunately, at present we lack analytical instruments capable of directly revealing a network-like structure, so we decided to apply a classical spatial interaction model to these data, in order to highlight differences between observed and expected values: those discrepancies, according to the hypothesis undertaken by this work, have been interpreted as hints of non–hierarchical elements of territorial organization.

In this study, telephone flows are compared with data obtained by application of a spatial interaction model à la Wilson (Wilson, 1974). The model redistributes flows among the sectors according to a gravitational logic, under a few constraints: row and column marginal totals of the flows matrix (the sum of outgoing and incoming flows from/to each zone) are preserved. It is, therefore, a double-constraint model obeying the following equation:

$$T_{ij} = A_i \cdot B_j \cdot O_i \cdot D_j \, e^{-\beta c_{ij}} \; ;$$

This second formula is derived from the previous one, substituting the generic notation of the two mass terms (W_i and W_j) with O_i and D_j, equal to total incoming and outgoing flows; and introducing the two calibration constants A_i and B_j instead of K, in order to guarantee respect of the constraints, which are expressed as follows:

$$O_i = \sum_j T_{ij}$$

$$D_j = \sum_i T_{ij}$$

As for the distance decay function, we chose an exponential function, fitting quite well observed data and generally preferred to mere gravitational forms. The model needs to be calibrated by assigning to the two vectors of parameters A_i and B_j, and to the scalar parameter β, appropriate values in order to maximize the fitness between observed and calculated data, with the additional constraint of maintaining the same total interaction cost (distance weighted by corresponding flow). Thus we tried to preserve the maximum similarity between model and reality: when such likeness fails, this should not be ascribed to an intrinsic inadequacy of this sort of models to explain non–hierarchical phenomena.

Table 8.2
Model Fitting

			With Milan	Without Milan
Padania		r2	0.88	0.45
(Threshold = 0)		r	0.94	0.67
		b	1.61	0.89
Lombardy		r2	0.73	0.46
(Threshold = 0.05)		r	0.85	0.68
		b	1.35	0.75

Let us say a few words about model fitting: Table 8.2 shows model fitness: we isolated the mass effect of Milan, and took into consideration only flows greater than a threshold (the median value, which turned out to be very low), thus focusing attention only on the more relevant relations; where observations and predicted flows match a gravitational structure as expected, whilst discrepancies are to be taken as hints of selective synergetic interactions (when real flows are higher than expected), or of relative isolation (predictions overcome reality).

8.3   Telephone flow analysis

8.3.1   The macro level: inter-district flows

In this section the network of connections linking together the districts of the compartment of Milan is presented. In addition to the network of internal flows, connections from the districts of Lombardy directed to all other Norther Italian districts are considered, as well. Nothing can be said about flows linking couples of districts belonging to compartments other than that of Milan, because no data of this kind is available yet. All districts considered amount to 119, among which 36 constitute the compartment of Milan: therefore, we operated on a rectangular, 119 wide by 36 high origin/destination matrix.

8.3.1.1 Networks, chains and other loops

In Figure 8.1 all major relations are shown, but for those with origin or destination in Milan (for readability purposes shown apart, in Figure 8.2). Because of the foretold limitations of the database, flows having origin and destinations in other compartments are not to be found here.

The centripetal role of the metropolis is clear: all flows converge towards the centre of the metropolitan area. Let us take this for granted for a while, and focus on the underlying rich and complex structure of relations among secondary and tertiary nodes. The results suggest a first confirmation of our hypotheses: that telephone flow data should allow the identification of network elements in the Lombardy system. We observed, in fact, a strong transverse integration among the centres belonging to an arch from North to North-East of

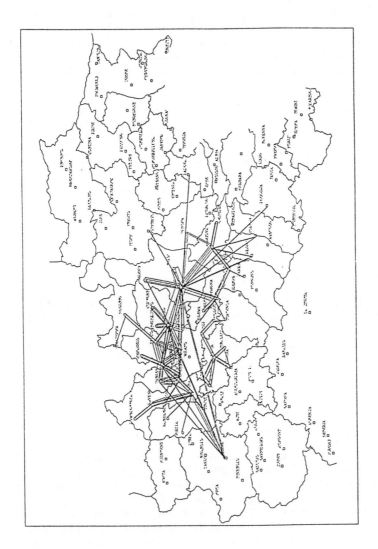

Figure 8.1 Macrolevel telephone flows in the Po Valley. Interactions with Milan are not shown (see Figure 8.2), which would hide the underlying structure of interactions. Flows tend to cluster in the north of the metropolitan region of Milan, comparing with the relative isolation of the rural districts (Pavia, Voghera, Cremona). Extra - regional connections concentrate on Torino (Piedmont), Verona (Veneto) and the neighbouring provinces of Emilia (Bologna, Piacenza, Modena).

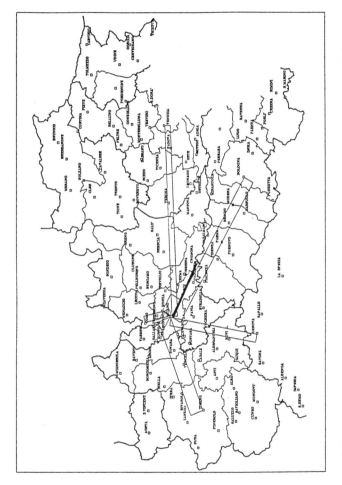

Figure 8.2 Comparison of observed and predicted flows. By comparing observed data with the predictions of a spatial interaction model it was possible to highlight nonlinearities in the structure of flows, such as amplifications due to synergetic effects (empty bars) and, on the opposite side, weak or missing linkages (solid bars). Here only relations concerning Milan are accounted for, showing the super-gravitational effect of the metropolis (predominance of empty bars), which plays the role of a gateway between the regional systems (Bergamo, Como, partly Brescia) and all major cities of Northern Italy (Torino, Genova, Venezia and Bologna).

Milan, including - beside the main towns (Como, Lecco, Bergamo, Brescia) - also the sub-metropolitan pole of Monza. Varese and Olonia (with this name, after the Olona river, the industrial area of Legnano, Busto Arsizio and Galarate is usually addressed) form another evident functional region with low, yet significant relations with further districts such as Brescia. Relevant are also flows between non-neighbouring districts: Busto and Lagnano with Brescia, Como with Bergamo and Brescia, Varese with Bergamo. These flows are comparable with those generated by the metropolis, and take part of the main structure of the region, introducing non hierarchical elements. Certainly marginal are all alpine districts (Sondrio, Clusone, Breno).

Non marginal, but poorly connected, are the systems of South Padania (Pavia, Cremona, Mantova). Pavia especially, despite of being the greater district, is a perfectly closed, hierarchical system (safe for the connections with Milan, that is with the central place of higher rank). The systems of Crema, Cremona and Mantova, though being less isolated, do not show any relation with non-neighbouring districts: the only linkage is given by those districts belonging to more than one system at the same time, and by Brescia, attracting all of them.

It is easy to remark, even at this first level of analysis, the simultaneous presence of two (competing?) structuring principles: the hierarchy and the network, dominating different portions of the region. If an areal-like logic appears to be still ruling the rural areas, with Pavia as an example, in the band between Milan and the Alps the structure of communication flows is such to make it difficult to achieve the enucleation of isolated systems; we could not find, at this scale, domination/dependence relationships revealing hierarchical sub-structures, each district seems to be connected with each other in a network of functional circuits, strictly linked.

It would be very hard, however, to speak of a large network, covering the whole territory of the Po Valley, or even of the Lombardy region. Network formation appears to be a local phenomenon in Northern Italy. Nevertheless, local systems are not isolated, but cluster together around a few nodes: usually this is a primate city common to more than one local system (Brescia, Bergamo, Como); but it could be a centre having no local network of his own, seeming to play uniquely the role of a functional link among separate local networks. These nodes, in order to connect differently specialized clusters, must be able to produce multipurpose services and to exchange information between 'client' systems. This behavioural model causes the single districts to participate in no more than one network, and to communicate with other systems mainly via the primate city, polymorphic enough to serve as a connective tissue.

In order to explain the formation of this kind of structure we must admit that the genesis of a network be formerly led by an innovator node: this, once attained a specialization, selects his partners and inhibits the development of similar specializations outside the network, in a process of cooperation–competition finally leading to the observed pattern. In a 'geometrical' interpretation which takes into account the rank of the nodes, diagonal relations between centres of different levels are not allowed, networks are formed by centres of the same rank, and stratify overlapping in the primate nodes, having a function of horizontal and vertical connection.

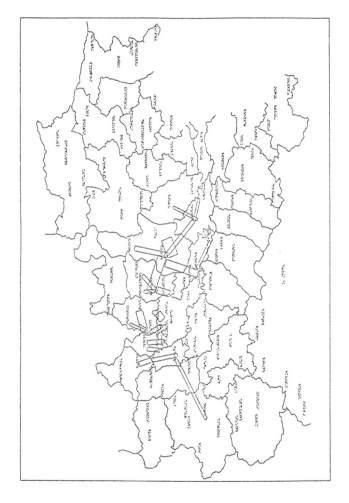

Figure 8.3 **Regional networks at the district (macro level).** Regional networks at the district (macro) level. The existence of network-like interactions is revealed by the study of the discrepancies between real and predicted data: white bars indicate underestimated flows, i.e. flows that overcome the model's prediction and therefore are supposed to be amplified by the presence of network synergies. Regional networks are to be found mostly in the north of Milan, drawing an arc from Novara to Brescia across the Brianza area, and appear to be isolated from each other; extra regional connections are provided mainly via Milan (see Figure 8.2) and partly by Brescia, Novara and Mantova. See also Figure 8.4.

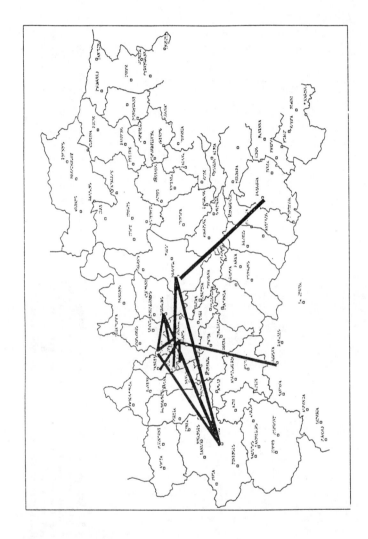

Figure 8.4 Deficiencies in the structure of spatial relations. Flows that do not even reach the predicted (gravitational) value help in identifying deficiencies in the structure of relations. Such defective connections, represented as solid bars, show the weak attitude of regional poles for external relations, and highlight the separation between local systems in Lombardia (Brescia Bergamo, Como Lecco, Varese Busto, Novara). See also Figure 8.3.

This model, still consistent with some elements of the hierarchical logic of the well-known areal model *à la* Christaller, introduces important innovative elements: namely it allows for the network-like structure of the single circuits, such as the specialized local districts in the north of Milan or the larger interregional networks, assembling together in larger compounds: chains of networks and hierarchies of networks, through the condivision of *gateways*.

8.3.1.2 Milan: the regional gateway

In Figure 8.2 (analysis of the exchanges of Milan) the polarization effect of the regional main town is evident: all flows converging towards the centre of the metropolitan area turn out to be higher than predicted. We defined this phenomenon as a supergravitation effect of the metropolis, probably due to the concentration of higher-rank strategic functions - operating in super-regional and international networks - which give to Milan the role of a gate towards external systems. This hypothesis is reinforced by studying Figures 8.3 and 8.4, which show the analysis of flows in the entire Northern Italian territory (interactions with Milan are hidden, to increase readability of these maps).

The main extra-regional destinations of flows coming from Milan are primarily the main towns of Torino, Bologna and Genoa, secondarily Venice, Verona and Trento. Connections to this poles coming from other districts than Milan are very scarce, with the significant exception of Torino, strongly interconnected with the districts in the area of Novara. With no exception at all, however, as shown in Figures 8.3 and 8.4 the outward attitude of Lombardy's districts is very low, being privileged to the communication with the metropolis. Not only is Milan a gateway to the whole region, but it turns out to be the only one, too; only Brescia, Bergamo and Como seem to maintain a relative autonomy in their extra-regional connections.

Moreover, total absence of flows directed towards lower-rank centres outside Lombardy suggests that a similar mechanism of exclusive gateways rule the structure of the external systems, about which, though, little can be said due to lack of empirical data.

8.3.1.3 Specialized districts and multi-functional nodes

Some regional nodes play the role of a pivot, connecting local networks in wider systems. These presumably are service centres or multi-specialized poles, able to process information of different species, coming from different systems. Thanks to their polymorphic nature they play a key role as information exchangers among networks. Many higher-rank towns (like Bergamo and Brescia) are such, but also a few secondary poles, lacking a gravitational system of their own, seem to behave in much the same ways: these are Lecco, pivoting between the Valtellina districts and the Brianze area, and Novara, which connects all the systems west of Milan (Olonia, Ossola) with Torino.

Even at the macro level the simultaneous presence of hierarchical and network–like elements, is clearly apparent. In the rural areas along the Po river a Christaller-like gravitational structure seems to be predominant (Pavia can be considered an almost pure instance of a Christaller system); in the wide belt

North of Milan and South of the mountains, where the industrialization process first started, having multicentric and pseudo-network features since its very beginning, the structure of telephone communications depict a very complex interconnected system, hardly decomposable in isolated elements, where no dominance-dependence relations are found: each district is linked to every other, forming a network of local functional circuits.

8.3.2   The micro level: inter-sector flows

By examining the distribution of real and computed data, it is possible to make a few remarks, which will further on be recognized to be structural characters of the network. Density distribution curves of observed and estimated flows reveal an important over-estimate of small flows (0-15 Erlang), accompanying a general underestimate of medium and large ones (more than 30 Erlang): this means that many important relations are ignored by the model, which depicts a number of weak flows, mostly non-existent. In order to understand the distribution of these 'phantom' interaction, which the model fails to point out, one needs to study flows distribution curves according to distance: it is short interactions (less than 20 km) that are underestimated, whilst flows over medium distances (20-75 km) are magnified. Differences between regional flows (over 100 km) fade away. As in gravity models interaction is directly proportional to masses (sum of produced/absorbed flows) and inversely proportional to distance between centres - willing to explain the behaviour just remarked - we need to introduce the hypothesis that many minor sectors, neighbours to each other, exchange intense relations in a preferential way, focusing their energies in a small area, confirming the hypothesis of non–hierarchical local networks. This hypothesis will find further support in the rest of the analysis.

Another outcome of the analysis of observed flow data is the inward propensity of the systems, and the short range of exterior relations: if we forget flows exchange with Milan, actually the sole pivot of the Lombardy urban system, all major systems 'grasp' only their neighbours, such that we were induced to think of a regional 'chain', rather than a regional network (Figure 8.5). These statements have to be smoothed when taking into account also minor flows, revealing a great richness of connections in the area at the north of Milan and towards Como, Bergamo and Brescia (in this last case, this is not the dominating tendency, rather the latent one).

8.3.2.1 Exchanges with the metropolis

With regard to telephone flows, not dislike any other kind of physical flows, the Milanese metropolis (Figure 8.6) acts like a whirlpool, what justifies us in leading two separate analyses: Milan against the rest of the region, and the whole of Lombardy with the exclusion of the main town. Otherwise, because of the great dimension and the quantity of Milan-bound flows would eclipse all non-centripetal interactions.

The three major urban systems of Lombardy (Milan, Bergamo, Brescia) behave, externally, much like hierarchical structures, each characterized by a star of interactions with their satellites and are linked to other systems strictly

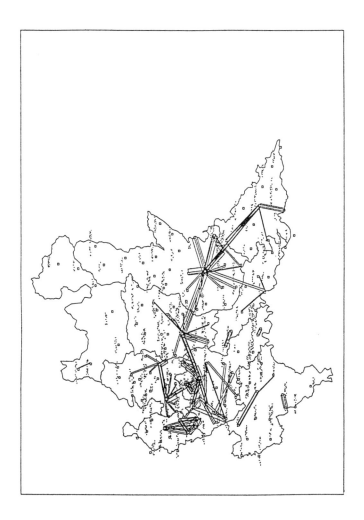

Figure 8.5 Macrolevel (inter-sector) telephone flows in the Po Valley. Microlevel (intersector) telephone flows in the Po Valley. Interactions with Milan have been masked for readability purposes. The structure of the local systems visible at the macro level appears in detail. Besides the semi-hierarchical systems of Brescia and Bergamo and the industrial clusters of Coma, Lecco and Olonia, a metropolitan network arises all around Milan, which was not represented at the district level.

141

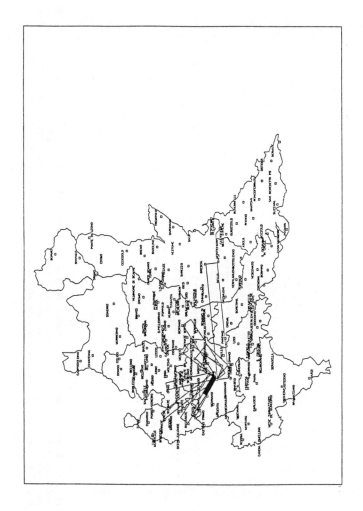

Figure 8.6 Centripetal structure of spatial relations. The strong centripetal structure of regional relations is evident also at micro level: most of the connections focus on the metropolis to such an extent that observed flows greatly overcome the model's forecasts. White bars show positive differences, i.e. model's underestimates; there is only one case of overestimation of the flow's intensity: between Milan and Rho.

through the central place. As for Bergamo and Brescia, this argument needs no corrections, but for Milan, this is only true when disregarding the highly complex structure formed by the flows having origin and destination in the centres of the ring and of the band between Milan and the Alps (Figures 8.7 and 8.8).

Flows originated and absorbed by the metropolis are guite well-balanced, the only exceptions appear to be Vegevano and Treviglio, both, however with values of the flow near to the lower threshold of shown flows (50 Erland, for flows to/from Milan). Major partners for the metropolis are some municipalities of the surrounding region: Monza, as the first, then the Olonia region and Merate; finally the centres of the other regional systems: Bergamo, Brescia, Como, Varese, Pavia and in the end Vigevano, Lodi e Lecco. As for Brescia and Bergamo, it is worthwhile remarking that they represent the two cases of greater discrepancy between observed data and the model. The flow between Milan and Bregamo is indeed underestimated, such as that between Bergamo and Brescia: this suggested that the the structure formed by the three major main towns of the region might embody elements of functional integration, being the only mesh of a regional macro-network. An analysis extented to other regions could tell us whether other meshes can be added to form an interregional network linking major cities.

8.3.2.2 Local Marshallian districts

If differences between real and modelled data were the exception in the Milanese centripetal system, they are quite the rule in the regional structure at a finer level (see Figure 8.7), which we could point out only by excluding Milan, having such a mass to obscure any other phenomena at a finer scale.

By observing the network of flows thus produced, and filtering out all weaker interactions (which are however - as it was previously shown - in contradiction with the hierarchical-gravitational model), three different sets of territorial structures appear: the hierarchical star of Brescia, much alike that of Milan at a finer scale, the network of centres belonging to the ring of the metropolis, the industrial districts at the feet of the Alp and in the Brianza area.

These two last structrues are of great interest with regard to their territorial organization, unseizable for any Christaller-like analytical schema, and it was possible to reveal them only by using peculiar flow-data such as telephone calls are (Figure 8.8). The gravity model fails because it stems from an hypothesis of territory in which local peculiarities do not take place, and only mass effects and distance (merely as a cost) play a role. In the reality of Lombardy, conversely, the existence of strong local synergies causes the formation of tiny networks (strongly resembling Marshall's 'industrial districts') involving few tens of municipalities, strongly interactive among them and with few, well–selected relations with the exterior. Take the case of Olonia as an example, being a small aggregation of no more than three sectors, having developed a specialization in light mechanics production, with connections restricted to Milan and, secondly, to Varese.

Other systems showing an alike structure are those of Como-Cantù-Erba (the silk *filière*), Desio-Seregno-Carate (furniture design and production district), Vimercate-Merate (which concentrate most of hi-tech production in Lombardy)

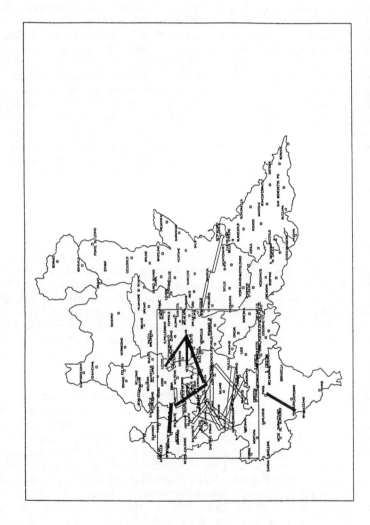

Figure 8.7 Network-like relations and missing connections. Network-like relations (empty bars) and missing connections (solid bars) are to be found mainly in a restricted area between Milan and the mountains, outlined in the map and examined in detail in Figure 8.8. The main exception is constituted by a few flows directed to Brescia, second regional town, probably due to a super-gravitation effect reproducing to a lesser scale that of Milan.

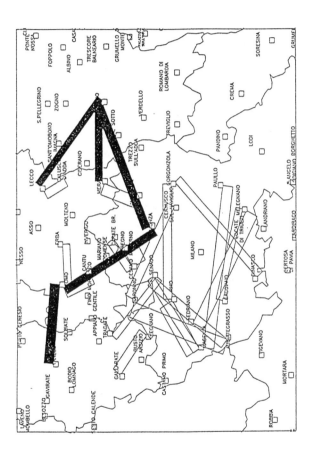

Figure 8.8 **Local orientation of network in Lombardia.** Networks in Lombardia appear to be an essentially local phenomena, linked to the presence of industrial districts or metropolitan synergies. To the former kind belong the systems of Como (silk), Lecco, Seregno (furniture design and production), Busto Gallarate Legnano (light mechanics) and Vimercate (hi tech). A strongly integrated network arises between all centres of the metropolitan ring, highlighting the nonhierarchical dynamics of this area's development model. The reciprocal isolation of these local structures is shown by dramatic lack of connections among the major regional nodes (solid black bars): Varese, Como, Monza, Bergamo and Lecco. Especially Monza, having the highest absolute value of exchanges, after Milan, besides showing relative isolation from all major systems, does not take part in any of the regional networks, showing an overall situation of remarkable weakness in the regional asset.

145

and Lecco-Calolzio Corte. All of them being isolated districts, endowed with strong specializations, scarcely or not at all connected among themselves, but with much stronger partners (that is Milan and, to a minor extent, Bergamo and Brescia).

Probing is the analysis of negative differences between reality and the model: false flows - expected to form the hierarchical mesh at a lower rank - pretned to link together Monza, Como and Varese (this last being the only main town completely forgotten by the network of real flows). Especially Monza, despite having the second largest amount of connections after Milan, not only appears to be isolated from all major systems, but it has not even developed a network of its own, nor does it take part in the metropolitan network, showing an overall condition of remarkable weakness in the regional asset.

Recalling the definitions given in the second paragraph above, it is possible to label these local networks, grown in a Marshallian 'industrial atmosphere' and taking advantage of 'milieu' effects, as 'complementarity networks'.

8.3.2.3 The metropolitan network

Beside the phenomenon of local districts, this analysis revealed a network encompassing a number of centres belonging to the ring of Milan (Figure 8.8). All major sector centres around Milan are involved: Saronno, Senago, Rho, Cernusco S/N, Gorgonzola, Paullo, Melegnano, Binasco, Gaggiano, Abbiategrasso, Magenta, Sedriano. All of them weave a mesh of relations forming a highly interconnected graph, especially in the north-western area, enveloping Milan. One could try to look at it as a great district concerning a higher number of centres, but the wider scale of the phenomenon, the proximity to the metropolis, the wide range of the interactions, crossing over the city as if it were a perfect connective element, depict a structure of different nature, living symbiotically with the 'centre', but in absence of a strong hierarchical dependence by it (in most cases, on the contrary, the interaction with Milan is only the second one in order of importance).

The centres involved in this second kind of city network, are mainly small and medium-size towns, similar to each other, and performing - thanks to cooperation - higher-rank service functions. According to the network logic recognized in the first part of this study, this structure seems to belong to 'synergy networks' category.

8.3.3 General remarks

Final remarks regarding this flow analysis can by no means be straightforward. During the study we met strong elements of hierarchical structuring: hierarchical is the macro-systems organization of Brescia, Bergamo and Milan. At a lower rank of the hierarchy surely belong all rural systems: Pavia, Cremona, Mantova; even the main centres of the pre-alpine band (Como, Lecco, Varese), show a centripetal-hierarchical component, but it is not the dominating one. There is a regional latent network, expressed by a more than gravitational synergy among the three poles of Milan, Bergamo and Brescia. and there is - in the most dynamic areas of the region - a component, probably latent in the case of Brescia, dominating in the areas of Milan and Como, strictly anti-hierarchical and anti-gravitational. It is precisely this component we desired to highlight, and traditional instruments, based on gravity-like logic, were unable to. In fact, a set of socioeconomic-cultural factors (the 'cultural factors of development' according to Mela), concur in determining the formation of local networks and districts, creating the local vocation. This process yields a strongly dishomogeneous territory (vs. that of gravity models), in which distance plays the ambiguous role of a filter (for all centres not belonging to the districts) and of an integration element (proximity). In other words, what the gravity model cannot explain is the intervention of elements of sociocultural identity (the 'milieu') as mass terms, and the synergetic effect of proximity, substituting decay due to distance.

The other case, clearly shown by data and by the comparison with the simulations, in which distance and masses play non-conventional roles, is that of the metropolitan area of Milan. Here it is the central city itself that encourages, instead of swallowing, a 'synergy network' of relations among minor poles surrounding it. It is possible to think of Milan as a sort of a super–conductor, reducing to zero distances between points situated on its border, but it recalls also the effect of 'gravitational sling', by which the gravity field of a great planet is used to greatly enhance the cynetic energy of a satellite skimming it.

Looking deeper inside the whole structure of relationships among urban centres, even if both hierarchical and network organizations are present in most territorial contexts, the second one, when it is prevailing, presents some specific features:

• the network structure does not connect centres of different rank, but yields in a context where city sizes are more or less equivalent (the regional main towns of second rank, the centres with 50-60 thousand inhabitants in the metropolitan area, the district clusters at the third rank);
• the strength of the network interconnections is higher among medium and small centres than among main towns;
• the information exchanges with higher rank poles are achieved through their closer higher central place, which acts as intermediate information exchanger from its dominated urban centres with respect to the other cities at the same rank.

In concluding this study we wish to summarize the general outcome yielded by the analysis: among the aims of this work there was the aim to identify the proper territorial scales for the observation of the various phenomena, moving from the remark that the dominating structure at a macro level might disappear at a reduced scale. Stepping backwards in the analysis, we recall how a principle of non-hierarchical functional integration was already shown by the analysis of aggregated district data; how the hierarchical structures linking together the centres of the single macro-systems appeared to be dominant at the sector level; how, finally, it was possible to point out, inside a large hierarchical mesh, a finer network of micro-systems, based on forms of organization related to the 'milieu' and the metropolitan network.

8.4 Conclusions

In this paper, it is shown how the logic that shapes the city-systems is more complicated than the simple 'territor1al' and hierarchical logic of the traditional central place model. The control of the market of outputs, inputs and innovative assets is performed by the firm not only in terms of management of a gravity area, but also and increasingly in terms of network relationships.

The new behavioural logic of the firm parallels and partly determines the new organizational logic of the city system, where phenomena of specialization and networking also appear.

Probability of interaction among cities may go far beyond what was expected on the basis of their size and distance. High density of information flows on a proximity basis, as the ones taking place within specialized industrial 'districts'; cooperation and spatial division of labour among specialized centres; and synergy among similarly specialized centres linked through high–performing information networks, are all elements calling for selected non-hierarchical linkages among centres, which we call 'city-networks'.

In the empirical realm of the Lombardy region, network relations among centres were discovered, mainly showing up in two specific spatial contexts:
• within the metropolitan area of Milan, shaping its emerging polycentric structure, and
• within sub-regional industrial districts.

In the first case, the empirical evidence suggests the existence of 'synergy networks', happening among similar centres performing headquarter and advanced production-services functions; in the second case, mainly 'complementarity networks' and 'milieu' type of interactions are revealed.

References

Bertelè, U, and Mariotti (1991), *Imprese e Competizione Dinamica*, Etas Libri.

Boyce, D, Nijkamp, P. and Shefer, D. (eds.) (1991), *Regional Science: Retrospects and Prospects*, Springer Verlag, Berlin.

Camagni, R. (1989), 'Technological Change, Uncertainty and Innovation Networks: Toward a Dynamic Theory of Economic Space', paper presented at II World Congress of the RSA,Jerusalem, April, Boyce, D. et al (eds.),1991, pp. 211-249.

Camagni, R. (1992), 'Organisation Economique et Réseaux de Villes', in Derycke, P.H. (ed.), *Espace et Dynamiques Territoriales*, Economica, Paris, pp.25-52.

Camagni, R. (1993), 'From City Hierarchy to City Networks: Reflections about an Emerging Paradigm', in Lakshmanan, T.R. and Nijkamp, P. (eds.), *Structure and Change in the Space Economy: Festschrift in honor of Martin Beckmann*, Springer Verlag, Berlin, pp. 66-87.

Camagni, R. and De Blasio, G (eds.) (1993), *Le Reti di Città: Teoria, Politiche e Analisi nell'Area Padana*, F. Angeli, Milano.

Capello, R. (1993), 'Una Tassonomia di Esternalità di Rete e una Teorizzazione del Loro Effetti sulla Performance delle Regioni', in. Bertuglia,

Capello, R. and Nijkamp, P. (1994), 'Corporate and Regional Advantages of Telecommunication Diffusion: the Role of Network Externalities', in Torre, A and Rallet, A. (eds.), *Industrial Organization and Spatial Economics*, Economica, Paris, forthcoming.

Dematteis, G. (1990), 'Modelli Urbani a Rete. Considerazioni Prelminari', in Curti, F. and Diappi, L. (eds.), *Gerarchie e Reti di Città: Tendenze e Politiche*, F. Angeli, Milano, pp. 27-48.

Dosi, G. and Orsenigo, L. (1988), 'Coordination and Transformation: an Overview of Structures, Behaviours and Change in Evolutionary Environments', in Dose, G. et al.(eds.) *Technical Change and Economic Theory*, Pinter Publishers, London, pp.13-37.

Fischer, M. (1992), 'Expert Systems and Artificial Neural Networks for Spatial Analysis and Modelling: Essential Components for Knowledge-Based Geographical Information Systems', *WSG Discussion Papers*, 17, Vienna University of Economics and Business Administration.

Fischer, M. and Gopal, S. (1992), 'Neural Network Models and Interregional Telephone Traffic: Comparative Performance Comparisons between Multilayer Feedforward Networks and the Conventional Spatial Interaction Model', *WSG Discussion Papers*, 27, Vienna University of Economics and Business Administration.

Hansen, N. (1992), 'Competition, Trust and Reciprocity in the Development of Innovative Regional Milieux', *Papers in Regional Science*, 2, pp. 95-105.

Van der Loewe, G. (1993), 'Information Theory and Urban Dynamics', in Lepetit B. and Pumain, D. (ed1.), *Témporalités Urbaines*, Economica, Paris.

Wilson, A.G. (1974), *Urban and Regional Models in Geography and Planning*, J. Wiley, London-New York.

Notes

1. This paper presents the main results of a research study carried out for I.RE.R of Milan on "City Networks in the Lombardy region", directed by Roberto Camagni and realised by an équipe encompassing, besides the present authors, Tomaso Pompili and Carlo Salone (Camagni and De Blasio, 1993). Though the paper is the result of a common research effort, R. Camagni has elaborated paragraph 8.1 and 8.4, L. Diappi paragraphs 8.2.2 and 8.3.3, S. Stabilini paragraphs 8.2.1 and 8.2.3 through 8.3.2. Cooperation of SIP, the Italian telephone carrier, in the supply of basic information and a financial support of the Italian Minister of University and Research is gratefully acknowledged.

9 Regional science and new transport infrastructure

R.W. Vickerman

9.1 Introduction

Across the world there is renewed interest in the effects of infrastructure, and new transport infrastructure in particular. There seem to be several reasons for this. In economically lagging regions infrastructure is seen as an essential prerequisite for economic development. This is nowhere more pronounced than in the countries of central and eastern Europe, as the experience of German unification has already shown. In older industrial regions the existing infrastructure is either reaching the end of its working life, or is increasingly inadequate to cope with the volume of traffic, leading to both congestion and environmental pollution. At the same time as this increased potential demand for infrastructure investment, governments are concerned with the cost of its provision and maintenance when there are pressures to reduce public expenditure. This has led in many countries to a cumulative underinvestment.

Ways are being sought to introduce more private sector finance into infrastructure provision as a means of overcoming the backlog in investment. The United Kingdom government has used this for bridge developments over major estuaries,as well as in the rather special case of the Channel Tunnel. It has also sought ways of introducing private capital into the provision of ordinary roads and new rapid transit links to Heathrow Airport and London Docklands. Since the private sector interest in such investment will, at least in part, arise out of development gain in the areas served this requires a more accurate assessment of the incidence of the wider economic benefits from infrastructure.

This paper addresses two broad areas of interest. First, there is the scale of analysis. Traditional approaches have looked at the impacts of individual infrastructure projects (bridges, tunnels, highways, airports) on the directly affected regions. Increasingly, new infrastructure is either so large (such as the Channel Tunnel) or is being planned as a major new network (such as the European High Speed Rail Network) that it will have impacts well outside a single region (Vickerman, 1993). This requires a different approach, since the individual regional impacts are fairly small, but the overall effect on the distribution of regional activity may be substantial (Vickerman, 1991b).

Secondly, there is a need to consider the appropriate methodology for

151

analysis. Traditionally, regional scientists have used economic potential or regional input-output studies as a means of measuring impacts. Both of these suffer from the difficulty of incorporating changing patterns of behaviour which are implicit in major infrastructure investments. Regional production function approaches have also been used in which public infrastructure is seen as enhancing the productivity of other factor inputs. This has the advantage of demonstrating clearly the likely return on new infrastructure, but raises complex measurement and estimation problems. Neither of these approaches fully captures the sort of change in both economic and spatial activity which may be associated with major changes and hence there is a role for more subjective studies. Thus far we have little ex post evidence of the changes induced by new infrastructures on which to base empirical analysis.

This paper does not claim to be a complete review of the literature on infrastructure (the reader is referred to Straszheim, 1972; Gwilliam, 1979; Botham, 1982; and Rietveld, 1989b for useful discussions and surveys). Its main purpose is to try and provide a framework within which the issues raised by new transport infrastructure can be considered and to highlight some of the areas where future research effort needs to be concentrated.

9.2   The scale of analysis of infrastructure impacts

9.2.1   Single region studies

Much analytical development in connection with the effects of new infrastructure has been closely related to regional policy making. This has meant that the analysis of regional impacts has concentrated on single region studies. In these one region, that where the infrastructure is located, provides the focus for analysis whilst all other regions are treated as something of a black box. There are good reasons for this. Since the essence of the regional science approach is captured in the notion of distance decay, it is clear that the impacts of any change will decay fairly rapidly as one moves away from their origin, hence the only measurable impacts will occur fairly close to the origin. This is compounded by data problems. With difficulty we can construct reasonable working descriptions of the economy of a single region, for example in terms of its input-output relations, but interregional input-output models on anything other than a fairly simplified level are much more problematic. Furthermore, it is often reasonable to argue that the impacts of some change in a regional economy are not likely to affect more than marginally the behavioural relationships which describe its links with other regions' economies.

This has been as true of transport infrastructure as of other types of change. We are typically interested in the impact of a marginal change in the transport system on the workings of a local economy. In an urban context therefore we look at the possible changes to a road network, or the introduction of a rapid transit or priority bus system. The impacts of these are seen to be on the efficiency of the urban economy through the workings of the labour market as measured in terms of time savings or the impact on property values. Although it is clear that such efficiency only matters in the context of competition for

152

resources, or over output, with other cities, it is only recently that such a wider context has been considered.

A transport infrastructure improvement which has a rather less local context is that of airport development. Here, however, the principal interest has been the extent to which a major investment of this type will affect employment in a region. It is therefore treated simply like any large scale investment which will have direct and multiplier effects on the local economy.

9.2.2 Networks and interregional effects

Where the one-region model starts to become seriously deficient is in the removal of a bottleneck in a network. The classic problem here is the impact of the construction of an estuarial or major river crossing or a fixed link to an offshore island. In the absence of such a crossing the two economies on either bank develop an independent existence which reflects the time and cost penalties imposed by the need either to use a ferry or to make a long detour. Whilst this is the model for a successful toll bridge in transport economics, it is also clear that where the separation is sufficiently great the effect of building a new link is marginal - unless it opens up a new corridor of transport between existing major generators of traffic (Marchetti, 1991). This is particularly likely to be the case if the new infrastructure is not just interregional, but also international in character.

This gives us a clue, however, about the scale and nature of effects. First we need to identify the relevant network into which the new infrastructure fits. Does it generate new traffic by making possible transport between any two points on that network which was previously impossible/excessively costly? Is it likely to lead to the diversion of traffic, either from one destination to another (which is like newly generated traffic on the link in question) or from an old route to the new route (either by traffic taking a shorter route by the same mode or by switching mode, especially from air to a surface mode)? Secondly we can examine the regional impacts of these effects on three types of region:

* the major traffic generators in the network, which will mainly benefit from increased accessibility, except that their dependence on air communications and the advantages derived from their domination of air networks may be reduced;
* the regions adjacent to the new infrastructure, which will gain from improved accessibility, but this may be reduced by their inability to benefit from these due to supply side rigidities and by the creation of corridor effects. The canalization of traffic through these regions, the desire to avoid the interference of local traffic with major centre to major centre traffic, can reduce actual accessibility below the potential whilst the growth of congestion on local networks associated with the new infrastructure reduces the economic advantage to such regions;
* other regions, which suffer from the diversion of traffic away from traditional routes, including coastal regions where port activities may be affected. Although this may have advantages symmetrical to the disadvantages faced by the newly served regions, the longer term effects of being perceived to be situated away from the major corridor of activity can cast a shadow. This shadow may also be felt in the adjacent regions as

part of an intraregional adjustment of activity between the narrow corridor and the wider region.

In summary therefore, the impacts of new infrastructure fall on major nodes of a network, on the major corridors between those nodes and their points of access, and on the interstitial or intervening areas (Vickerman, 1991b; 1993).

9.2.3 Macroeconomic effects of infrastructure

There is, however, an even wider scale which infrastructure addresses and which poses particular questions about the regional focus of many analyzes. Too often these are concerned with purely distributional questions within or between regions. This ignores the way in which the spatial question affects the overall performance of the economy, although it is also true of the way in which questions of performance have ignored the spatial question (Krugman, 1991b). The essence of a spatial economics lies in increasing returns since it is these which determine the degree of localization of industry (Krugman, 1991a). However, localization generates both agglomeration and urbanization economies which have a spinoff increasing competitiveness of a locality and thus having an effect on interregional (and international) trade and hence on growth (Henderson, 1988).

Infrastructure in such a system acts rather as a public good, part of the 'urbanization economies'. The argument over the role of infrastructure in economic growth involves the extent to which any lag in infrastructure investment (interpreted widely to include most 'public' capital) reduces the productivity of private sector investment and hence the rate of economic growth. Detailed studies of sectoral production functions tend to show that it is internal rather than such external economies which are mainly responsible for determining the degree of localization of industry (Henderson, 1988). However, these often tend to treat infrastructure in a rather aggregate way and thus fail to capture the differing specific role of infrastructure in different sectors. Furthermore, the indivisibilities present in much infrastructure lead to bottlenecks in its use which makes models based on continuous marginal adjustment inappropriate.

A further argument against the productivity enhancing role of infrastructure concerns the extent to which public sector infrastructure investment leads to 'crowding-out' of private sector investment through increasing public sector borrowing and raising interest rates. However, this is argued to be essentially a short run effect, the medium to long term effect is to increase private sector investment by making it more profitable.

Much of the empirical work on this has been done at a national level (Aschauer, 1989, 1990), although there have been studies which look at regional variations (Munnell, 1990). They look at infrastructure as an aggregate factor of production which combines with private capital, labour etc to produce output. Such studies produce almost unbelievably large implied marginal productivities for infrastructure. Indeed it is the size of the estimates which has originated much of the criticism. Aschauer's empirical work on US data suggests that the marginal product of public capital in the aggregate may have been over 200 per cent compared to a figure of 9 to 12 per cent for private capital. This suggests a need to invest at a rapid rate in infrastructure since over the 1970-88 period increased public investment would have raised the rate of return to private capital from 7.9% to 9.6% and the rate of productivity growth from 1.4% to 2.1% (i.e. by 50 per cent). These particular estimates seem to be unacceptably large and other work (including by Aschauer) has produced substantially lower figures, but nevertheless shows an important role for infrastructure. Disaggregating infrastructure and applying it on a regional basis, Munnell suggests that water and sewage systems had the greatest impact, followed by roads.

Much of the criticism of these results is based on the statistical analysis. The improper use of time series estimates is held to give rather spurious results (Aaron, 1990). Attempts to specify a fuller model have tended to produce rather unstable results, minor variations in the period analyzed give substantial variations in implied rates of return to public capital (Mehta et al. 1992). The role of infrastructure and other public capital is therefore ambiguous as a source of economic growth and its regional variations. The ambiguity of statistical estimates of the rate of return does not, however, confirm the unimportance of infrastructure. It may simply reflect the difficulty in measuring infrastructure appropriately for a given region.

Even the smaller estimates are interesting since they appear to contradict the traditional view that the rate of return to infrastructure is relatively small and it is this low return which requires such infrastructure to be a public sector responsibility. The problem of course is not the level of the rate of return, but the problem of capturing it to finance the investment. It is likely to be the case that better equipped areas, which are richer, are also likely to be in a better position to finance additional investment (Munnell, 1990; Duffy-Deno and Ebert, 1991). If the returns to infrastructure investment were so high, however, it would seem logical to argue that the private sector would gain sufficiently from the investment to wish to undertake it itself. A key tenet of the economic policies pursued by the Reagan and Thatcher governments in the US and UK during the 1980s was to make the private sector recognize this, and a large part of the current shortfall (though by no means all of it) in public infrastructure investment occurred during this period. Resorting to explanations through market imperfections, especially in terms of information, may not be an adequate response here.

These studies have concentrated on the directly productive role which infrastructure may play. An alternative approach is to consider the value of infrastructure as a public good to urban residents, and hence its capitalization in land values (Brueckner, 1979). In a recent paper Haughwout (1992) has combined the two approaches and demonstrated the way in which there is a significant simultaneous impact on both production and on the value of urban residence. The latter is reflected principally in land values but can also be identified in other input prices such as wages.

What these studies have done is to emphasize the role of infrastructure at a macroeconomic level - at least that there is a serious argument to be addressed. What regional science needs to do is to examine the spatial context of this. It is where that infrastructure is directed that is important in determining its effectiveness. To the extent that one product of the last decade is an increasing pressure for private sector funding of infrastructure wherever feasible, it is also important to recognize the one clear result from most regional impact studies of infrastructure - that the absence of infrastructure as an explanation of poor regional performance is always much easier to demonstrate than the direct beneficial impact of new infrastructure. This brings us to the question of modelling the impact of new infrastructure, which is the subject of the remainder of this paper.

9.3   Modelling the impact of new transport infrastructure

9.3.1   Economic potential approaches

The economic potential approach (Clark et al., 1969) is the obvious initial approach to the question of new infrastructure. What new infrastructure does first and foremost is change accessibility. The advantage of economic potential is that it is a multiregional analysis in which the relative change in accessibility and potential is as important as the absolute change for any one region (Keeble et al., 1982a, 1982b). Potential is a measure of a region's market area and hence the analysis is predominantly demand based. It does not allow for changes in either the mix of a region's output or for a change in technology which leads to increased efficiency and hence a price induced change in demand. For small changes in infrastructure which are marginal to the performance of a network this is an acceptable approach. For larger changes or continuing cumulative improvements in the efficiency of a network it is less satisfactory simply because these changes are likely to lead to changes in the supply side (Vickerman, 1989).

The problem of the economic potential approach is that it perpetuates the existing core-periphery relationships of an economy. Whilst it can be argued that there is clear evidence of the continuance of such regional disparities over long periods - the European Community being a case in point - this does not provide conclusive evidence for the economic potential approach as an explanation of either the initial divergence or its persistence. As Krugman and Venables (1990) have demonstrated with a simple model of integration in an economy with core and peripheral regions the removal of barriers to trade has ambiguous effects. Depending on the relative levels of factor prices, technology and transport costs and the changes in these brought about through the process of integration, the result could be either increasing or lessening peripheralization (Vickerman, 1992d). If the objective of policy were to reduce these regional divergences then a logical policy measure would be to destroy infrastructure since the evidence from economic potential is always that the core regions benefit sufficiently from new infrastructure to preserve disparities.

Traditional policy towards infrastructure has been to develop the new infrastructure to or in the more peripheral regions, recognizing that the possession of a given level of infrastructure is an essential prerequisite for economic growth. Frequently, however, it may be the absence of a critical link at some distance from the region with which we are concerned which may be the factor preventing growth. Economic potential measures cannot identify the difference between these two changes and could not help us, on an ex ante basis, to decide which would be more important to the region.

156

Thus, the economic potential approach provides essentially the most neutral picture of changes resulting from changing transport provision (Vickerman, 1987). To be more than just an initial indicator of the likely beneficiaries and losers from a change, a means of identifying those regions which need to be examined more closely, requires modelling of the supply side which will show how such changes will be translated into benefits by a region's economy. Some attempt has been made to allow for this by introducing an employment function which translates the basic potential change into employment changes (Evers et al., 1987, 1988). Rietveld (1989a) has shown how with some modification this can be given a more rigorous theoretical foundation. However, it is also desirable to analyze the impacts on the economy at a more disaggregate level. A first step towards this is input-output analysis.

9.3.2 Regional input-output studies

Input-output analysis is a second major analytical tool of the regional scientist after the gravity model which lies behind the economic potential approach. Put together, the input-output framework of a single region's economy coupled with a gravity-based model of trade between regions provides a powerful description of the sectoral and spatial structure of an economy. Where an input–output model with a trade sector scores over the potential approach is that it can identify the extent to which sectors in the regional economy are more or less trade dependent and hence how far they are likely to benefit from changing accessibility. This can help to differentiate between regions in similar locations, but with different economic structures. Secondly, the input-output approach enables a building up of the pattern of impacts on the regional economy through the internal linkages.

Recent examples of the application of input-output models relate to the Storebaelt crossing in Denmark (Madsen and Jensen-Butler, 1991), the development of a regional airport in the UK (Batey et al., 1993) and the Channel Tunnel (ACT Consultants et al., 1992). These are interesting because they show contrasting applications of the method. Madsen and Jensen-Butler and ACT Consultants develop multiregional models which can be used, inter alia, to predict traffic flows. The regional economic development derives from this. One of the problems with this approach is that input-output models are good at handling traditional trade in goods, but rather less good at handling service sector effects and the movement of people. The importance of service sector response to the Storebaelt has been emphasized by Illeris and Jakobsen (1991). The ACT Consultants work uses a multinational - multiregional model, which assumes constant technological relationships of the input-output model across countries. Batey et al adopt a more traditional single region model, but an extended model which deals in much greater detail with the household sector so as to be able to develop the employment impacts more fully.

A principal weakness of the input-output approach, however, is the focus that it puts on the traditional demand induced multiplier impacts on the economy through its existing (static) economic structure. This is frequently exacerbated by the need to assume similar input-output structures in competing regions because of the absence of adequate data. This may be reasonable in a comparison of similar regions, but is unlikely to be satisfactory for a comparison between, for example, a core region in one country and a peripheral region in another, where technology is likely to differ substantially to reflect different input prices, including that of transport. The effect of such an assumption of constancy is to reinforce the core-periphery relationships, since the latter can claim none of their advantages, whilst suffering the penalty of high transport costs. It is possible to introduce a more dynamic framework which allows for variable input-output coefficients (Liew and Liew, 1985), but usually only for a fairly coarse regional and sectoral structure.

One of the common fallacies about transport costs is that they vary with location to the extent that peripherality implies a substantial cost burden over less peripheral locations. Evidence generally suggests that transport costs faced by firms in more peripheral locations are not as much greater as the location would suggest (Chisholm, 1987; 1992). This arises partly because of the possibility of using more efficient modes of transport - traditionally UK firms faced lower transport costs than would have been expected because of the proportion of UK trade which could use cheap sea routes to gain close access to ultimate origins/destinations (Beckerman, 1956). It also depends on whether there are specific bottlenecks in the network which affect a particular region (Campisi and La Bella, 1988). Mainly, however, it is because firms adjust their technology to allow for potentially higher transport costs, producing goods requiring relatively less transport per unit value or by being more efficient in the way transport is used. This requires a much more detailed examination of appropriate production functions in understanding the response of the regional economy to changing transport conditions.

9.3.3 Production function approaches

The input-output approach is a production function approach, but one which assumes fixed coefficients. What we have argued above is that such coefficients are likely to differ between regions to reflect their different locations and that a likely response to changing transport opportunities is to change the appropriate technology. This can be better allowed for by explicit modelling of regional production functions.

The production function approach treats infrastructure in two ways. First, the existence of infrastructure as a common input to all activities in a region raises the productivity of other inputs to the production process. Regions with larger amounts of infrastructure thus have higher levels of output from a given quantity of other inputs than regions with smaller amounts of infrastructure. Secondly, the price at which infrastructure is available, or probably more correctly the price of the services provided by the given infrastructure, relative to the price of other inputs will lead to a substitution between the infrastructure services and other inputs. Abundant infrastructure providing cheap transport services will lead to a greater intensity of transport use ceteris paribus than in infrastructure starved areas.

These are rather like the usual income and substitution effects and it is crucial to understand the difference between these two effects to understand why higher levels of infrastructure provision are associated with higher levels of output, but that investing in infrastructure does not necessarily produce an automatic increase in regional performance. Since the answer is often primarily an empirical one, the specification and estimation of an appropriate production function has frequently dominated discussion of this approach (Rietveld, 1989b).

We have already discussed the more general macroeconomic effects of infrastructure in Section 9.2 of this paper, where we noted the potential ambiguity of its impact. An important variant of the production function approach is the use of production functions to estimate a region's productive potential and assess the degree to which it is failing to achieve its potential, usually as a result of bottlenecks within the production process (Blum, 1982). Such an approach can usefully identify where it is infrastructure which is the main bottleneck or where it is the lack of other factors (Biehl, 1991).

However, the main difficulty with a production function approach is achieving an appropriate measurement for the services provided by infrastructure. This is not unlike the difficulties faced in measuring capital, or even labour where quality variations are important. However, at least in these cases it is possible to use prices based on appropriate markets to provide some value measure. In the case of infrastructure we have the problem first of difficult to measure variations in the level of service provided by the infrastructure, then of distortions in the value of these caused by a lack of pricing or prices distorted by subsidy. Typical approaches are just to measure the physical size of infrastructure, length of roads, railways etc, usually measuring different categories separately such as motorways, main roads, other roads, multiple track, two track and single track railways. These are then weighted, for example by estimated passenger and tonne kilometres of use, in order to provide an aggregate measure. This provides only a measure of aggregate infrastructure capacity within the region. It does not indicate the degree of use of that capacity, or more importantly the extent to which appropriate links exist or do not exist.

It is this latter point which is the most relevant for understanding the specific impacts of a given new infrastructure, and for allocating investment in infrastructure optimally between regions (Anderstig and Mattsson, 1989). For the infrastructure to have an impact it must serve both the sectoral and the geographical needs of the region. But this identifies a further critical issue which was raised at the outset, that it is not just infrastructure within the region which is relevant to the needs of the regional economy - the relevant bottlenecks may be away from the region. The only way this can be incorporated is by explicit modelling of the trade sector including the direction of trade (Amano and Fujita, 1970). This implies a model integrating the features of accessibility/potential models, input-output models and production function models with an explicit trade model. A partial move in this direction has been used in a study on the impact of the Channel Tunnel on the regions of Europe (ACT Consultants et al., 1992). This used the framework of a Land Use Transportation Study Model with a multiregional input output character, combined with detailed transport flow modelling, calibrated on existing trade flows which feed into the input-output structure. This looks to have a promising future although as yet it suffers from many of the drawbacks of both static input-output and gravity based models.

Simple aggregate models are unlikely to be adequate for understanding complex effects specific to individual sectors and their responses to infrastructure. It seems to be this problem of the level of aggregation which lies behind our knowing that infrastructure is important for individual users, our ability to recognize that there is an overall relationship between levels of provision and regional performance, but our failure to identify and evaluate the regional benefits of new infrastructure in a convincing way.

Such a disaggregate approach is clearly both complex and expensive in data terms. We need some a priori help to decide how to proceed in specific circumstances and it is to this we now turn.

9.3.4 The scope for more subjective analysis

Economists are notoriously reluctant to rely on asking people about the effects of changes. There is some reason in this since it is likely that those questioned will attempt to second guess the interviewer's motives. If you think that by giving a particular answer you can influence policy to achieve what you want then you might bias your answer to this effect. Thus, since for most businesses improvements in infrastructure are likely to be beneficial, at least to the extent that they increase profits, then there is a strong bias towards making out that infrastructure needs improvement. Similarly, from the perspective of a regional or local government, if it is thought that there is development assistance to regions with inadequate infrastructure (and it must be remembered that 80% of ERDF funding has gone to infrastructure projects), the response is likely to be biased. This is limited by the fear that too negative a picture painted of a region may discourage possible inward investment (although a concerned local government fighting for improved access might be more influential).

As an example, there has been a general belief by most regions in the UK that they will lose as a result of the Channel Tunnel, either to other UK regions or that the UK will lose overall to France (Holliday and Vickerman, 1990). This loss is seen both as a natural outcome, based on a loose concept of increasing concentration, and as a result of specific policy action. Curiously, but not unexpectedly, the justification for policy action in France is seen partly as a response to the natural advantages accruing to the UK as the region with the greater change in accessibility.

To some extent this outcome is the product of an essentially static, zero-sum game world which most actors perceive. In a recent rather wider study for the European Commission, there was a general feeling that other regions would benefit from an infrastructure improvement, whether it was close or distant (ACT Consultants et al., 1992). It was also quite difficult to encourage respondents to address the question of how far changes in infrastructure might lead to more widespread impacts on the balance of mode usage which would have more direct impacts. Thus the creation of new links such as the Channel Tunnel, Storebaelt, and New Alpine Rail Axis carry a bias towards rail which may change both the level of service on the entire network, especially the range of accessible destinations, and the relative prices of different modes (Vickerman, 1993).

Nevertheless it is important to use subjective information as a way of making informed judgments about the changes in the coefficients of models estimated on the basis of existing behaviour. Work by both British Rail's Railfreight Distribution and Eurotunnel has shown that market research exercises which attempt to build up forecasts of use of the Channel Tunnel from individual markets provide a qualitatively different view of total demand than the traditional traffic forecasting approach which aims to estimate a total market and then allocate this between modes, routes etc on the basis of time and cost characteristics, even if total traffic forecasts are broadly consistent (Le Maire and Pevsner, 1992). The different submarkets have very different diversion rates, which aggregate forecasts fail to pick up. This is consistent with the argument developed above that it is important to separate out the different types of user of a given piece of infrastructure since they have different characteristics. Only when this is done can we hope to be able to develop a forecasting model which is adequate as the basis of appraisal of new infrastructure.

9.4   Appraisal frameworks for new infratructure

As was indicated at the beginning of this paper the new infrastructure that is being considered at the moment is large and consequently expensive. The Channel Tunnel will cost around £10 billion. The proposed rail link from the Tunnel to London, originally costed at about £1.5 billion is now thought to be likely to cost up to £2.5-3 billion. Schemes in the French TGV Schéma Directeur add up to FF 145 billion. Infrastructure costs of German unification have been put at over DM 200 billion. The Round Table of European Industrialists (1988) has suggested that an annual expenditure of between 32 and 40 billion ECU is needed to upgrade European transport infrastructure and the European Commission has identified a high speed rail master plan costing an estimated 150 billion ECU (Vickerman, 1991a).

Clearly a public sector facing increasing problems of controlling budget deficits is not going to be able to find finance on this scale. Indeed some of the problems of the deficit in infrastructure provision are themselves due to earlier cutbacks in public expenditure. In Europe concern about meeting the criteria for monetary convergence necessary for the transition to Economic and Monetary Union, plus the constraints put on all by the costs of German unification and the need to provide assistance to Central and Eastern European countries and the former Soviet Union, all provide added constraints. It is the large projects which tend to be the first casualties of this.

Indeed the 1970s proposal for a Channel Tunnel was a casualty of exactly this problem. It was to a large extent private sector pressure which brought the project back into discussion, showing how private sector funding could enable the project to proceed (Holliday et al., 1991; Vickerman, 1992b). The question is, however, whether the private sector can, and should, provide the finance alone and thus what the role of government is in such infrastructure funding. The advantages of private sector funding at a time of public sector funding constraint is that it may enable a project to be undertaken sooner and thus generate benefit sooner (Kay et al., 1989). However, it may be impossible to get the private sector to bear the risks associated with a complete network, and if the private sector is to finance specific links of the network then it is likely that it will require substantial guaranteed monopoly rents. The benefits to users, and to regions, derive largely from the network and not from specific

161

links. As the Channel Tunnel case clearly shows one of the major problems has been to ensure the adequate parallel development of both the Tunnel and its associated road and rail links. The absence of this may cause serious regional distributional problems (Vickerman, 1992a, c).

Usually only the public sector is in a position to finance projects for which the benefits are both long-term and substantially indirect. In the case of large infrastructure projects there is a substantial element of direct benefit which it is not unreasonable to expect users to finance, but it is rarely adequate to enable them to finance the project completely. This is especially true where there are important spillovers on to other parts of the network or major environmental considerations such as the bias to rail generally which major new projects may encompass.

What is thus required is a means of financing such large projects on a joint basis, the private sector financing that part from which it benefits. To achieve this implies a sophisticated and acceptable appraisal technique which can both identify aggregate benefits and attribute them. This is essentially the challenge for the analyst. This paper has attempted to set out the essential elements of a framework for that analysis.

References

Aaron H.J. (1990), Discussion, in Munnell, A.H. (ed) *'Is There a Shortfall in Public Capital Investment?'* Conference Series No 34, Federal Reserve Bank of Boston.

ACT Consultants, IRPUD, Marcial Echenique and Partners, (1992), *The Regional Impact of the Channel Tunnel Throughout the Community*, Final Report to DGXVI, Commission of the European Communities, February.

Amano K. and Fujita M. (1970), 'A long run economic effect analysis of alternative transportation facility plans - regional and national', *Journal of Regional Science*, 10, pp. 297-323.

Anderstig C. and Mattsson L.-G. (1989), 'Interregional allocation models of infrastructure investments', *Annals of Regional Science*, 23, pp. 287-298.

Aschauer D.A. (1989), 'Is public expenditure productive?', *Journal of Monetary Economics*, 23, pp. 177-200.

Aschauer D.A. (1990), 'Why is infrastructure important?' in Munnell, A.H. (ed) *Is There a Shortfall in Public Capital Investment?* Conference Series No 34, Federal Reserve Bank of Boston.

Batey P.W.J., Madden M. and Scholefield G. (1993), 'Socio-economic impact assessment of large-scale projects using input-output analysis: a case study of an airport', *Regional Studies*, 27, pp. 179-191.

Beckerman W. (1956), 'Distance and the pattern of intra-European trade', *Review of Economics and Statistics*, 38, pp. 31-40.

Biehl D. (1991), 'The role of infrastructure in regional development', in Vickerman, R.W. (ed) *Infrastructure and Regional Development*, European Research in Regional Science vol 1, Pion, London.

Blum U. (1982), 'Effects of transportation investments on regional growth: a theoretical and empirical analysis', *Papers of Regional Science Association*, 49, pp. 151-168.

Botham R. (1982), 'The road programme and regional development: the problem of the counter-factual', in Button, K.J. and Gillingwater, D. (eds) *Transport, Location and Spatial Policy*, Gower, Aldershot.

Brueckner J. (1979), 'Property values, local public expenditure and economic efficiency', *Journal of Public Economics*, 11, pp. 223-245.

Campisi D. and La Bella A. (1988), 'Transportation supply and economic growth in a multiregional system', *Environment and Planning A*, 20, pp. 925 - 936.

Chisholm M. (1987), 'Regional variations in transport costs in Britain with special reference to Scotland', *Transactions of the Institute of British Geographers*, 12, pp. 303-314.

Chisholm M. (1992), 'Britain, the European Community, and the centralisation of production: theory and evidence, freight movements', *Environment and Planning A*, 24, pp. 551-570.

Clark C., Wilson F. and Bradley J. (1969), 'Industrial location and economic potential in Western Europe', *Regional Studies*, 3, pp. 197-212.

Duffy-Deno K.T. and Ebert R.W. (1991), 'Public infrastructure and regional economic development: a simultaneous equations approach', *Journal of Urban Economics*, 30, pp. 329-343.

Evers G.H.M., van der Meer P.H., Oosterhaven J. and Polak J.B. (1987), 'Regional impacts of new transport infrastructure: a multi-sectoral potentials approach', *Transportation*, 14, pp. 113-126.

Evers G.H.M. and Oosterhaven J. (1988), 'Transportation, frontier effects and regional development in the Common Market', *Papers of Regional Science Association*, 64, pp. 37-51.

Gwilliam K.M. (1979), 'Transport infrastructure investment and regional development', in Bowers, J.K. (ed), *Inflation, Development and Integration*, Leeds University Press, Leeds.

Haughwout A. (1992), 'Measuring the impact of fiscal policy: a theoretical and empirical examination', Paper to 39th North American Annual Meetings, Regional Science Association International, Chicago, November.

Henderson J.V. (1988), *Urban Development: Theory, Fact and Illusion*, Oxford University Press, Oxford.

Holliday I.M., Marcou G. and Vickerman R.W. (1991), *The Channel Tunnel: Public Policy, Regional Development and European Integration*, Belhaven Press, London.

Holliday I.M. and Vickerman R.W. (1990), 'The Channel Tunnel and regional development: policy responses in Britain and France', *Regional Studies*, 24, pp. 455-466.

Illeris S. and Jakobsen L. (1991), 'The effects of the fixed link across the Great Belt', in Vickerman, R.W. (ed) *Infrastructure and Regional Development*, European Research in Regional Science vol 1, Pion, London.

Kay J.A., Manning A. and Szymanski S. (1989), 'The economic benefits of the Channel Tunnel', *Economic Policy*, 8, pp. 211-234.

Keeble D., Owens P.L. and Thompson C. (1982a), 'Regional accessibility and economic potential in the European Community', *Regional Studies*, 16, pp. 419-432.

Keeble D., Owens P.L. and Thompson C. (1982b), 'Economic potential and the Channel Tunnel', *Area*, 14, pp. 97-103.

163

Krugman P. (1991a), 'Increasing returns and economic geography', *Journal of Political Economy*, 99, pp. 483-499.

Krugman P. (1991b), *Geography and Trade*, MIT Press, Cambridge MA.

Krugman P. and Venables A.J. (1990), 'Integration and the competitiveness of peripheral industry', in Bliss, C.J. and Braga de Macedo, J. (eds) *Unity with Diversity in the European Community: the Community's Southern Frontier*, Cambridge University Press, Cambridge.

Le Maire D. and Pevsner M. (1992), 'Eurotunnel: the development of traffic forecasts for a private sector project', in Bovy, P.H.L. and Smit, H.G. (eds) *Financing European Transport*, European Transport Planning Colloquium Foundation, Delft.

Liew C.K. and Liew C.J. (1985), 'Measuring the development impact of a transportation system: a simplified approach', *Journal of Regional Science*, 25, pp. 241-257.

Madsen B. and Jensen-Butler C. (1991), 'The regional economic effects of the Danish Great Belt Link and related traffic system improvements', Paper to 31st European Congress of Regional Science Association, Lisbon, August.

Marchetti C. (1991), 'Building bridges and tunnels: the effects on the evolution of traffic', in Montanari, A. (ed) *Under and Over the Water: The Economic and Social Effects of Building Bridges and Tunnels*, Edizioni Scientifiche Italiane, Naples.

Mehta S., Crihfield J.B. and Giertz J.F. (1992), 'Economic growth in the American states: the end of convergence?', Working Paper No 20, Institute of Government and Public Affairs, University of Illinois, June.

Munnell A.H. (1990), 'How does public infrastructure affect regional economic performance?' in Munnell, A.H. (ed), *Is There a Shortfall in Public Capital Investment?* Conference Series No 34, Federal Reserve Bank of Boston.

Rietveld P. (1989a), 'Employment effects of changes in transportation infrastructure: methodological aspects of the gravity model', *Papers of Regional Science Association*, 66, pp. 19-30.

Rietveld P. (1989b), 'Infrastructure and regional development: a survey of multiregional economic models', *Annals of Regional Science*, 23, pp. 255–274.

Round Table of European Industrialists (1988) *Need for Renewing Transport Infrastructure in Europe*, Brussels.

Straszheim M. (1972), 'Researching the role of transport in regional development', *Land Economics*, 48, pp. 212-219.

Vickerman R.W. (1987), 'The Channel Tunnel: consequences for regional growth and development', *Regional Studies*, 21, pp. 187-197.

Vickerman R.W. (1989), 'Measuring changes in regional competitiveness: the effects of international infrastructure investments', *Annals of Regional Science*, 23, pp. 275-286.

Vickerman R.W. (1991a), 'Transport infrastructure in the European Community: new developments, regional implications and evaluation', in Vickerman, R.W. (ed), *Infrastructure and Regional Development*, European Research in Regional Science vol 1, Pion, London.

Vickerman R.W. (1991b), 'Other regions' infrastructure in a region's development', in Vickerman, R.W. (ed), *Infrastructure and Regional*

Development, European Research in Regional Science vol 1, Pion, London.

Vickerman R.W. (1992a), 'The impact of the Single European Market and new transport infrastructure in border regions', in Bovy, P.H.L. and Smit, H.G. (eds), *Financing European Transport*, European Transport Planning Colloquium Foundation, Delft.

Vickerman R.W. (1992b), 'Private provision of transport: lessons from the Channel Tunnel', in *Transport Policies*, vol III of selected Proceedings of 6th World Conference on Transport Research, Lyon, 1992, pp. 1757-1768, LET, Lyon, April 1993.

Vickerman R.W. (1992c), 'The regional impact of high speed railways in NW Europe', in *Demand, Traffic and Network Modelling*, vol II of selected Proceedings of 6th World Conference on Transport Research, Lyon 1992, pp.1247-1258, LET, Lyon, April 1993.

Vickerman R.W. (1992d), *The Single European Market: Prospects for Economic Integration*, Harvester Wheatsheaf, Hemel Hempstead.

Vickerman R.W. (1993), 'Changing European transport infrastructures and their regional implications', in Nijkamp, P. (ed) *New Borders and Old Barriers in Spatial Development*, Avebury, Aldershot, forthcoming.

10 Communication infrastructure and possible future spatial scenarios

R. Capello and A. Gillespie

10.1   Introduction

Few changes are having a greater impact on the ability of firms and countries to compete in global markets than the recent and ongoing revolution in telecommunications and transport. The new capabilities of information processing and transmission, as well as the enhanced mobility of people and the movement of freight, are profoundly altering features upon which the competitiveness of firms and the comparative advantages of regions depend.

The key forces generating a new industrial and spatial structuring are embodied in the radical technological changes currently underway in the telecommunications and transport industries. Communications and transport networks can be regarded as the 'carriers', in both literal and symbolic senses, of new systems of industrial and spatial organization.

The idea of communications and transport as the carriers of new industrial and spatial forms is of course not new. Many commentators have drawn attention to the historical association between advances in transport and/or communications technologies and changes in the nature of society, changes in the way the economy is organized, and changes in spatial structure and organization (see, among others, Giaoutzi and Nijkamp, 1988; Soekka et al., 1990; Nijkamp et al., 1990; Brunn and Leinback, 1991; Brotchie et al., 1991; Hepworth and Ducatel, 1991).

In one sense, the very existence of the city can be understood as the spatial response to the severe limitations upon the movement of people, and goods, and information which prevailed before, and during the early stages of, the industrial era (Moses and Williamson, 1967; Walker, 1981). As Schaeffer and Sclar (1975, p.8) put it, "to avoid transportation, mankind invented the city".

In contributing to this debate, our approach contains a number of points of departure from conventional approaches:

1   first of all, this study is based on a simultaneous analysis of both transport and communications. The analysis of technological innovation which we develop proceeds on the basis of a strong interrelationship existing between transport and telecommunications technologies, an interrelationship witnessed for example by a host of IT applications applied to the transport sector. This relationship goes well beyond simple

technological linkages and manifests itself in the joint capacities these technologies have to impact on the spatial structure of the economy;

2   secondly, the analysis is based on a constant awareness that, although technological changes in telecommunications and transport are the catalyst for spatial dynamics, they are only necessary but not sufficient conditions for these dynamics. The reason for this assumption is twofold;
- technological changes are developed and generated on the basis of economic, industrial and institutional forces governing their development trajectories. By this we mean, for example, the institutional changes governing the telecommunications sector, which acts in effect as a 'gatekeeper' for the development of new information technologies.
- even with a rapid development and diffusion of these new technologies, changes in spatial structure and organization only take place if they are accompanied by modifications in locational preferences at the level of the firm. This is also true at an industrial level, where locational patterns reflect the industrial and economic equilibria arising from interlinked locational preferences;

3   another distinct feature of the present study is that despite most frequent analyses trying to capture a direct link between technological changes and spatial patterns, this study stresses the interrelationship between technological changes, new organizational forms of production and spatial trajectories. The organizational variable is regarded as a fundamental and crucial 'bridge' to capture the linkages between technological changes and spatial dynamics. The relationship between these three variables are neither linear nor unidirectional, being best regarded as a circular set of interconnections, making the definition of the original causes of changes not easy to define (see Section 10.2 below);

4   the present study adopts a two level approach, a micro and a macro level, for studying changes in organizational and spatial structures, related respectively to the firm and the industrial system as a whole;

5   a final characteristic of the analysis is that no single, unique trajectory of change in the industrial and spatial structures can be identified for the future. The development trajectories for these industrial and spatial structures are obviously related to the development of transport and telecommunications technologies, but these in turn depend on the development trajectories of some other crucial elements, including technological innovation, the diffusion and application of technologies throughout the industrial system, and the institutional framework within which diffusion takes place - concerning for example the structure of markets and how they are regulated, standards issues, etc. These elements can follow a number of different development paths, each of them leading to a different pattern of usage of transport and telecommunication technologies and consequently to the constitution of different industrial and spatial structure scenarios. For these reasons, in this paper we refer to differing possible scenarios in the development of the industrial and spatial structure and we consider which of them is most likely to take place, given some key considerations. Before considering these scenarios, however, the next section explores in rather more detail the complex nature of causality in the relationships between transport and communications and

168

spatial organization.

10.2 Understanding the interrelationships and the circular nature of causality

As established in the previous section, our concern in this paper is with the nature of the interrelationships between transport and communications on the one hand, and organizational and spatial structures on the other, during a period of major structural change, change which is affecting all of these elements, and the relationships between them, simultaneously. With so many simultaneous changes taking place, understanding the direction(s) of causality is by no means straightforward. In this section, we begin to 'unpack' the complex interrelationships at work, and in so doing attempt to establish the framework which we will use in the following section for presenting a range of future transport and communication scenarios.

One of the driving forces affecting both transport and communications is of course technological innovation (Table 10.1). The interesting aspect analyzed in this paper is that technological innovation is not only affecting the development of transport and communications but also the interrelationship between them. New complementarities, as well as some new substitution possibilities, are being created by innovations in the physical movement of information, people and goods over transport networks, and their electronic communication over telecommunications networks.

From the point of view of our objectives in this paper, however, the significance of the types of technological innovation considered above lies in the way they interact with, or modify, or limit, the behaviour of organizations and, in the longer term, the spatial organization of the economic system. The complex nature of the interrelationships between these various elements, particularly as concerns causality, can best be illustrated by means of examples. Below three such examples are used to demonstrate the relationships between changes in transport/communications, organizational behaviour and spatial structure. Each has a different causal 'starting point', for there is no single direction of causality, the different elements being bound together in a web of two-way interactions.

Example 1: Technological innovation

The first example starts with a technological innovation, EDI, which is, simultaneously, both a transport/communication innovation, affecting the flow of information associated with the movement of goods, and an organizational innovation, affecting the relationship between customer and supplier. EDI can have significant implications for the behaviour of the firm and for organizational structure more generally; it can contribute to improving the internal efficiency of the firm, through automating existing labour intensive procedures; it can improve the competitive position of adopters, by speeding up their response to customer orders; and, in the longer term, through reducing transaction costs, it can even shift the boundary of the firm by affecting the 'make or buy' decision (Williamson, 1975).

Table 10.1
Major areas of innovation in Transport and Communication

MODE / MOVEMENT OF	(PHYSICAL) TRANSPORT	(ELECTRONICS) COMMUNICATION
INFORMATION	Express Courier services	High speed fax Electronic mail Computer networks (e.g. for CAD) Videotex/Teletex
PEOPLE	High speed trains Road informatics Information and booking systems	Work stations with slow–scan video images Video–conferencing
GOODS	Logistical systems	EDI Facsimile trasnmission of printed materials Computer networks for just–in–time delivery

EDI can also be expected to have implications for the spatial organization of production systems; by reducing one element of transaction costs, and by improving the overall efficiency of the transactional system, EDI is likely to contribute to the spatial extension of production linkages and, hence, to the viability of global production systems. Further, as EDI becomes more widely adopted and centrally embedded into the organization of production, the ability of locations to support sophisticated electronic communications for EDI will become a prerequisite for inward-investment. In the longer term, therefore, it can be suggested that EDI will affect, at a variety of scales from the urban-rural to the international, the relative locational attractions of different places for productive investments.

Finally, the 'wheel comes full circle' (appropriately enough, given the nature of the example), with these EDI-led organizational and spatial adaptations imposing new requirements upon the transport system, for example to support larger volumes of long-distance freight movement.

Example 2: Organizational change

Our second example, based on an actual firm (documented in more detail in Capello and Williams, 1990), breaks into the transport/ communication/ organizational behaviour/ spatial organization web of inter-relationships at a different point; it starts not with a technological innovation but with a perceived need for organizational change. The firm in question, which produces agricultural fertilizers and pesticides, recognized that its marketing effort was inconsistent and fragmented. The existing marketing effort was dispersed around its many production sites, and the firm decided to centralize the marketing function into three sites.

The reorganization of the marketing function within the firm thus had an explicit spatial dimension, and at once imposed new requirements upon the firms' communications infrastructure. A new computer communication network was implemented, linking the head office with the three new regional sales and marketing offices. At the same time the pattern of business travel within the firm changed substantially, both between the head office and the three marketing centres and between the sales offices and the firm's customers.

Example 3: Spatial restructuring

The final example, like the second an actual firm (documented in more detail in Goddard, 1990), starts from the need to reorganize the spatial structure of the firm, this time in response to a geographical shift in the firm's markets. The firm, based in the north of England and making timber doors and window frames, saw its existing northern market contract substantially with the demise of council-house building in the 1980s. Southern markets were growing vigorously with the boom in 'do-it-yourself', but serving these markets necessitated meeting much shorter order to delivery cycles than the firm was capable of with its existing production organization.

The geography of the firm's production organization was completely restructured, without having to close existing sites or open new ones, and a computer network implemented in order to support a very different set of interlinkages between the firm's production sites and with its final markets. As a result of this reorganization, patterns of movement of both intermediate and final products have changed completely, and the volumes of movement substantially increased. The higher transport costs have, however, been more than compensated for by production economies of scale and by the firm's improved responsiveness to customer orders which the computer network has made possible, resulting in increased market share and improved competitiveness.

As these examples demonstrate, there is no single direction of causality in the complex interactions between transport, communications, organizational behaviour and spatial structure. The circle by which they are interconnected can be broken into anywhere, in the sense of a change in any one element of the system then affecting each of the other elements. The 'starting point' adopted in any examination of these interrelationships is nevertheless significant, indicating a choice, a conceptualization of the main dynamics of the system of interconnections under investigation.

A familiar, indeed conventional, approach to understanding the types of interrelationships with which we are concerned would be to focus on the 'impacts' of new technology; starting therefore with the major changes taking place in the technologies of transport and communications, and following through their impacts upon organizational behaviour and spatial organization, an approach adopted for example in the EDI case outlined above.

In the remainder of this paper, however, we choose a different starting point, reflecting the conceptualization with which we interpreted of transport and communications as 'carriers' of particular paradigms of industrial and spatial organization. Our contention is that Europe is moving towards a new paradigm of industrial and spatial organization, one which is different in certain key respects from the model of growth which has been hegemonic in Europe since the 1950s, and which we labelled in the introduction as 'Fordism'. Just as transport and communications developed along certain paths during the Fordist era, helping indeed that paradigm to be realized, to be viable, so a new paradigm of economic organization, a successor to Fordism as it were, will make new demands upon the transport and communications system.

It follows that if we wish to try and understand what transport and communications will be like beyond the immediate and relatively predictable future, say in Europe 2020, then it will be necessary to attempt to understand first what type of industrial and spatial organization will be prevailing at that time. If we are right in our contention that the present period of restructuring is indicative of a new paradigm of economic organization, then a reading of what it is that is new about that paradigm (and indeed what it is that is not), at least as it is likely to effect the demand for transport and communications, will be an essential starting point.

This is not of course to deny the strong element of circular causality that we have discussed above, for future developments in transport and communications will no doubt facilitate forms of industrial and spatial organization which are not currently viable. Our belief, however, is that starting with the changes now occurring in such organization, and tracing through their implications for transport and communications, will prove to be a better choice in predictive terms than starting with a new technology-led prediction of transport and communication in the year 2020, and then trying to read off the 'impacts' they are likely to have on economic and spatial organization.

We are surely all too familiar with the inadequacies of futurological predictions based on the supposed power of new technologies to 'transform' society and its spatial organization. The strong element of wishful thinking behind such predictions often seems to be motivated by a sense of frustration with the complexities and perceived inadequacies of society as it is presently constituted. Rather than grappling with these complexities in the real world, how much easier it is to envisage a new society, constituted around the liberating potential of new technology. The field of transport and communications research is not unfamiliar with this type of discourse, which can be regarded as harmless or dangerous depending on your point of view; either way, it is not science, or social science, and should be left to the science fiction shelves.

Our own conceptual preference is then to start not with the impact of changes in transport and communication on economic and spatial organization, but rather with the less superficially exciting, albeit more challenging, task of considering the implications of changes in economic and spatial organization for transport and communications.

10.3 Transport and communications and the spatial structure of Fordism

The concept of 'Fordism' is a broad and farreaching attempt to capture the essential characteristics of what the French Regulation School define as a distinctive 'model of development' under capitalism. According to Leborgne and Lipietz (1988), a model of development involves a conjunction of three sets of relationships; firstly a 'technological paradigm', a set of general principles which govern the evolution of the organization of labour; secondly, a 'regime of accumulation', the macroeconomic principle describing the long-term compatibility between levels of production and of consumption; and, thirdly, a 'mode of regulation', the forms of individual and collective adjustment which enable the regime of accumulation to be sustained.

Fordism is one such conjunction, which Mathews (1991, p. 125) suggests "is now seen as the dominant political-economic framework of the twentieth century". This framework or growth model became established in the United States in the inter-war period and diffused to Europe in the period of post-war reconstruction, producing 'a twenty-five year golden age' of capitalism (Lipietz, 1986), but which has since the 1970s sustained a number of interrelated setbacks which have undermined its continued viability.

The dominant 'technological paradigm' under Fordism can be summarized as one of mass production and Taylorist work organization, the 'regime of accumulation' that of a mass consumption counterpart to mass production, and the 'mode of regulation' as the combination of collective wage bargaining, the hegemony of large corporations, Keynesian demand management and the welfare state (Leborgne and Lipietz, 1988; Boyer, 1988). Our concern below is only with the first of these three interlocking elements, that which deals with the organization of the Fordist system of production. We begin by outlining the main features of this system, paying particular attention to its spatial organization, before considering Fordism's transport and communications requirements (see Table 10.2 for a summary and a comparison with the two scenarios presented in Section 10.4).

10.3.1 Fordist industrial and spatial organization

The basic rationale behind mass production was the reduction of cost by standardizing the production of parts, and the use of repetitive methods to substitute for skilled labour. Piore and Sabel (1984) characterize the rise of the mass production system as a first 'industrial divide', differentiating it from craft and batch production methods. Although these previously established forms of industrialization continued to coexist with Fordist mass-production, the enormous productivity improvements which the latter made possible rapidly came to dominate in those sectors, such as cars and consumer durables, for which mass markets could be developed. As articulated by Scott (1988):

> "These sectors, in their classical form, are distinguished by a search for massive internal economies of scale based on assembly line methods, technical divisions of labour and standardization of outputs. The Fordist elements of the system comprise, in their essentials, the deskilling of labour by means of the fragmentation of work tasks while integrating the human operator into the whole machinery of production in such a manner as to reduce to the minimum discretionary control over motions and rhythms of work" (p.173).

The technical embodiment of Fordist production principles, the semiautomatic assembly line (Aglietta, 1982), can be seen as a device not only for increasing output but, as importantly, for gaining control over the pace and organization of production, combining the technical requirements of a shift from batch to flow production with a new drive for management control (Mathews, 1991).

This form of 'hard automation' proved very successful in achieving high rates of productivity growth for standardized, mass produced goods. An appropriate vehicular analogy for Fordist production organization at this microlevel would be the steamroller; a large, rather cumbersome, but crushingly efficient piece of machinery designed for and dedicated to a particular task, and extremely difficult to deflect once it is in motion. These same characteristics, however, proved rather less effective when the erosion of mass markets and the need for constant product innovation required not a steamroller but an adaptable all-terrain vehicle!

At the level of the industrial system as a whole, Fordism was characterized by large, vertically-integrated firms. Partly this stemmed from the internal economies of scale in production associated with its technological basis, but of considerable importance too was the need to coordinate and reintegrate the considerable technical division of labour which Fordism engendered. Quite simply, this coordination and reintegration task was more effectively handled, and with lower transaction costs, by the corporate hierarchy than by the external market.

The spatial form of the Fordist system of production organization was of course integral to that system, for, as Walker (1988, p.385) argues, "it is impossible to separate the organizational from the geographical", as "capitalist organization is constituted in and through spatial relations". At the broad regional scale, Allan Scott (1988) has described the spatial form of Fordism, at the peak of its development, as:

"associated with a series of great industrial regions in North America and western Europe, as represented by the Manufacturing Belt of the United States and the zone of industrial development in Europe stretching from the Midlands of England through northern France, Belgium and Holland to the Ruhr of West Germany, with many additional outlying districts at various locations. These locations were the locational foci of propulsive industrial sectors driving forward, through intricate input-output connections, dense systems of upstream producers" (p.173).

The geography of Fordism was associated in particular with major metropolitan regions, for it was the large city that provided the agglomerations of labour required for mass production. However, although this spatial form characterized what we might describe as 'early' Fordism, its spatial expression evolved and changed over time. Schoenberger (1988, p.255) suggests that this evolutionary tendency involved a shift from "initial massive industrial agglomerations in the core to decentralization and increasing dispersal of production towards the periphery".

This shift reflects an internal dynamic within Fordist production which, more so than any previous form of industrialization, came to use space and spatial differentiation as active elements of accumulation (Harvey, 1987). The Taylorist principles of work organization embodied in the Fordist mass production system involved a constant search for ways of improving profitability through the division of labour. The 'technical disintegration' of the production process, into separate shops within a plant and then into an interplant division of labour, was so sharp that it could be increasingly realized as a 'territorial disintegration' (Leborgne and Lipietz, 1988), in which different plants could be optimally located according to the type of labour they needed.

The spatial form of the industrial system thus underwent significant changes with the evolution of Fordism. The earlier form of geographical specialization based on sectors became a functional specialization associated with the increasing refinement of the division of labour within the firm, with certain regions coming to specialize as centres of corporate control, others as concentrations of research and development, others as semi- or unskilled production 'branch plants' (Hymer, 1972; Lipietz, 1975; Massey, 1984). The 'spatial division of labour' within 'late' Fordism soon became international as well as interregional, as the progressive deskilling of elements within the production process enabled the large vertically integrated Fordist corporation to take advantage of even cheaper unskilled labour in the Third World periphery (Frobel et al, 1980; Lipietz, 1986).

10.3.2 Fordism's transport and communications requirements

The increasingly complex spatial organization of production which evolved under Fordism imposed very considerable requirements upon the transport and communications system (Table 10.2). Indeed, it is clear that the pattern of production characterized above as 'late Fordism', with its high degree of territorial disaggregation and dispersed production, would not have been viable without significant innovation in both transport and telecommunications. As noted by Frobel et al (1980, p. 36), in their analysis of the new international division of labour, this form of industrial development is predicated upon "a technology which renders industrial location and the management of production itself largely independent of geographical distance".

How, and to what extent, were these requirements met? In the transport field, significant improvements have taken place since the 1960s which have benefited exactly the type of long-distance, regular, standardized commodity flow demanded by the (late) Fordist production system (Pedesen, 1985). Containerization, and the long-distance motorway networks which have so facilitated freight movement by truck, can be regarded then as the necessary transport concomitants of Fordist production organization. As van Hoogstraten and Janssen (1985) have argued in the case of the Netherlands:

> "it is more than contingent that the generalization of the network of motorways, spread from the western part of the Netherlands over the rest, has run concurrently with the decentralization of production".

In addition to the routinized long-distance movement of intermediate and final production, Fordism also required that reliable systems of voice communication be in place to permit the long-distance control and coordination of spatially dispersed production. Beyond voice telephony, the advent of computer networking in the 1970s clearly further facilitated the process of decentralization. Thus according to Perrons (1981, p.251), "neo-Fordist labour processes, based on electronic information systems with automatic feedback mechanisms... meant that locations in peripheral areas were technically feasible".

The vertically integrated nature of Fordist production organization places considerable emphasis on intracorporate flows of information. One of the main requirements of Fordism in terms of communications infrastructure is, in consequence, the provision of point-to-point voice and computer networks by means of leased circuits. The evidence concerning the geography of computer networking in the UK shows that such networks are indeed used almost exclusively for intraorganizational communication (Daniels, 1987), and suggests further that the use of dedicated private circuits is highest in those regions most clearly associated with the type of decentralized branch plant production associated with the late Fordist spatial division of labour (Diamond and Spence, 1989).

The Fordist system of production organization thus placed very considerable demands on transport and communication infrastructures and networks. Leaving aside the (rather sterile and probably unresolvable) question of whether the requirements of Fordism stimulated the necessary innovation and infrastructure investment, or whether this innovation and investment 'led' the development of new forms of production organization which evolved in order to exploit the new opportunities, it can be concluded that Fordism is clearly associated with major improvements in long distance transport and communication.

Without such improvements, it is evident that the model of decentralized production organization that we have characterized above as late Fordism would not have been viable, for this model demanded both the efficient long-distance movement of intermediate goods as well as final production, and the space-transcending control and coordination of complex multilocational enterprises.

10.3.3 The crisis of Fordist production organization

There is by now a substantial body of literature on the reasons why the Fordist system of mass-production ran, in the 1970s and 1980s, into increasing problems. Some see the breakup of mass markets due to changing consumer taste as the key; others the undermining of Fordism's production heartlands by the rise of low wage industrialization in the Third World; others again the technical rigidities of Fordist production organization itself.

The idea of Fordism reaching limits determined by its own internal logic is associated in particular with the French Regulation school, following and building upon the work of Aglietta (1982). He concentrated on the limits of Taylorist task fragmentation, and on the technical limitations of the assembly line in a period of unstable market conditions. Roobeek (1987) sees Fordism as coming up against a series of problems of control, problems which include not only the control over the labour process within the factory but also control over the complex spatial divisions of labour which Fordist production organization had engendered.

Although improvements in transport and communications had been instrumental in the emergence and evolution of Fordist production organization, there were clearly limits to the Fordist system's ability to transcend space and to overcome distance. As with so many of the other characteristics of Fordism, these limits became critical when more volatile and segmented market conditions necessitated much greater flexibility and responsiveness. Responses to the crisis of Fordism would thus need to address, inter alia, the limitations imposed by spatial organization and by transport and communication systems. It is to these responses, to the possible successors to Fordism, that we now turn.

10.4 Transport and communications and the possible successors to Fordism

10.4.1 A re-invigorated 'neo-Fordism'?

One significant possibility which needs evaluating is that developments in transport and communications networks and systems can help to resolve the crisis of Fordist production organization. Following Piore and Sabel (1984),

Rubery et al. (1987) argue that competitive success now depends not on achieving economies of scale in established mass markets, but rather on securing new markets, developing new competitive strategies for meeting changing demand requirements, and increasing the responsiveness of the organization to market changes. One of the present authors has suggested elsewhere (Gillespie and Williams, 1990; Gillespie, 1991) that developments in telematics offer important possibilities of achieving a more 'flexible Fordism'.

The scope for establishing a reinvigorated form of neo-Fordism has been considered in a number of recent contributions (see, for example, Leborgne and Lipietz, 1988; Mathews, 1991). However, even if some of the control and co-ordination problems of Fordism can be overcome by means of innovation in transport and communications systems, there remain questions over the long term viability of Fordist principles of production organization. As Mathews (1991, p.131-2) contends:

"Fordism, with its Taylorist fragmentation of jobs, deskilling and divorce of conception from execution, is becoming less and less relevant. It was 'productive' and 'efficient' only under the very special conditions prevailing within mass production".

In the new reality of segmented, rapidly changing markets, in which a considerable competitive premium is placed upon product innovation and upon responsiveness to market shifts, the hierarchical fragmentation of the Fordist system of production organization is simply no longer optimal. This of course is not to deny that 'Fordist' enterprises can adapt to the changing circumstances, and re-establish the basis for profitable production, as many clearly have been able to do. We would argue, however, that in so doing they have shed many of the key defining characteristics of Fordism. In the remainder of this paper, we turn our attention to two different interpretations of a post-Fordist industrial future, and to the transport and communication implications of these competing scenarios.

10.4.2 The 'Flexible Specialization' scenario

10.4.2.1 Industrial and spatial organization

The 'flexible specialization' model of industrial organization was formulated by Piore and Sabel (1984), drawing upon an interpretation of developments in the so called 'third Italy'. Conceptually, this model rests on the assumption that the economic weaknesses of Fordism need to be overcome, and a new industrial and spatial structure of the economy established, possessing a number of different, indeed oppositional, characteristics to that of Fordism. Thus if Fordism was primarily concerned with mass production and mass consumption and with the exploitation of economies of scale, the flexible specialization scenario rests on the idea of product customization, volatility of markets and demand, and the exploitation of economies of scope (Table 10.2).

Because of its oppositional view to Fordism, this school of thought is heralding, indeed often celebrating, a 'post-Fordist' future, one which marks a radical change and a break with the previous model of industrial development.

It is at once evident that the 'second industrial divide' predicted by Piore and Sabel conceptually implies the development of a new industrial order, in which the industrial and spatial forces of equilibrium are related to quite different economic and industrial features and to new corporate strategies. Moreover, associated with the flexible specialization scenario is the potential for the different development pattern of transport and communications systems, because of the different transactional and relational economic structures they will be required to support.

The generation of this scenario will thus have profound implications for both the micro and the macro level. At the micro level, the emergence of the 'flexible specialization' system rests on the assumption that mass production will be replaced by an industrial organizational model concerned rather with small batch production, regarded as a more suitable model of production organization for dealing with dynamic markets, displaying both high levels of vulnerability and volatility of demand.

A consequent outcome of batch production is the exploitation of economies of scope rather than the traditional economies of scale (directly concerned with mass production and consumption). Economies of scope are those economies of joint production resulting from the use of a single set of facilities to produce, or process, more than one product, under dynamic market conditions (Chandler, 1986; Teece, 1980; Jelinek and Goldhar, 1983).

Moreover, the flexible specialization scenario will generate a radical shift of demand away from mass consumption products in favour of differentiated, personalized outputs. Demand for a variety of products will increasingly replace demand for cheap and standardized products, and this will create more scope for the development of small, specialized firms. Demand needs will then more and more generate a process of customization of products, thus rejecting the idea of mass production and favouring a more differentiated production model.

In this scenario, the functional specialization of Fordism will be substituted by functional integration, conceptually overcoming once again the limits of the present structure. It has in fact long been recognized by organization scholars that the profound functional specialization of the large enterprise, designed to achieve economies of scale and higher professional knowhow, presents the risk of internal segmentation and bureaucratization, and in particular a loss in terms of the efficient exploitation of information arising from everyday operations in each department (Camagni, 1988). A functional integration model can, it is argued, overcome this inefficient and rigid structure, a structure which is completely inadequate in periods of high market volatility. Cross-functional work can generate useful synergies between functions, especially in terms of innovation.

The model of the large hierarchical firm, designed to be the most efficient industrial model of production, will increasingly give way to more decentralized organizational forms, in which the transfer of intermediate responsibility to lower levels in the organization takes place, assisted by the capabilities of the new technologies. By facilitating online remote communication and decision-support, these technologies can help to decentralize decision making processes to peripheral areas and to lower organizational levels.

All of these changes in intrafirm organization are supported and fostered by developments in so called 'soft' automation, by which is meant automation technologies consisting of a high percentage of software components and with a high reprogrammability capacity. The exploitation of economies of scope can be achieved only through the use of reprogrammable technologies, able to produce a variety of products with the same capital resource.

Major changes will also affect the industrial system as a whole, and, once again, the new rules governing the industrial and spatial structure of the economy will have characteristics that are opposed in many ways to those that prevailed under Fordism.

The large firm model of the vertically-integrated firm, with its strongly centralized decision making power, will be substituted by vertically-disintegrated systems, based on a series of specialized medium sized and small firms. Under this scenario we can thus envisage a radical segmentation of markets, reconstituted into 'firm networks': a group of small and medium sized firms, legally independent from one another, but very much vertically integrated within a particular production process through cooperative interfirm linkages. Moreover, these interfirm linkages are likely to be based on single sourcing relationships (Burns and Stalker, 1979; Antonelli, 1988).

On the basis of the characteristics of this industrial system it is relatively easy to configure its future spatial structure. The high degree of specialization of interlinked firms will lead towards the development of complementary regional and urban systems, specialized in different final products and based on local specialized labour market needs (Mouleart and Swyngedouw, 1988).

A spatial clustering will be the expected consequence, characterized by frequent linkages taking place over short distances; the development of specialized local areas, or 'industrial districts', such as Prato and Silicon Valley, in which the industrial system is governed by a high level of product specialization, can be regarded as contemporary exemplars of the flexible specialization scenario (Becattini, 1988; Scott, 1988; Camagni and Capello, 1990).

10.4.2.2 Transport and communications patterns and infrastructure requirements: policy options and priorities

The picture of the industrial and spatial system drawn above is the basis for the configuration of possible transport and communications development patterns, their future infrastructure requirements and appropriate policy options to support this scenario (summarized in Figure 10.2).

The high specialization level achieved by firms and production areas will generate long distance final product movement to markets, because of the highly spatially segmented market division. For intermediate goods, conversely, the spatial clustering phenomenon and the development of local industrial districts will result in short distance intermediate product movements (cf Pedersen, 1985).

Another consequence of the spatial clustering and of the development of local districts is the frequent, short-distance movement of people involved in meetings; frequent face-to-face contact can be regarded as essential for generating and maintaining the cooperative and trust based relationships upon which the flexible specialization model of production organization rests. For sales and marketing activities, conversely, long distance travel is to be expected, necessary because of local (urban and regional) product specialization and of the high degree of market segmentation.

Vertically disintegrated systems require a well developed information axis, around which both inter- and intracorporate information flows will be transmitted. These information flows, both intra- and intercorporate, will be used primarily to transport horizontal information, ie. information among functions at the same level in the hierarchical structure, or, in the case of intercorporate information flows, among firms at the same level in the production chain. This type of highly specialized and disintegrated production system requires a strong mechanism to ensure synergies, both between functions and firms, resting on a well-developed information system.

These patterns of transport and communication - of goods, people and information - require a future implementation of transport and communications systems able to cope with and support the new industrial and spatial structures. Unpredictable, fluctuating quantities of goods movement, for example, require a highly flexible transport system, able to cope with frequent movements of small quantities, rather than with the predictable, less frequent, larger volumes of transported goods that characterized Fordism.

The highly disintegrated local districts' model will thus increase both short distance, frequent, intermediate product movements as well as long distance, frequent, final product movements, and will necessitate reliable, frequent, regional interconnected passenger transport networks, efficient local telephone and fax networks and local computer networks.

Considerable effort is already being made in Europe to up-grade and improve long-distance transport and telecommunication networks. Consequent to the above discussion, however, a further important policy priority in the future development of transport and communications infrastructures would be to focus on the upgrading of local and regional transport and communications systems; the development of regional and metropolitan light railway networks, for example, or local digital telematics networks.

The Sprint project, developed in the Prato area (a local district in Italy), provides an interesting example of the latter. The attempt has been to create a local digitalized computer network, interconnecting all economic agents of the area and providing them with a local intercompany networked information axis (De Braband and Manacorda, 1985; Mazzonis, 1985; Rullani and Zanfei, 1988; Zanfei, 1986). The failure of the Sprint project can be explained, first, by its premature appearance in an area without a developed telematics culture and, second, by the threat it posed to the established power relationships embodied in the existing transactional structure (Camagni and Capello, 1991; Capello and Williams, 1992). However, in the 'flexible specialization' scenario of the future such limits will be likely to be overcome, both by a diffused telematics culture and by profound changes in the division of labour, in which more symmetrical and synergetic horizontal linkages will become established.

The development of this scenario will inevitably heighten the tension between the frequent freight movements required and the capacity of the road network to absorb such movements. Consequently, policy priorities should also be given to projects designed to improve roads at regional and national levels.

Table 10.2
Main features of the past industrial and spatial organization and of the two possible future scenarios: infrastructure requirements and policy options

	Fordist Organization	Organization Flexible Specialization Scenario	Scenario Local-Global
Industrial Organization	Economies of scale	Economies of scope	New equilibrium between economies of scale and scope
Micro	Mass production	Small batch production	Diversified mass production
Macro	Hard automation	Soft automation	Systems automation
	Vertically integrated systems	Vertically disintegrated systems	Quasi-vertical integration
	Large firms dominated	Firms network	Asymmetrical but stable linkage arrangements between producers and suppliers
Spatial Organization	Spatial division of labour within multilocational enterprises	Spatial clustering	New management of territory (same geography of the economic space of the firm with different functional locations) New logistical platforms
Transport and Communications Patterns	Long distance intermediate product movement to assembly sites	Long distance final product movement to markets	Long distance movement of both intermediate and final products
	Regional functional specialization	Short distance intermediate product movement	Increase in horizontal intercorporate information flows
Infrastructure requirements	Reliable long distance goods transport of standard quantity predictable in advance	Frequent face-to-face contacts	Long distance airfreight and other long distance goods movements coupled with short distance frequent delivery road based on local systems
	Reliable long distance communications	Long distance flexible final product movements	
		Increased short distance frequent intermediate transport system	Long distance computer networks
Policy Options and Priorities		Development of regional transport and digitalized local networks	Development of long distance transport and computer networks

182

10.4.3 The 'Network Firm' or 'Global-Local' scenario

10.4.3.1 Industrial and spatial organization

Some doubts must remain over the prospects for both the 'neo- Fordism' and the 'flexible specialization' scenarios. While the first rests on the assumption that the 'crisis of Fordism' can be internally resolved and overcome, and a new or at least modified regime built upon the old industrial and spatial organization, paradoxically the flexible specialization scenario is based on the over-idealistic view that a completely different industrial and spatial structure can be developed, with completely opposite features from those of Fordism (see Amin and Robins, 1990 for a critique of the empirical and theoretical validity of the flexible specialization scenario). Whereas the neo-Fordism view thus maintains that little of importance has changed, the flexible specialization view maintains that little of importance remains. Our own view lies somewhere between these oppositional extremes. On the basis of empirical evidence supporting it, a third and more likely scenario can be envisaged, which we term the 'network firm' or 'global-local' scenario, built on the assumption that the inadequacies of Fordist mass production are overcome, but with less radically oppositional outcomes than those predicted (advocated?) by the flexible specialization school.

This intermediate position is likely to appear both at micro and macro levels (Table 10.2). At the micro level, instead of envisaging the exploitation of either economies of scope or of scale, a new equilibrium between the two will be more likely. In fact, the development of economies of scope stem from the exploitation of reprogrammable production technologies, which require very substantial capital investment, thus necessarily requiring large scale production to be economically viable; ie. the exploitation of economies of scale. Thus, instead of completely substituting for economies of scale, economies of scope will rather compliment and coexist, exploited not only in the 'information handling activities sphere' (Jonscher, 1983), but also in the area of production activities (Capello and Williams, 1990).

Moreover, empirical evidence suggests that the development of new industrial systems strengthens a 'quasi-vertical integration' as the most efficient organizational form of production. There are various intermediate forms of 'quasi-organization' that are assuming an ever more important role as an alternative to full vertically-integrated or vertically-disintegrated production systems. In the terminology of Williamson (1975), these intermediate forms of organization will arise between the two opposite alternatives of 'make or buy', and can be described as the 'make-together' alternative (Camagni and Rabellotti, 1988).

The 'make-together' type of organizational form rests on the need to create synergies and complementarities through partnerships, due in part to the increased complexity and specialization of products and markets. The traditional models of the large, vertically-integrated company on the one hand, and of the small, autonomous, single-phase firm on the other, will be replaced by a new type of large 'network firm', with strongly centralized strategic functions and extending in several directions, and by a new type of small enterprise, integrated into a multicompany local network. Across the network, a system of constantly evolving power relationships governs both the dynamics of innovation and the appropriability of returns to the partners involved.

The 'network firm' will be attracted towards diversified mass production, which is the result of the contemporary exploitation of economies of both scope and scale, and by 'systems automation'; ie. not isolated 'islands of automation', but rather integrated automation systems, through local area networks (LANs) or wide area networks (WANs). Moreover, the integration process will take place between currently standalone procedures, with the positive consequence of an automation of intersphere and interfunction procedures. At the level of bureaucratic procedures, then, functional integration is likely to occur. The 'network firm' will inevitably centralize control at the level of strategic functions, but with the implementation of modern technologies, control over bureaucratic and routinized functions will be decentralized.

The industrial system coming out of this scenario is a reinforcement and generalization of the concept of the 'network firm', consisting of large firms, leading in their respective market specialization, competing with a host of smaller firms. At the level of suppliers, the existence of a 'network firm' will generate asymmetrical but stable linkage arrangements, the asymmetry depending necessarily on the unequal division of power among competing firms.

With respect to spatial organization, the outcome which can be envisaged from this scenario is far less dramatic and severe in its changes than the one suggested above by the 'flexible specialization' scenario. Despite the widespread assumption that the intrinsic capacities of new transport and communications technologies will reshape the geography of firms, it can be argued that the spatial extent of firms will remain, or at least could remain, largely the same.

This assertion is backed by empirical evidence, which suggests that a very different spatial organization can be achieved without the relocation of activities (Goddard, 1991). On the contrary, what will change is the way in which firms exploit their economic space, putting in place a new management of territory within the existing locational parameters of the firm (Williams and Taylor, 1991). In particular, following efficiency and effectiveness aims, firms will try to rationalize their fixed locational assets by physically integrating previously disjointed functions, thereby achieving better economic performance.

Another way of using and exploiting territory more effectively is through the development of new logistical systems, which may well lead to adjustments in the geography of corporate space. The development of central locations for stored goods helps in rationalizing materials purchases and intermediate goods movements, the efficiency of which derives from highly computerized storage systems (Ruijgrok, 1990).

10.4.3.2 Transport and communications and infrastructure requirements: policy options and priorities

A different development pattern emerges from this third configuration of a possible industrial and spatial system (see Table 10.2). This scenario requires long distance movement of both intermediate and final products, accompanied by an increase in short distance final product movement, coordinated through new logistical systems. The consequence is a more intense movement of both intermediate and final products from production sites to storage centres and from them to the final market. Globalization of markets strengthens this phenomenon, augmenting the spatial distribution of products and thus their physical movements.

A rather strong pressure for long distance business travel derives from this scenario, necessitating high volumes of movement between firms and (spatially diffused) customers, and between functions of multisite firms (each of which is expected to be located in one place, avoiding duplication and thus inefficiency). The 'network firm' scenario additionally implies a high volume of business travel associated with cooperative agreements, which may well be international in scope, complemented by well developed and advanced satellite based video conferencing systems.

Moreover, the 'make together' form of organization implies a high volume of information transmitted between firms, in the form of horizontal intercorporate information flows. At the same time, high volumes of vertical intercorporate information flows characterize this scenario, corresponding to the information requirements for asymmetrical but stable linkages with suppliers. Intensive intracorporate information flows will also be necessary in order to develop the types of 'new management of territory' outlined above, involving the relocation of part-functions in one place, thus rationalizing decision-making processes. It is clear that with such a relocation of activities in space, firms will need a constant flow of information, both horizontally (to develop decision making processes) and vertically (because of the decentralized control system).

From the above discussion, a simple consideration comes immediately to mind concerning the infrastructure requirements associated with this scenario. In an industrial and spatial system based on intense long distance movement of people, goods and information, a wide range of transport and communications systems infrastructures will be necessary, including air-freight systems, short distance frequent-delivery road based local systems, high speed trains, air passenger travel, long distance computer networks, and advanced personal communication services (ie. videoconferencing, electronic mail).

Some clear policy priorities emerge from this scenario and from these infrastructure requirements. All policies enhancing long distance transport and communications infrastructures are in this respect useful and efficient policies. The development of international computer networks with Electronic Data Interchange (EDI) applications will be required to deal with the mass of information associated with the new logistical platforms, as will the implementation of ISDN (the Integrated Services Digital Network). With respect to this scenario, then, a top-down policy approach to the development of advanced networks, rather than the bottom-up local network approach embodied in the previous scenario, is much more effective and efficient, dealing with the implementation of international 'information highways' rather than local telematics networks and applications.

This scenario has then clear implications for the development of transport and communications infrastructures. Not only is this new industrial and spatial scenario built on the assumption that long distance, reliable transport and communications networks are implemented, but it rests on the idea that these networks have to be 'integrated networks', both geographically and technologically speaking. The integration of these networks permits the development of the industrial and spatial system outlined above, for a 'quasi-vertically integrated' form of organization requires both an advanced communications infrastructure and a highly reliable complementary transport system.

The integration has to take place at both a geographical and technological level. At a spatial level, we are referring primarily to international networks, designed for long distance transport and communications. Networks which are confined to national territories, whether for the movement of information or people, will be of limited use in sustaining the types of industrial organization predicted under the network firm or global-local scenario. Technological integration is clearly vital for the development of international interconnected networks. Standards problems have to be overcome, both in the telecommunications and transport arenas, in order for genuinely borderless infrastructures to be developed.

With respect to this issue, a group of international experts have developed a project on 'Missing Networks in Europe' for the Round Table of Industrialists, primarily concerned with identifying the discontinuities which exist in international networks, both in transport and communications sectors. The result has pointed out that both telecommunications and transport networks could perform much better if missing networks were addressed, at five different levels (Maggi and Nijkamp, 1992):

- hardware (physical infrastructure)
- software (logistics and information)
- orgware (institutional and organizational setting)
- finware (financial and funding arrangements)
- ecoware (environmental and safety effects)

The interest in avoiding 'missing networks' becomes more crucial once a spatial and industrial system is envisaged in which economic transactions are developed primarily at an international scale and where synergies among firms take place globally.

10.5   Conclusions and policy recommendations

Of the three scenarios presented above, the most likely appears to be what we have described as the 'network firm' or 'global-local' scenario. There are few grounds for expecting that the Fordist model could be reinvigorated, even if some of its limits and weaknesses could be overcome. Once the nature of markets and of the regulatory system has shifted, as they have clearly done with Fordism, there are few reasons to suggest that the old system with its attendant model of production could return. However, the 'rejection' of the Fordist model for the future does not need to lead to accepting the directly opposing model envisaged in the 'flexible specialization' scenario. This scenario is idealistic but unrealistic, with little empirical evidence to suggest that we are moving towards this kind of regulatory system. On the contrary, the empirical evidence suggests rather a third kind of scenario, an intermediate model of production between the assumed rigidity of Fordism and the anticipated flexibility of 'post-Fordism'.

Some clear policy recommendations for the transport and communications infrastructure can be drawn, on the assumption that the 'global-local' scenario is the one most likely to be represented in Europe '2020'.

The transport and communications infrastructure requirements of this scenario go well beyond the geographical and technological integration of networks. The 'global-local' scenario rests on the assumption that a complete integration between transport and communication networks will be developed. The increasing importance of standardization and harmonization refers not only to the two sectors separately, but also to their cointegration. The strength of infrastructural development in this scenario is related to the implementation of technological and geographical integration of elements in both the transportation and communication systems. Spatial planning of transport infrastructure needs therefore to be developed in conjunction with the territorial planning of communications infrastructure. An efficient and reliable logistical system requires a contemporary existence of both advanced telecommunications systems and transportation networks. Integrated logistical systems require information systems and communication facilities that lead to improved control possibilities and to more efficient deliveries of stored goods in time and space (Ruijgrok, 1990).

A final consideration concerns the need for integrated transport and communication systems to be developed in conjunction with broader spatial (urban and regional) planning. Only in this way will transport and communication networks be developed on the basis of the real needs and necessities of the newly emerging industrial and spatial system. This assumption refers to the idea that transport and communication technologies in themselves are not sufficient forces for generating indigenous local economic development. On the contrary, they have to be thought of as strategic instruments to be exploited with reference to broader spatial economic planning. In this way, supply-driven transport and communications projects with little or no connection to real demand requirements and needs can be avoided, and the future development of these leading technological infrastructures can be conceived rather in terms of their contribution to the creation of an integrated economic system for 'Europe 2020'.

Acknowledgement

The support of an ESF NECTAR Twinning Grant is gratefully acknowledged. Section 1 of the paper is jointly authored. Sections 2 and 3 were written by A. Gillespie, Sections 4 and 5 by R. Capello.

References

Aglietta M. (1982), *Regulation et Crises du Capitalisme: l'Experience des Etats Unis*, Calmann-Levy, second edition, Paris.

Amin A. and Robins K. (1990), 'The re-emergence of regional economies? The mythical geography of flexible accumulation, Society and Space', *Environment and Planning D* 8(1) pp.7-34.

Antonelli C. (ed) (1988), *New Information Technology and Industrial Change: The Italian Case*, Kluwer Academic Publishers, London.

Aydalot P. and Keeble D. (eds) (1988), *High Technology Industry and Innovative Environments: The European Experience*, Routledge, London.

Becattini G. (ed) (1988), *Mercato e Forze Locali: il Distretto Industriale*, Il Mulino, Bologna.

Boyer R. (1988), 'Technical change and the theory of 'regulation'', in Dosi G., Freeman C., Nelson R., Silverberg G. and Soete L. (eds) *Technical Change and Economic Theory*, Frances Pinter, London.

Brotchie J., Batty M., Hall P. and Newton P. (eds) (1991), *Cities of the 21st Century*, Halstead Press, Longman, Cheshire.

Brunn S. D. and Leinbach T. R. (1991), *Collapsing Space and Time: Geographic Aspects of Communication and Information*, Harper Collins Academic, London.

Burns T. J. and Stalker G. M. (1979), *Direzione Aziendale ed Innovazione*, Franco Angeli, Milan.

Camagni R. (1988), 'Functional integration and locational shifts in new technology industry', in Aydalot P. and Keeble D. (eds) (1988), op cit.

Camagni R. and Capello R. (1990), 'Towards a definition of the manoeuvring space of local development initiatives: Italian success stories of local development - theoretical conditions and practical experiences', in Stohr W. (ed) 1990, *Global Challenge and Local Response, Mansell*, London.

Camagni R. and Capello R. (1991), 'Nuove tecnologie di comunicazione e cambiamenti nella localizzazione delle attivita industriali', in Lombardo S (ed), *Nuove Tecnologie dell'Informazione e Sistemi Urbani*, forthcoming.

Camagni R. and Rabellotti R. (1991), 'L'innovazione macro-organizzativa nel settore tessile-abbigliamento', *Sviluppo e Organizzazione*, 108, pp.2-8.

Capello R. and Williams H. (1990), 'Nuove strategie d'impresa, nuovi sistemi spaziali e nuove tecnologie dell' informazione come strumenti di riduzione della incertezza', *Economia e Politica Industriale*, 67, pp.43-70.

Capello R. and Williams H. (1992), 'Computer network trajectories and organisational dynamics: a cross-national review', in Antonelli C. (ed) (1992), *The Economics of Information Networks*, Elsevier, London.

Chandler A. (1986), Scale and scope: the dynamics of industrial enterprise (mimeo)

Daniels W. W. (1987), *Workplace Industrial Relations and Technical Change*, Frances Pinter, London.

De Braband F. and Manacorda P. (1985), 'Scenario telematico e territorio: lettura di un'esperienza in Corso', Research Report, October.

Diamond D. and Spence N. (1988), Infrastructural and Industrial Costs in British Industry, Report for the Department of Trade and Industry, HMSO, London.

Frobel F., Heinrichs J. and Kreye O. (1980), *The New International Division of Labour*, CUP, Cambridge.

Giaoutzi M. and Nijkamp P. (eds) (1988), *Informatics and Regional Development*, Avebury, Aldershot.

Gillespie A. E. (1991), 'Advanced communications networks, territorial integration and local development', in Camagni R (ed) *Innovation Networks: Spatial Perspectives*, Belhaven Press, London, pp.214-229.

Gillespie A. E. and Williams H. P. (1990), 'Telematics and the reorganisation of corporate space', in Soekkha H M, Bovy P.H.L., Drewe P. and Jansen G.R.M. (eds) *Telematics, Transportation and Spatial Development*, VSP, Utrecht, pp.257-274.

Goddard J. B. (1991), 'The geography of the information economy', *PICT Policy Research Paper No 11*, Programme on Information and Communications Technologies, ESRC, London.

Harvey D. (1987), Flexible accumulation through urbanisation: reflections on post-modernism in the American city', *Antipode*, 19.

Hepworth M. and Ducatel K. (1991), *Transport in the Information Society*, Belhaven Press.

Hoogstraten P. van and Janssen B. (1985), New forms of industrialisation and material infrastructure in the Netherlands (mimeo).

Hymer S. (1972), 'The multinational corporation and the law of uneven development', in Bhagwati J. (ed) *Economics and World Order*, Free Press, New York, 113-140.

Jelinek M. and Golhar J. (1983), 'The interface betwen strategy and manufacturing technology', *Columbia Journal of World Business*, Spring, pp.26-36.

Jonscher C. (1983), 'Information resources and economy productivity', *Information Economics and Policy*, no. 1.

Leborgne D. and Lipietz A. (1988), 'New technologies, new modes of regulation: some spatial implications', *Society and Space: Environment and Planning D*, 6, pp. 263-280.

Lipietz A. (1975), 'Structuration de l'espace, problème foncier et amenagement du territoire', *Environment and Planning A* 7 pp.415- 425; English translation in Carney J., Hudson R., Lewis J. (eds), 1980, *Regions in Crisis*, Croom Helm, Beckenham, Kent, pp.60-75.

Lipietz A. (1986), 'New tendencies in the international division of labour: regimes of accumulation and modes of regulation', in Scott A. J. and Storper M. (eds) *Production, Work, Territory: The Geographical Anatomy of Industrial Capitalism*, Allen & Unwin, Boston.

Maggi R. and Nijkamp P. (1992), 'Missing networks in Europe', *Transport Reviews*, Vol. 12, n. 4, pp. 311-21.

Massey D. (1984), *Spatial Divisions of Labour*, Macmillan, London.

Mathews, J. (1991), 'Mass production, the Fordist system and its crisis', in Mackay H., Young M. and Beynon J. (eds) *Understanding Technology in Education*, Falmer Press, London.

Mazzonis D. (1985), 'A project for innovation in Prato', paper presented at the Workshop of San Miniato, November 28-30.

Moses L. and Williamson H. F. (1967), 'The location of economic activity in cities', *American Economic Review*, 57 pp.211-222.

Moulaert F. and Swyngedouw E. (1988), 'A regulation approach to the geography of the flexible production system', *Society and Space: Environment and Planning D.*

Nijkamp P., Reichman S. and Wegener M. (eds) (1990), *Euromobile: Transport, Communications and Mobility in Europe*, Avebury, Aldershot.

Nijkamp P. and Salomon I. (1989), 'Future spatial impacts of telecommunications', *Transportation Planning and Technology*, vol. 13, pp 275-287.

Pedersen P.O. (1985), Communication and spatial interaction in an area of advanced technology - with special emphasis on the goods transport. Paper presented at the ESF Workshop on Transport Planning in an Era of Change, Zandvoort, April.

Perrons D. (1981), 'The role of Ireland in the new international division of labour: a proposed framework for regional analysis', *Regional Studies*, 15, 2, pp.81-100.

Piore M. and Sabel C. F. (1984), *The Second Industrial Divide: Possibilities for Prosperity*, Basic Books, New York.

Roobeek A.J. (1987), 'The crisis in Fordism and the rise of a new technical paradigm', *Futures* 19(2) pp.217-231.

Rubery J., Tarling R. and Wilkinson F. (1987), 'Flexibility, marketing and the organisation of production', *Labour and Society*, 12, 1.

Ruijgrok C. (1988), 'Recent developments in logistics, information technologies and spatial systems', in Giaoutzi M. and Nijkamp P. (eds.) 1988, op cit.

Ruijgrok C. (1990), 'Telematics in the goods logistics process' in Soekkha H. (ed.) 1990, *Telematics - Transportation and Spatial Development*, VSP, Utrecht.

Rullani E. and Zanfei A. (1988), 'Networks between manufacturing and demand: cases from textile and clothing industries', in Antonelli C (ed) (1988), *New Information Technology and Industrial Change: The Italian Case*, Kluwer Academic Publisher, London.

Schaeffer K.H. and Sclar E. (1975), *Access for All: Transportation and Urban Growth Pelican*, Harmondsworth, Middlesex.

Schoenberger E. (1988), 'From Fordism to flexible accumulation: technology, competitive strategies, and international location', *Society and Space: Environment and Planning D*, 6, pp.245-262.

Scott A.J. (1988), 'Flexible production systems and regional development: the rise of new industrial spaces in North America and Western Europe', *International Journal of Urban and Regional Research*, 12, 2.

Soekkha H.M., Bovy P.H.L., Drewe .P, and Jansen G.R.M. (1990), *Telematics- Transportation and Spatial Development*, VSP, Utrecht.

Teece D. (1980), 'Economies of scope and scope of the enterprise', *Journal of Economic Behaviour and Organisation*, 1, pp. 223-247.

Walker R.A. (1981), 'A theory of suburbanisation', in Dear M. and Scott A. (eds) *Urbanisation and Planning in Capitalist Society*, New York.

Walker R.A. (1988), 'The geographical organisation of production systems', *Society and Space: Environment and Planning D*, 7, pp.377-408.

Williams H.P. and Taylor J. (1991), 'ICTs and the management of territory', in Brotchie J., Batty M., Hall P. and Newton P. (eds) *Cities of the 21st*

Century, Halstead Press, Longman, Cheshire.

Williamson O. (1975), *Markets and Hierarchies: Analysis and Antitrust Implications*, Free Press, New York.

Zanfei A. (1986), 'I vincoli alla diffusione delle tecnologie dell'informazione in alcune esperienze di applicazione della telematica', *Economia e Politica Industriale*, n. 50, pp. 253-289.

11 From human capital formation to location of high-educated workers and knowledge-intensive firms

C. Anderstig and N.G. Lundgren

11.1 Introduction

In current discussions about the productivity growth slowdown in Sweden much attention has been paid to the role of the education system. The conventional opinion of a positive relationship between educational investment and productivity growth has been made topical and also gained support by results from special studies undertaken for an official report on the productivity problem; see, e.g., Bishop (1991), Wadensjö (1991).

Some problematic features of the Swedish education system should be outlined. While public spending on public education is currently about seven percent of GNP, which is at the top among OECD countries, the share spent on higher education is less than one percent, which is clearly below the average for OECD countries. Further, since the nineteen seventies Sweden applies a system with restricted intake for all kind of university education. It has also been observed that the individual earnings are very low for some university education.

These facts, the restricted intake and weak economic incentives to undergo higher education, partly explain why the share of Swedish youth entering university education has decreased for some years. What may have strengthened this tendency has been the state of an overheated labour market, especially during the late eighties.

The aim of this explorative paper is to examine some regional aspects of the stated problem, where we report on different, though related, research efforts. First, we know that the probability for entering university education is strongly varying among regions. Some explanations are obvious; we know from a large body of sociological and economic literature that the family background has a large effect on schooling (see, e.g., Hauser and Sewell, 1986), as well as we know that background variables, such as level of education and family income, show substantial variation among regions.

Background variables could, however, be more broadly conceived, including, e.g., the accessibility to and the quality of educational amenities, the state of the regional labour market etc. Starting from this assumption, the first section of the paper presents preliminary tests, examining the partial effects on schooling of some regional characteristics, in addition to variables representing

193

family background. The tests are performed with respect both to the probability for entering upper secondary school, and to the probability for entering university education.

Though the second part of the paper is self-contained, it is dealing with some closely related issues, viz. the location behaviour of labour with higher education and high-technology (knowledge-intensive) firms. Of course the dimensions and quality of the education system are matters of basic importance to bring about an expansion of higher education. And the question about the location behaviour of labour with higher education would not be very interesting if it could simply be established that people always follow jobs.

But, as Muth (1971) proposed, there is the chicken and egg problem - do people follow jobs or jobs follow people? And, as pointed out by Greenwood et al. (1991), a growing body of literature indicates that firms are increasingly drawn to specialized resources as labour skills and education. For high-technology firms in particular, traditional location factors, such as accessibility of markets and raw materials, are of small interest for the location decision, whereas the ability to obtain and retain individuals with specific knowledge occupations is of growing importance.

In principle, examining the location decisions of workers with higher education and specific occupations may thus give better insight into the location determinants of knowledge-intensive firms. In this paper the approach is, however, more limited. Based on a ten percent sample of workers with specific, knowledge-handling occupations, we model their decision to relocate over a five-year period, where the location decision is determined by a number of personal and regional characteristics. The location decisions of both firms and workers are, of course, interdependent. To shed some light upon this 'chicken and egg problem', we apply a simple joint location model to knowledge-intensive firms and workers with specific educations.

11.2 Regional differences in educational participation

A lot of various economic, social and cultural factors influence the individuals decision to invest in human capital (i.e. upper secondary school and university education). We have touched on some economic factors that may partly explain why the share of Swedish youth passing on to university education has decreased by about 17 percent between the late seventies and late eighties.

However, the focus of the present paper concerns the regional variation of transition rates to higher education. We will examine the transition rate from the nine-year Compulsory school to Upper secondary school, and the transition rate from Upper secondary school to University. The analysis is based on cross section data from all 284 municipalities in Sweden.

The regional variation in transition rates is illustrated in Figure 11.1, where municipalities are sorted in ascending order. The upper curve shows a substantial variation in transition rates to Upper secondary school in 1982-89. E.g., in the municipality of Danderyd, in the Stockholm region, the rate is about 70 percent, whereas the rate is only about 17 percent in Vindeln, a municipality in the north of Sweden. The lower curve in Figure 11.1 illustrates the transition rate (within three years) from Upper secondary school (1982-86)

to University. Again Danderyd has the highest rate, about 30 percent, while
Lessebo, located in the south-east of Sweden, has the lowest, about 7 percent.

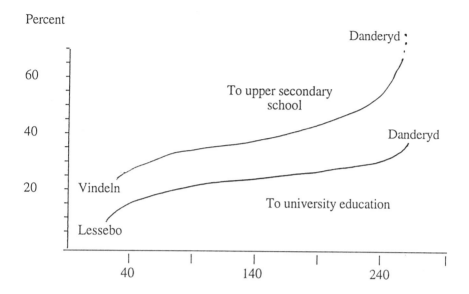

**Figure 11.1 Transition probabilities. Swedish municipalities
sorted in ascending order. (N = 284)**

11.2.1 A model approach to determine transition probabilities

In order to explain the observed regional variation in transition rates to Upper
secondary school and University, respectively, we have applied some simple
probability models (linear logit). Unfortunately, since we are lacking individual
microdata, the analysis is based on aggregate data (transition rates) with
municipalities (284) as observation units. Thus, denoting the transition rate in
municipality i Pi, the model applied takes the simple form

$$\log [P_i/(1-P_i)] = a + b\, X_i,$$

where X_i is a vector of explanatory factors in region i, and a and b parameters
to be estimated.

The drawbacks of using aggregate data in choice modelling are obvious, in
particular with respect to one of the explanatory factors, viz. the family
background. It is a well established fact that this factor is of vital importance to
the childrens' future education. A proper specification of the factor would claim
a number of characteristics. However, in our case we use mainly one proxy
variable to take this factor into account, viz. the share of total population in the
municipality with university education (three years or more). The transition

probability, both for Upper secondary school and for University education, is expected to increase as the share of population with university education increases.

In addition to the theoretical variable 'family background', it is assumed that other regional background variables also may have influence on the transition probabilities. (Of course, using aggregate data means that there is no strict distinction between empirical variables pertaining to the 'family' and 'region', respectively.) One type of variable is assumed to mainly reflect employment opportunities (or lack of) in the regional labour market. If the labour market in the municipality is dominated by industries with low demands on formal education, there is reason to expect low transition probabilities. This factor is taken into account by two variables. First, the share of total employment in Agriculture and Forestry; second, a binary variable taking the value 1 if more than half of manufacturing employment is within natural resource based industries (sawmills, paper and pulp mills, mining and steel plants).

Another category of regional variables refers to the access to and quality of educational amenities in the municipality. The first is a binary (1/0) variable, taking the value 1 if an Upper secondary school is located in the municipality. A second binary variable represents local access to a university. Transition probabilities are expected to increase with respect to both variables. A third variable represents regional access to a university education, using a weighted accessibility measure. (This measure is defined in Section 11.3 below.)

Two variables represent qualitative aspects of the schools in the municipality, viz. the share of unauthorized teachers in Compulsory school and in Upper secondary school, respectively. The rationale of including these variables is the usage of screened admission to university education in Sweden. The marks from Upper secondary school are thus of general importance to compete for a university education. Accordingly, reduced transition probabilities to university are expected in municipalities with high shares of unauthorized teachers.

Finally, the propensity to invest in additional years of education, after completed Upper secondary school, may be influenced by the state of the labour market. This is controlled for by two variables. One is reflecting the unemployment rate among persons aged 20-24. The other variable reflects the number of vacancies in percent of total employment in the labour market region of the municipality. It is expected that the transition probability is augmented by high unemployment rates, while reduced in face of a large number of vacancies, i.e. good employment opportunities.

Separate models have been estimated for males and females. Some overall statistics of the data set are presented in Table 11.1.

11.2.2 Transition to Upper secondary school

Table 11.2 shows the OLS estimates of the equations for transition probabilities to Upper secondary school. As expected the share of university educated in the total population is a highly significant factor, with the coefficient 0.052 (female) and 0.072 (male). The direct point elasticities of the transition probability with respect to a marginal change in the variable, evaluated at the mean values, are 0.18 and 0.22, respectively. Let us as a numerical example apply the elasticities to a non-marginal increase of the share of university educated, from 5 percent (mean value) to 10 percent. According to the estimated models this would imply that the transition probability increases from 0.31 to 0.37 for females, and from 0.38 to 0.47 for males.

Table 11.1a
Summary statistics. Means, standard deviation, min. and max.

	Mean	Std.dev.	Min	Max
Transition rate:				
To upper secondary school 1986-1989				
Male	38.4	8.3	17.1	76.7
Female	31.4	7.7	10.3	67.5
To university 1985089, 3 years or more				
Male	21.3	5.5	3.0	37.5
Female	18.3	5.1	6.1	31.8
To university 1985-89				
Male	35.1	7.9	10.6	70.2
Female	40.5	7.9	15.7	70.4
V1 Share of pop. with uni. edu. %	5.0	3.0	2.0	26.0
V2 Share of tot. empl. in Agri/Forest.%	7.3	5.2	0.3	24.4
Rate of unemployment %				
V3 Female age 20-24	6.4	3.6	0.5	18.3
V4 Male age 20-24	5.2	3.4	0.3	20.8
Unauthorized teachers %				
V5 Compulsory school	12.8	5.1	1.9	33.2
V6 Upper secondary school	10.2	6.0	0.0	45.0
V7 Accessibility to Univ. education	7.5	15.9	0.0	89.9
V8 Vacancies in lab. market region %	2.0	2.0	0.0	10.0

Table 11.1b
Simple correlation coefficients between independent variables

	V1	V2	V3	V4	V5	V6	V7	V8
V1	1.00							
V2	-0.41	1.00						
V3	-0.37	0.02	1.00					
V4	-0.21	0.03	0.71	1.00				
V5	-0.19	-0.04	-0.08	-0.03	1.00			
V6	-0.20	0.01	0.13	0.15	0.09	1.00		
V7	0.72	0.40	-0.43	-0.32	0.13	-0.17	1.00	
V8	0.22	-0.18	-0.17	-0.19	-0.22	-0.23	0.22	1.00

Table 11.2
OLS estimates of transition probability models.
Transition probability P to Upper Secondary School 1982-86 in 284 municipalities (t-values)

Dependent variable = $\log(P/1-P)$	Female		Male	
Constant	-0.620	***	-0.697	***
	(-15.4)		(-14.9)	
Share of total population with university education	0.052	***	0.072	***
	(8.6)		(13.5)	
Share of total employment in Agriculture/Forestry	-0.009	***	-0.017	***
	(-3.1)		(-4.7)	
Manufacturing employment mainly in nautral resource based industries (I/O)	-0.125	***	-0.119	***
	(-4.8)		(-3.9)	
Upper secondary school (I/O)	-		0.071	**
	-		(2.2)	
University (I/O)	-		-	
Accessibility to university education	0.003	***	-	
	(3.1)			
R^2	0.59		0.57	

* * t-test significant at 5%
***t-test significant at 1%

198

The two variables indicating a labour market dominated by industries with low demands on formal education both are significant and show the expected negative signs.

The results indicate that accessibility to university education may have a positive effect on the transition probability for Upper secondary school among females, while this variable is not significant among males. Note, however, that the inclusion of this variable affects the parameter for share of university educated; e.g., the estimated parameter for females is 0.062 when accessibility to university education is not included in the equation. (As shown in Table 11.1, the accessibility measure is highly correlated (0.72) with the share of university educated.) It can also be noted that local access to a university has no influence on the transition probabilities, whereas local access to an upper secondary school slightly influences the probability for males.

11.2.3 Transition to University

The results from the equations estimating transition probabilities to university education are presented in Table 11.3. Again it is obvious that the proxy variable of 'family background', i.e. the share of university educated in the total population, is the most significant factor; the coefficients 0.039 and 0.041, for females and males, respectively. The corresponding direct point elasticities, evaluated at mean values, are 0.12 and 0.14. In this case an increase in the share of university educated, from 5 to 10 percent, would imply that the transition probability to university increases from 0.41 to 0.45 for females and from 0.35 to 0.40 for males.

Contrary to the previous case, the two variables representing local labour market with low demands on formal education has no discernible effect on the transition probability. Nor have the variables representing local or regional access to university any effect.

The state of the labour market obviously has a significant impact on the transition probability, especially with respect to the impact of vacancies. Note however, that among males a higher unemployment rate slightly augments the transition probability to university education. As expected, the transition probability is reduced in labour markets where employment opportunities are good. As the state of the labour market has dramatically changed since the period 1985-89, we could give a hint of what this change implies. E.g., according to the estimated equation for females, a reduction of vacancies, from 2 percent (mean) to 1 percent, implies that the transition probability increases from 0.41 (mean) to 0.45.

It can also be noted that a high share of unauthorized teachers means that the transition probability to university education significantly decreases. E.g., the estimates imply that halving the average share of unauthorized teachers in Compulsory school, increases the transition probability from 0.35 to 0.37 for males, and from 0.41 to 0.43 for females.

These results may be of some interest also from a policy point of view. Formerly, the authorization rules for the teachers, as well as their salaries, have been a responsibility for the state. From 1992, this and other responsibilities for the schools are decentralized and transferred to the municipalities. Up to now almost all schools in Sweden have been under public administration and ownership. At the same time a debate is going on whether the schools to some extent ought to be privatized. According to the results above it is relevant to stress that authorized, i.e. well educated, teachers in a municipality seem to have an obvious and significant effect on the compatibility of the pupils on the 'educational market'. The policy for equalization, which has been the most important argument for a public school system in Sweden, organized by the central state authorities, has obviously not reached its goals.

Table 11.3
OLS estimates of transition probability models.
Transition probability P to University 1982-86
in 284 municipalities (t-values)

Dependent variable = log (P/1-P)	Female	Male
Constant	-1.584 ***	-1.598 ***
	(-20.7)	(-17.3)
Share of total population with university education	0.039 ***	0.042 ***
	(5.5)	(5.4)
Share of total employment in Agriculture/Forestry	-	-
Manufacturing employment mainly in natural resource based industries (I/O)	-	-
Upper secondary school (I/O)	-	-
Share of unauthorized teachers in Compulsory school	-0.014 ***	-0.014 ***
	(-3.9)	(-3.5)
Share of unauthorized teachers in Upper secondary school	-0.009 ***	-0.010 ***
	(-3.1)	(-2.8)
University (I/O)	-	-
Accessibility to university education	-	-
Rate of unemployment in municipality (20-24 years)	-	0.019 ***
		(3.0)
Vacancies as a percentage of employed in the labour market region	-0.20 ***	-0.15 ***
	(-3.7)	(-2.0)
R^2	0.18	0.20

* * t-test significant at 5%
***t-test significant at 1%

After having examined some regional aspects of the formation of human capital, we shall now turn to the issue of location decisions for high-educated workers, among whom those entering the labour market.

11.3 Migration of high-educated workers and location of knowledge-intensive firms

Results from surveys asking high-technology firms to rate various regional characteristics as to significance in their location decision show that the location factors considered most important relate, directly or indirectly, to the ability of these firms to attract and retain a highly skilled work force (Premus 1982; Rees 1986). Analyzing the location decisions of high-technology workers may thus give important knowledge about the location decisions of corresponding firms.

This issue will be addressed in the first part of this section, where we examine the migration decision of high-technology workers, using an approach similar to Herzog and Schlottman (1989). However, the definition of 'High-technology' is somewhat broader as our (wider) interest concerns the location of high-educated workers and knowledge-intensive firms. In the definition of high-technology workers, four sub-groups have been classified; 1) Computer specialists, 2) Engineers, engineering and science technicians, 3) Economists and statisticians, and 4) Life and Physical scientists.

11.3.1 Modelling the migration decision of high-educated workers

The analysis is based on microdata on households for the period 1980 - 1985 obtained from a ten percent sample of the 1980 and 1985 Censuses, with complementary regional data from 1980. This microdata was processed to extract householders aged 24 - 60 in 1985 who were members of the labour force in 1985. The sample was drawn from the total population, stratified into subpopulations according to outmigration 1980 - 1985 (w.r.t. labour market region, 'A-region',), and permanent address (Sweden subdivided into eight county-blocks). Although the definition of high-technology workers is relatively broad, the definition of higher education is strict; householders with less than 3 years of university education in 1985 have been excluded. The remaining sample consists of 5188 householders, 731 of which aged less than 30 in 1985.

An industry-by-occupation matrix for the four high-technology occupations defined above is presented in Table 11.4. It can be noticed that almost 50 percent of all high-technology workers are employed in Public services. Among younger high-technology workers, however, employment in Manufacturing is more frequent. The share of public employment may seem high, given the definition of high-technology occupations. Yet, for high-educated workers irrespective of occupation, the share is well above 60 percent.

Table 11.4
High-technology occupation/Industry distribution
in 1985, percent.
(Aged less than 30)[a]

Industry

Occupation	Manufacturing	Private Services	Public Services	Total
Computer specialists	3.4 (5.6)	7.4 (9.0)	1.5 (0.8)	12.3 (15.5)
Engineers, eng-ineering & science technicians	20.8 (27.8)	4.9 (6.4)	1.8 (3.3)	27.4 (37.5)
Economists and statisticians	3.1 (6.0)	6.5 (8.1)	3.7 (3.2)	13.3 (17.2)
Life and Physical scientists	3.8 (3.0)	3.1 (1.6)	40.0 (25.2)	47.0 (29.8)
Total	31.1 (42.2)	21.9 (25.2)	47.0 (32.4)	100.0 (100.0)

[a] Based on the sample of 5188 (731) householders

Regional characteristics determining migration should, in general, refer to conditions both in labour and housing markets, or, put in other words, to dimensions of work and life quality. Since, in our case, the analysis concerns determinants of interregional migration, with regions defined as labour market regions, we focus on characteristics that mainly pertain to labour market conditions.

One type of variable represents the specific employment opportunity for high-educated workers. In essence this (accessibility) measure reflects the intensity of higher-education workplaces. The accessibility measure is a weighted sum of the time distance from region i to all regions j; the weights being defined by the quotient between the number of higher-education workplaces and the accessibility to all workplaces in region j; the distance parameter is derived from estimated models of commuting trips. Two measures are used; accessibility with respect to all kind of higher-education workplaces and accessibility with respect to such workplaces in manufacturing,

202

respectively. Other variables are included to reflect the general economic conditions in the region (total employment growth) and regional scale (the size of population).

The 1980-1985 outmigration of high-technology workers is expected to decrease as the access to such jobs increases. It is also expected that high-technology workers in their location decision prefer the opportunities and diversity offered by large, and rapidly growing regions.

In addition to these mainly labour market oriented variables, one pertains to the housing market, or quality of life dimension, viz. home prices (average price in the municipality). If it is assumed that home prices solely reflect cost of living the intuitive expectation would be that migration is augmented by high home prices. The results obtained by Herzog and Schlottman (1989) give some support to this notion, when they let the local costs of living be represented by home prices. (This variable is included with reference to the fact that cost of living is listed among the more important location determinants of high-technology firms).

On the other hand, as discussed in Evans (1990, p. 516), in recent research on migration "it has been argued that since differences in ... property values capture environmental ... differences, they can be used as proxies for these differences and as indicators of the attractiveness of areas to migrants". With this amenity approach, migration of high-technology workers is, reversely, expected to decrease as home prices increase. Though interregional differences in amenities are capitalized into interregional differences in property values (home prices), and thus influence migration, it is also true that high prices are a consequence of migration. In an interregional perspective it may therefore be difficult to know to what extent high home prices reflect amenity-richness or general economic conditions in the region.

Table 11.5 presents migration rates for the total sample, for subgroups of younger householders and entrants to labour market, and, as a comparative figure, the migration rate for the total population, i.e. householders in all occupations and educations. Net migration figures of the metropolitan and university regions, and summary statistics for the personal characteristics, are also shown.

Of the 5188 high-technology workers described above, 1128 (21.7 percent) relocated between 1980 and 1985. Among those who were studying or unemployed in 1980, or aged less than 30, quite half relocated during the period. These high rates of mobility for high-technology workers can be compared to the figures for all workers, irrespective of occupation/education: 24 percent for entrants, and 8 percent for the total population.

Among all high-technology workers relocating, about 40 percent moved to a metropolitan region (Stockholm, Uppsala, Gothenburg or Malmö/Lund); among entrants this figure is almost 50 percent. This pattern is also reflected in the net migration figures, showing that, e.g., Stockholm gains 12 percent in migrating entrants, while the northern university regions Umeå and Luleå are loosing 47 and 27 percent, respectively. As expected, gains and losses are less with respect to migration of all high-technology workers.

The results of four estimated logit equations are reported, referring to the migration decision of the group aged less than 30 (I and II), and all high-technology workers (III and IV). It should be noticed that the majority of

Table 11.5
Migration rate 1980-1985 and summary statistics

	High-technology occupations[a]			All occupations[b]	
	Entrants	<30	All	Entrants	All
Migration rate, percent	52.6	50.0	21.7	24.0	8.0

Net migration, percent:

Stockholm	+ 12	+ 27	+ 2
Gothenburg	+ 3	+ 10	+ 1
Malmö/Lund	+ 1	+ 16	- 3
Uppsala	- 4	+ 32	- 2
Linköping	+ 6	- 11	+ 2
Umeå	- 47	- 26	- 27
Luleå	- 27	- 25	- 14

Personal charactistics percentage:

Female	13.7	14.0	7.4
Age (mean)	30.4	27.4	38.9
Married	23.7	12.9	64.6
Employed spouse	15.5	7.7	53.3
Spouse with knowl.occ.	8.0	5.5	27.3
School age children	9.9	1.6	40.3
Long-distance commuter	0.0	3.0	6.7
Entrant to labour market	100.0	70.9	16.9
Prior migration	44.3	37.8	56.7

[a] The occupations are defined in Table 11.4 and in the text. The total sample is 5188 householders, of which 878 are entrants to the labour market and 731 are aged less than 30.

[b] Based on a one percent sample of 19895 householders. This sample includes all occupations and education.

the entrants to labour market are aged less than 30, and more than two thirds of the younger group are entrants. In Model I only personal characteristics are included. In Model II the variable representing intensity of higher-education workplaces (manufacturing) is added. Model III is similar, while Model IV includes additional regional characteristics. The binary logit estimates of the determinants of migration are provided in Table 11.6. Asymptotic t-values and significance levels for each coefficient estimate are also reported.

For the group aged less than 30 it can be noted (I and II) that very few coefficients related to personal characteristics are significant. Mobility is augmented by long-distance commuting, by non-employment (entrant) and by prior experience of migration. The fact that personal characteristics perform very weakly is partially due to the grouping by age, which take account of most of the age generated variation in life-cycle components.

As shown in the second model (II), access to higher-education workplaces in manufacturing performs very strongly in determining migration, and inclusion of this variable means a marked improvement in the overall performance of the model. The result reported means that young high-technology workers are less likely to relocate in face of good employment opportunity in manufacturing. The same result is obtained using the alternative formulation of the variable, representing access to higher-education workplaces in all industries.

Turning to the determinants of migration of all high-technology workers, III and IV in Table 11.7, we find that nearly all coefficients related to personal characteristics are significant. The results demonstrate negative age coefficients, and that mobility is reduced among female workers, by a working spouse and by school-age children. On the other hand, mobility is augmented by long-distance commuting, by non-employment (entrant) and by prior experience of migration. It can also be noted that Life or physical scientists are more likely to relocate than workers in other high-technology occupations. (This may partly be due to the element of regulated mobility in the careers of physicians.)

As to the regional characteristics it can be noted (III) that the coefficient of access to higher-education workplaces is strongly significant. However, in the present case the inclusion of this variable means only a modest improvement in the overall performance of the model, compared to the model merely including the personal characteristics (not reported).

Additional regional characteristics (IV) only marginally improve the overall performance of the model. While two of the added characteristics are significant, demonstrating the preference of high-technology workers for large regions and high home prices (conceived as a proxy), it should be noted that the coefficient of access to higher-education workplaces is not significant in this model. Obviously, the strong interdependence between the regional characteristics (correlation coefficients about 0.7 - 0.8) makes it difficult to find out the partial effect of each variable.

To sum up, according to the revealed migration decision preferences, high-technology workers are less likely to relocate from larger regions, where the specific employment opportunities are good. It has also been shown that mobility significantly decreases with high home prices. However, in this model setting it cannot be determined to what extent home prices reflect capitalized amenities, or general economic conditions in the region.

Table 11.6
Determinants of 1980-1985 migration of High-Technology Workers:
Binary logit estimates[a], aged less than 30

Variable	Model I Coefficient	Asympt. t-value	Model II Coefficient	Asympt t-value
Constant	0.6462	0.4	3.3940	1.9*
Personal characteristics				
Female	-0.2495	-1.1	0.2100	0.8
Age	-0.0738	-1.3	-0.1001	-1.5
Married	-0.4173	-1.1	0.4219	1.0
Employed spouse	0.3535	0.8	-0.1855	-0.4
Spouse with knowl.occ.	0.0056	0.0	-0.1285	-0.6
School age children	-0.6587	-1.0	-0.7401	-1.0
Long-distance commuter	2.1990	4.1***	2.1090	3.6***
Entrant to labour market	1.1910	6.2***	1.0590	5.0***
Prior migrant	0.3884	2.4***	0.2785	1.5
Occupation:[b]				
Computer specialist	-0.1650	-0.6	-0.0745	-0.2
Engineering	0.1633	0.7	0.0997	0.4
Life or physical scientist	0.3145	1.3	0.4595	1.7*
Regional characteristics[c]				
Access to higher education workplaces (10^2)	-	-	-	-
- in manufacturing industry (10^2)	-	-	-0.3912	-11.0***
Empl.growth 1975-85(10^{-4})	-	-	-	-
Population size (10^{-6})	-	-	-	-
Home prices (10^{-3})	-	-	-	-
Likelihood	-470.11		-394.36	
Rho square	0.0722		0.2217	

*   t-test significant at 10%
**   t-test significant at 5%
*** t-test significant at 1%

a   High educated workers are listed by occupation and industry in Table 11.4. The analysis was based upon 730 observations.
b   The excluded occupation is economists and statisticians.
c   These variables assume 1980 values except where noted.

Table 11.7
Determinants of 1980-1985 migration of High-Technology Workers:
Binary logit estimates[a]

Variable	Model III Coefficient	Model III Asympt. t-value	Model IV Coefficient	Model IV Asympt. t-value
Constant	2.2350	7.1***	2.2410	6.3***
Personal characteristics				
Female	-0.3895	-2.6***	-0.3632	2.4**
Age	-0.0900	-13.3***	-0.0871	-12.9***
Married	-0.0071	-0.1	0.0179	-0.1
Employed spouse	-0.3981	-3.2***	-0.4217	-3.3***
Spouse with knowl.occ.	0.0143	0.2	-0.0018	-0.0
School age children	-0.2845	-2.8***	-0.2793	-2.8***
Long distance commuter	1.0680	8.3***	0.9808	7.6***
Entrant to labour market	1.1410	11.2***	1.1220	10.8***
Prior migrant	0.5464	6.7***	0.4942	5.9***
Occupation:[b]				
Computer specialist	-0.0085	-0.1	-0.0144	0.1
Engineering	0.1434	1.1	0.1693	1.3
Life or physical scientist	0.4369	3.5***	0.3778	3.0***
Regional characteristics[c]				
Access to higher education workplaces (10^2)	-0.1180	-11.2**	-0.0133	-0.8
- in manufacturing industry (10^2)	-	-	-	-
Empl.growth 1975-85(10^{-4})	-	-	-0.1131	-0.9
Population size (10^{-6})	-	-	-0.8419	-2.8***
Home prices (10^{-3})	-	-	-0.1941	-2.4**
Likelihood	-2168.67		-2125.99	
Rho square	0.3969		0.4088	

*   t-test significant at 10%
**   t-test significant at 5%
*** t-test significant at 1%

a High educated workers are listed by occupation and industry in Table 11.4. The analysis was based upon 5188 observations.
b The excluded occupation is economists and statisticians.
c These variables assume 1980 values except where noted.

11.3.2 The joint location of high-educated workers and knowledge-intensive firms

It has been contended above that high-technology firms, in particular, are drawn to the location of labour skills and education. Thus, by examining the location decisions of high-technology workers one can gain a better insight into the location determinants of knowledge-intensive firms. However, what has been demonstrated so far is mainly the influence of labour market conditions on the location decisions of workers. Since the location decisions of firms and workers are interdependent an analysis of the joint location is called for. An approach towards this kind of analysis is presented below. Although the issue is essentially dynamic, the theoretical framework is a simple two-equation static model.

Two-stage least square is the estimator employed. A basic location model is applied to both higher-education and lower-education workers/workplaces. Higher education is defined as above, i.e. 3 years or more of university education; Lower education is in this context defined as completed secondary school. The estimations are based on data from 1985 (location of workers and workplaces) and 1980 (three exogenous variables), of 284 municipalities.

Two of the exogenous variables used as instrumental variables are accessibility measures; accessibility to university education and to airport capacity. The accessibility measures are defined as a weighted sum of the time distance from region i to all regions j; the weights being defined by the number of students at universities in j (1980-1981), and the number of flights from j (1980), respectively. Nor in this context do we know to what extent the third variable, home prices, reflect capitalized amenities. If it could be assumed that the interregional system is in equilibrium the home prices differentials could serve as a proxy for differentials in environmental quality. (On the other hand, as noted by Evans (1990), it is difficult to reconcile this equilibrium assumption with the persistence of migration between regions.)

The four endogenous variables are all accessibility measures, intended to reflect the intensity of higher-education/lower-education workers/workplaces in the region. One of these measures, Accessibility to higher-education workplaces in manufacturing, was used above. The other are similarly defined; e.g., as to Accessibility to higher-education workers, the weight is defined by the quotient between the number of higher-education workers and the accessibility to all workers in region j.

A log-linear functional form is assumed for all equations. Table 11.8 reports 2SLS estimates. According to results shown in Table 11.8 there is a marked difference between location of higher-education and lower-education workers/workplaces, as to the strength in the interdependence. Whereas the interdependence between location of lower-education workers (LEW) and workplaces (LEWP) is equally strong, the location of higher-education workplaces (HEWP) is considerably more dependent on the location of workers (HEW) than the location of workers on workplaces, coefficient estimates 1.288 and 0.363, respectively.

Further, there is a significant influence of Accessibility to university education on the location of HEWP, while not on the location of LEWP. Access to airport capacity also seems to be somewhat more important for the location of

HEWP. In all, these results are in support of the contention that high-technology firms are drawn to the location of labour skills and education.

As expected, the results indicate that location of HEW is augmented by high home prices, while this is not a significant location determinant of LEW. However, as pointed out above, the interpretation of the effect of high home prices on location is ambiguous.

11.4 Concluding remarks

Since other European countries make large investments in higher education, it has been urged that it is necessary for Sweden to expand higher education, in order to maintain its international economic competitiveness. It goes without saying that the dimensions and quality of the university system are matters of crucial importance to bring about such an expansion. However, improving the availability of high-educated workers is not only a matter of expanding the total number and quality of course places. The issue also involves important regional aspects, that we have called attention to in this explorative paper.

First, the examinations that have been performed indicate that there is a regional variation in transition rates to higher education that cannot only be attributed to the effect of varying socioeconomic, or 'family background', factors. It is interesting to note that while there is only a very minor effect of good local or regional access to a university, if any, our results indicate that regional variations in the quality of the basic school system have a significant effect on the transition probability to university education. Although this effect probably represents various factors, the policy implication is obvious, viz. upgrading and improving the quality of schooling gives an impetus to higher transition rates to university education.

Second, it has been argued that high-technology and knowledge-intensive firms increasingly are drawn to the location of labour skills and education, i.e. to the location of high-educated workers. Thus, the location of high-educated workers is not only a matter of where the corresponding workplaces are located, but also a matter of environmental quality and the location of various amenities. Although most important in an intraregional or urban context, the issue is also of significance in an interregional perspective. Admittedly, the research presented in this paper has only touched upon the role of regional amenities in the location decision of high-educated workers. Yet, the results are in support of the contention that high-technology firms are drawn to the location of high-educated workers.

As to further empirical research in this field it would be desirable to improve both on data and methods. The choice modelling of transition probabilities would gain significantly on using individual microdata, most of all if longitudinal data were available. With respect to the location models a natural next step would be modelling the choice of migration and intraregional location, inter alia to gain further insight into the role of amenities.

Table 11.8
Estimates of location models of manufacturing workplaces and workers, specified by level of education.[a](t-values)

Location of Higher education Workplaces (HEWP)		Location of Lower education Workplaces (LEWP)
Dep. var. = log Acc. to workplaces[b]		
Constant	-0.906 (-1.39)	-0.390 (-0.93)
log Acc. to workers[c]	1.288*** (7.45)	0.878*** (6.97)
log Acc. to university education	0.066*** (5.08)	0.004 (0.53)
log Acc. to airport capacity	0.050 (1.61)	0.020 (0.92)
R^2	0.74	0.60

Location of Higher education Workers (HEW)		Location of Lower education Workers (LEW)
Dep. var. = log Acc. to workplaces[c]		
Constant	-3.103*** (-5.29)	-0.872 (-1.55)
log Acc. to workplaces[b]	0.363*** (10.23)	0.895*** (12.78)
log Home prices	0.234*** (3.90)	0.077 (1.41)
R^2	0.57	0.65

***t-test significant at 1%
[a] Higher education is defined as 3 years of university education; Lower education is defined as completed secondary school.
[b] Refers to Higher education workplaces (HEWP) and Lower education workplaces (LEWP), respectively.
[c] Refers to Higher education workers (HEW) and Lower education workers (LEW), respectively.

Acknowledgement

Support for this research from the Expert Group on Regional and Urban Studies (ERU) is gratefully acknowledged.

References

Bishop, J. (1991), 'Productivity and knowledge from education', in *Labour, labour market and productivity, Experts'* report No. 4 to the Commission on Productivity, pp. 179-223, Stockholm: Allmänna förlaget. (in Swedish.)

Evans, A.W. (1990), 'The assumption of equilibrium in the analysis of migration and interregional differences: A review of some recent research', *Journal of Regional Science* 30, 515-531.

Greenwood, M.J. (1985), 'Human migration: Theory, models and empirical studies', *Journal of Regional Science* 25, 521-543.

Greenwood, M.J., Mueser, P.R., Plane, D.A. and Schlottman, A.M. (1991), 'New directions in migration research', *The Annals of Regional Science*, 25, 237-270.

Hauser, R.M. and Sewell, W.H. (1986), 'Family effects in simple models of education, occupation status and earnings: Findings from the Wisconsin and Kalamazoo studies', *Journal of Labour Economics*, 4, 83-115.

Herzog, H.W. Jr. and Schlottman, A.M. (1989), 'High-technology location and worker mobility in the U.S.', in Andersson, Å.E., Batten, D.F., and Karlsson, C. (eds.), *Knowledege and Industrial Organization*, Heidelberg, Springer-Verlag.

Muth, R.F. (1971), 'Migration: Chicken or egg?', *Southern Economic Journal*, 37, 295-306.

Premus, R. (1982), 'Location of High Technology Firms and Regional Economic Development', *G.P.O.*, Washington, D.C.

Rees, J. (1986), 'Technology, regions, and policy', Totowa, Rowman and Littlefield.

Wadensjö, E. (1991), 'Labour, labour market and productivity: Introduction and summary', in *Labour, labour market and productivity*, Experts' report No. 4 to the Commission on Productivity, pp. 7-19, Stockholm: Allmänna förlaget. (in Swedish.)

12 Common knowledge, inter-organizational networking and local economic development

M. Borman, J. Taylor and H. Williams

12.1 Introduction

Over recent years two distinct but related phenomena have emerged. First there are changing patterns of industrial organization which it has been argued are giving rise to 'networked firms', the move away from **both** hierarchically structured organizations and market based activities. Secondly, there is the increasingly widespread adoption and diffusion in firms of new information and communication technologies, in particular computer networks, that is the synthesis of telecommunications and computing technologies.

The focus of this paper is upon inter-organizational networks (IONs) and the development of common knowledge. The argument advanced here is that much of the debate on the use of inter-organizational networks and the creation of 'non market - non hierarchical' arrangements is heroic. At least two areas of concern can be identified. First, there is the implicit assumption about the development of common knowledge. The argument here is that the development of common knowledge is axiomatic to the development of 'non market - non hierarchical' structures, yet the emergence of common knowledge is not necessarily secured simply by the flow of information between firms. Second, are the assumptions that firms are able to construct IONs, and that their construction carries relatively low costs so as neither to prejudice entry or exit from a particular trading relationship. The central argument here that unless the structures for the development of common knowledge are created - and entry and exit costs are minimized - inter-organizational networks will reinforce existing hierarchical or market based arrangements.

There has been a growing literature concerned with the uptake and use of new information and communication technologies in both the transformation of corporate behaviour (Davenport 1993, Keen 1986,1991, Antonelli 1988, 1992, Capello and Williams 1991, Taylor and Williams 1991) and processes of local economic development (e.g. Gillespie & Williams, 1987, Hepworth 1989). Inevitably, this concern with the uptake and use of new information and communications technologies has brought into focus new issues surrounding the nature of the firm, the organization of economic activity and patterns of local economic development. In essence, the technological transformations that have occurred through the adoption of digital technologies in computing and communications have laid the foundations for new patterns of transactional activity within and between firms and in and between localities.

This potential for the transformation of economic and social activity has not escaped contemporary novelists. For example, Jay McInerney in one of his novels writes about the transformation of social relationships in New York.

"After nearly collapsing in bankruptcy during the Seventies, their adoptive city had experienced a gold rush of sorts; prospecting with computers and telephones, financial miners had discovered fat veins of money coursing beneath the cliffs and canyons of the southern tip of Manhattan. As geologic and meteorological forces conspire to deposit diamonds at the tip of one continent and to expose gold at the edge of another, so a variety of manmade conditions intersected more or less at the beginning of the new decade to create a newly rich class based in New York, with a radical new scale of financial well-being. The electronic buzz of fast money hummed beneath the wired streets, affecting all the inhabitants, making some of them crazy with lust and ambition, others angrily impoverished, and making the comfortable majority feel poorer. Late at night, Russell or Corrine would sometimes hear that buzz - in between the sirens and the alarms and the car horns - worrying vaguely, clinging to the very edge of the credit limits on their charge cards."(Brightness Falls)

This quotation brings into focus questions over the conceptualization of new information and communication technologies and the information flows they support. In particular is the need to interpret new information flows supported by the technology in the context of economic and social processes. Williams and Taylor (1991, 1992) have tended to see the information flows supported over computer networks on two levels, firstly as flows of capital and labour and secondly as abstractions and representations of organizational phenomena, including decision making processes and heuristic frameworks for understanding and interpreting the business environment.

This paper is set out around four further sections. The next section, albeit briefly, considers some of the recent debate over the nature of inter–organizational activity and the relationship between the firm and its locality. The third section deals with the nature of inter-organizational networks through a review of the literature. The fourth section considers the development of common knowledge. Finally, the fifth section considers some of the telecommunication policy implications of inter-organizational networking and the need to secure common knowledge.

12.2 Inter-organizational behaviour

Across a broad range of perspectives (engineering, production management, operational research, economics, geography) there appears to be a consensus (at least in terms of description) that the nature of economic activity, especially that within firms, is subject to profound challenge, if not undergoing change. The hierarchical and bureaucratic organizational monoliths that were once seen as the foundation stones of advanced capitalist societies are being challenged and new forms of organizational behaviour are emerging. For some observers this debate is characterized by certain controversies, for example, debates over the future of fordism, neo-fordism and the rise of new regimes of accumulation and modes of regulation.

The emergence of 'non market-non hierarchical' forms of industrial organization has also fuelled the debate over the relationship between firms and their localities - the nature and extent of the space economy of individual firms. The debate over the networked firm and its relationship to the local economy and 'milieu' has brought into question traditional explanatory frameworks which account for the location of economic activity. The traditional *frictional* variables (i.e. those concerned with the distance between one place and another) and *area* variables (i.e. those specific attributes of areas ostensibly favourable to the development of firms, such as local institutional arrangements, local levels of scientific and technical expertise, venture capital and 'quality of life' amenities) are being challenged by those that see location as a product of industrial organization. Gordon (1991), who in turn draws from Bianchi(1986), Bellini(1987), Storper and Christopherson(1987) and Scott(1988), observes that

> "Advocates of spatial reconcentration alternatively assert that location is a product of industrial organisation rather than spatial attributes. Flexible production systems are built around congresses of small firms, each highly specialised in a particular process or phase of production. The vertical disintegration of industry promotes spatial agglomeration as specialised producers achieve returns to scale through external division of labour, locating in close proximity to reduce the cost of their unstandardised and unstable exchanges". (p.178).

Thus new forms of industrial organization predicated upon novel patterns of inter-organizational behaviour can be seen to offer up new opportunities for local economic development as well as challenges to existing patterns of industrial location. A fuller discussion of this phenomena can be found in numerous sources, such as, Piore and Sabel (1984), Amin and Robins (1991).

Much of this literature on flexible-specialization, the growth of the networked firm and the emergence of new patterns of economic activity is predicated upon a particular view of both the transactions occurring between firms and the nature of firms themselves. In essence this literature sees the transactions between firms as being centred upon the trade of products and services and mediated by prices. Thus even in the context of inter-organizational networking such transactions and trading can be seen to approximate a market. In such conditions firms are seen as little more than production functions standing free from the complexities of organizational phenomena.

This perspective, which is resonant with a neo-classical economist's view of the firm, has begun to be challenged in a number of ways. Nelson and Winter (1982) have introduced the notion of an evolutionary theory of economic change and by using the concept of organizational routines have sought to develop a more sensitive understanding of economic activity within firms. This literature stresses that though routines embrace the basic processes of the organization, that is workflow, information flow, cost flow and value flow,

215

they embody more than these processes. Routines are not 'organization-free' analytical constructs, rather they embrace, reflect and act upon organizational characteristics - structure, culture, and domains, or spheres of activity. It is within organizational routines that the basic capability of an organization exists.

This evolutionary literature emphasizes that at the heart of any organization lie sets of more or less complex routines which embrace basic processes, and organizational structures and are infused by organizational culture(s). Historically arrived at, routines represent a set of long standing working relationships between organizational subunits. Moreover, they represent the intellectual basis of the organization. They are thus the skills, memory and knowledge base of the organization, both capturing and conveying an accumulation of information and wisdom and introducing it into day-to-day activity. Furthermore, the concept of routines become an invaluable heuristic through which the organization is able both to analyze change, and to lay the foundation of response to change.

Camagni (1991) has sought to review critically the relationships in and between firms and the local milieu using the analytical constructs provided by evolutionary theory, in particular routines. Camagni argues that the firms faces five areas of uncertainty, namely:

i   an information gap which is limited to the complexity and cost of information collection.
ii   an assessment gap which is related to the difficulty of inspecting ex-ante the qualitative characteristics of inputs, such as technical equipment.
iii a competence gap, which is linked to the firm's limited ability to process and understand available information.
iv   a competence-decision gap which stems from the impossibility of precisely assessing the outcomes of alternative actions.
v   a control gap which stems from the dynamic interaction among independent actors and their decisions.

To counter these uncertainties Camagni argues that a firm develops specific functions to reduce uncertainty. Importantly, he argues that the *routines* of a firm can be seen as the key mechanism by which the firm both addresses the internal aspects of reducing uncertainty (e.g. through the development of skills, the use of memory) as well as managing the inter-relationships between a firm and its external environment. Camagni recognizes that through routines an organization is able to use the local milieu as an uncertainty reducing device.

In developing an understanding of organizational activity on routines the transactions both within and between an organization are necessarily imbued with specific sets of knowledge and understandings. The transactions of any firm are shaped and understood through routines. Therefore the nature and extent of the understanding the routines of different firms by trading partners (or departments or functional groupings within a single organization) is become an important determinant in the nature and development of activity between firms. In essence, it is in this process of understanding the rich ecology of different routines (and therefore semantic structures) that the development of common knowledge is best understood.

12.3 Inter-organizational networks

Concern with the transactional structure of the firm leads to a conceptual interpretation of the information flows over a computer network as flows of capital and labour. The insights derived from this conceptual framework are discussed elsewhere (Williams and Taylor(1991), Capello, Taylor and Williams(1990), Hepworth(1989)). These studies all point up patterns of restructuring and profound organizational change associated with the adoption and diffusion of computer networks. However, these patterns of organizational change appear not to be uniformly or evenly distributed between firms, sectors and localities. In this sense this conceptualization based around the representation of flows of information over IONs as flows of capital and labour provides only a partial analysis of change processes. Moreover, such a conceptualization does not provide insights into the diffusion of new technologies beyond that provided by the rubric of transaction cost minimization.

Extending the conceptual understanding of flows of information over computer networks to embrace the routinization and codification of decision making begins to offer up further opportunities for analysis. Particularly a focus on decision making provides a stepping stone to understand flows of information over computer networks as embodying a wide range of organizational phenomena. In short, information flows over computer networks can be seen as both a resource deployed in a complex array of resource-dependency relationships and as patterns of perception, the embodiment of meaning systems.

It is within this perspective that information flows are seen as abstractions and representations of organizational behaviour and, the flow of information within and between firms as expressions of organizational processes. Thus inter–organizational networking is seen as the exchange not of outputs such as in products/prices but the exchange and interlacing of organizational routines. It is in this context of the interlacing the routines of different organizations that the development and use of common knowledge is critical.

The development of inter-organizational networking has taken a number of paths depending upon, for example, the nature of the externalities, technological constraints and the patterns of industrial organization and concentration. Of particular interest here are those inter-organizational networks that permit and facilitate the broad exchange of information between different firms and are used to underpin long standing relationships between firms. As such inter-organizational network can be seen to both support and sustain the spatial division of labour and capital between firms but, in so doing, the information flows they support also become a challenge to the extant relationships.

> "What distinguishes such technologies is that they institute systems and as such are shaped through a process of iteration between the organization and the technology. Thus the adoption and widespread use of such technologies can bring about, and may in fact be dependent upon, organizational change. In effect, the adoption of computer networks and their intersection with the existing transactional structure of the firm

217

provides a set of heuristics with which to reconceptualise this transactional structure and thus deliver organizational change." (Capello and Williams 1992 p. 351).

"Like traditional inter-organization media such as telephone, paper and face–to-face meetings, an ION is a medium for communication and interchange among organizations. However, because of its technical characteristics, an ION changes the economics of inter-organization communication and interchange" (p. 3) Estrin 1986

It is important to note, however, that inter-organizational networks are not being defined by reference to their technological characteristics but in terms of the information flows they support and the extent to which membership of the network is restricted. However an area of concern, which has important policy implications, is the extent to which membership of the network, that is both the cost of entry and exit are strongly influenced by technological phenomena, for example the quality, cost and availability of advanced telecommunication services.

A number of approaches have been made to the problem of conceptualizing inter-organizational networks. The first perspective to be considered is that of writers such as Estrin (1986) who place particular emphasis upon the technological capabilities of inter-organizational networks. The concern here is with the technical design issues that are raised when a computer network transcends a company's administrative boundaries. Accordingly the electronic links are categorized along dimensions such as speed, accessibility and functionality.

Another school of thought, articulated by Barrett and Konsynski (1982) among others, focuses upon network management issues which they suggest are largely independent of the system's technology. Their central argument is that the level of participation of individual organizations within the information system differs with regard to the degree of responsibility, cost, commitment and complexity of the operating environment. Thus while an inter–organizational network may appear to be a homogeneous entity from a technical standpoint the organizations involved will differ with regard to the roles they have adopted, or been assigned, and their degree of integration into the network. As such it is not the networks themselves that are categorized but their participants. Thus of importance here is both the decision to participate in an inter-organizational network and the level of participation that is chosen. For example, if the first two levels of Barrett and Konsynki's (1982) classification scheme are considered, where the first level organization acts as an input–output node and the second level organization provides an application such as an order processing system.

> " .. a dependency relationship may be formed whereby the level one participants change their internal business procedures to conform with those of the IS (information system/computer network). This makes the level two participant less vulnerable in its primary business activity. However, if an insufficient number of level one participants join the IS, the level two participant will fail to achieve the volume of usage necessary for cost recovery .. " (p. 97) Barrett and Konsynski (1986)

A refinement to this theory is presented by Forengo (1988) who distinguishes between inter-organizational networks with regard to whether they are 'centred' or 'non-centred'. The former are implemented by a single organization so as to enable it to interact with its suppliers or customers while the latter are created and managed by a federation of organizations.

While all of these contributions can be seen to be valuable in their own right it is necessary to recognize that the frameworks they represent are descriptive rather than explanatory. They describe respectively the capabilities, organization and outcomes of inter-organizational networks but they fail to enlighten with respect to their purpose. To achieve this it is necessary to look beyond the technological system itself to examine the nature of the information flows supported by the network. The technical and organizational aspects of an inter-organizational network serve to delimit the nature, immediacy and direction of information flows acting to restrict or enhance the potentialities of the network accordingly. However it is the actual information that flows over the network that has the potential to facilitate the transformation of modes of production both organizationally and geographically.

12.4 Common knowledge

It is in the context of the argument above that the interpretation of information flows over computer networks goes beyond the revelation of economic transactions to embrace the juxtaposition of organizational processes and phenomena that the question of the development of common knowledge is germane.

The central thesis here is that the extent to which the development of common knowledge occurs is a key measure of the economic, social and organizational relationships embodied in the inter-organizational network. Moreover, the processes by which common knowledge emerges and evolves can be seen to reveal the extent to which non market-non hierarchical organizational forms are beginning to emerge and thereby create new opportunities for local economic development.

The underlying theoretical constructs of common knowledge emanate from concerns about the interrelationship between individual decision making and the payoff for the organization as a whole. Where the payoff to an organization as a whole depends upon individual decision making, and where these decisions are non-additive, as is typically the case, then the optimal decision for any one agent within the organization will, in general, depend on the way in which the other members of the organization take their decisions. There is, therefore, an interdependence of payoffs which is without problems only in those contexts where agents can communicate without costs, or alternatively where agents can collect information about the environment faced by others and interpret this information in the same way as other agents. Given that such conditions cannot be met there remains the difficulty of aligning the (non–additive) decision making of individuals to the performance of the organization as a whole.

This perspective is resonant with understanding the firm not as a single production function, or as a single, large, all-encompassing contract, but as a 'nexus of treaties'(Aoki et al 1990) and as an array of complex activities and relationships embodied within routines.

Common knowledge can be seen to have three component parts; first, a common knowledge of 'new facts', that is of facts usually understood in common language; secondly, a common knowledge of, and adherence to, a number of rules and, finally, knowledge of a language, or coding. A more a detailed level common knowledge can be understood as follows; namely

  i   Knowledge of facts
  ii Knowledge of the same facts
  iii Same knowledge of facts
  iv Knowledge of rules
  v Knowledge of language.

Within the context of a single organization where the information flows over computer networks are embedded and emanate from organizational routines then the development of common knowledge can be seen to be primarily concerned with the first three facets set out above, namely, knowledge of facts, knowledge of the same facts, and the same knowledge of facts.

The following example from Ford illustrates this argument(Hammer 1990). The review of the accounts payable system at Ford in the late 1980s was part of a more general concern to reduce cost in the light of intense competitive markets. It was commented that Ford(North America) employed some 500 people in its accounts payable system compared to just five in Mazada. The original system at Ford was based upon a complex set of information flows between different departments and the frequent reconciliation of the data. Therefore the system was essentially designed to capture mismatches and rework existing processes. The introduction of a computer network allowed the company of simplify the procedures and migrate onto the network those reconciliation activities. In building the computer network application around an existing routine Ford was able to focus upon ensuring that the knowledge of facts was common across different functional departments. Issues over the development of knowledge of rules and language did not surface as the new application was embedded in the organizational routine which itself created and sustained these characteristics. In cases such as this flows of information over the network and their close relationship to routines ensures that both the knowledge of rules and knowledge of language are understood both within the system and by the constellation of users. In such cases it is axiomatic that the information system is embedded within the routine and as such the knowledge of rules and knowledge of language are also in the system and are transparent to users.

In the development of inter-organizational networking the emergence of common knowledge is complex. Through the development of inter–organizational networks not only are issues over the knowledge of facts, knowledge of the same facts and same knowledge of facts brought into question but also the structure upon which such facts can be made sense of, that is, the knowledge of rules and the knowledge of language. Inevitably inter–organizational networking brings together the different meaning systems, in that they are embedded in the information system of the routines in different organizations.

The complexities of establishing common knowledge across organizations through inter-organizational networking can be seen to affect the way in which such networks evolve. One of the key issues here appears to be the extent to which the transactions between firms can be abstracted. The process of abstraction can be seen to have two motivations. The first is to facilitate moving from one perspective to another and therefore can be seen to support the development of common knowledge. The second view of abstraction is that it can be used to reduce 'search space', to reduce the complexities of transactions. In the context of inter-organizational networking this latter perspective can be seen to manifest itself in a number of ways. Firstly, the diffusion of inter-organizational networking is biased towards those situations where abstraction is possible. The most notable example here is the financial services markets. Secondly, there is the desire to create inter-organizational networks based upon some set of standards which impose a meaning system onto members of the network. An example here is the development of EDI networks.

12.5 Telecommunications policy

The argument developed so far has sought to position new flows of information and their mediation over communication networks at the heart of economic and managerial changes, particularly the relationships between firms and in the creation of non market-non hierarchical organizational forms.

These arguments rest on the assumption that the communication infrastructure is available, that organizations can actually build inter-organizational networks without incurring prohibitive entry or exit costs. Thus conditions under which the telecommunications infrastructure is developed becomes of central importance to the economic well being of firms, processes of transformation and the development of localities(Williams 1992).

It is only for a single establishment, that questions over the provision of the communication infrastructure lie outwith the telecommunications regulatory framework - that is outside the public policy debate. In all other cases, a complex set of issues emerge around the provision of the telecommunications infrastructure. The range of services provided over the network, their costs and the quality of service are contingent upon the decision of other organizations (Taylor and Williams 1990). In the UK these other organizations include not just BT and Mercury Communications Limited (MCL) but also the operators of cellular telephone networks, the cable TV providers, the behaviours of large companies and the decision of the 'Regulators', Office of Telecommunications, Department of Trade and Industry, the European Commission in Brussels, the International Telecommunications Union in Geneva (an agency of the UN) and the international standard setting bodies.

One of the successes of the telecommunications industry in most OECD countries has been the delivery of universal voice telecommunication services. This has been an axiom of regulatory development, and coupled with technical change, the telephony service over recent years has tended to become of relatively high quality. However, the nature and scope of new information flows and their mediation over communication networks creates demands on the telecommunications network that go well beyond the provision of dial tone, and the making of telephone calls.

Moving away from this basic provision of service through to the provision of increasingly advanced services the concept of universal service as a structure for regulating the provision of telecommunication services starts to come problematic, initially in terms of its meaning, but ultimately in terms of its relevance. It is here that not only do the costs of entry and exit of inter–organizational networks begin to be an issue but also the ability to construct such networks in the first place is a major concern.

This difficulty of building such networks is well illustrated by the following example from the defence industries in the UK[1]. For a variety of reasons both technical and administrative, the Ministry of Defence Liverpool Directorate which distributes some £12bn (about 50% of the total defence budget) is unable to offer Electronic Funds Transfer. Electronic Funds Transfer would allow for the instantaneous transfer of funds from the MOD bank accounts to those of the contractors rather than waiting for the cheque in the post. Where the sums involved are rather larger than most of us are used to dealing with a 'cheque in the post' can be expensive, for example, in terms of lost interest. Therefore the large defence contractors operate a 'helicopter club'. At 11.27 a.m. on the third Friday of each month a helicopter descends on the Liverpool directorate to collect the cheques for the major contractors which are released at 11.30 a.m. These cheques are then flown to London where the contractors have negotiated special clearing procedures with the Bank of England so that the cheques can be cleared over the lunchtime thereby enhancing the cashflows of the major contractors. Obviously the sums involved are large and the gains to the companies more than offset the £5000 charged for each helicopter flight. Such practices are more common that we may realize, for example, Rolls Royce is cited as regularly using small aircraft within the UK to effect funds transfer.

In focusing upon universal service questions over the availability, cost and quality of telecommunication services are thrown into stark relief. The answers to such questions are not neutral in that they do have a profound influence on the development of inter-organizational networking and the emergence of new organizational forms. In the context of voice telephony, universal service is largely defined around the ubiquitous availability of dial tone, the relatively rapid connection of customers to the network at a regulated price, common quality standards across the network and common tariffs for both access (rental) and use.

However, these characteristics of universal service are not cast in stone for all telecommunication services. In fact voice telephony can be seen as a special case and the norm for all other services is that provision is based upon the specifics of customer needs (and their ability to pay) rather than in anticipation of service requirements, or other economic and social topics. In the competitive market that now determines the provision of telecommunication services these behaviours are only to be expected and are, perhaps, well illustrated by the development of ISDN services in Europe.

The regulatory structure and its interpretation by the service providers have important implications for the uptake and use of networks, the forging of inter–organization networks, and thus the way in which firms and hence localities adjust to a new competitive environment. Without the regulatory authority of universal service being defined for each and every service, competitive behaviour in the telecommunications market may lead to distorted and uneven patterns in the availability of telecommunications services and hence the ability of firms to build or join inter-organizational networks.

12.6 Conclusion

This paper has sought to bring together a number of strands of recent work concerned with the development of inter-organizational networking and the emergence of new forms of organizational behaviour. The paper has sought to argue that our understanding of the behaviour of firms and the transactions between firms is best understood through the analysis of routines. Further, this analysis of routines provides a framework within which to understand the development of information systems. Within this theoretical framework information systems are to be understood not merely as transactional systems but abstractions and representations of organizational processes. In consequence the development of inter-organizational networking necessarily involves the inter-lacing of the routines of different organizations. It is in this context that the development of common knowledge is seen as necessary but yet complex to achieve. The simplistic assumption that interconnecting computer systems leads to new forms of organizational behaviour is shown to be naive. The emergence of new forms of non-market and non-hierarchical organizational behaviour requires a sensitivity to the interconnection of routines as well as the technical infrastructures of different firms. Finally the paper brings into focus the importance of the telecommunications policy debate and points up the poverty of seeing telecommunication infrastructure development independently of the both industrial and regional policy.

References

Amin, A. and K. Robins (1991), 'Marshallian Industrial Districts' *CURDS*, University of Newcastle upon Tyne.

Antonelli, C. (1988), *New Information Technology and Industrial Change : The Italian Case,* Kluwer Academic, Dordrecht.

Antonelli, C. (1992), *The Economics of Information Networks,* North–Holland, Amsterdam.

Aoki, M. et al (1990), *The Firm as a Nexus of Treaties,* Sage London

Barrett, S. and B. Konsynski (1982), 'Inter-organizational Information Sharing Systems',*Management Information Systems Quarterly,* Dec pp 93–105.

Bianchi, P. (1986), 'Industrial Restructuring within an Italian Perspective' Working Paper No. 2, *Nomisma,* Sept.

Bellini N. (1987), 'Intermediaries and Structural Change in Small Firm Areas. The Italian, Experience' Stanford University, June.

Camagni R. (1991), *Innovation Networks : Spatial Perspective,* Belhaven, London.

Capello,R.and H. Williams, (1992), 'Network Trajectories and Organisational

Dynamics', *The Economics of Information Networks*, pp 347-362.

Capello,R. and H. Williams (1990), 'Nuove strategie di impresa, nuovi sistemi spaziali e nuove teccnologie dell'informazione come strmenti di riduzione della incertezza', *Economia e Politica Industriale*, 67 september pp 43-72.

Capello,R., Taylor,J. and H. Williams (1990), 'Computer networks and Competitive Advantage in the Building Societies', *International Journal of Information Management*, 10 (54-66).

Cremer, J. (1990), 'Common Knowledge and the Co-ordination of Economic Activities', *The Firm as a Nexus of Treaties,* Sage London, pp 53-76.

Davenport,T. (1992), *Process Innovation: Re-engineering Work Through Information Technology*, Harvard University Press.

Forengo (1988), 'Inter-organisational Networks and Market Structures', *New Information Technology and Industrial Change: The Italian Case,* Kluwer, Dordrecht.

Gillespie, A.G. and H. Williams (1988), 'Telecommunications and the Reconstruction of Regional Comparative Advantage', *Environment and Planning A*, 20, pp. 1311-1321.

Gordon, R. (1991), 'Innovation Industrial Networks and High Tech Regions', *Innovation Networks*, (op cit) pp 174-195.

Hammer, M. (1990), 'Re-engineering Work: Don't Automate, Obliterate', *Harvard Business Review*, July-August, pp 104-112.

Hepworth M.E. (1989), *Geography of the Information Economy*, Belhaven, London.

Keen, P (1986), *Competing in Time*, Ballinger Publishing Cambridge, Mass.

Keen, P. (1991), *Shaping The Future: Business Design Through information Technology*, Harvard Business School Press.

McInerney, J. (1991), *Brightness Falls,* Bloomsbury.

Nelson,R. and S. Winter, (1982), *An Evolutionary Theory of Economic Change,* The Belknap Press of Harvard University Press, Cambridge, Mass.

Piore, M.J. and C.F. Sable, (1984), *The Second Industrial Divide Possibilities for Prosperity*, Basic Books, New York.

Scott, A.T. (1988), 'Flexible Production Systems & Regional Development', *International Journal of Urban and Regional Research,* 12, 2, pp. 171-185.

Storper M and S. Chrisopherson, (1987), Flexible Specialisation and Regional Industrial Agglomeration : The Case of the US Motion Picture Industry, *Annual of the Association of American Geographers*, 77, 1, 104-117.

Taylor J and H. Williams (1991), 'The Networked Firm', in Williams B and B. Spaul, (eds.), *IT and Accounting,,* Chapman Hall, London.

Taylor J. and H. Williams (1990), 'The Scottish Highlands and Islands Initiative: An Alternative Model for Development', *Telecommunications Policy,* June, pp. 189-192.

Williams, H. (1992), 'Firm Boundaries and Soft Edges' Inaugural Lecture, University of Strathclyde, Glasgow.

Note

1. A more detailed account of this example can be found in either reports from the National Audit Office or in the Financial Times, 21/2/92.

13 Knowledge networks, science parks and regional development: An international comparative analysis of critical success factors

P. Nijkamp, G. van Oirschot and A. Oosterman

13.1 The changing scene of regional development

In the past decade the scope and substance of regional development have drastically changed. The traditional viewpoints and policy strategies on problem regions - characterized by high unemployment, low income and low productivity, poor accessibility and insufficient level of public services - have shifted from passive support measures to active self-reliance strategies. The awareness has grown that regions are no islands in a calm sea, but part of a spatial economic network dominated by competitive forces (Nijkamp 1993). Regions which - through their competitive advantage - are able to attract a considerable share of the national and international market will become the winners in this game (cf. Biehl 1986; Porter 1991). Thus regions may in principle be regarded as islands of innovation and entrepreneurial spirit in a broader spatial network context.

This regional focus has often been advocated from the viewpoint of locational efficiency induced by both a reduction in transaction costs as a result of geographical proximity and the presence of external economies stimulating an industrial atmosphere and incubation climate. But it is increasingly recognized (see Camagni 1991) that the regional scene is extremely dynamic, which offers two more potential benefits for innovative regions:

- a collective learning process that stimulates local creativity and technogenesis through local synergies (see also Kamann and Nijkamp 1990).
- a decline *in dynamic uncertainty* intrinsic in technological developments and innovative processes.

Clearly, emphasis on dynamic development processes in a competitive and innovative setting leads directly to an evolutionary approach to spatial dynamics.

An important element of recent theory building in the field of regional dynamics is based on network concepts, not only in terms of material infrastructure and communication networks favouring the competitive advantages of regions, but also in terms of new network configurations of firms and services institutions aiming at achieving dynamic excellence

Networks provide proper channels for efficient logistics, marketing and sales policies, as well as for information gathering and processing.

The relevance of network views on spatial competition has also been illustrated by the subdivision of regions into promising regions, called 3C+ regions (regions characterized by connectivity, creativity, and competence), and lagging regions, called 3C- regions (regions characterized by congestion, claustrophobia and criminality) (see also Andersson 1985, and Nijkamp 1993). Networks are able to offer an incubation function for new entrepreneurial strategies through an efficient interchange of knowledge and information, goods and people. In conclusion, access to a high quality knowledge, information, telecommunication and infrastructure network offers many opportunities for creative and new decisions and strategies of firms. This observation is once more important, as the increasing share of the service sector and the knowledge component in industrial products suggests that learning principles (learning-by-examining, learning-by-doing and learning–by–using) become a critical competitive tool: reduction of uncertainty is most probably the highest benefit in an information society.

Traditionally, firms are supposed to face five types of uncertainty (Camagni 1991):
- information gaps caused by real world complexities
- assessment gaps caused by lack of ex ante qualitative information
- competence gaps caused by insufficient information processing abilities of decision makers
- competence-decision gaps caused by imperfect foresight into future strategic possibilities
- control gaps caused by lack of control or power on new actions.

In coping with such a wide range of static and dynamic uncertainties firms are trying to minimize risk and incorrect decisions through various activities:
- search functions
- screening functions
- transcoding functions
- selection functions
- control functions.

In doing so, firms are intrinsically dependent on their local environment, which may provide the following support mechanisms for these five functions, respectively:
- collective information - gathering and screening functions
- signalling functions
- collective learning processes
- collective processes of developing managerial styles and decision routines
- informal decision coordination functions.

In conclusion, information and knowledge are becoming one of the most critical success factors in regional development policies. This issue will be further discussed in the next section.

13.2 Knowledge infrastructure and regional development

The increasing knowledge and information intensity of modern production has provoked an increasing orientation of regional policy towards the creation of R&D centres, research laboratories, science parks, universities, transfer centres and related institutes for higher education (see Andersson et al. 1989). The regional economic interest in such knowledge-intensive institutes was not so much determined by the related expenditure patterns of the (relatively high income) employees of such institutes, but rather by the push effects of knowledge intensive areas. Silicon Valley, the Research Triangle, Route 128 in Boston, Tsukuba, Sophia Antipolis, and the Cambridge Science Park are well known examples of successful initiatives (cf. Hall and Markusen 1985, Rogers and Larsen 1984). Consequently, the concept of a knowledge network has increasingly come to the fore as an instrument in a regional development strategy (see also Batten et al. 1989). Such knowledge networks generate, collect and transfer scientific information via a multitude of channels and hence generate an information-rich incubator function for knowledge-based activities in both the private and the public sector. Especially the above mentioned 3C+ regions offer the necessary favourable conditions for competitive advantage. As shown by Batten et al. (1989) such regions are nodes in both material and non-material networks (see Figure 13.1).

The assessment of the socioeconomic impacts of knowledge centres is not an easy task (see Charles and Howells 1992; Luger and Goldstein 1991; Trow and Nybom 1991), because statistical information is scarce, many spill-overs to other areas exist and the real effects have a long lead time. A very interesting example of university impact analysis in the Netherlands using sophisticated regional economic models can be found in Florax (1992). Even though the direct regional economic benefits are not always impressive, the generative effects of knowledge centres - in terms of attracting high tech activities - are in general regarded as the most important cornerstones of regional R&D strategies.

It is indeed noteworthy that from the viewpoint of the private sector, the presence of a knowledge network is increasingly regarded as a primary locational factor (see Aydalot 1984, Malecki 1984, Nijkamp 1986, Oakey et al. 1987 and Premus 1982), as it allows entrepreneurs to benefit from the availability of new information, while at the same time a linkage to a knowledge and information node provides access to broader national and international networks.

It is therefore no surprise that many regions in the industrialized world are increasingly reaping the fruits of a network economy in which regions play a central role in an international competitive system. It is evident that a prerequisite for becoming a 'winner' in this competitive game is to build up a flexible and innovative high-technology and high-knowledge economy. Recent experiences show that there are various alternative development options in policies regarding knowledge creation, technological restructuring and innovation. They range from large-scale top down driven initiatives (e.g., the Airbus consortium in Europe) to small-scale local initiatives (e.g., regional information systems for local retailers).

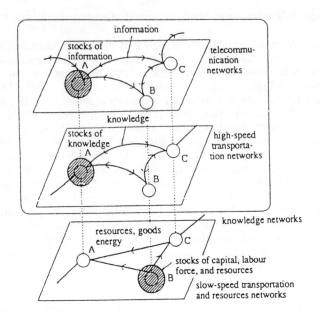

Figure 13.1 Knowledge and information in a networked society
Source: Batten et al. (1989)

Despite the diversity in these initiatives, there is one lesson which has become a common belief among both private and public decision-makers: technological innovation (and knowledge) is not 'manna from heaven', but can be stimulated and induced by well focused initiatives. The provision of incentives and the creation of favourable incubation conditions can generate creative and innovative behaviour of entrepreneurs. One of such stimuli is offered by the *science park* concept which is the focal point of the present paper. This concept is based on a synergetic view on scientific research and technological progress: innovations can be stimulated by locating new entrepreneurial activities in 3C+ regions (see Section 1). Such regions are a typical product of a competitive network economy. The success of a 3C+ region depends in particular on:

1   the availability of technological *hardware*, such as the existence of a good transport and communications system and the availability of land;

2   the existence and use of advanced *software*, such as the availability of a skilled and dedicated labour force, a population that is receptive to technical progress, and access to research institutes, end users and supply markets;

3   the implementation of appropriate *orgware*, e.g. the presence of supporting services and government policies favouring entrepreneurship;

4   the presence of a favourable *ecoware*, e.g., in terms of residential and cultural amenities;

5   the availability of *finware*, such as the availability of seed capital and venture capital.

228

The previous elements can be incorporated in a so-called *pentagon* model representing the decisive factors for successful 3C+ regions (see Figure 13.2).

It is interesting to observe that the long history of Europe clearly demonstrates that the rise and fall of 3C+ regions depend to a large extent on the factors mentioned in Figure 13.2. The places favoured in the Hanseatic period, the Industrial Revolution, and the current Information Age were able to generate new activities as a result of favourable incubator conditions embedded in the above five pentagon factors.

Seen from the above angles, it is evident that knowledge and information nodes, which are often located in accessible industrial and commercial centres with a diverse labour market and a creative climate, are to be regarded as obvious candidates for membership of the 3C+ regions family. In this context, the phenomenon of a science park has to be understood which has become a popular policy tool in many countries. In addition to exploiting the strong features of 3C+ regions via science park initiatives, in many countries science parks have also become a part of regional policy regarding 3C- regions. This difference will undoubtedly have implications for the success and performance of science parks, as will be shown in subsequent sections.

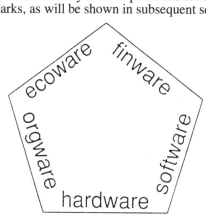

Figure 13.2 The pentagon model

13.3 Pathways to science parks

Technological development and economic growth are becoming increasingly intertwined phenomena. Technologically advanced products determine to a large extent the country's international competitiveness and therefore its welfare. In addition, it is also recognized that our world is at the brink of a technological revolution based on a high knowledge intensity. The impact of information technology on other sectors of the economy is expected to lead to an upswing in economic activity, and ultimately to a so called 'information society' or 'network society'.

Public decision makers and economists have become aware of this important relationship and feel that technological development ought to be stimulated. Many (especially regional) governments have therefore extended the visible hand of the state by assisting 'high tech' industries and individual companies by means of new policy instruments. Many of these instruments are aimed at the formation and growth of small new technology based firms, which are considered as seedcorn of the technological revolution.

This rising interest in technology policy has been accompanied by a general belief that universities and other research institutes represent a resource, in terms of knowledge and research, that can be tapped in order to promote high technology-based growth. Some authors have even compared the role of the research institute in an information society with that of a factory in an industrial society. The increased attention for technological development and the role of research institutes in this process has led to the rise of a new concept, viz. the science park.

Science parks are property developments alongside a knowledge or research institute. Their aim is to encourage the growth and formation of both new technology based firms and research institutes or knowledge centres. To accomplish this aim a science park facilitates the transfer of knowledge between research and business life; their function is that of *engineering creativity*.

Although a large number of science parks have been set up by various government agencies - often for reasons of regional technology development -, they are by no means the only founders. Universities have been among the first park founders and in the 1980s private companies have also become actively involved in science park development.

A government agency, a research institute or a private firm participates in a science park for the simple reason that it expects to benefit from its involvement (cf. Currie 1985, Dunford 1992, van Geenhuizen 1986, Gibb 1985, Klurfain–Spyridakis 1992, and Lacave 1992). To mention a few examples: a university may become more involved in industrial problems and practice, a small high-tech firm can use a university's computing facilities, and a city council may effectively promote technological development. A very interesting question then is: under what circumstances can the benefits of a science park be maximized; in other words *what are the critical success factors of a science park?* This is the central issue of this paper.

Many regional government agencies aim to build up a flexible and innovative high-technology economy by means of various customized incentives for the region at hand. The science park concept is one such incentive. It should be noted however, that nowadays various terms, such as science park, business park or incubator are being used to describe broadly the same phenomenon. We will start with some definitional and terminological remarks (see Nijkamp et al. 1992).

According to the widely used definition of the United Kingdom Science Park Association (UKSPA), a science park is:

A property based initiative which:
- has formal operational links with a university, other higher educational institutions, or a *major centre of research* (hereafter HEIs);
- is designed to encourage the formation and growth of *knowledge-based businesses* and other organizations normally resident on site;
- has a *management function* which is actively engaged in the transfer of technology and business skills to the organizations on site.

We use the term 'science park' for every such property based initiative, but it can be useful to differentiate between four different types of science and creativity based policy initiatives.

1   *Incubators* are 'breeding grounds' for young scientists who want to commercialize their own research. An incubator centre is small, provides financial, managerial and technical assistance to the new entrepreneurs and is usually created by an HEI.
2   *Science parks* are set up to promote the cooperation between HEIs and innovative enterprises. In order to improve the chances of a fruitful cross–fertilization of the ideas of entrepreneurs and scientists, most science parks are set up in the neighbourhood of HEIs. Although a science park often has an incubator on its site, its efforts are aimed at attracting existing enterprises.
3   A *technopolis* encompasses the concept of a science park. Apart from promoting the commercialization of science, it tries to create a general 'receptiveness' to a society based on technology. A true technopolis has a scientific, an economic as well as a social dimension. At this moment, the only cities that qualify as a technopolis are Tsukuba in Japan and Sophia Antipolis in France. All other configurations are of a much smaller scale.
4   A *business park* tries to promote the establishment of knowledge-based firms, but has no formal operational links with HEIs. It is therefore by definition not a science park. Foreign experience show that science parks of this type have a much higher failure rate than incubators and 'real' science parks.

The first science parks emerged in the United States during the 1950s. Europe followed in the 1970s, but science parks only started to grow rapidly in the past decade. Nowadays we find science parks - with different sizes and different degrees of specialization - in many countries, especially in France, Great Britain, Germany, the United States, Canada, Sweden, Japan and The Netherlands.

The period of rapid growth of science parks did not emerge until the eighties. Member states of the European Community, impressed by the success of the parks in the United States, attempted to create their own Silicon Valleys. Empirical evidence from the United States of substantial high technology growth in the vicinity of certain research institutes had made European politicians, facing serious economic problems and high unemployment rates in the traditional industrial areas, enthusiastic about the potential offered by science parks.

While in Europe policy makers often focused on job creation, the Japanese government announced a project aimed at economic restructuring. This so called Technopolis project was implemented to restructure the national economy from a traditional industrial manufacturing to knowledge intensive, high value-added production (cf. Stöhr and Ponighaus 1992). The number of science parks in Japan (technopoles included) jumped from zero in 1980 to one hundred and three in 1990 (see Masuda 1990). In the United States, science parks boomed as well. Although they were originally a university initiative, state and local governments as well as real estate developers joined the science park carousel. Figures 13.3 and 13.4 show the rise of science parks in the United States and the European Community, respectively (time series are not available for Japan).

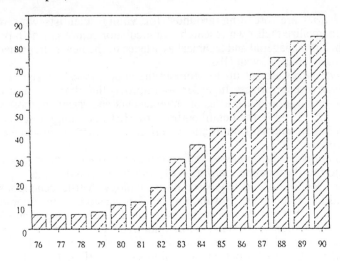

Figure 13.3 **Cumulative science park development in the United States**

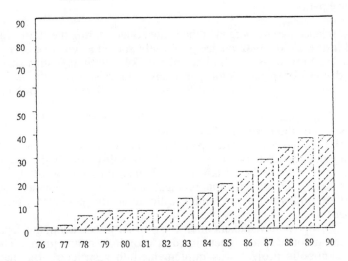

Figure 13.4 **Cumulative science park development in the European Community**

In spite of very different historical backgrounds, and of different social and economic conditions, it seems that three basic causes have led to the rapid growth of science parks in most industrialized countries: (a) a growing impact of technological development on economic growth, (b) the growing belief that universities and knowledge centres are underutilized sources of technological innovation, and (c) a change in regional policies (i.e., more bottom-up initiatives).

It was estimated by Van Oirschot and Oosterman (1992) that direct employment offered by science parks is nowadays about 150,000 in the United States, 50,000 in the European Community and 25,000 in Japan. Since reliable and comprehensive data about science parks are hard to find, these estimates are rather crude. Although science parks have been growing very fast in recent years, their impact on economic development should not be overestimated. They represent only a small fraction of jobs in the high-technology sectors and a negligible percentage of total employment in the major industrial countries.

Apart from these basic causes, a number of other factors have facilitated the boom. In the 1980s universities and public research institutes in almost all industrial countries faced drastic budget cuts. It was felt that science parks could grow into an additional source of income for these institutions: a direct source, through the sale or lease of land, as well as an indirect source, because an improved image would allow a university to compete better for research funds and for bright students. In a number of countries, such as the United States and the United Kingdom, universities possessed land which they were only allowed to use for academic purposes. A side-effect of these budget cuts was an increased work-pressure on academics accompanied by an increased income differential between the private and public sector, which in turn would increase their willingness to become engaged in the commercialization of scientific research.

In addition, universities and private companies show an increasing social responsibility. They are more and more inclined to pursue goals which are outside their original fields of interest, viz. education/research and profit, respectively. In some instances, the motivation of a founder to set up a science park is even to contribute to the local community.

Finally, there is an increasing 'receptivity' of society towards technology, as well as an increasing awareness of the paramount impact of technological development on economic welfare. This eases the path for governments, universities and private sector parties to promote science parks.

In many regions all over the world, policy makers appear to have turned to the upgrading of *indigenous* regional resources, which may trigger new - often knowledge-based - activities (cf. Davelaar 1991, Rothwell and Zegveld 1985, MITI 1990). The motives for indigenous development can be summarized as follows: (a) local firms are more firmly committed to local interests than branch plants; (b) new technology based firms, especially small ones, contribute considerably more than proportionally to the net growth of new jobs (see Birch 1979); (c) new technology based firms are expected to offer higher salaries and higher quality jobs than relocated branch plants; (d) new technology based firms are considered to be 'footloose' (in contrast to the industries associated with the fourth Kondratieff wave, they need not be located near sources of raw materials, energy, water, etc), and (e) in providing employment stability in under-industrialized regions, small local firms are superior to manufacturing divisions or branches of large firms.

Government agencies in most industrialized countries have thus turned to the promotion of new and small high technology firms and the attraction of high technology investment as the new means of promoting regional development. In some of these countries, science parks have become an instrument of regional development. The majority of parks in Great Britain (see Henneberry 1984) and Japan (see Tatsuno 1986), for instance, has been created to relieve regional imbalances. In all cases, science parks appear to serve simultaneously a research function, a commercial function and a knowledge transfer function (see also Figure 13.5).

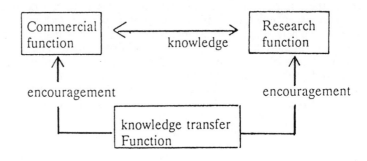

Figure 13.5 The science park concept

13.4 Critical success factors of science parks

The stages from planning a science park to its implementation as a sustainable success story of engineering creativity are manifold and long lasting. Here we will report on findings from a recent postal survey questionnaire among several science parks all over the world (see Van Oirschot and Oosterman 1992), with a special view on the following phases:
- strategic planning
- organization
- financing
- design and architecture
- management, and
- external environment

All these phases will succinctly be dealt with. For each of the stages, it is attempted to identify critical success factors.

13.4.1 Strategic planning

The strategic planning process which forms the first necessary step to start-up a science park is represented in Table 13.1.

Given the multiplicity of actors involved, due attention has to be given to potential conflicts between objectives of various parties. Although every founding party seems to have its own individual goal, three distinct groups of

234

founders each having similar types of goals can be distinguished: (1) government agencies (local, regional and central), (2) research institutes, and (3) private companies.

Government agencies are involved in the vast majority of science parks, be it as founder, financier or otherwise. Their interest in science park development can be seen as a 'confluence' of structural changes in the world economy and of changes in regional policies. Government agencies mention various motives for their interest in science park development, such as job creation, economic growth, the restructuring of a region's economy, technology transfer, the creation or support of new technology based firms, the enhancement of research opportunities for universities, etc., but in the end these motives are derived from the wish to (1) stimulate technological development, or (2) to stimulate regional development.

Universities (or, in several cases, public research institutes) have been the very first organizations to create a science park. First generation parks, such as Stanford Research Park, Cambridge Science Park and the Research Park Triangle have all been initiated by universities, partly to use idle land or to invest capital. In other instances, universities or other higher educational institutions have not taken the initiative, but have been approached by government agencies or private companies to perform the research function of the park. The reasons for their involvement are many.

Table 13.1
The strategic planning process of a science park

PHASE	ACTIVITY	PERIOD
Goal setting	Definition of product	
Strategy formulation	Identification of product and market	Before construction
Strategy implementation	Organization	
	Financing	
		During construction
	Park design	
		After construction
	(Operational) Management	

The private sector has so far played a modest, though increasingly important role in science park development. In general, it has followed a wait-and-see policy. The private firms which have already been involved in the establishment of a science park can be subdivided into three groups: (1) real estate developers operating purely for profit; (2) venture capitalists and high–technology firms aiming to have a 'window on technology' (this group appears to be small, probably because it is more efficient for them to invest in one of the companies located on the park than in the park itself); (3) large local firms investing in science parks for reasons of public relations and social responsibility (job creation, regional technological development). Table 13.2 lists the founders and their objectives.

Table 13.2
Goals and founders of science parks

FOUNDER	GOALS
Government agencies	Regional development Technological development
Universities	Regional development Technological development Financial returns Expand employment opportunities Enhance prestige Use idle land Invest capital
Private firms	Regional development Technological development Financial returns Window on technology Public relations

Table 13.3
Partnerships of science park founders

Control → Funding ↓	Government	Research institute	Private firm	Property developer
Government	control by government but universities have often creative leadership (formal co-operation)	joint-venture; often a loose co operation: more or less sponta - neous develop - ment	public private partnership; government funding lowers the risks	public private partnership: gov - ernment lowers risk and provides appropriate conditions
Research Institute	–	entirely owned & privately financed venture; spontaneous developed	–	–
Firms	–	firms doing part of the property development	–	private firms pro - vide a part of the property
Property develop-er	–	joint-venture on a formal base; both involved in decision making	not present: science park too risky to be financed by private sector firms only	not present: science park too risky to be financed by one private firm

All parties involved share also a responsibility in terms of the science park product and the market by selecting the proper candidates. The large variety of related names (e.g., incubation centre, innovation centre, technology park, business park, brain park or research park) indicates that the actual practice shows a wide diversity of policy orientations of science parks.

It turns out that during the strategic planning stage the most important critical success factors from a managerial viewpoint are:
- harmonious working relationships among founding parties (including long term commitment)
- flexible and creative planning practices
- early establishment of formal links with a high quality research institute.

13.4.2 Organization

Science parks - once established - appear to exhibit a great variety of organizational configurations and cooperative modes. Table 13.3 gives a systematic typology of modes of cooperation by looking into both control and funding.

This table gives in a pairwise way the most common and feasible modes of partnership among the main parties involved in the development of a science park.

The extent to which a science park is planned or is the result of a spontaneous development is of decisive importance for strategic planning, which in turn influences the organizational structure. The differences in strategic planning between European parks - where governments have a clear role in science park establishment - and the United States - where governments have only marginally been involved in science park development - are usually reflected in the legal structure of the park. For example, in the United States approximately 25 per cent is owned by for-profit corporations (see Luger and Goldstein 1991). In Europe, on the other hand, more than 60 percent of the science parks is under governmental control, while the remainder is mainly controlled by universities. In Europe, public financing and other government assistance have played a more pronounced role in science park development.

The various founding parties are able to create different types of partnerships. Since hardly any initiator, be it a research institute, government agency or private firm, has all managerial, technical and financial resources to develop a science park, it follows that critical success factors for the organization are:
- parties with complementary resources must cooperate;
- the organization structure must be chosen in accordance with the strategy of the founders.

13.4.3 Financing

Science parks are primarily financed by public authorities and by universities. The private sector considers them as financially unattractive. From a societal point of view, science parks can nevertheless be very attractive. We will see that this inconsistency often justifies government interference.

A science park can be seen as an investment decision with the following characteristics:

Long gestation period: it typically takes 10 to 25 years before a science park breaks even or becomes profitable. This requires sufficient patience of all parties involved; it also requires financial instruments tuned to the expected cash flow pattern of the park and the ability of the investors to provide funds in subsequent stages of development.

High capital investment amounts: especially in the first stage of development large amounts of money are required to finance land, site infrastructure and buildings of a fullsize science park.

Involvement of various parties: the multiparty model makes the financing decision more complex than a common business investment decision.

Lack of liquidity: a financial participation in a park can only be sold after the science park turns out to be successful. In other words, exit options are virtually non-existent. This is of course an obstacle for private investors.

The cash outlays of a science park are relatively high, concentrated at the beginning of the project and can be estimated with reasonable accuracy. The cash revenues, however, are spread over the entire lifetime of the park and are difficult to estimate, because of the unique character of a science park (in terms of stated goals, location, and parties involved). The future cash revenues depend mainly on the number of tenants a science park is able to attract; it is difficult to assess this number. For these reasons, science parks are risky investment projects. The perception of the private sector is that the expected return of an equity participation in a science park cannot compensate for this risk.

Private firms, including banks, are neither inclined to extend loans to science park founders. A park often lacks collateral; if a park fails, there will be hardly any assets that can be sold to pay off debts. This is because buildings and site infrastructure are adapted to the specific needs of tenant firms and are therefore difficult to sell in case of failure.

The financing of science parks is therefore largely marked by the absence of private investors. In the United Kingdom, government agencies account for about 50 per cent of total financing of science parks; the figures for the United States and Japan are 50 and 94 per cent, respectively (see Masuda 1990, and Luger and Goldstein 1991). Figures about investments by research institutes are not available. Investments by the private sector are concentrated in a small number of parks which are located in areas which are already characterized by the presence of technology based firms. Both private parks in Japan and the seventeen fully privately financed parks in the US have all been set up in such areas; a similar situation exists in Europe, though in a less extreme form. In these cases the potential market for the product - space and services - is high, so that revenues can be estimated with more accuracy and the gestation period is likely to be relatively shorter. In addition, the value of land in these 'high tech' areas is relatively high and can serve as collateral.

Since few regions are endowed with a critical mass of new technology based firms, the vast majority of science parks is primarily financed with government money. Especially in the economically less developed regions science parks are heavily relying on public funding or semi-public funding (via state banks, e.g.).

Clearly, a science park passes through different stages of its life time and the type of financing is dependent on its evolution. This is briefly summarized in Table 13.4, where a distinction is made between internal (i.e., directly committed via the management of a park) and external (only financially interested) investors.

In retrospect, the most important critical success factors in the financing stages of a science park are:

- substantial financial support of government authorities
- long-term commitment of all financiers
- willingness by financiers to absorb significant losses in the initial stages of a park development.

Table 13.4
An overview of financiers in different stages of development of a science park

Financiers	Pre-construction	Land	Construction	Marketing	Operation
Internal investors					
Central governments	X	X	X	?	?
Local governments	XX	X	XX	?	?
Universities	XX	XX	XX	X	X
Private firms	O	O	X	?	?
Property developers	?	?	X	?	O
Venture capitalists	O	O	?	?	O
External investors					
Central governments	?	?	?	0	O
Local governments	XX	XX	XX	?	?
Universities	?	?	O	O	O
Private firms	O	O	O	O	O
Property developers	O	O	X	O	O
Venture capitalists	O	O	O	O	O

XX Financing important   ? Financing possible
X   Financing available O Financing not available

13.4.4 Park design

The physical design and outer architecture of a science park is generally regarded as a major factor contributing to the image of a park. Landscaping is the process of making the site suitable for the science park to function. Many parks have formulated restrictions on land use are density.

Virtually all successful science parks have restricted on site manufacturing. Most of them do not allow manufacturing at all, while others only allow light manufacturing or prototype production. Polluting and dangerous activities are almost always restricted or prohibited. Landscaping issues that effect a park's image are listed in Table 13.5.

In terms of critical success factors, the following conditions can be mentioned:

239

- a prestigious outlook and imaginative architecturing
- flexible and low cost buildings that are appropriate for innovative activities and knowledge transfer.

Table 13.5
Image related landscape issues

Land available for development
Volumetric ratio (floorspace / site area)
Ecological / environmental issues
Provision of residential areas and shopping centres
Provision of leisure facilities
Zoning restrictions

13.4.5 Management

The management of a science park is different from that of a conventional industrial park in that it undertakes efforts to stimulate cooperation between its tenants and to help its tenants grow. To encourage the transfer of technological knowledge between the commercial and research function and assist on site organizations, the management team provides for various services.

Managing the park during the operational phase is considered to be a critical phase, as in this stage the park management has to prove that it is able to sell its product and become a profitable organization. It is hard however to demonstrate a positive impact of the supply of non-property elements on the benefits of the commercial, research and knowledge transfer functions. Some even doubt whether on-site management is required to stimulate interactions between tenants and the university and whether assisting tenants will resolve particular business problems (Luger and Goldstein 1991). There are however some studies which suggest a positive contribution of services to the success of a science park. For example, in the United Kingdom, one third of companies located on a science park mentioned on-site management as a reason to locate on the site. Luger and Goldstein (1991) found that US parks consider the provision of services as one of the three most important location factors.

Henneberry (1984) has divided the services that a management team can provide into four groups. The first group is *basic unsophisticated services*. These are the general secretarial services such as typing, reception, photocopying, telephone answering etc. Fax and electronic mail are also increasingly required by tenants and if provided centrally, they are cost–effective to tenants. Although science parks are set up to accommodate high tech firms, the tenant demand for these 'low tech' services is higher than the demand for more advanced services.

The second group is *technology and training services*. Contrary to basic services, technology support and training services are rarely provided on conventional industrial estates. For this reason, new high tech firms regard these services as an 'added value' of the science park concept. Tenants have access to university libraries and databases and are sometimes advised on patents and other forms of intellectual property; research institutes might also be able to carry out subcontracted R&D. Technology support can be offered by

240

an on-site company or research institute or by an external organization.

The third group of services is *business services,* such as business planning, management consulting and marketing assistance. A particularly weak point of small firms is the formulation of a corporate business strategy and the implementation of this strategy. The management of a firm is often insufficiently aware of product/technology trends and the size of its target market, which can have considerable consequences for its future prospects. Marketing assistance is also important, as small firms are often unable to promote their products and to create the sales channels required to reach the national or international markets and thus fully exploit their products's profit potential.

Financial services is the last group of services. They are of utmost importance to small firms. Many small firms or persons with promising ideas lack the cash to realize them. Banks and other private investors are reluctant to finance them for various reasons.

As Table 13.6 shows, in most developed countries private funding and bank loans are the most important financing options for start-ups. Because of their modest financing requirements and high risk, venture capital is only available for the most promising small firms. A problem related to venture capital is the unwillingness of owners to lose control. A venture capital investment involves (quasi-) equity participation, which means that the firms are no longer fully owned by the founder(s). Furthermore, the concept of venture capital implies active involvement in the companies they finance until they are sufficiently developed for disposition. This involvement varies from the presence of a member in the board of directors to hands-on management, to cope with problems such as marketing and financial matters. One can therefore say, that the equity gap experienced in this stage of development is mainly the result of a management gap.

Government assistance (grants, loan guarantees, interest subsidies, etc.) is a small but growing source of finance for small firms. Unfortunately, small firms find it extremely difficult to obtain the support they are entitled to. The application process is sometimes so complicated and time consuming that most firms do not even apply for government grants.

To recapitulate the critical factors then for a successful management of science parks are:
- provision of services consistent with the science park's profile
- strict orientation of management strategies towards the park's needs
- attraction of some key firms ('anchor companies').

Table 13.6
Sources of finance for new SMEs (%)

	UK	Japan	US
Personal savings	55.0	60.2	66.2
Banks	17.1	22.4	25.0
Government agencies	16.9	2.3	3.5
Manufacturing companies	2.5	NA	NA

Sources: Monck (1988)

241

13.4.6 External environment

Given the diversity and types of science parks, various important external factors can be distinguished that enhance the viability of a science park. They are summarized in Table 13.7.

Table 13.7
External success factors of science parks

Economic factors	Social factors	Environmental factors
Risk capital Skilled labour force Related industries Infrastructure	Local support groups Entrepreneurial spirit	Desirable living environment

Most founders and managers of science parks are aware of the impact of these factors on the success of their park. If the region in which the park is located is not endowed with (all) external success factors, they sometimes attempt to 'internalize' these factors. Some parks, for instance, have created a venture capital fund to be invested in their own tenants, others organize courses in entrepreneurial management, or provide high quality telecommunication facilities.

The assumption that the availability of external success factors is positively correlated with per capita regional income is supported by Henneberry (1984) and Masuda (1990). They have shown that science parks (and especially the total acreage of parks) in the United Kingdom and Japan respectively are highly concentrated in regions with a per capita income above average. This is also confirmed by data from the US and the EC (see Table 13.8).

Table 13.8
Science parks in regions with a per capita income above national average

	Number of parks (%)	Total acreage of parks (%)
Japan	66,0	86,7
United States	65,4	81,5
European Community	49,7	68,4
United Kingdom	55,8	76,2

Source: Calculations based on Henneberry (1984); Masuda (1990)

Thus in conclusion the abovementioned economic, social and environmental factors may be seen as critical external success factors for science parks.

242

13.4.7 Concluding remarks

The above mentioned critical success factor have been identified from a broad survey among various science parks in various parts of the world. After this exploratory stage these results have been further investigated by in depth analysis of five specific science parks: Sophia Antipolis (France), the Stanford Research Park (USA), the Technopolis Project (Japan), the Hsinchu Science Based Industrial Park (Taiwan), and the Research Triangle Park (USA). The experiences from these cases supported the above exploratory notions.

Science parks appear to differ enormously with respect to their strategic goals, their formulated strategy in terms of products and markets, and in the implementation of their strategies. At first sight, it seems impossible to formulate a list of critical success factors with general validity. But in practice, most science parks do pay attention to a number of common factors which are critical for their successful development.

General speaking, science parks may act as the incubator of new technological development in a region, or they may be the result of such a development. In the first case, the region has already experienced the growth of technology based firms; then science parks, often set up by market-oriented universities or property developers, can take advantage of this situation by offering them space and services. Thus these parks have spontaneously developed. But the vast majority of science parks is set up in a region without the presence of a critical mass of technology based firms. Primarily because of the difficulty to demonstrate a market need for science parks in regions without a 'high tech' industrial base, the private sector has been reluctant to invest in such developments.

Thus, as a stand-alone project, a science park is usually not viable from a purely financial point of view: the expected return is not commensurate with the perceived risk. But the benefits of these 'forerunners of high-tech growth' must be seen in a broader context. From a long term perspective, science parks can contribute to the technological development of a region's or nation's economy. But since private investors do usually not obtain most of these benefits, many governments agencies and universities have financed the development of science parks, notably in Japan and Europe. Without this assistance it is unlikely that science park development would have existed at its current level.

There are several factors which depend on the availability of financing: a prestigious outlook, the provision of services, and the provision of basic infrastructure. Science parks can create an attractive, prestigious image to attract large knowledge-intensive companies. Such companies are often able to generate a considerable and relatively riskless stream of income. A prestigious outlook can also be created to attract skilled labour force (e.g., the Hsinchu Science Based Industrial Park, Sophia Antipolis and various Japanese technopoles). This is important, because large firms are not willing to locate in an area with a shortage of skilled manpower. It must be noted however, that a prestigious outlook is expensive; if prices rise above a certain threshold, small technology based firms will no longer be able to pay the rent. In other words, a strong emphasis on the prestige and overall image of the park may become at odds with its technology transfer function.

243

The physical characteristics of a science park should of course meet evident conditions to attract tenant organizations, such as the presence of a good road infrastructure.

To encourage the formation and growth of small high tech firms, science parks should also provide more advanced services. We stress the importance of basic services (such as shared fax or a centralized switchboard), technical and training services, business services and financial services. Financial assistance is especially important, since the problems of starting firms are primarily financial in nature.

Contrary to most other organizations, science parks are usually set up by different institutions with different backgrounds and different strategic goals. The reason is that hardly any organization has all managerial, technical and financial resources at its disposal to develop a park.

The goals of the different founders may conflict with one another. These conflicts must be resolved, before the science park can function as a coordinated entity. Since an organization cannot exist without agreement among the founders about its desired state, it is of utmost importance to build consensus in the strategic planning process. Needless to say that short-sighted, fragmented policy making among the government, business and university components of a science park will do harm to the achievements of a park. If research institutes and companies are to benefit from each other's strengths, a real 'think collaboration culture' has to be developed.

The importance of harmonious working relationships is reinforced by the fact that founders have to cooperate for a long period of time. The typical gestation period for a park to become profitable or to break even is between 10 to 25 years and exit options hardly exist. Especially the commitment of financiers in science park development is critical for its success. They must be able to absorb substantial losses during the gestation period. Financiers do not only need to finance the construction of the park, but also the park's management team. We have seen that government agencies are regularly involved in the financing of a park.

The goals of an organization are best realized if strategy formulation and strategy implementation are congruent with these goals ('consistent fit'). The identification of product and target market, the organizational structure, the financing mechanisms, the physical characteristics of the park, as well as the services offered, are all to be determined by the goals set by the founders. Strategic planning practices must however, be flexible enough to respond easily to economic and technological changes.

What, as a summary question, appear to be the critical success factors of a science parks? After a careful analysis of the theory and practice of science parks, they can all be traced back to:
• The availability of government financing (in particular, for science parks in regions without a critical mass of high-tech firms).
• A consistent strategy, which leaves room for flexibility and creative management.
• Harmonious, long term working relations, which are safeguarded by a nucleus of dedicated people.

In conclusion, science parks can be seen as potentially powerful policy tools for regional development, but the road towards successful engineering creativity is paved with many stumbling blocks. Overcoming such bottlenecks in each development stage of the life cycle of a science park is a sine qua non.

Acknowledgement

The authors wish to thank Marina van Geenhuizen for her constructive comments on a previous draft of this paper.

References

AURRP and IASP (1990), *Research Park Directory*, AURRP and IASP, London.

Andersson, A.E. (1985), 'Creativity and Regional Development', *Papers of the Regional Science Association*, Vol. 56, pp. 5-20.

Andersson, A.E., Batten, D.F. and Karlsson, C. (eds) (1989), *Knowledge and Industrial Organization*, Springer, Berlin.

Aydalot, Ph. (1984), 'Crise and Espace', *Economica*, Paris.

Batten, D.F., Koboyashi, K. and Andersson, A.E. (1989), 'Knowledge, Nodes and Networks: An Analytical Perspective', *Knowledge and Industrial Organization*, (A.E. Andersson, K.F. Batten and C. Karlsson, eds.), Springer, Berlin, pp. 1-18.

Biehl, D. (1986), *The Contribution of Infrastructure to Regional Development*, DG XVI, EC, Brussels.

Birch, D. (1979), 'The Job Generation Process', *MIT Program on Neighbourhood and Regional Change*, Cambridge.

Camagni, R. (ed.) (1991), *Innovation Networks: Spatial Perspectives*, Belhaven, London.

Charles, D., and Howells, J. (1992), *Technology Transfer in Europe*, Belhaven, London.

Currie, J. (1985), *Science Parks in Britain*, CSP Economic Publications, Cardiff.

Davelaar, E.J. (1991), *Regional Economic Analysis of Innovation and Incubation*, Avebury, Aldershot, UK.

Dunford, M. (1992), 'Technopoles: Research, Innovation and Skills in Comparative Perspectives', *Topos*, vol. 5, pp. 29-54.

Florax, R. (1992), *The University: A Regional Booster?*, Avebury, Aldershot, UK.

Geenhuizen, M.S. van (1986), 'Science Parks, Prospects for Success?', *Proceedings IFHP International Congress*, Malmö.

Gibb, J.M. (ed.) (1985), *Science Parks and Innovation Centres*, Elsevier, Amsterdam.

Hall, P., and Markusen A. (eds.) (1984), *Silicon Landscapes*, Allen & Unwin, Boston.

Henneberry, J.M. (1984), 'Property for High Technology Industry', *Land Development Studies*, vol. 1, pp. 145-168.

Kamann, D.J., and P. Nijkamp (1990), 'Technogenesis: Incubation and

Diffusion', *The Spatial Context of Technological Development* (R. Cappellin and P. Nijkamp, eds.), Avebury, Aldershot, U.K., pp. 257-302.

Klurfain-Spyridakis, L. (1992), 'Technopoles and Science Parks', *Topos*, vol. 5, pp. 71-92.

Lacave, M. (1992), 'Science Park and University', *Topos*, vol. 5, pp. 107–116.

Luger, M.I., and Goldstein, H.A. (1991), *Technology in the Garden*, University of North Carolina Press, Chapel Hill.

Malecki, E.J. (1984), 'High Technology and Local Economic Development', *Journal of the American Planning Association*, vol. 50, pp. 262-269.

Masuda, S.(1990), Nihon No Saiensu Paku 1990 Nen No Genjo (The State of Science Parks in Japan in 1990), TIT-CRI Report, CRI-6, Tokyo.

MITI (1990), Outline and Present Status of the Technopolis Project, MITI, Tokyo.

Nijkamp, P. (ed.) (1986), *Technological Change, Employment and Spatial Dynamics*, Springer, Berlin.

Nijkamp, P. (1993), 'The United States of Europe', *European Planning Studies*, (forthcoming).

Nijkamp, P., G. van Oirschot and A. Oosterman, Technopolis and Spatial Development, *Topos*, vol. 5, 1992, pp. 93-106.

Oakey, R.P., Rothwell, M., Beesley, M. and Cooper, S.Y. (1987), 'Research and Development and Competitive Performance in British and American High Technology Small Firms', *Innovation: Adaptation and Growth, An International Perspective* (R. Rothwell and J. Bessan, eds.), Elsevier, Amsterdam, pp. 193-210.

Oirschot, G. van and Oosterman, A. (1992), *Engineering Creativity*, Master's Thesis, Dept. of Regional Economics, Free University, Amsterdam.

Porter, M. (1991), *The Competitive Advantage of Nations*, Free Press, New York.

Premus, R. (1982), *Location of High Technology Firms and Regional Economic Development*, US Government Printing Office, Washington, D.C.

Rogers, E.M. and Larsen, J.K. (1984), *Silicon Valley Fever*, New York.

Rothwell, R. and Zegveld, W. (1985), *Reindustrialization and Technology*, Longman, Harlow, Essex.

Stöhr, W. and Ponighaus, R. (1992), 'Towards a Data-Based Evolution of the Japanese Technopolis Policy', *Regional Studies*, vol. 26, no. 7, pp. 605-18.

Tatsuno, S. (1986), *The Technopolis Strategy: Japan, High Technology and the Control of the 21st Century*, Prentice Hall, Englewood Cliffs.

Trow, M.A. and Nybon, T. (1991), *University and Society*, Jessica Kingsley, London.

14 Barriers to technology transfer: The role of intermediary organizations

M. van Geenhuizen

14.1 Introduction

Since the late 1970s a growing scientific interest has become evident in the role of technology and innovation in long term economic growth and structural economic transformation. In addition, a growing awareness has emerged about the entrepreneurial framework of innovation and restructuring (cf. Freeman, 1982; Nelson and Winter, 1982). In this behaviourial line of inquiry, innovations are conceived of as entrepreneurial decisions and concomitantly, attention is drawn to the decision environment, organizational routine and search behaviour of companies. Key issues in this approach are uncertainty and risk, as well as the relevance of *knowledge* (cf. Thomas, 1987; Camagni, 19–91) and *creativity* (cf. Andersson, 1991).

Companies face generally different amounts of uncertainty, dependent on the newness of their economic activities (sector), as well as on their age (Figure 14.1). Regarding the sector, it is commonly acknowledged in product life cycle theory that in the stage of introduction of new products uncertainty is relatively large. This is true for the technology which is still unstable, and for the market which still has to be created (cf. Davelaar, 1989; Rothwell and Zegveld, 1985; Vernon, 1966). At the same time, the amount of uncertainty changes with the age of companies. Particularly in the early years, there is a lack of organizational experience (cf. Hannan and Freeman, 1989) and a shortage of marketing knowhow.

In the past decades there has been a general increase of uncertainty and risk faced by companies. First of all, new technologies pervasively changed advanced industrial economies. Information and communication technology, biotechnology and new materials had impacts which go clearly beyond the use of the technology self, for example, in new modes of organization of production and new work practices. A crucial development was also the increasing globalization. A major response to global competition has been to place more emphasis on the development of new product and new process technology to improve long term competition. At the same time, the lifespan of products was shortening progressively, for example, in microelectronics. As a result of these developments, companies had and have a growing need for technological know how.

Also of interest is the increased complexity of R&D in a number of sectors, for example, in pharmaceutical industry (Van Geenhuizen, 1993; Howells, 1992). Various R&D trajectories appear to be completed, and therefore, new products can only be invented at much higher costs and in a much longer timespan than before.

| | | COMPANY LIFE CYCLE | |
		young	older
PRODUCT LIFE CYCLE	introduction	large uncertainty	intermediate uncertainty
	growth maturity	intermediate uncertainty	small uncertainty

Figure 14.1 A two-way classification of companies

Moreover, development times are lengthened in specific sectors due to increased safety and testing requirements, such as in aircraft and space industry, and again pharmaceutical industry.

Companies use different sources in order to supply their need for technological knowledge. These sources are either internal or external, and operate with a large variety of institutionalization (Table 14.1). For example, inhouse generation and accumulation of knowledge may take place in separate R & D departments but also incorporated in production functions as a process of doing by learning. With regard to *external* sources, customers have achieved an increasingly important role in production modes where manufacturing is on their specification or in co-makership with them. These types of collaboration clearly followed from the general trend for risk-minimization and withdrawal on core-activities since the early 1980s. In this framework, also joint R & D with similar companies and use of professional services increased in importance (cf. Tordoir, 1993). The previous discussion indicates that companies have progressively moved to external knowledge sources over the past several years.

It is generally agreed that innovative behaviour and risk minimization are unequally dispersed over *space*, not only because of sectoral or socioeconomic variation among companies in different areas but also because of spatial differences in opportunities to reduce uncertainty and spatially discriminating urban and regional policies.

In the past decade the scope of regional policy has drastically changed. For example, the Dutch policy shifted from equality to efficiency and an appeal to the socalled self-organizing potentials of regions since the mid 1980s. This new approach emphasized regional endogenous growth, for example, by means of local initiatives. It is increasingly recognized that this type of growth may be strongly supported by the regional scene through benefits from localized collective learning processes (Camagni, 1991). Accordingly, the regional setting offers strong potentials for the reduction of various types of uncertainty that companies are currently facing. As a result, information and knowledge are becoming one of the major critical success factors in regional development policies.

Table 14.1
Sources of technological knowledge from a company perspective

Internal
-    R & D departments
-    R & D incorporated in production
-    Employees
-    Equipment
External
-    Customers
-    Suppliers of equipment, material
-    Non-profit business and branch organizations
-    Temporary staff or students
-    Other manufacturing companies (joint activities)
-    Universities and other public knowledge institutions
-    Profit and non-profit intermediary institutions
-    Professional service companies
-    Conferences and fairs
-    Sources of written information
-    Informal networks

One of the components of such regional policies is the identification of potentials of technology transfer between knowledge institutions and the (regional) business world, as well as barriers to this transfer. In the framework of regional policy, transfer centres and science parks are instruments aimed at advancing the specific technology flow between universities and industry, whereas innovation centres serve a broader process of technology transfer.

This paper falls apart into results of a conceptual exploration and results of an empirical analysis. First, the concepts of technology transfer and intermediation will be considered, in particular their structural characteristics and process characteristics (Section 14.2). Barriers to technology transfer will receive particular attention in Section 14.3. Section 14.4 explores then the specific form of technology transfer from universities to the business world. In the second part, first, the basis of the empirical analysis is explained (Section 14.5). This analysis will focus on barriers to technology transfer in the Netherlands as experienced in the specific flow from universities to industry

(Section 14.6) and in one broad flow to industry (Section 14.7). This paper concludes with a summary of the major conceptual and empirical findings, and with some policy implications (Section 14.8).

14.2 Characteristics of technology transfer

Technology transfer is one process in a chain of interaction processes between knowledge and economy, including also the generation of ideas (creativity) and innovation by prototyping (cf. Andersson, 1991). Technology transfer can be defined as the diffusion of the bundle of knowledge which surrounds a level and type of technology (cf. Charles and Howells, 1992). This definition is rather broad, including various types of knowledge, various forms of transfer, as well as a variety of organizational and spatial scales.

The types of knowledge have a strong influence on the forms of transfer. In this respect the distinction is important between embodied knowledge, i.e., in physical products, plants and equipment, and disembodied knowledge, for example, in patents, experience and learning, and know how. It makes sense whether the information is articulated in such a way that it is transferable by written documentation and oral teaching, or is tacit and only transferable by being learned through practice. Based upon the various types of knowledge, five forms of transfer can be identified (Table 14.2). In each of the forms the vehicle of transfer is different, e.g., human beings, written language, spoken language, hardware, and (images of) practical acts.

Table 14.2
Forms of technology transfer

Form (vehicle)	Examples
- Human capital transfer	Ideas, skills and routines in employees
- Written transfer	Data, manuals, patents, specifications
- Oral transfer	Understanding, abilities, competence
- Hardware transfer	Devices, equipment, materials
- Tacit transfer	Learning by doing

Basically, three actors are involved in the process of technology transfer, i.e., (1) the source of knowledge, (2) the receiver of knowledge, and (3) the intermediary organization (Figure 14.2). Whereas the source and receiver are crucial actors, the intermediary organization can be considered as optional. Technology transfer may equally run by means of intermediation and without intermediation, directly from source to receiver.

The relationship of intermediary organizations with source and receiver may be very different, i.e., regarding the following (interconnected) dimensions:
- Strength
- Duration
- Number of sources/receivers
- Orientation.

As concerns a different strength, relationships are usually weak in situations of temporary and incidental intermediation, whereas strong relationships develop on the basis of permanent arrangements. Important in this respect is the number of institutions on which behalf the intermediary organizations are acting. This may vary from one single institution to an undefined number of institutions. Thus, intermediary organizations may be single-linked or multiple–linked. A good example of the former category is the academic transfer centre because it is exclusively linked to one single source: the university. Innovation centres are good examples of the latter category because they intermediate between a large variety of institutions. As concerns the dominant orientation, a distinction can be made between source oriented and receiver oriented intermediaries. Academic transfer centres are good examples of the former category. Branch (innovation) organizations are good examples of the latter, because they focus on companies as receivers within specific branches of production

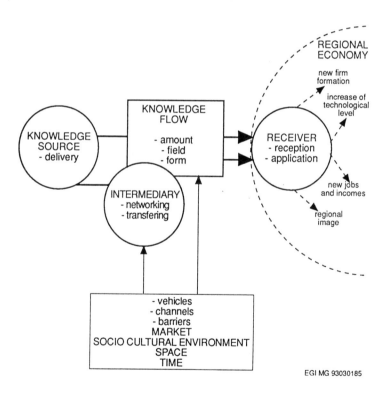

EGI MG 93030185

Figure 14.2   Actors in the process of technology transfer

251

The amount of linkages and the dominant orientation seem to be most influential thus far. Therefore, these two dimensions are used in a first classification of intermediaries regarding their structural position in relation to sources and receivers (Figure 14.3).

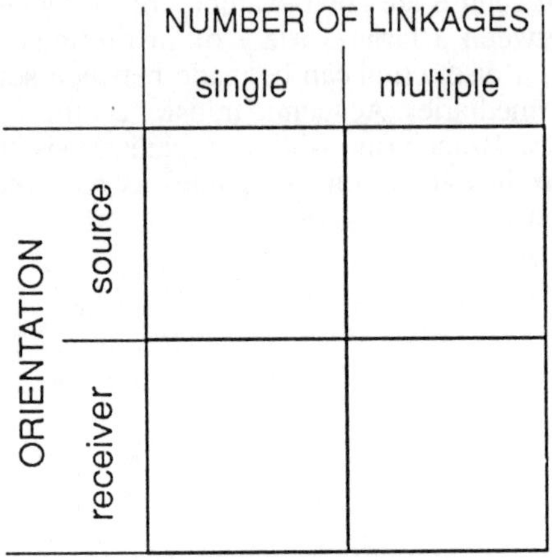

	NUMBER OF LINKAGES	
	single	multiple
ORIENTATION — source		
ORIENTATION — receiver		

Figure 14.3 A two-way classification of intermediary organizations in technology transfer

When technology transfer is viewed as a **process**, various stages can be distinguished (Table 14.3). It should be stressed that these stages may overlap in practice to a certain degree while also various loops may occur.

Technology transfer is hardly possible without the first two stages. The actors in the process should know each other and have an appropriate image towards each other. This includes a sufficient level of information about potential supply and demand, and about broad conditions under which transfer may occur, such as cost and form. The next necessary step in the process includes actual contacts between (potential) sources and receivers. Intermediary organizations have prominent roles in these two stages, which can be labelled as *active networking*. A further step in technology transfer includes specific preparatory work in order to guarantee a smooth flow of knowledge. A good example of activities in this stage is the establishment of contractual arrangements and the selection of the most appropriate form(s) of flow.

Table 14.3
Stages in technology transfer as a process

Stage	Characteristics
1.	Building of public relations and image (networking)
2.	Establishing contact between specific sources and receivers (networking)
3.	Finding forms (vehicles) and channels, as well as removing barriers
4.	Delivery of knowledge
5.	Reception of knowledge
6.	Use and application of knowledge

Within the framework of regional policy, the last stage in technology transfer is extremely important. The primary aim includes the actual use and *application* of the technology by the receiver, in order to raise the technological level of regional business. Other major aims in this respect are to advance the creation of new firms, new jobs and incomes. Building an attractive image as a region or town is also a popular goal of regional (local) policy in this respect.

Various structural characteristics of technology transfer can be distinguished, dependent on the 'environment' which is taken into consideration. The market, the sociocultural environment, space, and time are relevant in this respect. In a market perspective, emphasize is put on price and quality of technological knowledge as a product, nature of supply and demand, and market imperfections such as the lack of information, etc. This perspective also includes the labour market for academic graduates.

From the perspective of the sociocultural environment, technology transfer involves a variety of organizational scales. It operates within and between organizations. It operates also on a variety of scopes, i.e., between the same types of organization, for example universities, and between different types of organization, for example between universities and private companies, and between public sector institutes and individual households. Within this approach to technology transfer, *network* analysis has increasingly received attention over the past decades (cf. Williams and Gibson, 1990). Network analysis brings to the surface the webs of relationships between organizations involved in technology transfer. The analysis focuses on networks in terms of their size, density, diversity, reachability and stability (or dynamics). The analysis may also include various levels of networks, for example the individual organization level and the macro (population) level.

As concerns the third perspective, space, technology transfer operates on a large variety of scales, ranging from intra-urban such as local industry–university links, to transcontinental such as technology assistance between developed and less developed nations. From a spatial perspective, technology transfer can take three forms of networks which are basic to all types of flow, i.e., branched, circuit and barrier networks (cf. Suarez-Villa et al., 1992).

Technology transfer has also a time dimension. Different patterns of transfer can be distinguished in this respect, for example, one singular event and a sequence of events, the latter being divided into regular and irregular patterns.

The time dimension of technology transfer depends very much on the nature of the transfer activity. For example, courses and training are usually organised on a sequential basis, whereas the transfer of patents may take place as singular events. Also, the type of channel used in the transfer is important. Insufficient links may prevent transfer during certain times when there is a large demand for communication, such as in telephone networks. With this example, however, attention is already shifting towards barriers. First, then, it is necessary to consider this concept.

14.3 Barriers to technology transfer

Barriers to technology transfer may be interpreted as all constraints that impede a smooth flow of information on technology in space and time (Nijkamp, et al., 1990). Barriers have a disruptive influence on knowledge transfer and are, therefore, indicated by discontinuities in the intensity of this transfer.

The definition used here, includes explicitly a notion on needs or desires for transfer, for example, on one or both sides of the potential flow, or among politicians. Thus, when there is a need to increase information transfer but additional flows are hampered, barriers are indicated. However, when there is no transfer simply because any need or desire is absent or is decreasing strongly, the question of barriers is not relevant.

Within each of the above indicated 'environments' of technology transfer various potential barriers can be identified (Table 14.4). These barriers are associated with the various stages in the process of transfer as discussed in Section 14.2. An important distinction can be made between general barriers which are inherent in the nature of the interactions, and intentional barriers which have the specific aim of protection against access often in the first process stages. A common general barrier results from the very nature of networks, i.e., *inertia* (cf. Håkansson, 1988).

From a *market* perspective, transfer may be hampered by a lack of supply or demand. Barriers to transfer in the first stages may also be caused by low skill levels on the supply and the demand side of the market, for example, with regard to the image of the actors (cf. Brown, 1981). In addition, the nature of the knowledge itself may well contribute to friction on transfer. In innovation diffusion theory, it is emphasized that the higher the level of complexity and cost, the more time it takes before the technology has reached all potential adopters (cf. Davies, 1979). A different type of barriers occurs further in the process of transfer, namely as a result of discrepancies between demand and supply in communication channels, i.e., congestion (Nijkamp, et al., 1990). Congestion is, however, strongly time dependent due to fluctuation between peak and offpeak hours. An important category of barriers from a market perspective aims at protection for economic reasons. This type of barriers may take various forms. For example, patent protection simply forbids others than the patent holder to produce the involved product for a certain number of years. Similarly, tests and certification of new products by importing countries prevent an immediate introduction of new product technology to the market and cause considerable delay and cost.

Table 14.4
Potential barriers to technology transfer

Origin	Type of Barrier
Market	
a. General	Low supply/demand of knowledge
	Small skill to identify supply/demand
	Small skill to marketing of knowledge
	Small skill to use transfer channels
	High complexity of knowledge
	High cost of knowledge
	Unknown knowledge
	Congestion
	Network inertia
b. Protection	Market regulation
	Trade borders and (fiscal) tariffs
	Secrecy and intellectual property protection
	Standardization and certification of products
Sociocultural environment	
a. General	Language and vocabulary disparities
	Educational and income disparities
	Cultural behaviour disparities
	Network inertia
b. Protection	National borders
	Social group protection
	Political and ideological protection
Space	Long distance (micro- to macroscale)
	Low population density
	Natural barriers
Time	Peak and offpeak hours
	Divergent time-zones

Many barriers to technology transfer originate in the *sociocultural environment*. Language is far the most important barrier, preventing networking as well as reception and use of knowledge. Language barriers include spoken, written and computer language, as well as the vocabulary used in the communication. The latter barrier type follows, for example, from different stages in the development of the technology (basic and applied), and from differences in the organizational culture between source and receiver (Williams and Gibson, 1990). A further category of barriers is concerned with social class differences due to educational and income divergencies or religion. Purposive protection against access to technology is realized by means of keeping group membership exclusive, for example, of schools, clubs and societies. These types of barrier prevent networking already in the early stages of the process. With regard to remote regions or islands, sociocultural barriers have often come into existence due to centuries of isolation from the core-area. This may be reflected in a different dialect and lower educational levels, but more importantly, also in divergent attitudes following from social class differences or ideological differences. Over the past several years, the importance of sociocultural obstacles has been increasingly emphasized in research on technology transfer (cf. Lundvall, 1988; Malecki, 1991; Gertler, 1993).

A large number of researchers has chronicled the influence of geographical *space* (See Charles and Howells, 1992), both at the microscale (within a building, on a site) and the meso- and macroscales (regional, national and international context). On the latter scales, the diffusion of knowledge is thought to follow two spatial patterns, namely contagious and hierarchical diffusion (cf. Hägerstrand, 1965; Florax and Folmer, 1990). In the contagious pattern, the diffusion of knowledge is concentrated in the vicinity of the originating source and decays strongly with distance. In the hierarchical diffusion pattern, knowledge transfer is first found in central places whereas it trickles down to places of lower order later in time. From the preceding it follows that large distances and low population densities cause friction to technology transfer. In addition, various natural barriers should be mentioned. Good examples are mountain areas, islands and areas under unfavourable climatic conditions. Natural access obstacles have declined in importance in the previous decades due to tremendous advances in transportation and telecommunication. The sociocultural barriers caused by (former) natural obstacles may, nevertheless, survive for a long time.

The fourth origin of barriers, *time*, causes potential constraints in two ways. Within daytime, the transfer infrastructure may not be able to handle all demand during a number of peak hours. This obstacle is most obvious in telecommunication. The second source of time constraints rests on the system of global time-zones. Knowledge transfer may be hampered by a lack of overlap of working times between the two sides of the potential flow. This holds largely for flows by telephone and is clearly visible in world-embracing services such as stock transaction, although lack of overlap is reduced as much as possible (Warf, 1989). Above discussion indicates that time barriers usually occur when the first stages of the transfer process have been passed.

To conclude, a large variety of potential barriers hamper technology transfer. Natural barriers, or broadly, spatial barriers seem to have lost importance, whereas evidence increases on the relevance of sociocultural barriers. Barriers occur in various stages of the transfer process by preventing active networking (early stages), delivery and reception, as well as use and application of the knowledge. The next section will explore specifically the characteristics of technology transfer from universities, in order to set a framework for the analysis of barriers and success factors for this transfer further in this article.

14.4 University transfer

University-industry transfer of technology operates either directly between academics and companies, or by means of intermediary institutions. The general forms of technology transfer, discussed in Section 14.2, are clearly applicable to university-industry flows (Charles and Howells, 1992; Dalton, 1992), although tacit information transfer may be scarce at the first sight. Table 14.5 lists the major forms of university-industry knowledge transfer and a few examples of them by focusing on the one-way flow from university to industry.

Table 14.5
Forms of university-industry technology flows

1. *Human capital*: academics parttime appointed in industry; academic graduates working in industry; academics founding a new company based on an innovation (possibly) in science parks.
2. *Written documents*: academic invention taken up by existing industry (licensing, patents, specifications); publication in scientific journals, textbooks or manuals; reports on contract research results, etcetera.
3. *Oral transfer*: academic training, courses, presentation at conferences, consultancy.
4. *Hardware*: supply of accommodation and equipment, such as laboratories, clinical trial facilities, devices, computers and entire information systems.
5. *Tacit*: (images of) acts in laboratory routines, engineering, design, treatment of medical patients, etcetera.

Various forms of knowledge transfer have always been a major component in the role of universities in society, notably education of graduates, publication in scientific journals and reports, and presentation of results at conferences. Since the early 1980s, however, many universities intensified their links with industry, whereas they also sought new modes of collaboration and intermediation of transfer.

Academic transfer agencies have the primary task of intermediation for transfer which involves a combination of written, oral and hardware knowledge. Science park organizations are largely concerned with transfer by means of human capital in that they foster direct formation of companies by academic staff or graduates (spinoffs). A second difference between transfer centres and science park organizations is the fact that the latter are usually involved in a whole range of aims and activities, of which technology transfer is only one.

257

University transfer agencies have largely been established since the early 1980s. They operate as intermediary agencies alongside direct transfer by individual academics and direct transfer within various kind of university–industry institutions, such as jointly operated research facilities and research consortia. With regard to modern knowledge transfer, Charles and Howells (1992) point to the emergence of a new profession and a new branch of services. The major components of these services are listed in Table 14.6, according to a division into general and specialist services. The former clearly reflects the first stages of the transfer process discussed in Section 14.2 (networking), whereas there is also an emphasis on contractual arrangements. Specialist services are found in agencies with specific additional functions. For example, transfer agencies may provide assistance to the design of business plans when they are involved in attracting academic spinoff. Furthermore, in the United States, patenting and licensing have become a specialism of various university agencies, named Office of Technology Licensing (OTLs) (Parker and Zilberman, 1993).

Table 14.6
Major components in academic knowledge transfer services

Type of services	
General	- Internal (university) and external contacts (networking) - Missionary work and marketing (networking) - Negotiation on behalf of the university or other institute that is represented (finding forms and channels) - Drawing up and administering of legal agreements, patents, licences and other forms of contract (finding forms and channels)
Specialist	- Identifying matches between supply and demand of various client groups by means of databases - Pursuing opportunities for obtaining grants from private and public bodies - Business planning and advice - Patenting and licensing

In the publicity surrounding university-industry links, science parks and spinoffs have received a great deal of attention. Science parks are among the most popular regional development strategies currently in use, in Western Europe, the United States and increasingly, the Pacific Rim. The fast majority of science parks has been established since the early 1980s. However, particularly the ones that attracted much attention are clearly older, such as Stanford (1952) and Research Triangle (1959) in the United States, and Heriot–Watt Edinburgh (1971) and Cambridge (1972) in Great Britain.

In the literature the term science parks is used both in a broad and a narrow sense. In a broad sense it covers a wide range of hightech developments, including university 'incubator blocks' as well as the Japanese phenomenon of the comprehensive Technopolis. In the present analysis the term science park

will be used in a rather narrow sense by following the definition of the United Kingdom Science Park Association (cf. Dalton, 1992). Accordingly, a science park is a property based initiative which:
- has formal and operational links with a university or other higher educational or research institute;
- is designed to encourage the foundation and growth of knowledge based business and related organizations;
- has a management function which is actively engaged in the transfer of technology and business skills to the residents on site.

Despite above definition, science parks may still be different in size, type of accommodation, and mode of management selected to suit the needs of specific situations. A further distinction between science parks concerns their regional location. Science parks have been established both in economic core-areas and in peripherally located regions. This divergent location causes differences in proximity to (other) first order knowledge centres, and also differences in the size of the regional input and output markets. In addition, there may be a diverse benefit from comprehensive regional or urban policies, including, for example, investment grants.

Unlike academic transfer agencies, science parks are usually founded by different parties (Van Geenhuizen, 1986; Nijkamp et al., 1992) (Table 14.7). Universities and government agencies have been involved in the establishment of the vast majority of science parks. The private sector has thus far not been very active in science park development. Private firms which already play a role nowadays, can be subdivided into two major categories: (1) real estate developers and investment banks, largely operating for profit and, particularly the latter, also for prestige and public relation (Currie, 1985); (2) large local firms, investing in science parks for reasons of public relation and social responsibility.

The inventory in Table 14.7 indicates that the principal actors share only a few goals, e.g., regional development and technological development. At the same time, they give divergent priorities to these objectives. Such a multiple objective situation causes a limited chance for consensus about the definition of *success* of science parks among the principal actors. This observation leads on to the issue of evaluation of science parks or other intermediaries in terms of success or failure.

There are many reasons why success or failure cannot be defined easily (cf. Luger, 1992). First of all, success is a normative concept, including a notion about a 'standard' which should be satisfied. In addition, when success is defined in terms of, for example, net job creation or net increase of university research budgets, the problem of counterfactuality arises. Outcomes are observed where a park is located and a transfer agency is operating, while it should be known what the outcomes would have been when both did not exist (zero-case). Special evaluation procedures must be applied in order to solve this methodological problem.

A further issue is concerned with the time-dependency of success and failure. Due to the changing nature of the processes over time, success must be measured in different ways over the various development stages of transfer agencies and science parks. In the case of the latter, the 'standard' for the first

259

few years may be to recruit at least one R & D organization, whereas the 'standard' for later stages may be in terms of employment growth. Success in early stages is, then, no guarantee for success in later stages.

Table 14.7
Founders of science parks and their goals

Founder	Goals a
University	Financial returns
	Use of idle land
	Enhance prestige
	Improve industrial liaison
	Expand employment opportunities
	Expand academic expertise
	Regional development
	Invest capital
Government	Regional development
	Technological development
	Real estate development
	Enhance prestige of city or region
Private sector	Real estate development
	Enhance prestige
	Public relation
	Financial returns
	Regional development
	Window on technology
	Technological development

a A 'maximum' list, based upon large numbers of science parks in Europe and the United States.

In the light of these methodological issues, the following analysis will merely focus on the performance of intermediary organizations and avoid a strict evaluation in terms of success or failure.

14.5 Empirical basis

The following sections will explore barriers to technology transfer experienced in the Netherlands. To this purpose the focus will be on two different forms of transfer, i.e., the flow of academic knowledge towards the business world by means of transfer centres and science parks, and the broad flow of knowledge to the business world by means of innovation centres. Regarding academic transfer centres, one specific town will be taken as an example, namely Groningen (Note 1).

Groningen is a mediumsized town (around 170,000 inhabitants) located in the socalled Outer Zone in the Netherlands (Appendix 14.1). The region of Groningen has been included in regional development programs for a long time, due to a onesided economy and relatively high unemployment. Unemployment in the Province of Groningen varies between 13.0 and 16.5% of the labour force, whereas the national average is 9.1% (1990) (Labour Force Survey, 1990). The advancement of technology transfer is clearly one instrument in the regional policy for this area.

Regarding the second type of technology transfer, the one via innovation centres, the current empirical analysis draws heavily on a recently published evaluation study of the Dutch system (Bureau voor Economische Argumentatie, 1993). The results are based on a sample of all small and mediumsized firms, and samples of specifically manufacturing and construction firms in the Netherlands.

14.6 Transfer centres and science parks

The system of academic transfer centres was founded in the Netherlands in 1981 (Buck Consultants Int., 1987) (Appendix 14.2). In the first years, the system has been fully subsidized by the central government. After 1986, however, subsidies were decreased by 25% per year and at the end, terminated. This shift in policy caused a rather divergent development of academic transfer organizations in the late 1980s. With regard to (legal) status and type of activities, different models came into being. For example, Groningen remained closely integrated within its university whereas it became also fully financed by this university. On the other hand, a transfer agency with a strong commercial orientation emerged in Tilburg. This agency adopted the status of legal firm with limited liability.

As far as activities are concerned, transfer centres have put a different emphasis on requests for transfer by the university and on that by external target groups. On the whole there was, however, a move to activities initiated by the university. For example, a number of centres became stronger active in patenting university innovations (University Leiden, 1989, 1990). Thus, university transfer centres in the Netherlands developed a stronger source–orientation in the late 1980s. At the same time, a *downward* trend has become evident in the amount of transfer. This can be illustrated with the number of projects carried out by the Transfer Centre Groningen in the years 1984 to 1991 (Table 14.8). One can observe an initial increase followed by a clear decrease of activity: the number of transfer projects amounted to almost 300 in 1987, whereas it felt down to around 200 in 1991.

The above indicated development can easily be explained with the emergence of new categories of sources or intermediaries in the market for technical knowledge since the late 1980s. In 1986, various higher educational institutes across the country established their own transfer agencies. In addition, since 1988, the national system of innovation centres came into being. As a consequence, transfer centres at a short distance from a new innovation centre may have experienced a certain amount of 'catching' of activities by the latter. At the same time, also a number of commercial consultancies started activities in the field of technology transfer. It can be concluded that the emergence of new sources and intermediaries has led to a loss of potential activities among academic transfer centres. Further consequences may have been the rise of missing links between the different transfer networks, as well as a decrease of transparency of the supply structure towards potential receivers.

Apart from changes on the supply side of the market, one important change could be observed on the demand side. In the course of time, a certain 'upgrading' of the quality of the transfer questions became evident. As a consequence of this development, a larger number of less relevant questions were not taken into consideration by the academic transfer centres and directed to other institutions.

Table 14.8
Number of projects carried out by the Transfer Centre Groningen

	Absolute	Index Number
1984	231	100
1985	269	116
1986	283	123
1987	297	129
1988	239	103
1989	239	103
1990	245	106
1991	193	84

Source: Annual Reports

In expanding knowledge networks from universities, generally, a large degree of *inertia* is encountered, resting on the largely stable and conservative nature of contact networks (Charles and Howells, 1992). This phenomenon can be illustrated with the establishing of new contacts by the Transfer Centre Groningen (Table 14.9). The most important basis for new contacts is in existing relationships. In addition, many new contacts rest on recommendation given by various other parties. Accordingly, the fast majority of all new contacts (75%) follows from previous knowledge about the Transfer Centre.

A further type of barriers to technology flow from universities can be summarized as *'mental'* barriers. These include, for example, a lack of invitation to participate, or a lack of awareness among firms about potentials of collaboration (Charles and Howells, 1992). Regarding the inert character of networks, this means that very strong efforts are needed in missionary work and marketing in order to increase the size of transfer networks.

Table 14.10 summarizes the major barriers to technology transfer from universities, discussed thus far. It also summarizes barriers to the development of science parks, particularly the growth of academic spinoff which will be discussed in the remaining part of this section. Within this framework the science park in Groningen, Zernike Science Park, will serve as an example of the successful avoiding of various barriers.

Table 14.9
Basis of contacts with the Transfer Centre Groningen (1990)

	Percentage	Ranking
Based on previous knowledge		
Previous customer's relationship	47	1
Recommendation by third party a	28	2
Based on new knowledge		
Presentation on conferences, fairs	13	3
Otherwise (advertisement etc.)	12	4
Totals	100	

a.   Personal recommendation included.
Source: Annual Report 1990.

Table 14.10
Potential barriers to academic technology transfer

Intermediary	Type of barrier
Transfer centre	Low university potentials for commercialization
	Competition from new sources or intermediaries
	Missing links between various sources or intermediaries
	Lack of transparency of technology supply structure for potential receivers
	Inertia of contact networks
	Lack of knowledge about and appropriate image of university potentials among receivers
Science park	*University:*
	Low potentials for commercialization
	Lack of contractual arrangements which advance a shift of academic staff to business
	Low responsiveness and flexibility in supply of supportive services
	Science park organization:
	Inappropriate accommodation for spinoff
	Accommodation types which are also offered elsewhere in the region
	Target firms which are not appropriate to potentials of the region
	Lack of supportive services
	Management 'gap' after initial success
	Relaxation on selection criteria for future occupants
	Low level of coordination between various actors (founders)
	Passive role in identifying potentials for commercialization

In an inventory of obstacles to science park growth, a distinction can be made between universities and science park organizations, the latter being involved in development and management (cf. Gibb, 1985; Van Geenhuizen, 1986; Nijkamp, et al., 1993). The actors involved in Zernike Science Park have clearly been aware of a number of obstacles and organised the science park accordingly (Table 14.11). The park was founded in 1984, as a 'second generation' park, in which could be built on experiences from older ones. In the first years emphasis was strongly put on the fostering of commercial projects and startup firms, whereas later, priority was given to realestate development (De Lange, 1992). The park faced a strong growth, regarding the number of occupants after nine years (45 in 1993). The fast majority of them (almost 90%) is spinoff from the local university or related institutes.

As concerns universities, it is obvious but sometimes overlooked that there should be inhouse expertise which has strong potentials for commercialization. Thus, universities with a weak orientation on, for example, applied informatics, biotechnology and advanced materials have a less favourable outlook for technology transfer to industry than other universities. In addition, a lack of inviting arrangements hampers a smooth shift of potential academic entrepreneurs to (parttime) involvement in commercial ventures. A major component in this respect is the creation of attractive legal and contractual conditions for a partial shift of university staff towards own business. In Groningen, a number of contractual agreements is being developed between university departments and startup companies, as concerns salary cost and share ownership (De Lange, 1992). A factor which may in general discourage the rise of spinoff firms, is a low flexibility and responsiveness of universities in the dealings with them. This concerns also the use of university facilities such as computers, laboratories and their equipment, which would otherwise be out of reach for small firms.

With regard to science park organizations, a useful distinction can be made between two types of 'seedbed' conditions, namely physical factors and organizational factors. Regarding the former, it is of utmost importance that small and cheap accommodation is available for rent, usually in 'incubator blocks'. These units are preferably flexible in order to provide room for potential expansion, which is particularly important for new biotechnology ventures and their laboratories (Feldman, 1986). Also, the type of rent contract should give some flexibility to starting companies. A very important further consideration regarding the type of accommodation, is concerned with the nature of the regional (local) market for business accommodation. From experiences in Britain it appears that too much supply of accommodation of the same type within one area may hamper the growth of science parks (Van Geen - huizen, 1987). One other point of attention in this respect is the regional location of the park. In remote regions, the large distance to an international airport may be an obstacle to science park development. It is advisable, therefore, to exclude companies which prefer close proximity to international airports as a target group in remote regions.

As concerns organizational factors, first of all, a range of supportive services needs to be made available to startups, such as advice in firm foundation, management and marketing advice, as well as financial supportive services such as venture capital. Firms on science parks typically face a large amount of uncertainty, due to their new technologies and young age (see Section 14.1). Therefore, a strong focus of the science park organization on advice and problem solving is very important. It should be stressed that problems faced by science park occupants are not the same for all categories. For example, foreign subsidiaries encounter small barriers, while independent startups usually face a large amount of difficulties. In particular, independent startups in modern biotechnology are very vulnerable. Their investment level is relatively high, due to the need for advanced laboratory equipment. When DNA technology and the use of radio-nuclides are involved, laboratories should also meet specific standards. In addition, particular problems are faced in the often global marketing (Daly, 1985; Hagedoorn and Schakenraad, 1990).

Table 14.11
Key features of Zernike Science Park in Groningen

Feature	Comment
Year of foundation	1984
Concept	- Supportive organization for academic spin-off - In a later stage, priority given to real-estate development.

Organizational features	- Comprehensive approach (accommodation, venture capital, business training etc.)
	- Own tools to advance the start-up of firms
	- Strong ties between responsible institutions (Zernike Foundation, University, Regional Development Agency, Northern Provinces etc.)
	  - Large commitment of key managers.
	  - Active screening of university on potentials for commercialization

Accommodation	60 hectare ground 10,000 m2 incubator floor
Number of firms	45
Type of firms regarding origin	Relocated from elsewhere: 7% Subsidiary (foreign): 4% Academic spin-off: 89%

Source: Interview

Zernike Science Park in Groningen has two major tools available to foster new hightech enterprises (De Lange, 1992). It actively coordinates and manages projects which are expected to result in commercial products, processes, or new companies. It also supports individual researchers with a bright idea, by means of a grant or fellowship. Accordingly, access is given to

265

research facilities whereas also a stipend may be granted in order to develop ideas into convincing prototypes or processes.

A further point of concern is the quality of the management on the long term. The success of science parks in the first years usually rests on the shoulders of one or two strong managers. It is important to realise that these managers are often 'bought' by other organizations after the success of the park has become evident. Therefore, it is advisable to pay close attention to the succession of the first managers, in order to prevent danger from a management 'gap'.

A factor which is often overlooked in science park development, concerns a consequent selection of potential occupants of the park. The history of older parks indicates that the concept of 'seedbed' for hightech business is in many cases relaxed and general business or lowtech manufacturing is coming in, in order to maintain the park's viability as a real estate project. With regard to the United States, Luger and Goldstein (1989) found that only around 25% of the parks continued in existence as originally planned. The prospect of a future shift in type of occupants, however, may decrease the attractiveness of the park as concerns the preservation of its image and the continuation of its service supply.

A further barrier to growth of science parks is strongly connected with the different actors involved in the establishment (see Section 14.4). From the beginning, constructive ties should be kept between them in order to prevent the development of too divergent policies.

With regard to spatial barriers, the performance of Zernike Science Park in Groningen indicates that a remote or peripheral location is certainly not a major obstacle to science park development, and when such obstacles do exist, they may be 'compensated' by means of a strong organization. The particular organizational strength of Zernike Science Park includes a comprehensive approach to firm formation, strong ties with other responsible parties, a strict application of the original concept, an active role in the identification of academic potentials for commercialization, and a strong commitment of the organization's managers.

14.7 Innovation centres

The Dutch system of innovation centres has become operational in 1989. It includes a decentralised network of 18 regional offices (Appendix 14.2) and three offices with a specialist function, namely for invention, protection of intellectual property and patents, and central (coordinative) facilities.

The basis for this system was an advice given by the Commission Dekker (1987), which recommended to improve the knowledge infrastructure for the socalled 'technology following' small and mediumsized enterprises. Accordingly, the major aim of the innovation centres was and still is to increase accessibility and applicability of technological knowledge for this category of firms. Key activities in this respect are the providing of information, first-line advice, and intermediation. These activities require also a great deal of networking in the sense of building a regional knowledge network. In terms of the typology discussed in Section 14.2 innovation centres can be qualified as multilinked receiver oriented intermediaries. The receiver categories include manufacturing and construction companies, sized less than 200 workers, as well as parts of the service sector such as transports and business services.

Most recently, technology transfer by means of innovation centres has been subject of an evaluation study (Bureau voor Economische Argumentatie, 1993). In the methodology, technology transfer is approached as a process by taking three stages or layers into account, i.e., (1) public relation and image, (2) establishment of specific contacts, and (3) use and application of the knowledge. The analysis involves an assessment of effectiveness based upon the share of firms that progresses from one stage into the next. The major results of this analysis are shown in Figure 14.4.

TOTAL SME[a]

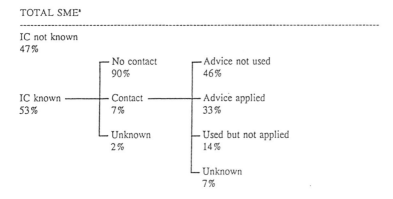

TOTAL SME IN MANUFACTURING[b], CONSTRUCTION[c]

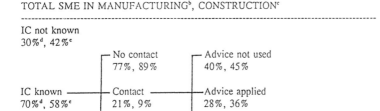

Figure 14.4 Effectiveness of Dutch Innovation Centres (IC) in various steps of transfer

a   n = 4.504 (sample size)
b   n = 956 (idem)
c   n = 816 (idem)
d   manufacturing
e   construction
Source: BEA (1993), p. 49-50.

The effectiveness of innovation centres varies strongly with the type of firms taken into consideration. The effectiveness in the first stage is higher among the target groups of manufacturing and construction than among all SME's. The shares of 'being known' are 70 and 58%, against 53%, respectively. In the stage of 'established contact', the share is relatively high only in manufacturing, i.e., 21%, versus 7% among all SME's. An important result of the analysis is that effectiveness is far the lowest in the step from 'being known' to 'established contact'. Among the target groups, the fast majority (77% of manufacturing and 89% of construction firms) established no contact with innovation centres. When once contacts have been established, however, 38% of manufacturing firms and 46% of construction firms actually use the information in practice.

Above analysis indicates that barriers to technology transfer are strongest in the step from knowledge about the intermediaries toward making contact with them. The most important barrier in this respect appears to be a lack of demand for technology assistance (73%), in general and particularly from innovation centres. 'Mental' barriers as discussed in previous sections, seem to be less important but not negligible (15%). Particularly in this respect, a strong effort is needed to adjust the image of innovation centres.

The importance of lack of demand for advice from innovation centres may reflect the current plentiful supply of this service. When demand barriers also exist in relation to other types of sources and intermediaries, it may be relevant to 'bundle up' activities in a smaller number of transfer organizations.

14.8 Conclusion

The availability of technology in a region is increasingly a crucial asset to economic development. Within this framework, this paper explored the concepts of technology transfer and intermediation, their features as a process and their structural characteristics. Intermediary organizations hold a position between knowledge sources and knowledge receivers. Their relationship with these two types of actors may, however, be very different regarding the amount of linkages and dominant orientation. By conceiving technology transfer as a process, six different stages can be distinguished, running from public relation (including image building) to application of the technology by the receiver. Intermediary organizations have prominent tasks in the first stages, i.e., in active networking.

Barriers have been defined in this paper as all constraints that prevent a smooth flow of information. Various structural barriers to technology transfer could be identified by adopting a process approach and four different perspectives, i.e., the market, sociocultural environment, space and time. Spatial barriers, particularly small natural access, have increasingly lost importance, whereas market and sociocultural barriers still exert a significan influence on technology flows. Language constitutes the most important barrier at work in all stages of the transfer process. This also includes the vocabulary used in different implementation stages of technology and in organizational cultures of source and receiver. Unlike language, purposive protection against access to technology has its major impact in the first stages of transfer.

This paper focused also on empirical findings in the Netherlands about various intermediaries. As a result, an inventory of barriers to technology transfer from universities could be designed. This inventory can serve as a 'checklist' which may be helpful in future decisions on academic transfer centres and science parks.

Regarding university transfer centres, various barriers have recently arisen due to the emergence of new sources and new intermediaries. These barriers include loss of receivers, (potentially) missing links between networks, and small transparency of networks. In addition, structural barriers involve a lack of awareness and appropriate images ('mental' barriers), and resistance to new contacts (inertia), all at work in the early stages of the transfer process. Regarding innovation centres, 'mental' barriers are less important. Instead, a low demand for intermediation among potential receivers seems to be a crucial obstacle to technology transfer.

In the light of above barriers, it is advisable to target policy efforts on the following:
- To remove 'mental' barriers by intensifying networking between intermediaries and small and medium-sized firms.
- To investigate demand for technology transfer as experienced by various sources and intermediaries, and when necessary, to investigate the best way to 'bundle up' a number of these institutions.

This paper has also examined university science parks in detail. The barriers in this respect are structurally different from the ones discussed above because the transfer involves largely human capital, in the form of firm foundation by (ex)academics. The growth of this spinoff may be hampered by low commercialization potentials of the university and less attractive conditions for academics to start own business. Barriers may also rise on the side of the science park organization. An essential ingredient for success of it is the supply of 'customized' accommodation and supporting services to young firms. A point of concern in this respect is the position of the accommodation in the local and regional real estate market.

This study has taken Groningen, located in the Dutch Outer Zone, as an example. It appeared that technology transfer from universities in remote regions to the business world is not structurally different from technology transfer in Core-regions. The Zernike Science Park illustrated that science park development is quite well possible in remote regions. Spatial barriers, if any, can be 'compensated' by the quality of the science park organization and management.

Note

With almost 20,000 students, the State University of Groningen is one of the largest universities of the Netherlands. It holds a third position after the University of Amsterdam and the State University of Utrecht. Unlike many other general universities, Groningen provides education in a number of applied technical fields, such as technical physics and technical chemistry. This difference gives Groningen a relatively large potential for commercialization of its academic knowledge.

References

Andersson, Å.E. (1991), 'Creation, innovation, and diffusion of knowledge - General and specific economic impacts', *Sistemi Urbani*, 1-2-3, pp.5–28.

Buck Consultants Int. (1987), Availing the Knowledge Potential of Universities for Regional Development, Nijmegen.

Bureau voor Economische Argumentatie (1993), Evaluatie netwerk van Innovatie Centra, Hoofddorp.

Camagni, R. (1991), 'Local 'milieu', uncertainty and innovation networks: towards a new dynamic theory of economic space', in Camagni, R. (ed) *Innovation networks: spatial perspectives*. pp. 121-144, Belhaven Press, London.

Charles, D., and Howells, J. (1992), *Technology transfer in Europe, public and private networks*, Belhaven Press, London.

Commission Dekker (1987), *Wissel tussen kennis en markt*, The Hague.

Currie, J. (1985), *Science Parks in Britain: Their Role for the Late 1980s*, CSP Economic Publications, Cardiff.

Daly, P. (1985), *The Biotechnology Business; A strategic analysis*, Frances Pinter, London.

Davelaar, E.J. (1989), *Incubation and Innovation. A Spatial Perspective*, Free University (PhD Thesis), Amsterdam.

Davies, S. (1979), *The diffusion of process innovation*, Cambridge University Press, Cambridge.

Dunford, M. (1992), 'Technopoles: research, innovation and skills in comparative perspective', in *Topos Review of urban and regional studies*, 5/92, pp. 29-54.

Feldman M.M.A. (1985), 'Biotechnology and local economic growth: The American Pattern', in Hall, P. and Markusen, A. (eds) *Silicon Landscapes*, Allen & Unwin, Boston, pp. 65-79.

Florax R., (1992), *The University: A Regional Booster?*, Avebury, Aldershot.

Florax, R. and Folmer, H. (1990), *Knowledge impacts of universities on investment behavior of industry*, Agricultural University, Wageningen.

Freeman, C. (1982), *The Economics of Industrial Innovation*, Frances Pinter, London.

Geenhuizen, M. van (1986), Science Parks, Prospects for Success? *Papers and Proceedings of International Congress Malmö Sweden*, The Hague, International Federation for Housing and Planning.

Geenhuizen, M.S. van (1987), 'Science Parks, een eerste inventarisatie', in: *Stedebouw en Volkshuisvesting*, nr.5.

Geenhuizen M.S. van (1993), *A longitudinal analysis of the growth of firms, The case of the Netherlands*, Erasmus University (PhD Thesis), Rotterdam.

Gertler, M.S. (1993), 'Being There: Proximity, organization, and culture in the development and adoption of advanced manufacturing technologies', Paper presented at the Annual Meetings of the Association of American Geographers, Atlanta, April 1993.

Gibb, J.M. (1985), (ed) *Science Parks and Innovation Centres: Their Economic and Social Impact*, Elsevier Science Publications, Amsterdam.

Hagedoorn, J. and Schakenraad, J. (1990), 'Interfirm partnerships and cooperative strategies in core-technologies', in Freeman, C. and Soete, L.

(eds) *New explorations in the economics of technological change*, p. 3-37, Pinter, London.

Hägerstrand, T. (1965), 'Aspects of the Spatial Structure of Social Communication and the Diffusion of Information', *Papers of the Regional Science Association*, 16, 27-42.

Hakansson, H. (1988), *Industrial Technological Development. A Network Approach*, Croom Helm, London.

Hannan, M.T. and Freeman, J. (1989), *Organizational Ecology*, Harvard University Press, Cambridge, Mass.

Labour Force Survey (1990), Netherlands Central Bureau of Statistics, Voorburg.

Lange, L. de (1992), Establishing a Science Park in the Netherlands: the case of the Zernike Science Park, Paper presented at the Conference of the International Association of Science Parks in Groningen, 5-7 February 1992.

Luger, M., and Goldstein, H.A. (1989), *Research (Science) Parks as Public Investment. A Critical Assessment*, Wirtschaftsuniversität, Vienna.

Luger, M. (1992), Methodological Issues in the Evaluation of US Technology Parks, in Bozzo, U., Elias de Freitas, J. and Higgins, T. (eds) *Proceedings of the International Workshop on Science Park Evaluation*, Commission of the European Communities, Luxemburg.

Lundvall, B-A (1988), Innovation as an interactive process: from user producer interaction to the national system of innovation, in Dosi, G. (ed) *Technological Change and Economic Theory*,. Frances Pinter, London, pp. 349-369.

Malecki, E.J. (1991), Culture's Influence on Technological Development and Economic Growth, Paper prepared for the Conference of the Commission on Industrial Change of the International Geographical Union, Penang, Malaysia, August 1991.

Nelson, R.R. and Winter, S.G. (1982), *An evolutionary theory of economic change*, Harvard University Press, Cambridge.

Nijkamp, P., Rietveld, P. and Salomon, I. (1990), Barriers in spatial interactions and communications, A conceptual exploration, *The Annals of Regional Science*, 24, pp. 237-252.

Nijkamp, P., Oirschot, G. van and Oosterman, A. (1992), 'Technopolis and spatial development', *Topos Review of urban and regional studies*, 5/92, pp. 93-106.

Parker, D.D. and Zilberman, D. (1993), 'University Technology Transfers', *Contemporary Policy Issues*, Volume XI, nr. 2, pp. 87-99.

Premus, R. (1986), 'The strategic role of university Science Parks in the hightech strategies of state and local governments in the United States', Seminar on Science Parks and Technology Complexes in relation to regional development, Venice, June 1986.

Roobeek, A.J.M. (1990), *Beyond the Technology Race*, Elsevier, Amsterdam.

Rothwell, R. and Zegveld, W. (1985), *Reindustrialization and Technology*, Longman, Harlow Essex.

Suarez-Villa, L., Giaoutzi, M. and Stratigea, A. (1992), 'Territorial and border barriers in information and communication networks: a conceptual exploration', *Tijdschrift voor Econ. en Soc. Geografie*, 83, no. 2, pp. 93–119.

271

Thomas, M.D. (1987), 'The innovation factor in the process of microeconomic industrial change: conceptual explorations', Knaap, G.A. van der and Wever, E. (eds) *New Technology and Regional Development*, pp. 21–43, Croom Helm, London.

Tordoir, P.P. (1993), *The Professional Knowledge Economy*, University of Amsterdam (PhD Thesis), Amsterdam.

Transfer Centre State University Groningen, *Annual Report 1984–1991*, Groningen.

University Leiden, *Annual Report 1989, 1990,*. Leiden.

Vernon, R. (1966), International investment and international trade in the product cycle, *Quarterly Journal of Economics*, 80, pp.190-207.

Warf, B. (1989), Telecommunications and the globalization of financial services, *Professional Geographer* 41, pp. 257-271.

Williams, F. and Gibson, D.V. (1990), *Technology Transfer. A Communication Perspective*, Sage, Newbury Park.

Appendix 14.1

The Netherlands in three zones

Location of Groningen in the Netherlands

For Dutch standards, the distance between the Core-area where the major cities are located, and Groningen is rather large. There are no flights from Amsterdam International Airport to Groningen (Eelde), but there are regular flights from Rotterdam Airport. These have a frequency of three times a day and a duration of 45 minutes. By train, Groningen is directly connected with the major cities in the Core-area. This intercity train runs once an hour from Amsterdam, and once in two hours from Rotterdam and The Hague. Travelling time is around two and a half hour. As concerns road traffic, Groningen is at a distance of around 220 kilometres from Amsterdam and 260 kilometres from Rotterdam and The Hague.

Traffic infrastructure between Groningen and the Dutch Core-area

	Connection	Frequency	Travelling time/ distance
Air	Rotterdam	3x per day	0.45 minutes
Intercity train	Amsterdam	1x per hour	2.20 minutes
	Rotterdam	1x per two hours	2.35 minutes
	The Hague	1x per two hours	2.40 minutes
Highway	Amsterdam	-	220 kilometres
	Rotterdam	-	260 kilometres
	The Hague	-	260 kilometres

Appendix 14.2

The Dutch system of university transfer centres (1993)

Amsterdam (2x)
Groningen
Leiden
Utrecht
Enschede
Delft
Wageningen
Rotterdam
Nijmegen
Tilburg
Eindhoven
Maastricht

EGI MG 93030186

The Dutch system of Innovation Centres (1993)

EGI MG 93030187

276

Part C

MODELLING SPATIAL NETWORKS AND DEVELOPMENT

15 The diffusion of telecommunication technologies in the European countries

D. Campisi, C. Tesauro and A. Vulterini

15.1 Introduction

The diffusion of telecommunication technologies is rapidly increasing in both industrialized and developing countries, so producing remarkable effects on the socioeconomic environment and the spatial organization of society. The main effect of the present rates of adoption is related to the evolution of both the traditional localizing factors and the internal structure of organizations, and produces centralizing or decentralizing processes driven by new necessities. A secondary effect, further discussed in this paper, is related to an increasing transportation demand and the need of a reorganization of physical movement.

The telecommunication market can be divided in two main sectors: services and equipment. Services are provided to the end-users by licensed operators, while equipments are supplied to both end-users and operators.

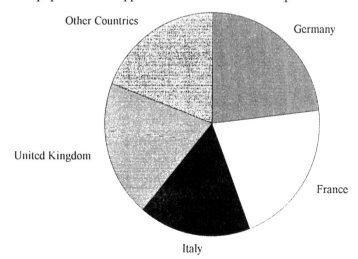

Figure 15.1 The settlement of the European telephone market
Source: direct computation of SIP data

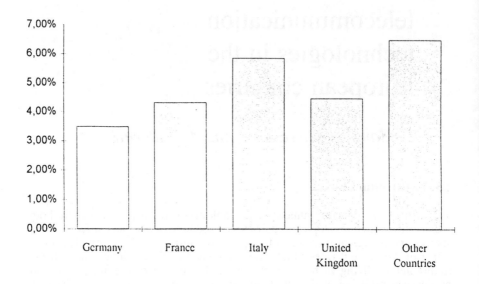

Figure 15.2 The growth rates of the European telephone market
Source: direct computation of SIP Data

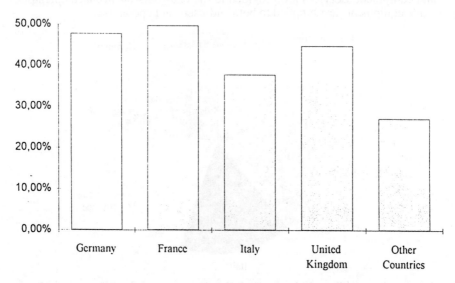

Figure 15.3 Penetration levels of the European telephone market
Source: direct computation of SIP data

Figure 15.1 shows how the installation market is distributed among the European countries. It can be seen that the most industrialized countries (Germany, France, UK and Italy) heavily lead the market, reaching a cumulative share over the 70%. Figure 15.2 evidences that the national growth rates of "Other Countries" exceed the average annual growth rate presenting a factor over the 7%, followed by Italy (6%), France and United Kingdom (over 4%). Notice also that the average growth rates for equipment sales in the "other countries" of Europe outstrip those of the four most industrialized European countries. This indicates that the "other countries" are going to become more significant in the continental market.

A further parameter to be analyzed is the telephone density, which gives a measure of the penetration degree of the most conventional services (the structural bases for the adoption of advanced technologies in the field). This parameter is presented in Figure 15.3 where the very different shapes of eight European countries are compared. France, with 50 main lines for 100 people, leads the EEC ranking, followed by Germany and UK (over 40).

We can further evidence the penetration indices of Italy (47), whereas "Other Countries" are far below the entering threshold of developed countries.

The largest proportion of telecommunications revenues accrues from the sale of basic services, mainly voice telephony. Apart from the UK, which has introduced a second carrier for basic services, the rest of Europe has indicated that basic services will continue to be provided by national monopoly carriers, largely immune from competition. In the area of equipment and systems sales, approximately one-quarter of sales relates to central office switching (Antonelli, 1989), so showing the absence of a complete deregulated market.

In the following sections an analysis of the diffusion process of telecommunications equipment in EEC is carried out to obtain general insights on the infrastructural endowment of each country and their relationships with the socioeconomic development.

Thus, starting with a forecast of the diffusion of telecommunication equipments (which can give some indication of the increasing rate of the market share of these products) we proceed with a verification of the index of market penetration reached in each EEC country, and finally, analyze the most meaningful socioeconomic components of this phenomenon. Our aim is to verify concordances and discrepancies in the development degree of telecommunication and transportation networks of the European countries and relate the different national realities to the different socioeconomic environments.

The paper is organized in three sections: section 15.2 is devoted to introducing the analytical framework, while section 15.3 deals with a discussion of the numerical results.

15.2 Analytical framework

15.2.1 Technology and innovation

The correlation between technological innovation and economic development was used by Schumpeter (1939) to explain the long economic cycle. The

281

behaviour of the pair of technological innovation and market request is opposite in terms of formal position, but equal in terms of substance because the increase of the technological offer is coupled with an equal development of the market demand. However it is often difficult to point out the roles played by technology and market, especially when the changes involved are multi-causal. Thus, when these situations occur, a redefinition of roles is required, starting from the new existing reality.

Subsequently, Rogers (1983) and others discovered that in most cases the adopters' distribution over time follows a standard normal distribution; so that the cumulative number of adopters, with respect to time, can be obtained from the mathematical integration of the distribution namely the diffusion curve.

Again from the Schumpeter model, the difference was introduced between innovation and imitation, because the origin of first step of the diffusion process is strictly related to the "innovators" and only in a second step, when knowledge about innovation increases, it is possible to verify the effect of imitation.

With Fisher and Pry (1971) we observed the first concept of "substitution effect", based on the idea that the innovation diffusion is the result of a competitive replacement of a method satisfying a need by a newer one. The substitution process will proceed to completion once started and it is possible to identify a take over point of this process at the inflection point of the curve that is equal to half-process time. The formula proposed by the authors is:

$$df/dt = C_1 f (1 - f) \tag{15.1}$$

where f=f(t) is the number of adopters or the market share of a product at time t, and df/dt the step of adoption. C_1 is a constant that identifies the diffusion parameter, namely the number of adopters or the market share gained in each time unit (this parameter is inversely proportional to the take-over time).

For reading convenience, we report the integral form of (1): its plotting in a logarithmic scale enables a straightforward interpretation of the phenomena under investigation

$$\ln[f/(1-f)] = C_1 + C_2 t \tag{15.2}$$

Models (15.1) or (15.2) are widely used in technological forecasting, using the market share gained from the new product or technology as dependent variable (an estimate of the overall market).

15.2.2 Infrastructural and socioeconomic indicators

Initially, the Christaller indicator (Christaller, 1933) was introduced to measure the relative intensity of telephone diffusion in a segmented area of interest. This estimator expresses the intensity of the diffusion phenomenon in each sub-area with respect to the mean value of the area of interest. Nevertheless, it is already possible to read the results obtained by the Christaller indicator as an estimate of the excess of services' offer with respect to the local demand. This excess, usually viewed as the importance of the place, can also be explained as a surplus of service available for the demand of the peripheral areas.

The usual formulation for the Christaller indicator is:

$$Z_Z = T_Z - P_Z (T_R / P_R) \qquad (15.3)$$

where:
T_Z is the number of users of the zone z;
P_Z is the population of the zone z;
T_R is the number of users of the total area r;
P_R is the population of the total area r.

The ratio T_R/P_R indicates the overall mean density, whereas its product with the population of a particular zone will give the theoretical value of T_Z for the zone z. The centrality, or the surplus of service, is estimated as a proxy of phenomenon intensity and then defined as the difference between the real value and the theoretical value calculated as the mean value of the area.

The presence of a positive value of the indicator expresses an active balance for offer/demand of a zone that is an excess of service available for export. Vice versa, a negative value of the indicator expresses a deficiency of balance for the zone showing the need of buying elsewhere the necessary services.

The Christaller indicator, then, expresses a sort of regional balance on demand and offer of services, enabling an analysis of intra-regional phenomena. In the following section the same indicator will be used also for Telefax and Data Transmission systems.

The development of these network services will be also compared with the development of the more conventional transportation infrastructures (rail and road). In order to proceed with this assessment we need some further definitions. On the basis of the following formulas (both for rail and road transport), we can calculate two different indicators respectively related to population and territorial size:

$$R1_Z = A_Z - P_Z (A_R / P_R) \qquad (15.4)$$

$$R2_Z = A_Z - S_Z (A_R / S_R) \qquad (15.5)$$

where:
A_Z is the number of rail (road) kilometres of the zone z;
A_R is the number of rail (road) kilometres of the total area r;
S_Z is the surface area of the zone z;
S_R is the surface area of the total area r.

The ratios A_R/P_R and A_R/S_R indicate the mean densities for total area, while its product with the population or the surface area of a particular zone will give the theoretical values for the zone z.

These indicators are then defined as the difference between the observed and the theoretical value. The second one is calculated with respect to the theoretical mean value of the total area.

The specific infrastructural equipment of a zone is represented by a positive value indicating an active balance with respect to the total area. Vice versa, negative values represent a deficit showing the absence of specific infrastructural equipments.

The above indicators enable a straightforward comparison of telecommunication and transport infrastructures within a regressive scheme:

$$Z_Z = a + bR1_Z + gR2_Z + dR3_Z + eR4_Z \qquad (15.6)$$

$$FX_Z = a + bR1_Z + gR2_Z + dR3_Z + eR4_Z \qquad (15.7)$$

$$DT_Z = a + bR1_Z + gR2_Z + dR3_Z + eR4_Z \qquad (15.8)$$

Furthermore, in order to focus the relationships between technological change in telecommunications and the existing socioeconomic levels, a larger set of variables has been analyzed within the regressive scheme (15.9 - 15.11):

$$Z_Z = a + bDW_Z + gSW_Z + dPD_Z + eRD_Z + zMW_Z + hCI_Z + qIN_Z + iSV_Z \qquad (15.9)$$

$$FX_Z = a + bDW_Z + gSW_Z + dPD_Z + eRD_Z + zMW_Z + hCI_Z + qIN_Z + iSV_Z \qquad (15.10)$$

$$DT_Z = a + bDW_Z + gSW_Z + dPD_Z + eRD_Z + zMW_Z + hCI_Z + qIN_Z + iSV_Z \qquad (15.11)$$

where:

DW_Z = employment rate for each zone;
SW_Z = self-employment rate for each zone;
PD_Z = population density of each zone;
RD_Z = mean regional density of each zone;
MW_Z = mean wages of each zone;
CI_Z = percentage of inhabitants of cities with population greater than 500,000 with respect to total population of the zone;
IN_Z = industrial indicator of each zone;
SV_Z = services indicators of each zone;
FX_Z = the telefax indicator;
DT_Z = the data transmission indicator.

The employee and self-employee rates indicate the single job organizations. The population and the mean regional density, together with the percentage of inhabitants of large cities, are indices for the character of each country. Moreover, the mean wage of each zone, together with industrial and services indicators, can identify a proxy for labour quality.

15.3 Numerical results

The first group of results represents the outcomes of the Fisher-Pry model (2) in analyzing the telecommunication diffusion through the EEC countries. Fig. 15.4 (a and b) both show the trend of the telephone diffusion process from 1980 to 1989 and the resulting forecast until 1995. From these figures it is

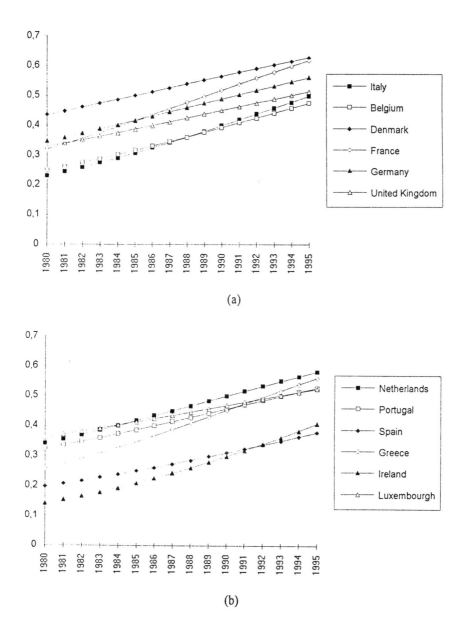

(a)

(b)

Figure 15.4 Telephone diffusion in EEC countries and forecast until 1995
Source: direct computation of SIP data

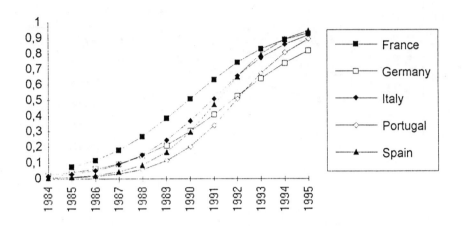

Figure 15.5 Telefax diffusion in EEC countries and forecast until 1995

Source: direct computation of SIP data

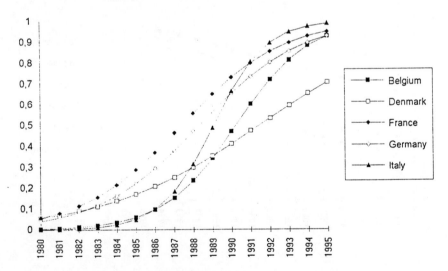

Figure 15.6 Data transmission diffusion in EEC countries and forecast until 1995

Source: direct computation of SIP data

possible to sketch effects of the existing difference among European countries. This difference is related to two main components: the initial value in the available time-series, that is the market share gained from telephone technology in 1980, while the second component is represented by the different national growth-rates.

With reference to the first analytical element, we notice that Denmark presents the only value grater than 40% of the market share, followed by Luxembourg, Germany, the Netherlands, United Kingdom, Portugal and France that which reached a market share greater than 30%.

Note also the second analytical element: the growth rates of France, Greece and Ireland, that will double their values in 1995 with respect to 1980, while Denmark, Germany, Luxembourg, United Kingdom and Spain will follow with slower rates.

Figures 15.5 and 15.6 show the diffusion of telefax and data transmission (for available data only). Note the difference between the shapes of these curves with respect to the telephone ones. Note also that Italy always shows the greatest growth rates, while Germany always depicts the slowest ones.

The second group of results is related to Christallerian indicators. The telephone indicator (Figure 15.7) shows that only five of the twelve EEC countries have a strictly positive value, namely Germany, France, United Kingdom, Denmark and the Netherlands, while Belgium and Luxembourg are close to the mean value. On the contrary, the results related to the telefax system (Figure 15.8) depict a different scenario characterized by more homogeneous performances: only the United Kingdom and Netherlands indicators assume positive values, whereas six countries are close to the mean value. Finally, the results related to data transmission (Figure 15.9) depict a third alternative scenario characterized by positive indices related to France, Germany and Denmark, the Dutch index only being close to the mean one. Thus the above results finally show a turbulent market, differently segmented with strong disparities between the North-Continental countries and the Southern ones. These results mismatch with the ones arising from the outcomes derived from the analysis of the more conventional transportation infrastructures. With the exception of Germany, United Kingdom and France the rail indicators related to the national surface, in facts, show a uniform development degree (Figure 15.10).

A similar result is derived with reference to national populations, where only the French indicator assumes a positive value with an alignment of the remaining eight indices (Figure 15.11). Similar results are obtained from the road indicators. Figures 15.12-15.13 show positive values referring to the total surface (population) indicators France, Germany and Belgium (France) assume(s). For each simple index, more than six countries assume values strictly close to the mean ones so indicating the attainment of a certain development degree of transportation infrastructures in Western Europe. Potentially, the same result could be reached in the telecommunication field although performance and efficiency should be further investigated.

The last group of results analyzes the relationship between telecommunications and both infrastructural and socioeconomic indicators. Table 15.1 shows the results obtained from regression (15.6) that analyzes the telephone distribution with respect to rail and road distribution. The results

287

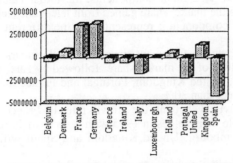

Figure 15.7 Telephone distribution in EEC countries
Source: direct computation of CENSIS and SIP data

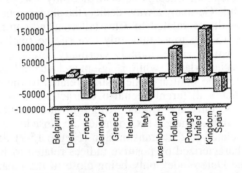

Figure 15.8 Telefax distribution in EEC countries
Source: direct computation of CENSIS and SIP data

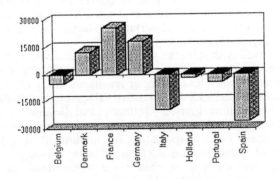

Figure 15.9 Data transmission distribution in EEC countries
Source: direct computation of CENSIS and SIP data

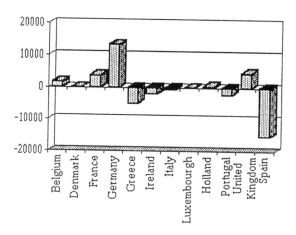

Figure 15.10 Rail distribution with respect to the total surface area in EEC countries
Source: direct computation of CENSIS data

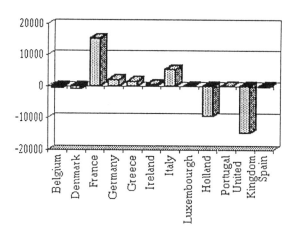

Figure 15.11 Rail distribution with respect to population in EEC countries
Source: direct computation of CENSIS data

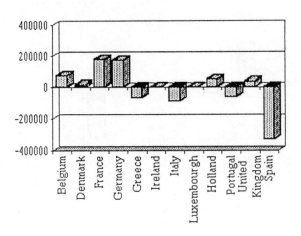

Figure 15.12 Road distribution with respect to total surface area in EEC countries
Source: direct computation of CENSIS data

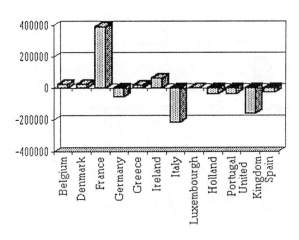

Figure 15.13 Road distribution with respect to population in EEC countries
Source: direct computation of CENSIS data

show how the variance of the telephone sample is well explained by the variance of the model, since the adjusted R^2 value is meaningful (0.87). A better more significant is obtained while substituting telephone with telefax distribution in regression (15.7) (Table 15.2); the explained percentage of sample's variance increases until the maximum level (0.99). Also for the data transmission indicator, as in regression (8), the obtained adjusted R^2 value, as reported in Table 15.3, reaches meaningful level (0.87).

The result of the relationships between telecommunication indicators and socioeconomic estimators are then presented in Tables 15.4-15.6. The selected indicators are not assertive to the variance of each telecommunication indicator as the previous ones. However they give some interesting results. For the telephone sample the adjusted R^2 value obtained by regression (9) is 0.60, whereas for telefax and data transmission indicator (regressions 10 and 11) the adjusted R^2 are 0.84 and 0.59 respectively.

Tables 15.1 and 15.2 show that the telephone and fax variables respectively, are positively related to the existing wage and employment levels only. In addition table 15.3 shows that both wage and employment levels are positively related to the explanation of data transmission variables whereas the mean regional density joined with the industrial and the services indicators significantly contribute but with a negative sign. The latter result than shows that data transmission equipments in comparison with the more conventional ones have a larger diffusion in the less crowded european countries. We can therefore conclude that the telephone and fax systems seem to follow the existing human and industrial settlements whereas the data transmission networks more effectively may contribute to the creation of a more homogeneous organizational and behavioral customs.

Table 15.1
Model fitting results for Z variable
Source: SIP and CENSIS data

INDEPENDENT VARIABLE	COEFFICIENT	STD. ERROR	T-VALUE
CONSTANT	-117.370167	2.303991E5	-0.0005
R1	-63.374938	49.837703	-1.2716
R2	9.318002	4.310846	2.1615
R3	378.439875	171.548764	2.2060
R4	-5.03288	9.334182	-0.5392
R-SQ. (ADJ.)	0.8714		

Table 15.2
Model fitting results for FX variable
Source: SIP and CENSIS data

INDEPENDENT VARIABLE	COEFFICIENT	STD. ERROR	T-VALUE
CONSTANT	-30.805785	35.805105	-0.8604
R1	-15.917193	0.007745	-2055.1538
R2	0.679627	0.00067	1014.4811
R3	15.941355	0.026659	597.9619
R4	-0.680651	0.001451	-469.2284
R-SQ. (ADJ.)	0.99		

Table 15.3
Model fitting results for TD variable
Source: SIP and CENSIS data

INDEPENDENT VARIABLE	COEFFICIENT	STD. ERROR	T-VALUE
CONSTANT	-444.723964	2855.050769	-0.1558
R1	-0.668272	0.663528	-1.0071
R2	0.101252	0.04665	2.1705
R3	3.147977	1.958801	1.6071
R4	-0.083529	0.10287	-0.8120
R-SQ. (ADJ.)	0.8099		

Table 15.4
Model fitting results for Z variable
Source: CENSIS data

INDEPENDENT VARIABLE	COEFFICIENT	STD. ERROR	T VALUE
CI	3.079127E7	1.39659E7	2.2047
MW	12927.469172	4766.029515	2.7124
DW	-1.099876E5	1.884045E5	-0.5838
SW	-2.191555E5	1.10607E5	-1.9814
PD	1.021364E5	4.239535E4	2.4091
RD	-1.144317E8	4.768825E7	-2.3996
IN	1.901422E5	2.103695E5	0.9038
SV	-6.256954E4	1.242318E5	-0.5037
R-SQ. (ADJ.)	0.6016		

Table 15.5
Model fitting results for FX variable
Source: CENSIS data

INDEPENDENT VARIABLE	COEFFICIENT	STD. ERROR	T VALUE
CI	1.784587E6	3.31738E5	5.3795
MW	-494.31799	113.209564	-4.3664
DW	24699.995143	4475.252635	5.5192
SW	-9349.520296	2627.296673	-3.5586
PD	-1422.181456	1007.035075	-1.4122
RD	1.624527E6	1.13276E6	1.4341
IN	-2.512161E4	4996.997585	-5.0273
SV	-1.191027E4	2950.931701	-4.0361
R-SQ. (ADJ.)	0.8447		

Table 15.6
Model fitting results for TD variable
Source: CENSIS data

INDEPENDENT VARIABLE	COEFFICIENT	STD. ERROR	T VALUE
MW	69.530085	67.403264	1.0316
DW	1741.089795	996.732092	1.7468
SW	1241.924133	2487.000547	0.4994
RD	-2.550556E4	5.392765E4	-0.4730
IN	-1888.995489	1858.879029	-1.0162
SV	-2180.452406	1433.803215	-1.5207
R-SQ. (ADJ.)	0.5895		

293

References

Antonelli, C. (1989), 'Induced Adoption and Externalities in the Regional Diffusion of information Technology', *Regional Studies*, 24, pp. 31-40.

Blackman, A.W. (1974), 'A Mathematical Model for Trend Forecasts', *Technological Forecasting and Social Change*, 6, pp. 41-63.

Campisi, D., Tesauro, C. (1992), 'The Diffusion and Spatial Distribution of New Telecommunication Technologies in the Italian Region of Campania', *Technovation*, 12, 6, pp. 355-368.

Censis, (1991), 24° Rapporto sulla Situazione Sociale nel Paese - 1990, Franco Angeli, Milano.

Christaller, W.(1933), *Die Zentralen Orte in Suddeutschland*, Jena.

Fisher, J.C. and Pry, R.H. (1971), 'A simple Substitution Model of Technological Change', *Technological Forecasting and Social Change*, 3, pp. 75-88.

Holsgrove, T. (1990), 'European Opportunities in Telecommunications', *International Journal of Technology Management*, Vol. 5, No. 1.

Marchetti, C. (1980), 'Society as Learning System: Discovery, Invention, and Innovation Cycles Revisited', *Technological Forecasting and Social Change*, 18, pp.267-282.

Rogers, E.M. (1983), *Diffusion of Innovation*, 3rd Edition, The Free Press, New York.

Schumpeter, J.A.(1939), *Business Cycles*, McGraw -Hill, New York.

Skiadas, C. (1985), 'Two Generalized Rational Model for Forecasting Innovation Diffusion', *Technological Forecasting and Social Change*, 27, pp. 39-61.

Vervest, P.H.M. (1987), *Innovation in Electronic Mail*, North-Holland.

Yokoy, M., Kojina, M. and Hoken, J. (1986), 'Comparative Studies of Telecommunication and Computer Penetration', in Kuhn, P. (ed.), *New Communication Services: A Challenge to Computer Technology*, Elsevier Science Publishers, North-Holland.

16 Revealing network properties of Sweden's trade with Europe

B. Johansson and L. Westin

16.1 Introduction

Classical models of the Ricardo type and Heckscher-Ohlin trade models indicate for each country whether a specific commodity group is exported to or imported from an anonymous world market. To which countries are the export flows directed and from which countries do the imports originate? Standard as well as modern trade models in the above tradition are not designed to answer such questions. They abstract from frictions, inertia and barriers of trade links and may thus not explain bilateral patterns of flows in a network. However, they suggest for each trading node, factors which are important for the generation of inter-industry trade in homogenous commodities.

In this paper we outline a theoretical framework for analyzing size and direction of trade flows in a network of trading nodes. This framework identifies frictions on links as well as affinities between pairs of nodes. The latter enhance the propensity to trade. Two regions or countries with low frictions for interaction and joint barriers vis-a-vis third parties tend to display high affinities. Moreover, cultural similarities and joint communication facilities are other affinity factors. These factors may be described as link properties or network characteristics. Such a framework is applied in the empirical part of this paper. There we estimate how various network attributes influence Sweden's export and import flows, specified for supply and demand nodes in Europe. Moreover, the trade is clustered into different product groups, each with particular market characteristics.

In this study we deal with the relation between node and link related network properties and the export pattern of four commodity aggregates. In order to reveal such properties of aggregated flows we use different versions of a model which is inspired by so called gravity models. The gravity model has been used in empirical analysis of international and interregional trade with great success. Generally, such a model may include a characterization of nodes by means of variables which represent market size, per capita income, population and internal costs of communication. Links may be described by trade barriers, distance frictions, measures of accessibility including cultural affinity and communication conditions, membership of trade preference areas, as well as common borders.

The selected model framework makes it possible to incorporate the existence of cross-hauling. In Europe more than 60-70 per cent of all trade is characterized by two-way flows of cross-hauling type, often recognized as intra-industry trade (Greenway and Hine, 1991). Such exchange refers to differentiated commodities where product attributes are at least as important as product prices. We call competition by means of product and delivery attributes product competition, distinguished from price competition. For both types of trade we investigate the importance of trade links between countries.

The models reported in this paper have been estimated on a panel of Swedish export data consisting of seven years between 1970 and 1987. Commodities are defined with regard to their market performance, into product competitive and price competitive aggregates. Product competition is often associated with markets in the early stage of the product cycle where product attributes and customization determine the success of sales while the commodity price is the primary attribute for more standardized products, often in the later stages of the product cycle.

The estimations give support in favour of our initial assumptions that the pattern of trade is sensitive to a mix of three factors, the accessibility and affinity features on the links connecting nodes, the attributes of the nodes and the market performance of commodities. Especially, our results indicate that successful trade in product competitive commodities is favoured by similarities with regard to cultural affinities. Price competitive commodities are instead more sensitive to distance and the existence of common borders between the trading nodes. However, we can also observe some contradictions compared with standard assumptions. These observations indicate where further research may be directed.

The paper is organized as follows. In section two, we present how the gravity model may be used in the analysis of trade patterns in a network economy. Section three introduces assumptions regarding the relation between trade patterns and market performance. Our data set and the Swedish export pattern are introduced in section four. The estimated models and the econometric results are presented in sections five and six while section seven concludes the paper.

16.2 Characteristics in a network economy

Two main features of current trade flows are in the focus of this paper. Firstly, one may observe the growth and dominance of differentiated commodities in the trade among industrialized countries. This represents a major change away from the trade of bulk and other standardized goods in earlier parts of the 20th century. In the case of Sweden, the growing share of intra-industrial trade in relation to inter-industrial trade in the gross trade confirms this observation (Petersson, 1984).

A second feature which may be observed is the increased formation of economic networks among producers and subcontractors and between producers and consumers of final products. Establishment of such networks is connected with investments in links between deliverer and customer. An increased emphasis devoted to the network aspects of the economy, in replacement of the traditional price-oriented market view, implies that link properties will increase in importance relative to node attributes as explanations of trade patterns, service networks and spatially distributed production systems. The archetype model of a market economy with independent actors, in which a quantity of a commodity is bought from the seller who offers the lowest price at the point of delivery focuses, in a myopic way, on production costs in nodes and, if at all, on the transportation costs without observing the dynamic inter-dependencies between actors at the demand and supply sides of a market.

The network economy is thus based on existence of reciprocity at the micro level over time and emphasizes mutual investments in the link between customer and deliverer. (Johansson, 1991; Teubal and Zuscovitch, 1993). Such investments represent sunk costs and introduce rigidities in customer relations which are reflected by inertia in the trade flows. The amount of investment needed to establish and strengthen a producer/customer relation is obviously negatively related to existing affinities between nodes and a positive function of the friction on mutual links. The dominating flows of a specific product category will thus follow links which have the most appropriate attributes for the products, while the total volume is constrained by barriers, frictions and diversities.

The two processes of commodity differentiation and emergence of economic networks are highly integrated. Demand for differentiated commodities is a function of income levels and social identification while supply of differentiated products is motivated by the profitability of forming niches which establish a temporary monopoly for each customer relation. Hence, both sellers and buyers have incentives to develop long-standing links of communication and close interaction in order to secure development of products which fulfil their individual goals. Customer networks with service, financial assistance and information exchange are visual responses to this demand. In Johansson and Westin (1993), it is suggested that this behaviour may be modelled by a logit formulation based on discrete choice at the micro level. At the aggregate level such a model would be cast into a gravity formulation of flows in a network.

Gravity models have in various versions successfully been used in analysis of interregional as well as international trade and barriers to communication analysis. They may both capture dispersions of flows and cross-hauling caused by differentiated commodities and the inertia in flows which is a consequence of strong links between actors in the market. Hence, they address questions about with whom does a country trade, and how much? Early studies may be found in Tinbergen (1962), Leontief and Strout (1963), Linnemann (1966), Gruber and Vernon (1970), Aitken (1973) and Leamer (1974) while more resent studies are Bröcker (1984), Rietveld and Janssen (1990) as well as Bröcker and Rohweder (1990).

The empirical success of the gravity model has not been followed by an equally elaborate theoretical support. However, recently the relation between discrete choice, multinominal logit, entropy and gravity models has been understood more fully (Batten and Boyce, 1986; Batten and Westin 1990). This research has also given the gravity formulation a stronger theoretical support with a foundation in discrete choice theory. Bröcker (1989) also analyzes and develops the relation between a model of partial spatial price equilibrium with differentiated goods and various gravity models. As Bröcker observes, this will improve the possibility to specify the structural form of a trade model which can then be transformed to a reduced form of gravity type, designed for estimation of actual trade flows.

The unconstrained gravity model may be formulated in the following way:

$$x_{rs} = A(Z_r)^\alpha (Z_s)^\beta f_{rs}. \tag{16.1}$$

The notation in (16.1) should be interpreted as follows:

x_{rs} Commodity flow from node r to node s, measured in quantities.
A   Intercept coefficient
Z_r Attributes related to origin node r
Z_s Attributes related to destination node s
α, β Parameters
f_{rs} A function of attributes of the link between r and s, representing friction, affinity and properties of micro links between agents in r and s.

In a specific estimation, a vector of variables may represent node attributes. Variables such as population, market area, income, and educational level may be used. Other attributes of nodes relate to transaction and communication costs caused by frictions inside each node. The number of telephones, telephone calls, vehicles, passenger miles and similar variables may after normalization be indicators of internal interaction capacity and friction. Table 16.1 presents variables describing various node related attributes.

Table 16.1
Variables describing attributes of node r

GDP_r	Gross domestic product (GDP)
N_r	Population
$GDPC_r$	GDP per capita
$\Delta GDPC_{rs}$	Difference in GDP per capita between r and s as a measure of similarity in income and taste
INF_r	Measures of internal friction inside a node

The link related function in equation (16.1), contains attributes of the links between nodes. In an ordinary linear regression this may be modelled either by an additive, multiplicative or by a combined function. We may thus write,

$$f_{rs} = \tau_{rs} w_{rs} + \exp\left\{ \hat{\tau}_{rs} \hat{w}_{rs} \right\} \tag{16.2}$$

In equation (16.2) w_{rs} and $\bar{w}_{rs}$ are attributes related to the link between r and s while τ_{rs} and $\hat{\tau}_{rs}$ are parameters. Table 16.2 contains variables which characterize link attributes. Distance is generally measured as the crow flies between capitals of nations or between large harbours. The cost of transportation would be an appropriate alternative but is often difficult to measure. Dummy variables are appropriate to estimate effects of common borders and membership in trade agreements. Dummy variables are also used to represent such things as cultural affinities. Such an approach partly reflects the problems of finding suitable measures in this area. In this paper we highlight this issue by assessing results from different model specifications.

Table 16.2
Variables which describe link attributes between node r and s

d_{rs} Distance between r and s as a measure of accessibility

c_{rs} Transport cost between r and s

D_T A dummy variable for membership in a trade agreement

D_B A dummy variable for common borders

D_L A dummy variable for language and other cultural affinities between r
           and s

An alternative to the formulation in (16.1), with actual trade flows as the dependent variable, is to use fractions of total trade flows on links. In panel data, such a procedure eliminates cycles and trends over time in the trade. Instead, processes of substitution and complementarity between flows on different links are stressed. When the fraction of total export from region r is analysed one may then study the following variable:

$$\theta_{rs} = x_{rs} / \sum_s x_{rs}$$

(16.3)

Having introduced the variable in (16.3), the standard approach is to specify a logistic function and use

$$\ln(\theta_{rs} / (1 - \theta_{rs}))$$

as dependent variable in a linear regression. Some of the econometric results that we discuss below are based on this approach. Our own exercises will altogether be based on the formulation in (16.1-16.2).

One of the central assumptions with regard to differentiated commodities is the correlation between trade and income per capita as argued and demonstrated by Burenstam-Linder (1961), Krugman (1979), Lancaster (1980), Helpman

(1981) and Balassa and Bauwens (1988). These studies indicate that demand and supply of differentiated products are positively associated with income. The market size is also assumed to be positively correlated with the number of commodities produced. Small countries with low accessibility to large markets have to find their comparative advantage in production of homogeneous commodities.

A successful development of differentiated products depends on the possibility of establishing intense or close interaction between suppliers and customers. In international trade both parties are firms or other types of organizations. As a consequence, the production of differentiated commodities can be assumed to display a negative correlation with the amount of internal friction in a node.

Following Balassa and Bauwens (1988), one may furthermore assume that trade with differentiated products between two nodes is positively correlated with link related factors such as,

* Similarities in language and culture.
* Similarities with regard to the size of two interacting economies.
* Participation in common trade agreements.
* Common borders between nations.
* Similarities in income per capita and thus in taste.
* Accessibility with respect to transportation.

With the exception of similarities in income per capita, which partly represents similarities in factor proportions, one should expect that also trade in homogeneous commodities is positively correlated with those factors. The important question is thus if it is possible to show that significant differences exists between homogeneous and differentiated commodities with respect to the above barriers and friction factors. The following section establishes our hypotheses about the form and strength of such differences.

16.3   Trade patterns and categories of product markets

Increased product differentiation on a market implies that the price of a commodity, although still important, loses its dominance as a means of competition. From a product cycle perspective one may argue that products in the early stage of their life-cycle are characterized by attributes which are important complements to the price as attractors vis-à-vis the customer. The market performance is then characterized by product competition which could be described as competition by means of differentiation. In the later phases of the product cycle where products are standardized, returns to scale can be exploited and larger volumes sold. Then the importance of relative prices increases.

In order to test our assumptions about market performance and trade patterns a classification of commodities with regard to market performance is needed. Such a classification may be accomplished in a number of ways. Our classifica - tion is based on estimated growth rates of export prices relative to import prices and the relative growth of the volumes of export, compared to import volumes.

The analysis comprises a large set of specific commodities during the years 1970-1985. Four categories of commodities are identified by combining such growth rates with the growth of employment in the pertinent industrial sectors (Appendix I). The four categories are:

1 Product competitive commodities with increasing employment (expansive)
2 Product competitive commodities with decreasing employment (contractive)
3 Price competitive commodities with increasing employment (expansive)
4 Price competitive commodities with decreasing employment (contractive)

As a first step we exclude all products with a low proportion of trade, compared with the domestic production and consumption. For all other products the above classification can be applied. We may start with the product competitive group, which is defined to consist of commodities for which the following two change patterns apply simultaneously:

i   The ratio between the export and import price has not decreased.
ii The ratio between the export and import volumes has increased.

For these products the market size has expanded without any price cuts. Remaining sectors are classified as price competitive. For them the relative price is decreased – with or without growing sales volume. Commodities with both falling prices and sales may be regarded as examples of unsuccessful price competition.

The second division into expansive and contractive categories is made on the basis of employment growth rates. Each commodity has then been associated with the industrial sector which dominates its production. The division is made in order to identify differences between growing and contracting sectors, in terms of employment. Increasing employment is assumed to be associated with the expansive part of the product cycle. Category one, with expansive product competition, contains the most successful commodities during the examined period, according to the model assumptions. Employment contraction may in this respect be a first sign of ageing and an outcome of labour saving investments, but also of an unsuccessful market performance in general.

Our hypotheses may be presented as follows. Recall first the network require - ments specified for trade in differentiated commodities. We assume that the same requirements apply with regard to product competitive commodities, since they compete by means of attribute differentiation and other forms of customization. We also assume that affinities and network accessibility are more important for the expanding than the contracting segment of product competitive commodities. Moreover, in general the sensitivity for variations in network qualities is assumed to be significantly lower under the regime of price competition. In summary:

i   Trade with product competitive commodities is sensitive to link-specific affinities
ii Price competitive commodities are elastic with respect to prices and transportation costs but less affected by cultural affinities and barriers.

In this way elements from product cycle theory and models of differentiated competition are integrated with recent developments of modern trade models and theories of economic networks.

16.4 Sweden's export to Europe

The foreign trade data used in the econometric part of our study are organized according to the CCCN statistics of Sweden's export of mining and manufacturing commodities. They refer to the years 1970, 1975, 1980, 1982, 1985, 1986, 1987. As stated in the preceding section, commodities produced in sectors under direct and indirect trade protection have been excluded from the material. Such sectors have been identified by the share of international trade in relation to Swedish production. Unit prices (f.o.b.) on each link may be calculated from data on exported and imported quantities of each commodity, as well as the pertinent volumes in value terms. In this way we obtain export and import prices.

Commodities are aggregated into the four categories discussed in the previous section. The European countries are aggregated into ten regions as described in Table 16.3 below. This division reflects the geographical orientation in the Swedish export, with a separate specification of Nordic countries.

The export in metric tons from Sweden to each of those ten trade-regions is given in Table 16.4. The table describes for each region the share of each of the four categories. Product groups with increasing and decreasing employment are indicated by (+) and (-) signs.

Table 16.3
European countries grouped into ten Swedish trade regions
The full name of a country aggregate is given within parentheses.

TRADE REGION		COUNTRIES
NOR		Norway
DEN		Denmark
FIN		Finland
ATL	(Atlantic countries)	Iceland, Faroe Islands, Greenland
FRG		Federal Republic of Germany
SWC	(Small West and Central European countries)	Netherlands, Belgium, Luxembourg, Ireland, Switzerland, Austria
UK		United Kingdom
FRA		France
WME	(West Mediterranean countries)	Spain, Portugal, Italy, Malta
EME	(East Mediterranean countries)	Yugoslavia, Greece, Turkey, Israel

302

Table 16.4
Export volumes in metric tons 1985. Per cent of total flows
to each export region

EXPORT REGION	1 PROD(+)	2 PROD(-)	3 PRICE(+)	4 PRICE(-)
NOR	21.8	23.6	22.5	32.1
ATL	19.4	23.1	34.3	23.1
FIN	12.1	5.8	5.7	76.5
EME	4.9	17.5	0.9	76.7
SWC	4.9	6.6	12.7	75.7
UK	4.5	25.3	15.2	55.0
DEN	3.9	12.7	44.3	39.1
FRA	3.6	7.3	1.7	87.5
VMW	3.5	20.6	9.7	66.2
FRG	3.0	6.7	12.7	77.6
TOTAL EUROPE	6.0	12.0	16.0	66.0
REST OF WORLD	7.6	11.2	2.0	79.2

Remark: Expanding categories are signified by (+), and contracting by (-).

The regions are ordered with respect to their share of expansive product competitive commodities in total trade. The table shows that Sweden's trade with Norway and Finland contains a relatively large share of these commodities, while the trade with Denmark is dominated by successful price competitive commodities.

The Swedish export to central and southern Europe is on the other hand dominated by contractive price competitive commodities. If this aggregate is elastic with respect to distance, this observation provides an argument in favour of increasing the efficiency in the transport connections with those regions as a means to strengthen the competitive situation for a large share of Swedish trade.

As is shown by Table 16.5 a different pattern occurs when flows are measured in values instead of quantities. Still, around 40% of the total trade consists of contractive price competing commodities. However, the share of the expanding product competitive commodities is more then a quarter of the total export in value terms. Moreover, one may observe that in value terms the export to the rest of the world is dominated by product competitive commodities.

The fifth column in Table 16.5 contains the ratio between expanding product competitive and contracting price competitive trade on each link, in values 1985. The figures confirm the results from the analysis of volumes and indicate that the Nordic countries and the SWC region have shares above the average, while Sweden's trade with Germany is dominated by commodities characterized by price competition with decreasing employment.

Table 16.5
Sweden's export value to ten regions in Europe 1985.
Percent of the total trade value 156 billion SEK.
Manufacturing and mining products

	1	2	3	4	
EXPORT-REGION	PROD(+)	PROD(-)	PRICE(+)	PRICE(-)	1/4
SWC	7.2	2.3	2.2	6.2	1.2
NOR	3.9	2.7	2.1	5.5	0.7
UK	3.8	2.9	1.3	6.4	0.6
FRG	3.0	2.5	2.4	9.0	0.3
FIN	2.8	1.5	1.0	2.7	1.0
DEN	2.6	2.1	3.3	3.9	0.7
WMT	1.7	1.3	0.6	3.5	0.5
FRA	1.4	1.3	0.5	4.0	0.4
EME	0.6	0.3	0.2	0.8	0.8
ATL	0.1	0.1	0.1	0.1	1.0
EUROPE	27.2	16.9	13.7	42.2	0.7
REST OF WORLD[a]	45.7	16.1	4.8	28.4	1.6

a) The total export value to the rest of the world is 68 billion SEK.

The difference between patterns measured in volumes and in values confirms the assumption that product competition refers to lighter, more valuable and thus more expensive commodities than other trade flows. This pattern is also compatible with arguments from product cycle theory. The f.o.b. prices of commodities in this material are presented in Table 16.6.

As may be expected, the low weight of expanding product competitive commodities is associated with high unit values. However, one should also observe the relatively low prices on contracting product competitive commodities. This fact may explain why employment in this category decreases. It may also indicate that Sweden should specialize even more on the expensive part of the segments with product competition. The small flows to the Mediterranean regions are correlated with high unit values which give them their top positions in the table.

304

Table 16.6
Average prices (f.o.b.) of Sweden's export to European export regions 1985.SEK/KG.

EXPORT-REGION	1 PROD(+)	2 PROD(-)	3 PRICE(+)	4 PRICE(-)	AVERAGE
WME	49.0	6.2	6.2	5.3	7.1
EME	38.0	6.5	64.1	3.6	6.5
UK	28.8	3.9	3.0	3.9	4.9
SWC	24.2	5.7	2.8	1.3	3.0
DEN	20.6	5.1	2.3	3.1	3.8
FRG	16.6	6.1	3.1	1.9	2.9
FRA	14.0	6.4	11.2	1.6	2.6
FIN	13.9	15.7	10.2	2.1	4.5
NOR	7.6	4.8	4.0	7.3	5.3
ATL	6.9	5.6	2.7	8.5	5.4
MEDIAN	18.6	5.9	3.6 (3.1)[a]	3.4	4.5
STANDARD DEVIATION	13.5	3.3	19.0 (3.4)[a]	2.5	1.5

a) When the price of EME is excluded.

In international trade studies the standard deviation of the unit prices to different destinations is often used as a measure of the degree of product differentiation. The standard deviations in Table 16.6 indicate that the classification of aggregates is reasonable according to this test. A comparison with the flows in Table 16.4, indicate that the high standard deviation of the expanding price competing aggregate is mainly due to the small export to the eastern Mediterranean countries. An exclusion of this flow reduces the standard deviation to 3.4, which is at an expected level. The standard deviation for the group contracting product competition is low although its average price exceeds the prices of the two price competitive aggregates. This suggests a careful use of the standard deviation as a measure of product differentiation, at least at aggregated levels.

Interesting enough, trade patterns, unit prices and standard deviations are all within bounds which may be expected from a priori assumptions. This suggests that the very rough classification which has been obtained from the trade and employment statistics provides a reasonable picture of a trade pattern with properties which are predicted by product cycle models.

16.5 Import and export affinities

In order to examine the existence and strength of affinity relations we have specified a set of fixed-effect models for Sweden's import from and export to the European regions in Table 16.3. Let us start with the import flows. They are analysed by means of the following two equations:

$$\ln x_{rs} = \hat{\beta}_r + \beta_1 t + \beta_2 \ln P_{rs} \tag{16.4}$$

$$\ln x_{rs} = \hat{\alpha}_r + \alpha_1 \ln Y_s + \alpha_2 \ln Y_r + \alpha_3 \ln P_{rs} \tag{16.5}$$

By x_{rs} we denote the annual import flow to Sweden, s, from a Europan trade region, r. The flow x_{rs} is measured in quantity terms (weight units). The independent variables in (16.4-16.5) are defined as follows:

$\hat{\beta}_r$ = fixed effect referring to Sweden's propensity to import from r according to (16.4)
$\hat{\alpha}_r$ = fixed effect in equation (16.5)
t = denotes years in the period 1970-1987 (time trend), $t(1970) = 1$
P_{rs} = price of Sweden's import from r
Y_s = GDP each year in Sweden
Y_r = GDP each year in region r. $\tag{16.6}$

Although the model in (16.5) has strong similarities with a traditional gravity model, it also contains some specific qualities. Data only consists of that row in the European trade matrix which refers to Sweden. Hence, Y_s does not act as an attractor in the model. Secondly, gravity models are often estimated on a one - year basis over cross-sections. Both (16.4) and (16.5) are estimated on a set of panel data with 10 trade relations over 7 years. This feature motivates the inclusion of a time trend in (16.4) and Y_s in (16.5), since Y_s develops over time.

In equation (16.4) the economic size of each trade region, r, will be captured by the fixed-effect parameter $\hat{\beta}_r$. In equation (16.5) the size of each region is represented by the GDP-variable Y_r. Hence, $\hat{\alpha}_r$ will reflect affinities in a more profound sense than $\hat{\beta}_r$.

The time coefficient β_1 in equation (16.4) will differentiate the four product groups as regards their market growth. In equation (16.5) the time variable has been replaced by $Y_s(t)$, i.e., the annual GDP-level in Sweden. We should expect α_1 to be negative, reflecting a process in which the value per weight unit increases as Y_s grows. In other words, the weight per value unit is negatively correlated with Y_s.

Table 16.7 presents the econometric result with regard to equation (16.4). The Swedish exports of the group PROD(+) grew fast in the analysed period. By definition we shall expect a slow growth of the imports of the same group.

From Table 16.7 we can conclude that this group has the lowest β_1-value. Next we observe that the largest price elasticities are found for the contracting segments PROD(-) and PRICE(-). Finally, the propensity to import is highest for Germany and lowest for the East Mediterranean territory.

Table 16.7
Import propensities according to model (16.4)
Metric tons 1970-1987

Parameters	1 PROD(+)	2 PROD(-)	3 PRICE(+)	4 PRICE(-)
Time trend, β_1	0.019	0.024	0.052	0.025
	(3.0)	(3.1)	(3.7)	(4.6)
Import price, β_2	-0.53	-0.93	-0.75	-0.91
	(6.0)	(8.2)	(11.9)	(8.1)
Fixed effect, $\hat{\beta}_r$:				
FRG	7.1	6.9	5.9	7.4
SWC	6.4	6.2	6.0	6.9
NOR	6.1	5.3	4.9	6.3
UK	6.0	5.9	6.1	6.8
FIN	5.7	5.6	5.1	6.5
FRA	5.4	5.2	4.2	6.3
WME	5.3	5.3	4.6	6.5
DEN	5.2	5.7	5.5	6.5
EME	4.0	2.7	2.3	4.5
Adjusted R^2	0.97	0.98	0.95	0.97

Remark: t-values are given within parentheses. The $\hat{\beta}_r$-estimates have all very high t-values. The number of observations = 70. In this table the small Atlantic region has been excluded.

In Table 16.8 we control for the size of each exporting economy by introducing the GDP-variables Y_r. As a consequence the small Nordic countries now get larger affinity values ($\hat{\alpha}_r$) than most other countries. However, also in this case Sweden reveals a considerable import affinity vis-a-vis Germany. Moreover, also with model (16.5) the group PROD(+) has the lowest price elasticity, followed by PRICE(+). We may finally observe that equation 2 in Table 16.8 reveals a different behaviour compared with the other equations. The size of the export region, Y_r, is not significant, while the positive sign of α_1 associated with Sweden's GDP indicates a strong growth of this import flow. This is compatible with the observation that the employment in pertinent Swedish industries has decreased during the period.

Table 16.8
Import affinities according to model (16.5)
Metric tons 1970-1987.

Parameters	1 PROD(+)	2 PROD(-)	3 PRICE(+)	4 PRICE(-)
Sweden's GDP, α_1	-0.72	0.3	-1.46	-0.46
	(2.9)	(2.7)	(2.7)	(2.2
Exporter's GDP, α_2	0.80		1.60	0.79
	(3.8)		(3.5)	(4.6)
Import price, $\alpha 3$	-0.57	-1.19	-0.81	-0.93
	(5.8)	(15.1)	(14.7)	(8.9)
Affinity coefficient, $\hat{\alpha}_r$:				
NOR	6.0	2.4	4.9	3.3
FIN	5.7	2.7	5.2	3.6
DEN	5.0	2.8	5.4	3.4
FRG	5.0	4.2	2.4	2.4
SWC	4.8	3.4	3.3	2.4
UK	4.3	3.2	3.2	2.2
FRA	3.5	2.4	1.0	1.5
WME	3.3	2.4	1.3	1.6
EME	2.9	0.0	0.7	0.7
Adjusted R_2	0.97	0.98	0.95	0.97

Remark: t-values are recorded within parentheses. All $\hat{\alpha}_r$ -variables have very high t-values. The number of observations = 70.

If one calculates the average affinity position in a ranking test, the Nordic countries come out as number one, followed by Germany and SWC. To what extent are these affinity estimates reciprocal for import and export relations? In order to answer that question the following export equation was estimated:

$$\ln x_{sr} = \hat{\omega}_r + \omega_1 \ln Y_s + \omega_2 \ln Y_r + \omega_3 \ln P_{sr} + \omega_4 t \qquad (16.7)$$

where x_{sr} denotes Sweden's export to each region r, measured in metric tons. The variables Y_s, Y_r and t are defined in (16.6). New variables in (16.7) are

P_{sr} = Sweden's export price for the flow x_{sr}

$\hat{\omega}_r$ = Sweden's export affinity with regard to region r.

Table 16.9
Sweden's export affinities according to equation (16.7)
Metric tons 1970-1987

Parameters	1 PROD(+)	2 PROD(-)	3 PRICE(+)	4 PRICE(-)
Sweden's GDP, ω_1	-0.59	-0.73	-0.94	-0.65
	(2.4)	(4.0)	(3.0)	(3.7)
Importer's GDP, ω_2	0.69	0.89	1.10	0.73
	(2.9)	(6.5)	(4.3)	(3.7)
Export price, ω_3	-1.01	-1.09	-1.16	-0.93
	(12.4)	(36.4)	(28.6)	(16.7)
Time trend, ω_4	0.05	*	*	0.02
	(6.6)			(2.3)
Affinity coefficient, $\hat{\omega}_r$:				
NOR	5.8	4.6	5.4	6.8
FIN	5.6	4.2	4.9	6.4
DEN	5.4	4.3	5.3	6.5
SWC	5.0	2.6	3.0	5.7
UK	4.4	2.6	2.6	5.6
FRG	3.8	2.0	2.4	5.6
WME	3.4	1.6	2.6	4.7
FRA	3.1	1.6	2.6	4.9
EME	3.1	1.5	2.3	4.2
Adjusted R^2	0.98	0.99	0.98	0.99

The result in Table 16.9 reveals that the ranking of export and import affinities are not equivalent. First, the Swedish export flows tend to penetrate small regions like the SWC and the Nordic areas more easily than larger economies. Second, the export behaviour of the Swedish industry reveals a higher export affinity for UK than FRG.

We may observe that a growing GDP in Sweden seems to imply an increased value per weight unit, which explains the negative sign of ω_1. The export of product group PRICE(+) is more stimulated by large economies than the other groups. Finally, the time trend is significant and strong for the group PRODUCT(+)

16.6 Export affinities and network attributes

In this section export affinities are examined further. We add network attributes as explanatory factors. Some of these link attributes will reduce the importance of bilateral affinities. However, also with a detailed specification of link attributes, an export affinity pattern still remains as a determinant of export flows. The export equation for the four groups is specified as follows:

$$x_{sr} = A Y_s^{\theta_1} Y_r^{\theta_2} P_{sr}^{\theta_3} \exp\{\theta_4 t\} f_{sr} \qquad (16.8)$$

$$f_{sr} = \exp\{\theta_5 d_{sr} + \theta_6 D_L + \theta_7 D_B + \theta_8 D_A\} \qquad (16.9)$$

where Y_s, Y_r, P_{sr} and t are defined in (16.6) and (16.7). A denotes the intercept and f_{sr} reflects the combined consequence of frictions and accessibility factors. Obviously, f_{sr} refers to link-specific factors, which are specified in (16.10):

$d_{sr} =$ the distance as the crow flies between Sweden and each European region r,
$D_L =$ dummy for language and cultural similarities,
$D_B =$ dummy for countries with whom Sweden has a common border,
$D_A =$ dummy for the Atlantic trade region.   (16.10)

Formula (16.9) should be compared with (16.5) and especially (16.7). One may then conclude that (16.9) represents an attempt to explain the affinities observed in 16.6. These additional explanatory factors are specified in (16.10).

During the estimations of (16.9) the GDP variables have experimentally been replaced by or combined with income per capita variables. Generally, multi - colinearity prohibits a simultaneous use of income and income per capita variables. Differences in accessibility between regions and commodities are estimated through distance and dummy variables. The dummy, D_L, indicating language and cultural similarities is active for all regions with the exception of France and the two Mediterranean regions. The dummy for common border, D_B, contains Norway, Denmark, and Finland. A dummy for the Atlantic region, D_A, has been included since in the residual analysis the trade with those islands was shown to contain significant fixed effects compared with the average trade pattern. An alternative to the above procedure would have been to use the estimated fixed effect model in a first step and to regress the fixed effects against the link-specific variables in a second step.

The time trend, t, may be interpreted as an indicator of the correspondence between the preferences among consumers and the attributes of the commodities delivered from Sweden. It may also capture other trends, for example changes in the overall accessibility to the customers and a development towards lighter commodities not captured by the GDP variables. As discussed in Section 16.5, the Swedish GDP variable is included as a measure of the elasticity of exported volumes with respect to increased incomes in Sweden.

The price variable captures the static demand price elasticity with respect to Swedish export. The size of this elasticity reflects the degree of product differentiation and rigidities in the market due to long term contracts and producer/customer relations. Prices are measured at the Swedish border and should thus not double count for the link costs which are represented by distance and dummies. As discussed by e.g. Linnemann (1966) and Bröcker (1989), prices are often left out from gravity models, with the argument that the model represents the reduced form of a price equilibrium where prices may be eliminated and the exogenous attributes of nodes should explain the pattern of trade. In this case, the use of a time series of data implies that the notion of a single static equilibrium becomes inapplicable. Price changes reflect imbalances caused by devaluations, investments in new technology, demand shifts etc. As a consequence they will influence the annual variation in trade flows. The fact that we are not estimating a full origin-destination matrix gives a further argument in favour of a formulation with elements from a traditional demand function.

At this stage the model and its results should primarily be seen as a further step in the assessments made in Section 16.5. It is a model designed to test our previous hypotheses and to examine the empirical regularities which were identified in the preceding section.

The results of our estimations are presented in Table 16.10 below. Initially one may observe that all four regressions have a high degree of explanation and significant estimates are obtained for most variables. In particular we observe that income per capita differences have not, because of multicolinearity, been possible to integrate as an independent explanation of the trade pattern when GDP variables are included in the regressions.

The coefficient related to the Swedish GDP, Y_s, has for each category a negative elasticity. We interpret this as a confirmation of our assumption that less heavy products are substituted for heavier ones as Y_s increases. This process has been especially fast with regard to product category 4, PRICE(-).

The GDP elasticity with respect to the destination regions may be interpreted as a combined effect of the income in and the size of the destination markets. This elasticity is in all four cases positive but rather inelastic. However, contracting commodities are more elastic than expanding commodities.

The D_L-dummy supports our assumption that product competitive commodities are more sensitive to cultural affinities than price competitive products. The two first categories have both a relatively high θ_6 value, and the expansive aggregate is considerably more sensitive to such affinities. According to this result, Sweden's cultural barrier separates the Mediterranean countries from the rest of Europe's market economies.

Other factors are important for price competitive commodities. The contracting segment is the only category with a significant distance sensitivity. The dummy representing common borders refers to the Nordic market. The dummy reveals that there is a strong Nordic affinity, which stimulates Swedish export of all product categories to the Nordic market. The strongest effects are observed for PROD(-) and PRICE(+). The comparatively low value for the category expanding product competition was not expected. Although Sweden is more successful on the Nordic market also in this case, the tendency is that the growth of PROD(+) needs all of northern Europe as its nearby market.

Table 16.10
Node and link attributes of Sweden's export in metric tons to Europe
Product and price competitive commodities 1970-1987.

	1 PROD(+)	2 PROD(-)	3 PRICE(+)	4 PRICE(-)
A	3.97 (2.18)	1.56 (1.37)	2.09 (1.32)	6.15 (5.46)
Sweden's GDP, θ_1	-0.42 (-2.03)	-0.59 (-4.48)	-0.58 (-3.42)	-0.99 (-7.96)
GDP in r, θ_2	0.46 (3.83)	0.87 (12.30)	0.79 (7.54)	0.96 (15.88)
Time trend, θ_4	0.05 (6.60)			0.03 (4.42)
Culture, θ_6	1.31 (10.45)	0.81 (10.98)	0.62 (6.62)	0.69 (10.04)
Distance, θ_5				-0.0002 (-4.71)
Border, θ_7	0.74 (2.48)	1.68 (10.28)	1.79 (6.79)	1.18 (6.70)
Atlantic, θ_8	-1.57 (-2.45)	0.89 (2.47)	0.77 (1.40)	0.67 (2.18)
Export price, θ_4	-0.93 (-8.04)	-1.13 (-30.00)	-1.21 (-30.60)	-0.78 (-13.06)
R^2	0.95	0.98	0.98	0.98
F-value	176	499	451	645

Remark: t-values corrected for heteroscedasticity are presented within parentheses. Heteroscedasticity is taken care of through White's (1980) method. The number of observations = 70.

Finally, the price elasticity is shown to be relatively low for the expansive product competitive category. Although the elasticity is surprisingly high, the comparatively low value was an expected result from a product cycle point of view. However, the elasticity of contracting price competitive commodities is even lower. This was not assumed. One explanation may be that the measured elasticity is static. In cases when the market is characterized by long term contract, the short term effect of prices changes may be small. A dynamic measure of the price elasticity would then be higher. The unequal length of the periods between the years in the data set have prevented such a model. A second explanation to the observed elasticities may be that the demand function is not identified in an appropriate way.

16.7 Conclusions about link specific affinities

In this paper we have discussed why network properties, existence of appropriate links and barriers to trade and communication should be important components in the analysis of market performance and patterns of trade. Our assumptions regarding the impacts of cultural affinities and distance on the trade with commodities in price and product competition have gained some support from our estimations of the link and commodity dependent attributes in Sweden's export to Europe.

Table 16.11
Measures of link specific trade affinities

Trade region	Export affinities (Table 16.9)	(Table 16.10)	Import affinities (Table 16.8)
NOR	5.7	++	4.2
DEN	5.4	++	4.2
FIN	5.3	++	4.3
SWC	4.1	+	3.5
FRG	3.5	+	3.5
UK	3.8	+	3.2
FRA	2.9		3.1
WME	2.9		2.2
EME	2.8		1.1

Remark: The affinity values presented are averages across the four product categories.

Since accessibility on links between countries reflect investments in infra-structure, our results also have at least one policy implication. Expensive, differentiated products in the early stage of the product cycle may obtain a stronger comparative advantage from an adjustment of advertisement, design and standards to the tradition in each region of destination. For these products it may also be specially important that the firms are able to understand the foreign culture and subtleties of the language. Such efforts may depend on the quality of interregional infrastructure and interaction conditions. However, they cannot be substituted by investment in physical infrastructure. In Table 16.11 we summarize the affinity measures as obtained from tables 16.8, 16.9 and 16.10. The largest indicators of important affinity are registered for the Nordic group, Germany and the SWC-region. Export affinities are especially high for

Sweden's three Nordic neighbours and the SWC-region.

This study has identified areas where further work may be concentrated. Alternative measures of market performance is one such area. A second area would be to use our approach on less aggregated data both with regard to commodities and regions. We have not corrected our analysis for auto-correlation in time and space. The lack of regularity in our time series makes the first type of correlation difficult. The costs of completing the time series are considerable. However, a spatial correction may be included in future work.

Acknowledgements

The authors are thankful to Lena Sahlin and Jens Tjernström for their assistance in creating the database and in the econometric part of the paper.

References

Aitken, N.D. (1973), 'The Effect of the EEC and EFTA on European Trade: A Temporal Cross-Section Analysis', *American Economic Review*, pp. 881–91.

Balassa, B. and Bauwens, L. (1988), 'The Determinants of Intra-European Trade in Manufactured Goods', *European Economic Review*, 32, pp. 1421-37.

Batten, D.F. and Boyce, D. (1986), 'Spatial Interaction and Interregional Commodity Flow Models', in Nijkamp, P. (ed.), *Handbook of Regional and Urban Economics*, Vol. 1, North-Holland, Amsterdam.

Batten, D.F. and Westin, L. (1990), 'Modelling Commodity Flows on Trade Networks: Retrospect and Prospect', in Chatterji, M. and Kuenne, R.E., *New Frontiers in Regional Science*, Macmillan, London.

Burenstam-Linder, S. (1961), *An Essay on Trade and Transformation*, John Wiley and Sons, N.Y.

Bröcker, H. (1984), 'How do International Trade Barriers Affect Interregional Trade?', in Andersson, Å.E. et al. (eds.), *Regional and Industrial Development Theories, Models and Empirical Evidence*, North-Holland, Amsterdam.

Bröcker, J. (1989), 'Partial Equilibrium Theory of Interregional Trade and the Gravity Model', *Papers of the Regional Science* Ass., 66, pp. 7-18.

Böcker, J. and Rohweder, H.C. (1990), 'Barriers to International Trade. Methods of Measurement and Empirical Evidence', *Annals of Regional Science*, 24, pp. 289-305.

Deardorff, A.V. (1984), 'Testing Trade Theories and Predicting Trade Flows', in Jones and Kenen (eds.), *Handbook of International Economics*, Elsevier Science Publ., N.Y.

Gruber, W. and Vernon, R. (1970), 'The Technology Factor in a World Trade Matrix', in Vernon, R. (ed.), *The Technology Factor in International Trade*, Columbia University Press, N.Y.

Greenway, D. and Hince, R.C. (1991), 'Intra-Industry Specialization, Trade Expansion and Adjustment in the European Economic Space', *Journal of Common Market Studies*, XXIX, 6, pp. 603-622.

Helpman, E. (1981), 'International Trade in the Presence of Product Differentiation, Economies of Scale and Monopolistic Competition: A Chamberlin-Heckscher-Ohlin Approach', *Journal of International Economics*, 11, pp. 305-340.

Johansson, B. (1989), 'Innovation Processes in the Urban Network of Export and Import Nodes: a Swedish Example', in Nijkamp, P. (ed.), *Sustainability of Urban Systems*, Avebury, Aldershot.

Johansson, B. (1991), 'Economic Networks and Self-Organisation', in Bergman, E.M., Maier, G. and. Tödtling, F (eds.), *Regions Reconsidered*, Mansell, London.

Johansson, B. and Westin, L. (1993), *Affinities and Frictions of Trade Networks*, Royal Institute of Technology, Stockholm.

Krugman, P. (1979), 'Increasing Returns, Monopolistic Competition, and International Trade', *Journal of International Economics*, 9, pp. 469-79.

Lancaster, L. (1980), 'Intra-Industry Trade under Perfect Monopolistic Competition', *Journal of International Economics*, 10, pp. 151-75.

Leamer, E.E. (1974), 'The Commodity Composition of International Trade in Manufactures. An Empirical Analysis', *Oxford Economic Papers*, pp. 350-74.

Leontief, W. and Strout, A. (1968), 'Multiregional Input-Output Analysis' , in Barna. T. (ed.) *Structural Interdependence and Economic Development*, MacMillan, London.

Linnemann, H.J. (1966), *An Econometric Study of International Trade Flows*,

Peterson, L. (1984), *Svensk utrikeshandel 1871-1980: En studie i den intraindustriella handelns framväxt*, Lund Economic Studies, No. 30, Lund.

Reitveld, P. and Janssen, L. (1990), Telephone Calls and Communication Barriers. The Case of Netherlands', *Annals of Regional Science,* 24, pp. 307-18.

Tinbergen, J. (1962), *Shaping the World Economy: Suggestions for an International Economic Policy*, The Twentieth Century Fund, N.Y.

Teubal, M. and Zuscovitch (1993), 'Demand Revealing and Knowledge Differentiation Through Network Evolution', in Johansson, B., Karlsson, C. and Westin, L., *Patterns of a Network Economy*, Springer-Verlag, Berlin.

White, H. (1980), 'A Heteroskedasticity-Consistent Covariance Matrix Estimator and a Direct Test of Heteroskedasticity', *Econometrica*, 48, p. 4.

APPENDIX I SECTOR CLASSIFICATION

The classification is made according to the standard of Swedish classification of economic activities (SNI) as well as market and product cycle performances. Average export prices (1985) are also given in SEK/Kilo.

PRODUCT COMPETITIVE COMMODITIES:

INCREASING EMPLOYMENT		DECREASING EMPLOYMENT	
SNI	SEK/KILO	SN	SEK/KILO
2302	2.1	3212	64.9
2909	0.3	3215	6.4
3115	7.2	3219	40.0
3419	9.4	3232	580.1
3511	4.1	3311	2.2
3522	242.2	3319	8.2
3560	30.6	3513	8.7
3720	15.5	3521	8.2
3821	84.8	3829	55.0
3832	397.7	3831	74.3
3843	48.3	3844	82.3
3851	419.8	3845	3318.6
3852	531.9	3853	383.0

PRICE COMPETITIVE COMMODITIES:

INCREASING EMPLOYMENT		DECREASING EMPLOYMENT	
3119	21.5	2301	0.1
3529	6.4	2901	0.1
3530	1.8	3114	15.4
3540	2.8	3211	54.4
3811	150.0	3213	124.2
3824	70.2	3214	32.0
3833	59.4	3220	198.4
3849	29.6	3231	58.9
		3233	98.2
		3240	75.6
		3320	17.6
		3411	3.6
		3512	1.2
		3523	11.9
		3551	22.7
		3559	31.0
		3610	31.8
		3620	5.9
		3691	3.0
		3710	4.8
		3812	19.3
		3819	15.5
		3822	43.9
		3823	76.4
		3825	395.5
		3839	40.1
		3841	145.6
		3901	327.3
		3902	40.1
		3903	49.3
		3909	50.4

17 Regional development strategies and industrial policy making: A European example

K.E. Haynes, T. Dignan and Li Qiangsheng

17.1 Background

Uneven development of regions within a national state has, as one of its dimensions, an imbalance in the distribution of wealth and employment opportunities. Such an imbalance has often caused political concerns and led to legislative solutions. Even industrialized countries such as Italy, Ireland,the United Kingdom, Canada, and Belgium, among others, provide examples of this phenomenon.

In each of these countries there exists a locational problem - some regions (or set of regions) experience difficulty in attracting new economic activity. Recognizing this locational problem, a variety of national governments (including those cited above) have attempted to modify the relative attractiveness of regions to firms by offering inducements to locate in relatively disadvantaged regions. Typically, the inducement takes the form of a locational cost reduction mechanism. In Smith's (1966) terminology, the national government seeks to expand the spatial margins of profitability so as to include disadvantaged regions. Examples of such inducements are direct capital grants (utilized in Ireland), interest rate subsidies (utilized in Belgium), and employment premiums (utilized in the United Kingdom).

One of the empirical difficulties in assessing regional development strategies is the sources of variation that impact industrial policies. The first source of variation concerns the objectives underlying policy instruments. For example, the Industrial Development Certificate policy pursued in Britain sought to reduce 'congestion' in areas such as the Midlands and Greater London, as well as redistributing employment opportunities and capital investment away from these areas and to such problem areas as the Northeast of England. The second source of variation concerns the spatial scale at which policies operate. For example, the British government's Regional Employment Premium (REP) policy operates not just at the regional level but also at the international level since it would, in theory at least, have influenced mobile capital in choosing between Britain and competing nations. The third source of variation in location policies concerns the ways in which they affect a firm's production function. An example of this is the British government's REP policy which also serves to reduce the labour costs associated with a particular project, whereas the capital grants employed by the Irish Republic have a direct impact on the fixed asset investment costs of establishing a new enterprise (Table 17.1).

Even when these sources of variation in regional economic development strategies are articulated and tracked the levels of effectiveness vary. Regardless of the type of policy instrument employed, any framework for evaluating the efficiency of such policies must contain at least two basic elements, ie. 'microlevel effectiveness' and 'macrolevel effectiveness' (Yannopoulos & Dunning, 1976). **Microlevel effectiveness** of regional policies refers to the impact of a policy or set of policies on a firm's 'location choice behaviour'. Moses' (1958) classical integration of production theory with traditional location theory shows that, regardless of the firm's production function, a firm's cost function varies across locations in the presence of spatially differentiated delivered factor prices, and hence the optimal combination of inputs also varies across locations. This means, the capital grants differential policy tends to affect the spatial distribution of firms by attracting more capital intensive industry into the targeted region, or encouraging production firms to find factor replacements in favour of capital. In other words, the effect of the policy will vary across firms, depending on production characteristics, technologies and conditions.

Macrolevel effectiveness of a regionally-differentiated capital subsidy depends inter alia, on whether the subsidy has contributed to the growth of national income and employment as well as the improvement of social and economic conditions of the country, compared to the situation that would have otherwise been in the absence of the subsidy. Indirect effects on employment and income growth via backward linkages also requires attention.

Another effectiveness is on the mesolevel, or the employment and income effects at the regional level. This **mesolevel effectiveness** of a policy depends on the objective(s) underlying the use of a particular instrument. A wide variety of objectives can be pursued, though the reduction of regional per capita income and unemployment rate differentials are 'standard' objectives. For example, if a regional policy aims at reducing per capita income differences, then the 'gain' from employing location-deflecting incentives might be written as the contribution of incentive-leveraged employment to reducing the variance in regional per capita income. However, the consideration of macro- and mesolevel effects of an incentives policy can be integrated by means of a programming function which treats the macrolevel 'losses' and the mesolevel 'gain' (Table 17.2).

The implementation of industrial policy is made even more complex due to the characteristics of particular instruments. Methods for evaluating an instrument at its different levels of effectiveness need to be comprehensive and often interrelated. All national and regional development policies, particularly those that benefit the nation or regions at the expense of other regions, are limited by political and economic constraints.

Investment incentives of various forms are widely used in a number of developed and developing countries. Table 17.3 shows the types of regional investment incentives and the maximum assistance levels of the incentives in the countries of the EEC. The most popular form of subsidy would appear to be direct capital grants whereby the national government contributes some

318

proportion of the capital costs associated with a new development. Other forms of assistance to capital include accelerated depreciation allowances and low interest loans or interest rate subsidies. More recently, equity participation has been used as a means of attracting new investment (e.g., the Irish Industrial Development Authority, and the Welsh and Scottish Development Boards). The extent of coverage of regional policy programs in terms of impacted population in the EEC countries is also illustrated in Table 17.3.

17.2 Introduction

The policies cited above have in common a regional-level spatial orientation. Obviously, in microeconomic terms such policies should be effective to some degree if they significantly affect a firm's cost structure and are perceived to do so by the firms to which the policies are targeted. In this paper, we argue that an additional factor to be considered in determining the effectiveness of such regional-level policies is the structure of the decision making process of the firm. Specifically, we utilize a probabilistic model of the locational choice behaviour of individual firms which allows us to infer the nature of the decision making process based on the revealed preferences of firms for particular locations. The relationship between the structure of the decision making process and the level of effectiveness and/or applicability of a regionally based subsidy mechanism are explored from a policy perspective.

The model specifically illustrates how the capital grants program initiated by the Irish government was aimed at attracting new investment, and associated employment opportunities, from foreign-based companies to Ireland. The same program, by the regionally differentiated nature of the grants available, has the objective of diverting projects to disadvantaged areas and thus 'balanced out' the interregional distribution of employment opportunities in Ireland.

The empirical assessment utilizes the decision structure in competing destinations studies as adapted by Fotheringham (1984, 1986) in measuring airline passenger and migration flows in the United States, and by Ishikawa (1987) in studying regional interaction in Japan. This paper applies this model in a probabilistic framework to assess regional development policies as reflected by investment flows and industrial location destination decisions in Ireland.

In section three we outline the probabilistic choice model and the two alternative industrial decision processes to be evaluated. Section four describes the origin of the specification of these decision processes of simultaneous versus hierarchical and sequential choice. Irish regional economic development policy is reviewed in section five. This policy is formally modeled and evaluated for industrial decisions and regional development policy effectiveness in section six. Section seven contains concluding remarks relative to Irish programs and overall regional economic development strategies.

319

Table 17.1

Sources of variation in industrial development policy

I) Policy Objective
- Employment
- Growth (contribution to GDP)
- Horizontally redistributive (e.g., UK's IDC policy)
- Sectorally distributive (e.g., Irish IDC policy)
- Marginally distributive (e.g., Irish IDC policy)

II) Spatial Scale
- Local, regional
- National
- International

III) Production Function
- Labor costs (e.g., UK's REP policy)
- Capital costs (e.g., Irish CE policy)
- Resource costs (energy, materials, etc.)
- Substitution impact

Table 17.2

Dimensions of industrial development policy effectiveness

Microlevel
- Individual firm behavior
- Individual community impact

Macrolevel
- Cumulative consequences
- Opportunity cost
- Strategic competitive consequences

Mesolevel
- Regional objective
- Second order consequences
- Balancing objectives across regions

Table 17.3
Main Regional Incentives in EEC Countries

Country	Regional Population affected as % of national total	CG	IRS	TC	DA	LS	Problem region	Maximum aid as a net grant % or in EUA per job created by initial investment
Belgium	42%	2x			x		Development Zones	25% or 3,500EUA(up to 25%)
Denmark	27%	x	2x				Special development regions	25% or 4,500EUA(up to 30%)
France	35%	x		x			1.Overseas department	75% or 13,000 EUA
							2.Regional development Grant Area	30% or 5,500 EUA(up to 50%)
Germany	36%	2x	x	x			1. Berlin (West)	75% or 13,000 EUA
							2. Zonal Border Area	25% or 4,500 EUA(up to 30%)
Ireland	33%	2x					Designated Areas	75% or 13,000 EUA
Italy	35%	x	x	x		x	1. Mezzorgiorno	75% or 13,000 EUA
							2. aided center-north	30% or 5,500 EUA(up to 50%)
Luxemburg	17%	x		x			not designated	20% or 3,500 EUA(up to 25%)
Netherlands	45%	x		2x			investment premium area	20% or 3,500 EUA(up to 25%)
U.K.		x	2x				1.Northern Ireland	75% or 13,000 EUA
							2.Development areas	30% or 5,500 EUA(up to 30%)

a Abbreviations: CG stands for capital grant, including (re-)investment grant, allowance and premium, and development grant; IRS for interest related subsidy, including all kinds of soft loans; TC for tax concession, including export tax-relief; DA for depreciation allowance; and LS for labor subsidy.
When a country adopts two different incentive programs that belong to the same category, they are indicated as "2x".
Source: Yuill et al.(1980), Table 11.3.

17.3 A probabilistic choice model and alternative decision structures

Suppose that a particular country is divided into two regions, A and B. Region A is underdeveloped relative to Region B. The national government of the concerned country is actively engaged in attempting to induce foreign-based firms to locate within its national boundaries. The policy instrument underlying this effort consists of direct grants paid to new industry projects in proportion to the amount of investment made. Cognizant of the relation between A and B, and concerned to enhance the ability of Region A to attract investment, the proportion of the amount invested which is payable as a direct grant is higher in Region A than in Region B. Let G_{ij} be the amount payable to firm i if it locates in j. Given the scenario described above, there is a regional grant differential, $G_{iA} - G_{iB}$, where $G_{iA} > G_{iB}$.

Suppose that a firm, i, has decided to locate a plant somewhere in the abovementioned country. Ostensibly, the firm must make at least two decisions: it must choose a region (A or B) and a specific urban centre within the chosen region.

Assume that the firm is an optimizer and employs a utility function in choosing a location and that this function can be specified as:

$$U_{ijk_j} = Z'_{ij} \beta + X'_{kj} \alpha + \varepsilon_{ijk_j} \tag{17.1}$$

where,

U_{ijk_j}, is the utility accruing to firm i from a choice of region j and urban centre k within region j;

Z_{ij}, is a vector of variables operating at the regional level;

X_{kj}, is a vector of variables operating at the urban level;

ε_{ijk_j}, is the stochastic component of utility and is a function of uncertainty and (unmeasurable) firm-specific idiosyncrasies;

α, β are parameter vectors;

j subscripts regions, j = A, B;

k_j subscripts urban centres in j, $k_j = 1, S_j$;

Since utility contains a random component of firm i's locational preference, it can be predicted only up to a certain probability but always less than one.

Assuming that ε_{ijk_j} is distributed i.i.d. Weibull, then the selection probabilities corresponding to utility-maximizing behaviour can be specified as (McFadden, 1974; 1975):

$$P_{ijk_j} = \frac{\exp(Z'_{ij}\beta + X'_{kj}\alpha)}{\exp(Z'_{il} + I_l)} \tag{17.2}$$

where,

$$I_j = \ln(\sum_{k_j=1}^{S_j} \exp (X'_{k_j} \alpha))$$

The inclusive value, I_j, can be interpreted as a measure of the urban content of region j (Anas, 1982).

A problem with the specification (17.2) is that it assumes the independence of irrelevant alternatives (IIA), ie. the unobserved attributes of urban centres are uncorrelated. Mcfadden (1978) reparameterizes (17.2) in order to take account of possible violations of the IIA assumption. Thus (17.2) is respecified as:

$$P_{ijk_j} = \frac{\exp (Z'_{ij} \beta + X'_{kj} \alpha - \lambda I_j)}{\sum_l \exp (Z_{il} \beta + (1 - \lambda) I_l)} \qquad (17.3)$$

where,

λ is a parameter, $0 < \lambda < 1$.

The advantages and other issues relating to the specification (17.3) are discussed in detail in Mcfadden (1978), Anas (1982), and Haynes and Fotheringham (1991). Of concern here is the alternative decision making structures implied by various values of λ. In order to explore these decision structures, note that (17.3) can be decomposed as:

$$P_{ijk_j} = P_{ij} \times P_{ik_j|j} \qquad (17.4)$$

where,

$P_{ijk_j|j}$ is the conditional probability of k_j being chosen, given that j has been chosen;

$$P_{ij} = \sum_{k_j} P_{ik_j|j} \text{ is the marginal probability of region j being chi}$$

is the marginal probability of region *j* being chosen.

Figure 17.1 shows the decomposition of equation (17.3) implied by equation (17.4), as well as the probability specifications resulting from the extreme values, $\lambda=0$ and $\lambda=1$. Figure 17.2 illustrates the decision structures corresponding to these extreme values.

The case of $\lambda=0$ suggests a single-stage decision process whereby the firm simultaneously chooses both an urban centre and a region (see Figure 17.2). Examination of the appropriate row of Figure 17.1 shows that the marginal probabilities are a function of the inclusive value, I_j. That is, the regional choice depends on the characteristics of each set of urban centres within the

323

competing regions, as well as the regional-level characteristics. It should also be noted that, when $\lambda=0$, equation (17.3) reduces to equation (17.2), suggesting independence of errors across urban centres.

For $\lambda=1$, a hierarchical and sequential two-stage decision process is inferred. As can be seen from Figure 17.2 and the final row of Figure 17.1, the firm first chooses a region without regard to the characteristics of urban centres. Note the absence of the inclusive value from the regional probability when $\lambda=1$. At the second stage, the firm chooses between the urban centres within the chosen region.

To examine the implications of alternative decision structures for regional level policies, assume that the probability model described by equation (17.3), given that the linear predictor $Z'_{ij}\beta + X'_{kj}\alpha$ is properly specified, adequately describes the decision making process for a typical firm i. Second, assume that the parameterscan be estimated.

Selection Probability

(a) Regional P_{ij}	(b) Urban $P_{ijkj|j}$	(c) Joint P_{ikj}

$$0<\lambda<1 \qquad \frac{\exp (Z_{ij}\,\beta+(1-\lambda)\,I_j)}{\sum_l \exp (Z_{il}\,\beta+(1-\lambda)\,I_l)} \times \frac{\exp (X'_{k_j}\alpha)}{\exp (I_j)} = \frac{\exp (Z_{ij}\,\beta+X'_{k_j}\alpha-\lambda\,I_j)}{\sum_l \exp (Z_{il}\,\beta+(1-\lambda)\,I_l)}$$

$$\lambda=0 \qquad \frac{\exp (Z_{ij}\,\beta+(1-\lambda)\,I_j)}{\sum_l \exp (Z_{il}\,\beta+I_l)} \times \frac{\exp (X'_{k_j}\alpha)}{\exp (I_j)} = \frac{\exp (Z_{ij}\,\beta+X'_{k_j}\alpha)}{\sum_l \exp (Z_{il}\,\beta+I_l)}$$

$$\lambda=1 \qquad \frac{\exp (Z_{ij}\,\beta)}{\sum_l \exp (Z_{il}\,\beta)} \times \frac{\exp (X'_{k_j}\alpha)}{\exp (I_j)} = \frac{\exp (Z_{ij}\,\beta+X'_{k_j}\alpha-I_j)}{\sum_l \exp (Z_{il}\,\beta)}$$

Figure 17.1 Selection Probabilities Implies by Alternative Values of λ

Now, suppose that, for our hypothetical case, the only factor varying significantly at the regional level is the amount of direct grant which a firm receives. Further, suppose that, in terms of urban content or structure, Region B's attractiveness significantly outweighs Region A's. This second supposition is not unrealistic: it is intuitively plausible that uneven development of regions will be reflected in diverging urban structures. It implies:

$$I_B > I_A \tag{17.5}$$

Finally, in order to evaluate the degree of effectiveness of a regionally based subsidy mechanism, it is necessary to define the 'degree of effectiveness' operationally.

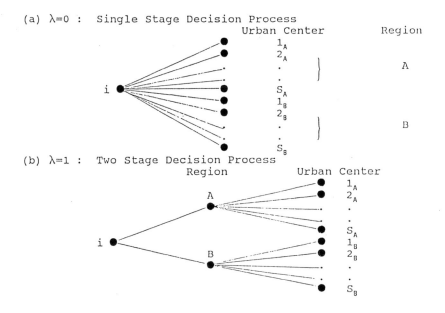

(a) λ=0 : Single Stage Decision Process

(b) λ=1 : Two Stage Decision Process

Figure 17.2 Alternative Decision Structures Implied by the Extreme Value of λ

The purpose of a regionally based grant subsidy mechanism is obviously the diversion of investment into relatively underdeveloped and/or disadvantaged regions. A policy is effective only insofar as firms are responsive to that mechanism in their location choice utility function. This suggests that we measure the effectiveness of a regionally based subsidy by its qualitative impact on the probability of a firm choosing to locate in a targeted region.

Given the above scenario of our hypothetical case, the probability of a location in Region A can be written as:

$$P_{iA} = \frac{1}{1 + \exp\left[(G_{iB} - G_{iA}) + (1-\lambda)(I_B - I_A)\right]} \qquad (17.6)$$

Obviously, if β=0 then, regardless of the firm's decision making process, the policy instrument should be re-evaluated. However, λ can be seen to affect the value of P_{iA} which the policy maker is trying to enhance. If λ=1, a two stage decision making process is inferred in which regions are first compared with respect to their characteristics, and then urban centres are evaluated. If the firm is employing a two-stage process then its regional location behaviour should be

325

susceptible to a regional level policy instrument. Conversely, if $\lambda=0$, then the firm is inferred to employ a single-stage decision process and to be basing its regional location decision, at least in part, on a comparison of the urban content of alternative regions. A finding of $\lambda=0$ and $\beta=0$ would therefore suggest that the spatial scale of the policy instrument be reoriented to the urban level, ie., it is the deficiencies in A's urban infrastructure that must be rectified in order for the region's attractiveness to be optimally enhanced.

If $\beta>0$ holds then the policy can be construed to be effective insofar as firms are responsive to the policy instrument. However, note that, for fixed β,

$$(P_{iA\,|\lambda=1} - P_{iA\,|\lambda=0})$$
$$= (P_{iA\,|\lambda=1} \times P_{iA\,|\lambda=0}) \times \exp[(G_{iA} - G_{iB})]\,[\exp(I_B - I_A) - 1] \qquad (17.7)$$

From (17.5) above, $I_B > I_A$. Therefore, $\exp(I_B - I_A) > 1$ and,

$$P_{iA\,|\lambda=1} > P_{iA\,|\lambda=0} \qquad (17.8)$$

Thus, for fixed β, the probability of choosing A is higher for $\lambda=1$ than for $\lambda=0$. This suggests that the effectiveness of a regionally based subsidy, in terms of its ability to divert firms to the target region, will be highest when firms employ a two-stage process. A finding of $\beta>0$ and $\lambda=0$ would suggest that the policy is having some impact at the regional level but also that there is a scope for some urban-oriented policy measures.

The above discussion is summarized in Figure 17.3.

(a) $\lambda=1$, $\beta=0$ Two-stage decision process, policy instrument ineffective, but there is scope for a regional level instrument.

(b) $\lambda=0$, $\beta=0$ Single-stage decision process, policy instrument ineffective, policy should be reoriented to urban level.

(c) $\lambda=1$, $\beta>0$ Two-stage decision process, policy instrument operating effectively.

(d) $\lambda=0$, $\beta>0$ Single-stage decision process, policy instrument at least partially effective at the regional level, potential scope for urban-based policies.

Figure 17.3 Alternative Combinations of the Policy Variable and Inclusive Value Coefficients and Implications

17.4 Other forms of the hierarchical destinations choice models

As has been mentioned earlier, the origin of this decision structure evaluation is found in the two-stage hierarchical destinations choice model used by Fotheringham (1984, 1986) to compute the airline passenger and migration flows in the United States. Ishikawa used the same concept (1987) to study regional interaction in Japan.

The competing destinations model has been suggested to replace the production-constrained gravity model which has been a poor specification of reality. The equivalent competing destinations model formulated by Fotheringham (1986) is:

$$P_{ik} = w_k^{\alpha_1} \exp{(\alpha_2\, d_{ik})}\, A_{ik}^{\alpha_3}\, [\sum_k w_k^{\alpha_1} \exp{(\alpha_2\, d_{ik})}\, A_{ik}^{\alpha_3}]^{-1}\; ; \tag{17.9}$$

where A_{ik} represents the accessibility of destination k relative to other potential destinations available to i in region j. Its utility function has been shown as follows:

$$U(i, k) = \alpha_1 \ln w_k + \alpha_2\, d_{ik} + \alpha_3 \ln A_k + \varepsilon_{ik}. \tag{17.10}$$

If the selection of a destination results from a two-stage process, the probability that i chooses region j is simply the sum of the attractiveness of each of the destinations within j:

$$P_{ij} = \frac{(\sum_{k \in j} w_k)^{\alpha_1} \exp{(\alpha_2\, d_{ij})}}{\sum_{j=1}^{x} (\sum_{k \in j} w_k)^{\alpha_1} \exp{(\alpha_2\, d_{ij})}}, \tag{17.11}$$

where α_1 and α_2 are parameters associated with the choice of region j, which includes all individual destinations k. Replacing d_{ij} with d_i for all j, (17.11) becomes:

$$P_{ij} = \frac{w_j^{\alpha_1}}{(\sum_{k=1}^{x} w_j^{\alpha_1})} \tag{17.12}$$

Differentiating with respect to w_j and reorganizing, we have

$$\frac{\partial P_{ij}}{\partial w_j} = \frac{\alpha_1 \, P_{ij} \, (1-P_{ij})}{w_j} = \frac{w_j^{\alpha_1 - 1} \, \alpha_1 \, (1-P_{ij})}{\sum\limits_{j=1}^{x} w_j^{\alpha_1}} \cdot$$

(17.13)

It now becomes clear that the relationship depends critically on the value of α_1, as Fotheringham has (1986) demonstrated,

$$\text{when } w_j \to 0, \; \frac{\partial P_{ij}}{\partial w_j} \to \begin{cases} \infty & \text{if } \alpha_1 < 1 \\ (\sum\limits_{k=1}^{x} w_k)^{-1} = \dfrac{1}{r_j} & \text{if } \alpha_1 = 1 \\ 0 & \text{if } \alpha_1 > 1 \end{cases}$$

where r_j represents the remainder.

Hence, the relationship between P_{ij} and w_j depends on α_1, which is a scale parameter associated with the choice of a region with n destinations. When $\alpha_1 < 1$, the relationship is logarithmic, a possible two-stage choice of destination with urban content being the primary consideration until competition among towns takes place; when $\alpha_1 = 1$, a logarithmic relationship with a single-stage destination choice; and when $\alpha > 1$, there is a logistic two-stage destination choice relationship with the region being the first consideration until agglomeration forces among towns begin to function. Following Fotheringham (1989), Figure 17.3 represents these three choices for our situations.

The nested logit model with a two-stage decision process corresponds conceptually to the decision structure in the competing destinations choice model. Following Ishikawa (1987), it assumes the utility function

$$U_{ij} = \alpha_1 \, \ln w_{ij} + \beta_1 \, \text{Ind}_{ij} + \varepsilon_{ij}$$

(17.14)

for the upper choice level, and

$$U_{ik} = \alpha_2 \, \ln w_{ik} + \beta_2 \, \text{Ind}_{ik} + \varepsilon_{ik}$$

(17.15)

for the lower choice level. W_{ij} and d_{ij} respectively denote the attractiveness of j for i and the distance to j and/or cost for i to choose j, ε_{ij} denotes random error. Thus, the nested logit model is formulated as follows:

$$P_{ij} = P(j) \cdot P(j/k) = \frac{W_{ij}^{\alpha_1} \, d_{ij}^{\beta_1} \, [\sum\limits_{k' \in j} (W_{ik'}^{\alpha_2} \, d_{ik'}^{\beta_2})]^{1-\sigma}}{\{\sum\limits_{j'} (W_{ij'}^{\alpha_1} \, d_{ij'}^{\beta_1})[\sum\limits_{k' \in j} (W_{ik'}^{\alpha_2} \, d_{ik'}^{\beta_2})]^{1-\sigma}\}} \times \frac{W_{ik}^{\alpha_2} \, d_{ik}^{\beta_2}}{\sum\limits_{k' \in j} (W_{ik'}^{\alpha_2} \, d_{ik'}^{\beta_2})}$$

(17.16)

Where $\sum_{k' \in j} (W_{ik'}^{\alpha 2} d_{ik'}^{\beta 2})$ is the inclusive value, which indicates the expected maximum utility of the nest, and σ is the parameter. When $\sigma = 0.0$, it implies that the destination choice is made by one-stage decision making. When $\sigma = 1.0$, the destination is chosen in a strictly hierarchical way. Therefore, if the value of the parameter σ ranges between 0.0 and 1.0, and is significantly different from 0.0, it can be perceived as a two-stage destination choice behaviour (Ishikawa, 1989; Fotheringham, 1986). This is directly parallel to the interpretation of λ in our model.

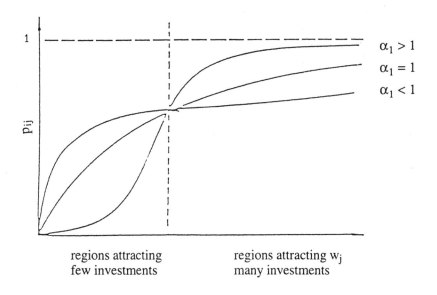

Figure 17.4   The relationship between P_{ij} and W_j when the decision structure is hierarchical.

17.5   Evolution of regional development policy in Ireland

Ireland is a comparatively less developed member country of the European Economic Community. Its lower investment costs and direct accessibility to the European market attracts foreign investors.

Since the mid 1950s, the Irish government has adopted an export-oriented economic policy by removing protectionist barriers and encouraging foreign investment and trade. Consequently, the Irish economy today is small, open, and highly dependent on international trade. The value of its gross merchandize trade (imports plus exports) is equivalent to 105 percent of its GNP figure, twice the European average. However, from a regional development perspective its previous self-sufficient and import substitution economic policy had left the country with a locationally concentrated industrial base and hence a polarization of industrial employment growth. (Ross 1978). In particular, the Dublin region and the Northeast shared most of the nation's industrial development, while counties along the Atlantic seaboard had failed to develop a significant industrial base (Haynes and Dignan, 1985).

To encourage industrial development in the poorer parts of the country, the Irish government passed the Undeveloped Areas Act in 1952, which initiated a program of state incentives designed to attract new industry to less developed areas, most notably counties west of the Shannon River, Donegal, Kerry, and West Cork. The Act was proposed to promote economic development and provide employment in these areas which were disadvantaged by their inadequate access to major population centres, underdevelopment of infrastructure and declining agricultural activities. The primary incentive introduced by the Act comprised nonrepayable cash-grants, with statutory limits of 50% and 100% towards, respectively, the cost of machinery/equipment, and land and buildings.

Industrial assistance was extended to all parts of the country with the passing of the Industrial Grants Act in 1956, which was intended to stimulate manufacturing employment and import substitution. However, the regional differential was maintained by offering assistance only towards the cost of buildings, with a statutory limit of 67% and a grant limit of £50,000. Such a regional differential was actually eroded by successive amendments to the basic Acts over the period 1959 to 1969. In 1969, both Acts were replaced by the Industrial Development Act, under which the country was divided into Designated Areas (DAs), Non-Designated Areas (NDAs) and Dublin (DUB), with DAs roughly corresponding to the former Undeveloped Areas. The primary purposes of the Act were to update and clarify the incentives available to industry, as well as to integrate the process of allocating grants with the promotional aspects of the so called New Industry Program. Further, the basic cash-grant system was streamlined and the regional differential was strengthened. The standard grants were set up to 40% of the cost of fixed assets invested for the DAs and up to 25% for the NDAs, with an additional 20% payable under 'exceptional' circumstances such as one with high growth potential. No limit was set on the level of grant which could be approved, but grants in excess of £350,000 required the consent of the government. Some modifications were made to this system in the 1970s and 80s, eg. the condition of employment generation was linked to the level of grant-giving. Thus, for a DA location, a firm could receive up to 50% of the cost of fixed asset investment as long as the grant cost per job created did not exceed £5,000. For counties in the NDAs outside Dublin and Dublin itself, the standard limits were set respectively at 35% and 25% of eligible costs, subject to a limit of respectively £4,000 and £3,000 per job. The rate for Dublin was changed to that for the NDAs in 1977 in the wake of the recession of the mid 1970s when Dublin was particularly hard hit by job losses.

Other incentives were also provided, including: a guaranteed 10% maximum corporation tax until the year 2000; depreciation allowances enabling both buildings and machinery to be written off against tax liability; all profits being allowed to be repatriated; grants for up to 100% of cost for labour training;

330

equity participation and provision of advance factories; and infrastructural assistance (Haynes and Dignan, 1985). These incentives have made Ireland a profitable and attractive location in Europe, attracting over 860 foreign companies (300 of them U.S.) in 20 years time (1967 - 1987).

17.6 Formal model and empirical evaluation

Based on the above scenario, the policy of differential capital grants was one of the measures to encourage a balanced regional development adopted by the Irish government and administered by the Industrial Development Authority (IDA). It can be formally described as follows:

$$\text{Max } G_{ij} = t_j \text{ EFA}_i \tag{17.27}$$

where, Max G_{ij}, is the maximum level of grant payable to firm i for locating in region j;

EFA$_i$, is the expected fixed asset investment of firm i;
t_j, is the maximum proportion of EFA$_i$ payable as a grant for location j, (j= DA, NDA, DUB).

Under this scheme, $t_{DA} > t_{NDA} > t_{DUB}$, but from 1977 onward it became $t_{DA} > (t_{NDA} = t_{DUB})$.

If EFA$_i$ can be assumed constant across regions, then (17.27) can be solved to give :

$$G_{ik} = (t_k/t_j) \ G_{ij}, \quad i \neq k. \tag{17.28}$$

Utilizing (17.28), the observed grant approved for firm i locating in region j can be used to compute an expected grant approval if the firm had located in region k rather than in region j.

Using a data set culled from the annual reports of the IDA, a probability model in the form of (17.3) was estimated by means of maximum likelihood using the Powell (1970) algorithm. The linear predictor utilized was:

$$Z'_{ij} \ \beta + X'k_j \alpha = \beta_1 G_{ij} + \beta_{2j} U_i + \beta_{3j} UK_i + \alpha_1 \ln\text{Popk}_j + \alpha_2 \ln Ak_j^{-i} \tag{17.29}$$

where,

U_i, is the national unemployment rate at the year of i's observed location;
UK_i, = 1 if i originated in the UK;
= 0 if otherwise.
Popk$_j$, is the population of town k in region j;
Ak$_j$, is the accessibility of town k to major ports of Ireland;
$\beta_{2, DA} = \beta_{3, DA} = 0$.

331

The results are presented in Table 17.4. As it shows, $\beta_1=0$, and α_2 is significantly different from both 0 and 1. However, λ is closer to 0 than to 1. The results suggest an effective policy measure, and a decision process which is closer to a single-stage than a two-stage process. In short, the results suggest the need for reorientation of policy toward the urban level. The estimate of β_1 is, however, surprising since the country is small in scale and the IDA seems quite confident that the policy was effective in terms of diverting firms to the DAs (O'Farrell, 1978).

Table 17.4
Parameter Estimates for the Joint Choice Model
(asymptotic 't-ratios' in brackets)

Variable	Grant	Unemp	UK	lnPop	lnA	I
$\ln[P_{NDA}/P_{DA}]$	.0003	.1381	-1.1753	.3744	.5913	.3651
	(.051)	(5.056)	(-2.349)	(4.079)	(7.688)	(2.525)
$\ln[P_{DUB}/P_{DA}]$		.2993	.4786			
		(8.994)	(1.034)			
$\ln[P_{NDA}/P_{DUB}]$		-.1612	-1.6539			
		(-2.764)	(-3.488)			

Notes: The coefficients of the variables Grant, I and A are constant across log - odds equations;
'Grant' is measured in 10,000 pound units;
UK = 1 if i is from the United Kingdom; = 0 otherwise;
Pop = population of town k in region j;
A = accessibility of town k in region j to major port outlets.

To explore the issue further, the grant variable was respecified as:

$$f(G_{ij}) = g_{ij}^{\phi}, \quad 0 < \phi < 1. \tag{17.13}$$

This formulation suggests that, the grant variable has a significant influence on regional location choice, but that, as the scale of investment increases, the marginal effect of the grant declines. The choice model was re-estimated for various values of ϕ. For $\phi = 0.25$, we obtained $\beta = 0.2922$ (t=2.115), as shown in Table 17.5. Interestingly, though all other parameter estimates were quite stable , the estimate for λ almost doubled, from 0.3651 (t=2.525) to 0.6836 (t=2.895). This value is also significantly different from zero and unity, but is much closer to a two-stage decision process than a one-stage process. This formulation also suggests national economic conditions to be significant, with the effect of urban structure being somewhat marginal at the regional level.

These results are obviously ambiguous. Additional data would seem to be needed in order to clarify the matter. In particular, note that, in generating the grant variable, G_{ij}, it was necessary to assume no regional variation in EFA_i. Since data on EFA_i was unavailable, this assumption could not be tested. Further, no data was available with respect to the level of employment each firm expected to generate. Thus, the implicit assumptions that this level did not vary across locations and was not a factor considered by firms could not be tested. The specification of (17.29) is obviously subject to the validity of these assumptions.

Table 17.5
Parameter Estimates for the Scale Adjusted Model

$$g(G_{ij}) = G_{ij}^{\phi}$$
(asymptotic 't-ratios'in brackets)

Variable	Grant	Unemp	UK	InPop	LnA	I
ln[P$_{PNDA}$/P$_{DA}$]	.2922	.2032	-1.3299	.3712	.5922	.6836
	(2.115)	(4.818)	(-2.6209)	(3.991)	(7.612)	(2.895)
ln[P$_{DUB}$/P$_{DA}$]		.2460	.3056			
		(4.7553)	(.6511)			
ln[P$_{PNDA}$/P$_{DUB}$]		-.0428	-1.6355			
		(.463)	(3.449)			

Notes: The coefficients of the variables Grant, I and A are constant across log-odds equations;

'Grant' is measured in 10,000 pound units;

UK = 1 if i is from the United Kingdom; = 0 otherwise;

Pop = population of town k in region j;

A = accessibility of town k in region j to major port outlets.

O'Farrell's (1975,1978) research suggests that the system of regionally differentiated grants did have the effect of dispersing industry throughout the country. Table 17.6 shows the distribution of capital grants as a percentage of fixed asset investment between DA and NDA projects for 1960-73. Grants in excess of 40% of fixed assets investment were made to 65% of the DA projects, compared to 26% to the NDA projects. And also in terms of the level of employment per £1,000 investment in fixed assets, DA (1.9) is significantly lower than NDA (2.1).

Table 17.6
New Industry Manufacturing Establishments Locating in Ireland between 1960 and 1973 Classified by Grants as a percentage of Assets

Location	Under 20%	20-29.9%	30-39.9%	over 40%	all	Employment per £1,000 of assets*
DAs	21	13	38	136	208	1.9
NDAs	20	53	82	55	210	2.1

* Results derived from random samples of 169 DA and 183 NDA projects

If the differentiated grants are the cause of the location choice, then the policy is effective at the microlevel; conversely, if the location is the cause for qualification for higher grants, then the differential grant policy is extraneous and unnecessary.

Despite the sharp increase in the number of foreign firms locating their plants in Ireland presumably as a result of the incentives, at the macrolevel, the country did not experience a high per capita GNP growth as desired. Throughout the 1970s, the growth rate of per capita GNP remained well below 3%, until it turned negative in four of the five consecutive years in the early 1980s, with its average growth rate (2.1%), below the OECD level (2.4%) (1979 - 1988). Unemployment rate peaked at 19% in 1978, and remained 18% in 1987 and 17% in 1989. This phenomenon seems to support Bornschier's arguments that foreign investment, in manufacturing in particular, is positively associated with economic growth, while the stock of foreign capital is negatively associated with growth; and that the total direct and indirect negative effect of foreign penetration tends to be greater than the positive effect of such investment. If these arguments hold, then the macrolevel effectiveness of the IDA's policy becomes doubtful and requires re-evaluation from a longer term perspective. But what appears to contradict Bornschier's arguments is the latest recovery of the Irish economy - an average GNP growth rate of 4% was reported for the period 1987-1989, 5% for 1990. Unemployment has tended to come down, and a better economic situation is expected for 1991 and thereafter through 2000.

17.7 Concluding remarks

This paper has introduced a probabilistic model for the study of the effectiveness of a regionally-based subsidy policy for diverting investment into disadvantaged areas. An empirical assessment is made of the Irish differential grants policy. The criterion of effectiveness employed was the quantitative impact of the policy on the probability of a firm locating in a disadvantaged region. The level of effectiveness, by this criterion, was suggested to vary according to the decision making process employed by the firm. It was argued that regionally-based subsidies will have maximum effect in terms of investment diversion if firms employ a two-stage decision process whereby regions and urban centres are evaluated hierarchically, sequentially and separately. In the case of a one-stage decision process it was argued that such a policy would need to be supplemented by urban-oriented policies.

Another issue implied in the differential grants and other investment incentives policies seems to have produced diverging effects on their microlevel and macrolevel effectiveness. On the microlevel, foreign firms have responded to such policies by utilizing the subsidized factor markets to gain high rates of return on their investment (average 23% for US firms) which is three to four times that of the EC average (6%). On the other hand, disadvantaged areas seemed to have gained the priority for foreign investment, which has helped reduce local unemployment and even though the policy encourages capital intensive investments it generates economic impetus through backward linkages. However, during this period, at the macrolevel, Ireland had not witnessed a proportionally high rate of per capita GNP growth, and unemployment remained high.

Regional development policy is a multilayered system that needs to integrate economic variables and industrial decision processes and must be evaluated in terms of effectiveness at both the microlevel of individual investment flows as well as in terms of aggregate macrolevel strategic effects. From this analysis it would seem that a third, meso- or intermediate, layer of evaluation may be worth investigating. Although this analysis covers a period of over twenty years, it is still unclear what the appropriate time horizon is for evaluating the effectiveness of regional development policies and this deserves increased attention if we are to develop appropriate strategies and properly assess their effectiveness.

References

Anas, A. (1982), *Residential Models and Urban Transportation: Economic Theory, Econometrics, and Policy Analysis with Discrete Choice Model*, Academic Press, New York.

Bradley, J. & Fitz Gerald, J. (1990), 'Production Structure in a Small Open Economy with Mobile and Indigenous Investment', *European Economic Review*, 34, pp. 364-74.

Fotheringham, A. S. (1986), 'A New Set of Spatial-interaction Models: the Theory of Competing Destinations', *Environment and Planning A*, 18, pp. 401-18.

Fotheringham, A. S. and O'Kelly, M. E. (1989), *Spatial Interaction models: Formulations and Applications*, Kluwer, Boston.

Haynes, K. E. and Dignan, T. (1988), 'Evaluating Capital Grants for Regional Development', *Essays in Honor of François Perroux*, Higgins, B. and Savoie D.J. (eds), Unwin Hyman, Boston, pp. 330-74

Haynes, K. E. and Fotheringham, A. S. (1991), 'The Impact of Space on the Application of Discrete Choice Models', *Review of Regional Studies*, 20, pp. 39-49

Ishikawa, Y. (1987), 'Exploration into the Two-stage Destination Choice', *Geographical Review of Japan*, Vol. 62, pp. 75-85.

McFadden, D. (1974), 'Conditional Logit Analysis of Qualitative Choice Behavior', in Zarembka, P. (ed.), *Frontiers in Econometrics*, Academic Press, New York.

McFadden, D. (1978), 'Modeling the Choice of Residential Location', in Karlqvist, A. *et al.* (eds), *Spatial Interaction Theory and Planning Models*, North Holland, Amsterdam.

McFadden, D. (1975), 'The Revealed Preferences of a Government Bureaucracy: Theory', *The Bell Journal of Economics*, 6.

O'Farrell, P.N. (1978), "An Analysis of New Industry Location: the Irish Case", *Progress in Planning*, UK, 9, pp. 129-229.

O'Hearn, D. (1990), 'TNCs, Intervening Mechanisms and Economic Growth in Ireland: a Longitudinal Test and Extension of the Bornschier Model', *World Development*, Vol. 18, No. 3, pp. 417-29.

Powell, M.J.D. (1970), 'A hybrid method for non-linear equations', in Rabinowitz, P. (ed.), *Methods for Non-linear Algebraic Equations*, Gordon and Breach, London.

Smith, D.M. (1966), 'A Theoretical Framework for Geographical Studies of Industrial Location', *Economic Geography*, 42.